BASKETBALL

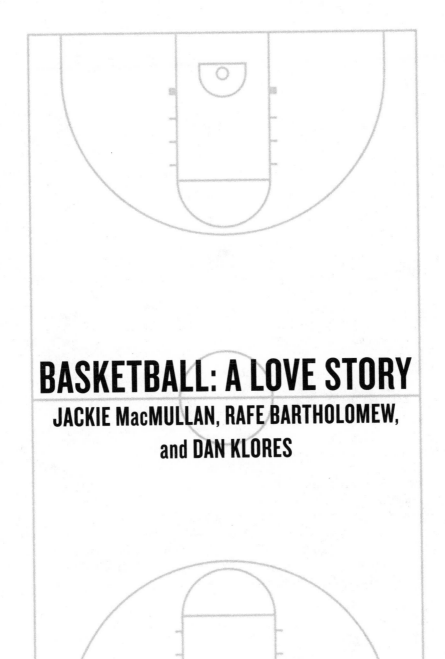

BASKETBALL: A LOVE STORY

JACKIE MacMULLAN, RAFE BARTHOLOMEW, and DAN KLORES

CROWN
ARCHETYPE
NEW YORK

Published in the United States by Crown Archetype, an imprint of the
Crown Publishing Group, a division of Penguin Random House LLC, New York.
crownpublishing.com

Crown Archetype and colophon is a registered trademark of
Penguin Random House LLC.

Library of Congress Cataloging-in-Publication Data is available upon request.

ISBN 978-1-5247-6178-3
Ebook ISBN 978-1-5247-6180-6

Printed in the United States of America

Book design: Lauren Dong
Jacket design: Rodrigo Corral Design
Jacket photographs: (Stephen Curry) Gregory Shamus/Getty Images; (LeBron
James) Ronald Martinez/Getty Images; (Lisa Leslie) Andrew D. Bernstein/National
Basketball Association/Getty Images; (Vlade Divac) The Sporting News/Getty
Images; (Walt Frasier) Focus on Sport/Getty Images; (Paul Pierce) Jeff Gross/Getty
Images; (Jerry West) Focus on Sports/Getty Images

10 9 8 7 6 5 4 3 2 1

First Edition

In loving memory of Ed Kleven. You are missed.

—JACKIE

*To Geoffrey Bartholomew for introducing me to the game,
to Ray Pagan for teaching me to play it, and to the Philippines
for showing me what it means to love it.*

—RAFE

To my cherished quartet: Abbe, Jake, Sam, and Luke.

—DAN

AUTHORS' NOTE

The story of how this book came together begins with a different project that shares the same name, ESPN Films' *Basketball: A Love Story*, directed by Dan Klores. At the heart of both projects is a landmark feat of basketball reporting—165 in-depth interviews, conducted between 2014 and 2017 by Dan and a number of renowned sports journalists, with a collection of basketball luminaries that ranged from Bill Russell and Oscar Robertson to Cheryl Miller and Mike Krzyzewski to LeBron James and Dirk Nowitzki. Together, these interviews resemble something like the Dead Sea Scrolls of basketball, containing 70 years of collected wisdom from the NBA, the women's game, college hoops, and international competition, and bound together by the overarching theme of the love of the game.

In early 2016, while working to complete the film, Dan enlisted Jackie MacMullan and Rafe Bartholomew to produce a book using the same cache of interviews. After reading through thousands of pages of interview transcripts, Jackie and Rafe began the difficult process of deciding what to include in this volume. The transcripts contained enough poignant, powerful, and revealing anecdotes to fill a book three times the size of this final version, but given the amount of space permitted, the authors did their best to represent the major events, movements, and dynasties in basketball history, from the 1930s through the present. The book is presented in oral history style, allowing the voices of the athletes, coaches, executives, and journalists who helped build basketball into a global game to speak for themselves, and only interjecting with the authors' prose to provide context. The interviews have been condensed and edited for clarity, but the authors have made every effort to preserve the sources' conversational and sometimes informal voices. Because the original interviews were not conducted with the intention of creating an oral history book, it would be improper to call *Basketball: A Love Story* an oral history in the strict sense of the form; likewise, it would be incorrect to describe this book as anything close to a definitive history of the sport—there is so, so much more.

We are thankful for the opportunity to work on this book, thankful to all of those who will read it, and, most of all, thankful to all the men and women interviewed, whose dreams and sacrifices have made basketball what it is today.

—Jackie MacMullan, Rafe Bartholomew, and Dan Klores

CONTENTS

BASKETBALL

FIRST LOVES

When James Naismith hung a peach basket in 1891 so his students at the Springfield, Massachusetts YMCA could play the first game of basketball, he couldn't possibly have known the millions of lives the sport would touch, that it would become the basis of a professional league worth billions of dollars, or that it would join soccer as one of the world's true global games. And the connective tissue that binds everyone who's ever devoted a part of his or her life to the sport of basketball—spanning generations and continents—is the love of the game.

EARVIN "MAGIC" JOHNSON (President of Basketball Operations, Los Angeles Lakers; 3-Time NBA MVP): I fell in love with basketball watching games with my dad in the living room. I was 3 or 4 years old. Him cheering for the Philadelphia 76ers—Wilt Chamberlain was his favorite player. I would go out and practice Wilt's ugly finger roll and try to be "the Big Dipper," and ever since that moment I just had to have a ball in my hand.

LeBRON JAMES (4-Time NBA MVP): When I was 4, 5 years old, I started playing on a crate. We cut the bottom out, nailed it to the light pole, me and my friends. No backboard, so every shot had to go straight in or you didn't make it. And I remember that joy—playing on the street, cars interrupting our game, the ball going into the woods. Playing basketball, it did something to me.

KOBE BRYANT (Shooting Guard, Los Angeles Lakers; 2008 NBA MVP): I have a basketball family—my father played in the NBA, my uncle played in the NBA, my grandma played, my sisters played, cousins played—and so when I picked the ball up, I literally could not stop. I was instantly attracted, almost like I was born to play.

KEVIN DURANT (2014 NBA MVP): My mom took me to a rec center and I walked into the gym, and it was like the gates of heaven opened up. I just jumped in. I don't even remember after that. Everything was so smooth and effortless, I didn't wanna leave. It felt like years were rolling past as I was playing, and that's how I could tell, "This is something I want to do every chance I get."

CHERYL MILLER (2-Time NCAA Champion; 1984 Olympic Gold Medalist): I just knew there was something bigger and greater out there for me through basketball. It wasn't until 1976. I remember seeing highlights of the women's Olympic team, and for the first time in my life I identified with other female basketball players. That's when that internal clock of something bigger and better out there for me began to tick. And it's been the driving force for me ever since.

CHRIS PAUL (9-Time NBA All-Star): My sophomore year [in high school], I killed. Oh my goodness—30-something every night, 10 assists, I was getting 10 steals, we went undefeated. I had this ultimate confidence [when] I finally dunked for the first time. Then it was on: I had to play no matter what.

STEPHEN CURRY (2-Time NBA MVP): When I was 5, my dad signed me up for the rec league in Charlotte, and it was my first time playing organized basketball. I loved to play on our Fisher-Price goals around the house and all that, but to play organized basketball, suitin' up with your jersey . . . I think I made one good pass, and the family went crazy in the stands. That's the first moment I knew I loved the game.

STEVE NASH (Point Guard, Dallas Mavericks/Phoenix Suns; 2-Time NBA MVP): I fell in love with it from the time I was 13 till I was 41. Almost every day in that 28-year period, there would be me, a ball, and a hoop, and I would practice. I would try to master my craft, and it was also very meditative and therapeutic. It was an extremely exciting and creative place for me. That feeling of being on my own in my imagination, having this burgeoning obsession—it's something I never lost. Every day, my own world: me, the ball, and the hoop. I could imagine and conjure and create, and that was at the heart of it all.

JERRY WEST (Shooting Guard, Los Angeles Lakers; 14-Time NBA All-Star): Where I grew up, there was really nothing to do. And I've always felt that the greatest thing a person can have is an imagination. When I picked that ball up, I was the referee, the timekeeper. If I missed three times in a row, I'd find a way to put a second back on the clock. When I was a little boy, that's where my satisfaction came from. I could use my imagination to be the hero of every game.

SHAQUILLE O'NEAL (Center, Orlando Magic/Los Angeles Lakers; 2000 NBA MVP): First time, it was a movie called *The Fish That Saved Pittsburgh*. Dr. J, Julius Erving, [was] in the movie, did great things with the basketball, but I didn't know he was a real person. So my father said, "Come on," and [we] jumped on the train to Madison Square Garden. I'm sitting there like, "That's the guy from the movie!" Then he goes baseline, throws it down, the crowd goes crazy. I look at my dad, I said, "That's what I want to be when I grow up."

ALLEN IVERSON (Guard, Philadelphia 76ers; 2001 NBA MVP): I was like 8 years old, and I've always been a football player, and one day I came home and my mom was like, "You going to basketball parks." And I was like, "Basketball? I don't like basketball. Basketball is soft." But she worked with a guy that ended up being real inspirational in my life, basically the type of guy that God sent to me. She talked to him about how good I was, so he came to our neighborhood and he seen me play, and he was like, "He got it."

MOSES MALONE (Power Forward; 3-Time NBA MVP; Died 2015): My favorite sports were football and baseball. I thought basketball was a sissy's game—too easy. When I first was introduced to basketball me and a couple of my buddies, we'd come around the playground, and we had a little rubber kickball. I threw the rubber ball up, and it went into the hoop. I said, "This might be a game I wanna try." All of a sudden, I left football, left baseball, and I really started loving the game.

CHARLES BARKLEY (Power Forward; 1993 NBA MVP): I started playing basketball because I felt like I was going down the wrong trails. I'm from a small town in Alabama, and I started stealing for no reason, but basketball got me out of trouble. Obviously, I was able to make a great life at it, but the really cool thing about basketball is it kept me out of jail.

ADAM SILVER (NBA Commissioner): When I was in second grade, we had a team that played against the other elementary schools, and I'll never forget: I shot the ball and it went in. I remember that feeling, I remember my hand shaking because I was so scared to shoot in front of all these people, and I remember the coach patting me on the back and saying, "Great shot." In terms of building character and confidence, [the] next time I ran up and down the court I was a different guy.

CAROL BLAZEJOWSKI (Forward, Montclair State College Red Hawks; 3-Time College All-American): I remember it vividly. I was 10 years old. I was a tomboy growing up, and I did football and baseball and the whole gamut, and it wasn't until my fifth-grade gym teacher threw the basketball out one day and said, "You're tall, you're athletic. I think you're gonna like this game." And I tell you, the second I picked that ball up, it really was love at first sight.

CALVIN MURPHY (Guard, Houston Rockets): I fell in love with basketball in the third grade. I walked in the gym, picked [the ball] up, and shot it. The first shot I ever took went in the basket. I don't know how, but it went in. Something just went all over me. It's like a beginning golfer that goes out and hits one great shot—you're hooked. I went home: "Mom, I want to play basketball." Mom goes out and gets one of those cheap balls that after two days forms the bubble. But nevertheless, it was a basketball, and it became my whole life.

BERNARD KING (Small Forward, New York Knicks/Washington Bullets; 4-Time NBA All-Star): I distinctly recall attempting my first basket. I'm in third grade with a bunch of kids in the Catholic school cafeteria, and there was a basket. Each of us attempted to make a goal, and one by one each of the kids faded away. No one could make a basket, and I refused to leave until I made that basket. Once I did, I wanted to feel it over and over and over again.

BILL BRADLEY (Small Forward, New York Knicks; U.S. Senator, 1979–97): I grew up in a small town in Missouri on the banks of the Mississippi River, about 3,400 people. I practiced alone a lot, and it was there that I felt the game enter my soul. Imagine you're alone: the bounce of the ball, the squeak of the shoes, and then that magic sound, *swish*, when it goes in.

JERRY COLANGELO (Managing Director, U.S. Men's National Team; 4-Time NBA Executive of the Year): When I was a kid, someone handed me a ball and I smelled it, and it was the beginning of a love affair that's lasted my entire lifetime. It becomes part of you. There weren't many games on TV back then, but I remember going to Chicago Stadium and watching college doubleheaders, thinking, "Someday, I'll be on that court."

GEORGE GERVIN (Small Forward; 4-Time NBA Scoring Champion): At a young age, whenever we used to see an NBA game, we wanted to go out and play ourselves, no matter if it's summer or winter. We used to go to the park, and [if] snow was on the ground, we'd sweep the snow off, then shoot till our hands got numb. We could stay out there for hours.

EARL MONROE (Guard, Baltimore Bullets/New York Knicks; 4-Time NBA All-Star): One day when I was walking down the hall [in] junior high school, the coach came [and] asked me if I could play basketball. I was 6'3" at that time, kind of big, so I said, "No, sir," and he said, "Well, come down to the gym this afternoon." So I went, couldn't play, everybody was beatin' up on me, but I got the bug. Even though I wasn't that good, I was out at the playground the next day, trying to get a run.

STEVE KERR (Guard, 16-Year NBA Veteran; Head Coach, Golden State Warriors): I fell in love with the game at Pauley Pavilion, watching UCLA during the heyday. My dad was a professor, we had two season tickets, and the first game I remember was UCLA-Maryland. Bill Walton was playing, [Maryland] had John Lucas and Len Elmore, and I was probably 6, 7 years old. Looking around, hearing the band, sold-out arena, incredible energy—it was like a drug.

BILL WALTON (Center, Portland Trail Blazers/Boston Celtics; 1978 NBA MVP): I grew up in this culture of non-sports, an unathletic family. I never shot a basket with my dad. My mom was a librarian, and my dad was a social worker and an adult educator and a music teacher. They loved literature and art and education. Then, all of a sudden, I found basketball and I just fell in love. It was endless—every possession was completely different, and I could play it out in my mind, I could visualize it. Basketball is a symphony, and we could take that ball and become artists ourselves.

TOMMY KEARNS (Point Guard, University of North Carolina Tar Heels, 1955–58): I didn't want to be a cop, a bartender, none of those things. I wanted to be a basketball player.

REBECCA LOBO (WNBA/NCAA Basketball Analyst, ESPN; Center, New York Liberty; 1999 WNBA All-Star): It can be hard to be the girl who is taller than all the other girls, taller than all the boys, and taller than all the teachers. I'm in eighth grade, and I'm already 6'2". You go to school dances, and no boy is asking the 6'2" girl with the big perm hair to slow-dance. People stared as I walked through the mall, not because they recognized me as a basketball player, but because I was an awkward, extraordinarily tall 14-year-old girl. But when I played basketball, I loved being tall. It gave me an advantage, helped me be better than other girls my age. Basketball was the place where I felt good about myself.

DALE BROWN (Head Coach, Louisiana State University Tigers, 1972–99): I grew up in a pretty good era in North Dakota. Roger Maris and I are the same age. Lute Olsen and I are the same age. And Maris, by the way, was a better football and basketball player than he was [a] baseball [player]. There was no television. We didn't own a radio, I don't think, until maybe [I was] 15 years old. I never mimicked anybody because there was no one to mimic. I just loved the game.

TOM THIBODEAU (Head Coach, Minnesota Timberwolves): I was 4 years old, and my dad gave me a basketball for Christmas. Best gift ever, and he shared his love for the game with me and my brothers and sisters and my mom. It's a game that you can play by yourself, you can go to any playground and join, and once it bites you, you never want to let it go.

SPENCER HAYWOOD (Center; 1970 ABA MVP; 4-Time NBA All-Star): We didn't get a basketball for Christmas because my mom could not afford it. With my father passing, we were poor. So she decided, "I'm going to make you boys a basketball," and we were like, "How are you going to make a basketball? A basketball's gotta bounce." So she made us a ball out of this croker sack, and she put cotton and everything into the sack, and we were allowed two bounces in our head to make the pass or make the shot. That's when I started to enjoy basketball. Of course, even though all of us were playing by the rules, my brother Andrew would get three bounces, and we would allow it because he was a little aggressive. We didn't have a real basket because that cost money. So we put a barrel rim on a telephone pole and played there. This was really rural basketball—no gym shoes, playing in the dust bowl barefooted.

GEORGE KARL (2013 NBA Coach of the Year): I still am in love. There's something extremely beautiful about the gifts of this game. I've been blessed by having a son that can play basketball, and watching him be the best player on a college court was one of the greatest gifts I've ever been given.

MIKE KRZYZEWSKI (Head Coach, Duke University Blue Devils; Head Coach, U.S. Men's National Team, 2006–16): I knew when I was a teenager that basketball was my friend. I could take my ball and go to the playground, and I didn't need anybody else. I could imagine. I could mimic. I could feel myself doing something that maybe I would never do in reality, but in my imagination, on that court, that was my friend. And it's been my friend for over 50 years.

CELTICS VS. LAKERS: Russell's Dominance, West's Heartbreak, and Those Balloons

The NBA may bask in an embarrassment of riches today, but the infancy of professional basketball left players so poorly compensated they required off-season jobs to pay their bills. Early NBA stars played before sparse, often raucous crowds that hurled insults—and occasionally objects—at the opponents. Travel was arduous, interest was tepid, and amenities were scarce.

The Boston Celtics played 10 forgettable seasons before their fortunes changed on April 30, 1956, the day coach Red Auerbach dealt the No. 7 pick, along with Ed Macauley and Cliff Hagan, to St. Louis for the No. 2 pick.

Auerbach fervently hoped to draft William Fenton Russell, a defensive specialist who played at the University of San Francisco, but first he had to convince the Rochester Royals, who had the No. 1 pick, not to snag Russell themselves. Celtics owner Walter Brown intervened, dialing up Royals owner Les Harrison and offering him a week of free performances by the Ice Capades (which Brown owned). Squeamish about Russell's demands for a $25,000 signing bonus, Harrison agreed to pass on the center.

Auerbach got his man, along with territorial pick Tommy Heinsohn and second-round steal K. C. Jones. The three future Hall of Famers, along with incumbent point guard Bob Cousy, ushered in a wave of dominance that remains unmatched in professional basketball history.

BOB COUSY (Point Guard, Boston Celtics; 13-Time All-Star; 1957 NBA MVP): The NBA was no glamour league at the start. But none of us complained. We were getting paid to play a child's game, and that was good enough.

TOMMY HEINSOHN (Power Forward, Boston Celtics; 6-Time NBA All-Star): If you played a game in Rochester [New York], the next night you were going to play in Fort Wayne [Indiana]. There was no direct way to get there. They would make an arrangement with one of the railroads that you took this train at 11 o'clock at night, and it would get into Indiana and it would pass through cornfields about 20 miles outside of Fort Wayne. They would stop the train, and you'd get off in the cornfield and thumb a ride from the high school kids to Fort Wayne.

COUSY: In Syracuse they'd boo you [even] if the bone was sticking out of your leg. There was no inch of sportsmanship in any way. They were hostile. Some fan got carried away, he must have had a couple of pops before the game, and this guy got onto the floor in a timeout. I took him and I shoved him in the middle of our huddle. Loscy [Jim Loscutoff] and everybody took a shot at him. They picked him back up and dumped him out, and they all ended up in court. I didn't have to go. Heinsohn, to this day, blames me.

HEINSOHN: Carl Braun was my roommate in 1962—everyone had a roommate on the road—and we got to L.A. and there weren't enough beds. They took some cots and moved them into this [room] and that one, and Carl Braun was left out. Here he is, a five-time All-Star, and he doesn't have a bed to sleep in. Red starts ranting and raving, "We had reservations, blah-blah-blah," so the manager says, "All I can think of is, I'll put this cot in the ballroom, and the first room that becomes available tomorrow morning, he can have it." Carl goes to the ballroom on the cot, falls asleep, and at 9 o'clock in the morning, he wakes up in the middle of a Communion breakfast.

TOM "SATCH" SANDERS (Power Forward, Boston Celtics; 8-Time NBA Champion): One of the first things that I encountered with the Celtics, which was a mystery to me, was that half the guys smoked. I said: How could they play at the level they were playing? How could they run? How could they press? How could they do the things that they were doing and smoke cigarettes? So I started smoking. At halftime everybody would light up. The worst part, of course, was Auerbach smoking those rope cigars.

COUSY: When we played on the road, Arnold [Red Auerbach] would sit there with a cop on each side protecting him and infuriate the fans, because he wouldn't light up his cigar until he knew we had the game won.

They were already pissed off, and now Arnold's sitting there smoking away, and the fans would throw things at us.

MARV ALBERT (NBA Broadcaster, TNT): I know guys in the NBA who really disliked Red because if you went to Boston in the springtime, the locker room, which consisted of a folding chair and a nail on the wall for each player, was sizzling hot, and if you were there in the winter, it would be below zero. There'd be no towels, no soap for the showers.

JOHN HAVLICEK (Small Forward, Boston Celtics; 13-Time NBA All-Star): We were playing Cincinnati in the playoffs and we won a tough, close game, and as we're leaving the floor, there's a rowdy fan who spit on Red, so Red punched him and broke his glasses. I don't know if he broke his nose and cracked his teeth or whatever, but the guy sued Red, and Red was going to have to go to court. I was following Red out at the time, and he said, "You saw that, didn't you? The guy spit on me and then I defended myself." I said, "Well, I guess." So we went to court and Red was thinking there was going to be a big ordeal, and he ended up settling out of court by paying for the guy's glasses and the dental work and giving him a couple Celtics key chains and beer mugs.

SANDERS: Auerbach was very pushy about winning. If we lost a couple games in a row—and that didn't happen that often—we would have to start having a training-camp-type session, a very long practice.

ALBERT: Red was the first guy who had a scouting system. He had friends all over the country. There was someone who told him, "Hey, there's this guy who's pretty good playing at the University of San Francisco. His name is Bill Russell; you oughta take a look at him."

HAVLICEK: I'll never forget when Russell was player/coach and missed the game because of a snowstorm. Red had to come out of the stands to coach the team, and Wayne [Embry] started for Bill while we played San Francisco with Nate Thurmond. We end up beating them, and Red really reamed Russ out. He said, "How can you be the coach and not show up for the game because of a snowstorm and everyone was here?"

Russ said, "Well, Red, my Lamborghini . . ." [Red] said, "Your Lamborghini? Take that Lamborghini and get yourself a jeep."

BOB RYAN (Columnist, *Boston Globe*; Retired): Red Auerbach played for Bill Reinhart at George Washington [University] and they were an up-tempo team. The NBA was still more "throw the ball in to the big guy," but Auerbach believed firmly in trying to beat the team down the floor. Cousy was the perfect mastermind for that. One of the reasons was, Cousy didn't hesitate to throw slingshot, sidearm 50-foot passes to advance the basketball.

HUBIE BROWN (NBA Broadcaster, ESPN; 2-Time NBA Coach of the Year): Cousy had Houdini-type talent, and he landed with the perfect team.

RYAN: Cousy was the innovator of the behind-the-back dribble. It was nothing he had practiced—total improvisation.

BOB PETTIT (Power Forward, Milwaukee/St. Louis Hawks; 2-Time NBA MVP): Going behind your back like that was unheard-of, and Cousy was very proficient at it. But I thought the big thing he could do was throw the ball the length of the court right on the nickel.

COUSY: I've never been a big self-promotion guy, but I would put my creativity, my imagination, my passing skills, with anyone who's played the game. In 1957, I thought I was the best damn player on the planet, frankly.

HUBIE BROWN: Cousy brought fans and winning [to Boston]. But the championships came with Russell.

BILL RUSSELL (Center, Boston Celtics; 5-Time NBA MVP): A couple weeks after I got to Boston, Cousy and I started collaborating. I was clearly at that time the best rebounder in the league, and he saw that. So he says, "When shots are taken, I'll go to that spot over there. Look there first when you get the rebound." Sometimes I would get a rebound and never land; just get it and redirect it. He would get the ball between the top of the foul circle and half-court on the run, so a lot of times we would have a layup within four seconds.

COUSY: The talk in Boston was "Yeah, the Celtics are good, they're entertaining, but in the playoffs, they die, ya know?"

HEINSOHN: We're playing in St. Louis [in Game 3 of] the 1957 Finals, and Bill Sharman comes over to Red and says, "Red, the basket's not 10 feet." Bill Sharman was a very precise person, so if he said it wasn't 10 feet, it's not 10 feet. So Auerbach, who had coached [Hawks owner] Ben Kerner's Tri-Cities [Blackhawks] team and had a falling-out with him, tells him about the basket. Kerner says, "You bush-league sucker," and he goes after Red. Red winds up and pops Ben Kerner right before the game even starts. Our coach belts the owner of the St. Louis Hawks—that's all we need. For the rest of the series, they were throwing eggs at us. I'll never forget the sight: they hit [Auerbach] right in the forehead. It must have hurt; it was all dribbling down his face.

RYAN: The series goes seven games. Cousy actually air-balled a free throw.

HEINSOHN: Russ and I were rookies, flying high and having fun. Cousy and Sharman were so anxious they tied themselves in knots. They were something like 5 for 40 from the floor. Cous had a chance to win the game if he made two free throws.

COUSY: It was the first time I ever remember choking in basketball. We're up 1 with 5 seconds left. I go to the line. I was a pretty good free throw shooter, 81 percent. I make the first one. Swish, we are up 2. [Player/coach Alex] Hannum—I don't know if it was by design to freeze [me]—calls timeout. I go back to the huddle. Now, seven years we have been waiting on a championship. It's celebration time. Hey, we got a championship! We got it, man. All you have to do is make the next free throw, because there were no three-point shots [then].

HEINSOHN: I had a little trick to get inside position on a missed free throw, where I would watch where the [shooter's] knees would go from the corner of my eyes. I would turn my shoulder, and the guy [on the block next to me] would bump me right in front of him. As I see Cousy's knees go up, I turn my shoulder, the guy pushes me into the middle, I look up, and there's no ball. The ball didn't travel halfway to the basket.

COUSY: I missed steel, OK? I missed steel! I got letters for many years after, saying, "Cous, what was Arnold's strategy? Why did he have you miss that on purpose?"

HEINSOHN: Cous was so anxious to win this thing, after six years of trying.

CLIFF HAGAN (Forward, St. Louis Hawks; 5-Time NBA All-Star): Alex Hannum is our player/coach, and he puts himself in the game and says, "I'm gonna throw the ball all the way down and hit the backboard, and hopefully [Bob] Pettit can tip it in." To hit something that far away with a basketball is wild.

COUSY: We're only up 2. For some inexplicable reason, we don't put some monster in front of Hannum to try to impede his pass. He had to throw it 94 feet. He throws the fastball right where he aims it. [It] hits the middle of the backboard and goes to the guy he wanted it to go to— his star, Pettit—right at the free throw line. He's gonna make the shot that he hasn't missed before in his life.

HAGAN: Bob goes up and tips it, but he misses, and the game is over. Boston, who has never won anything, has won its first NBA championship.

COUSY: [Pettit] choked as badly as I did. He hit the damn backboard, and it almost went back to half-court.

RYAN: They don't win without Tommy Heinsohn, who had 37 points and 21 rebounds.

HAVLICEK: They used to call Heinsohn "Tommy Gun" because he never took a shot he didn't like. His first step offensively was as good as anybody at the time because he could get to the basket, and he had great timing for the hook shot, the drive, and he could sort of cock his head and shoot that line-drive jump shot, too. He couldn't do more than one push-up, but somehow he had the tenacity to be a great basketball player.

SANDERS: I had to play against Tommy every day after practice. He kept saying, "Satch, you're supposed to be a good defensive player, so I know if I make these moves against you, it's gonna help my game. Let's play one-on-one." I'd say, "Heiny, I don't feel like playing anymore. Practice is over. Come on." He had moves inside, moves outside, and he certainly had the aggressive nature to take the shots. But what Tommy lacked in my estimation was the kind of stamina that could give him 40 minutes a game.

HAVLICEK: Red would tell Tommy, "You got to stop smoking, because I want to use you, but you get so tired that I can't use you." So Tommy would stop smoking and then he would gain weight, so Red would say, "You can't go because you're overweight, so go back to smoking." So he went back to smoking, and he never could get that stamina thing down.

SANDERS: Loscy, myself, Frank Ramsey, would sit beside Auerbach after a timeout anytime Heinsohn was playing, because when Tommy showed signs of being tired, Red would be upset and grab the closest forward and yell, "Get Heinsohn out of there!" Whoever was sitting closest to him would get the playing time.

The Celtics won their second championship in 1959 against what was, at the time, just another opponent, the Minneapolis Lakers. Yet, in the ensuing years, the Lakers came to symbolize an annual rite of passage for Boston. From 1962 to 1969 (by then the Lakers had moved to Los Angeles), the Celtics played L.A. for the championship six times—and won all six.

Boston was making history in other ways, too. The Celtics fielded the first all-black starting five in 1964, and when they named Russell as player/coach in 1966, he became the first African American head coach in the NBA.

The Lakers boasted their own talented duo in Jerry West and Elgin Baylor, but they were about to embark on a string of staggering futility.

JACK RAMSAY (Head Coach, NBA Champion Portland Trail Blazers, 1977; Died 2014): Elgin Baylor was a great one-on-one player. He became well-known for his ability to drive past his man and get to the basket, or drive into the paint and then shoot a pull-up jumper. He had a physical characteristic that helped him in this regard. He had a facial tic, so he would drive at you, give you that little twitch, go up and shoot his jump shot or drive past you to the basket.

SANDERS: My rookie year, Red says, "Go out there and guard Elgin." This is the first exhibition game against the Los Angeles Lakers. I go out and get real close to Elgin, 90 feet away from the basket. Elgin looks at me like, "You gotta be kidding me. This is an exhibition game. What in the hell is this nut doing?" I'm on him, hands working, so Elgin throws an elbow. Boom. It hits me, I fall back, but I'm right back up. That was the beginning of our, let's call it, relationship.

DON NELSON (Power Forward, Los Angeles Lakers/Boston Celtics; 3-Time NBA Coach of the Year): You couldn't stop Elgin around the basket. He had such a quick jump that he would shoot a little quick, and then his man would leave his feet to block the shot. Elgin would go down the other side of the basket and pick up his miss and score it. I'd never seen a guy do that before.

JERRY WEST: I used to watch Elgin in practice, and I would say to myself, "How in the world does he do this?" I would try to incorporate how he would shoot the ball off the board with spin on it, and I got to the point where I could not even look at the basket and shoot it because I watched him so much.

PETTIT: Elgin was ahead of his time as a forward. He would bring the ball up against the press, and very few forwards in that day could do that or even [wanted] to do that.

SONNY HILL (Philadelphia Basketball Legend; Founder of Sonny Hill Community Involvement League): You know what Elgin Baylor told me? When Jerry West first came to the Lakers, West couldn't bring the ball up the floor. The reason was that in high school and college, Jerry was a forward. So Elgin brought the ball up the first two years Jerry West was there.

NELSON: West was a fantastic player and teammate, but he worried about losing all the time. His fear of losing was far greater than the gift of winning. He was just petrified that he was gonna lose, so he would do all the extra work to keep from experiencing that loss.

PAT RILEY (President, Miami Heat; 3-Time NBA Coach of the Year; 2011 NBA Executive of the Year): The fact that Jerry never won in the '60s took him to a level mentally, when I got with him, where he was desperate to win. Even when we won the championship in 1972, he was a basket case in that Finals. He was nervous. He didn't shoot the ball well. He defended well and passed well, but he was like, "I know I'm gonna lose again." When we won, it was the greatest feeling I've ever had for another man, for him to get that off his back and not be haunted for the rest of his life.

NELSON: When we [the Lakers] played Boston in the '65 Finals, West was incredible. He averaged 40-something points a game and really carried us. But Dick Barnett went down with a groin pull, Elgin was already out with a knee injury, so we didn't have a lot of skill left. They put me in the backcourt, which I never had played before, and who does Auerbach put on me? K. C. Jones. Try to get the ball up court against K.C.

RUSSELL: I've never seen a better defensive player out on the floor than K. C. Jones. Nobody close.

COUSY: We had four Hall of Famers in the backcourt. That's never happened before and will never happen again. Poor K.C. was at the height of his career and he's sitting behind two guys, but I never sensed any resentment.

NELSON: We also had Sam Jones, who you had to force to take the shot, otherwise he would just play along and let somebody else do it.

HAVLICEK: Sam Jones had quirks about him that no one knew. We're in Philadelphia one time and Sam hadn't taken a shot, and Russell said, "Sam, you gotta take a shot, you're passing off too much, you got to shoot the ball, you're a scorer." He said, "I can't shoot the ball." Russell said, "What do you mean you can't shoot the ball? Why not?" He said, "My feet are cold."

RUSSELL: Sam used to tell me about this backboard that was made of wood. And there was a screw that wasn't painted over, and if he shot at [a] certain angle, if he hit the screw, the ball would automatically go in. So, while I was throwing it up there, he is aiming at this screw.

COUSY: Sam used to taunt Wilt [Chamberlain]. Wilt wouldn't come down on the break a lot of times, so he'd be the lone defender waiting while we attacked him. Sam would be on the wing in the corner, which was his best shot. I'd give it to him, and he'd say [to Wilt], "Come on, big guy, come on out here and get me." Wilt would start to come out a little bit, and just as he'd get there, Sam would launch it and say, "Too late!"

WAYNE EMBRY (Center, Cincinnati Royals/Boston Celtics; 5-Time NBA All-Star): When I was with Cincinnati, it was very frustrating [not to beat Boston], particularly knowing that their team wasn't gonna change and we had to change and make adjustments to try to beat them.

WEST: I'll liken it to a kid that walks up to a toy store or a candy store, and there's a piece of glass there. It separates you from getting something you desire or something you absolutely crave. That's what it was like for me after we would lose.

PETTIT: I've often said that if St. Louis had not traded Russell, there would have been a lot of cigars smoked in St. Louis, with a lot of banners hanging up there.

COUSY: I will go to my grave believing that Russ would not have gone to one of those other teams and won 11 out of 13 times. Arnold would not have been there. Let's not discount his contribution, his constant motivating factor, his relationship with the black players.

EMBRY: There was extreme mutual respect between Red and Russell. They were good for each other. Red recognized Russell's greatness, and Russell appreciated Red recognizing his greatness.

RUSSELL: The young Elgin Baylor, before he hurt his knees, I had never seen anybody better than that. Oscar Robertson? I had never seen anybody better. Both of those guys played in the same era where we won eight straight championships, so they don't get the credit [they deserve]. If it wasn't for us, they would have won five or six championships of their own.

EMBRY: The trump card was Bill Russell. I could contain him scoring, but as anyone in basketball knows, his greatest strength was on the defensive end—and not just against the man he was matched up against, but against the whole team.

NELSON: Every now and then we'd have these races, and Russ would race all the point guards. He'd beat them by two strides. He was just such an incredible athlete and didn't care about anything other than winning.

SANDERS: When this team lost, the guys were actually crying. That was phenomenal to me. I could not believe guys were actually crying about losing a game. I said, "These guys are kind of crazy. They wanna win all the games."

Even though Elgin Baylor played mostly only on weekends during the 1961–62 regular season because he was called to active military due to the Berlin crisis, he still averaged 38.2 points a game and 18.6 rebounds for the Lakers. West was emerging as one of the best shooters in the game (his likeness would later be used as the NBA logo) and earned the nickname "Mr. Clutch" because he hit so many game winners.

There was reason for optimism in the 1962 Finals when the Lakers took a 3–2 series lead after Baylor dropped 61 on the Celtics in Game 5. But then the Lakers blew a 17-point lead in Game 6.

In Game 7, Lakers guard Frank Selvy, who once scored 100 points for Furman University, knocked down two clutch jumpers to tie the game in the final minutes. The Lakers wound up with the ball and 5 seconds to win it. Selvy inbounded to teammate Hot Rod Hundley, who, upon seeing West was covered, threw it back to Selvy in the corner. He launched an open 14-footer that was on target but bounced high off the back of the rim as time expired. The Celtics went on to win the title in overtime.

A shattered West sat slumped, his head bowed, in the locker room as Selvy told reporters, "I'd give back all the shots that I've ever made just to hit that one."

COUSY: Jerry was obviously a fierce competitor. He met just about every challenge. He had all these skills, he could beat you offensively, and defensively he had great quickness. If you were putting down on paper what you'd want a 6'3" shooting guard to be, it'd be Jerry West.

RICK BARRY (Small Forward, Golden State Warriors; 8-Time NBA All-Star): Jerry West had incredibly long arms for his size. Jerry was 6'3". I was 6'7", but put our hands together, and they come up the same.

WEST: I could tell you what people were going to do even before they did it. It was a gift that was honed through experience. It was like you could read the other people's minds. It's a scary feeling to look at a player and say, "I know what he's going to do, so can I defend it?"

RILEY: Jerry West and I were best friends for five years. You talk about a great player? You talk about a competitor? You talk about a genius? He's also one of the most miserable people I've ever met in my life because he was so depressed and down when he would lose or fail. I don't know how I would have ever reacted if I was Jerry West and I had that level of ability to compete and to be that great and lose six times in a row in the Finals. I think it would have broken me.

WEST: People always show these winning locker rooms, guys celebrating. There are more stories in the losing locker room than there will ever be in a winning locker room.

COUSY: Looking back, the [1962] championship seems more unfair now because I ended up winning six of the suckers. I would've been happy with one. The thought process in Jerry's mind had to be that he came so close so often and didn't quite grab the brass ring.

HEINSOHN: People believe the Celtics Leprechaun is real. I keep tellin' them, before every game we would go down to the basement and pay him off in gold coins. He must have been sitting on the rim that night in '62, because Frank Selvy ended up with a clear shot. He was a great shooter, and it didn't go in.

COUSY: Frank had plenty of time. It might've been the only time in his career where he missed that shot. It hit the rim, bounced right side up. I'm thinking, "It's still gonna go in." But I see Russ grabbing the rebound, and I'd liked to have kissed him on the spot.

WEST: It was just a horrendous feeling to lose, to go into the summer thinking, "I don't wanna do this anymore." And that was in the height of my career. I didn't wanna do it. It hurt so much because, as they say, you put so much into it, and then there's nothing there.

COUSY: It's hard to feel sorry for opponents. I got to know Jerry West and Elgin [Baylor] pretty well afterwards. They were good guys, and you found yourself thinking, "Is there any fairness in sports? Shouldn't Elgin and Jerry—they're such great, great athletes—win one of these things?" Because we beat them in that manner, in that Selvy manner.

By 1968–69, the Celtics had won 10 championships in 12 seasons—all but 4 at the expense of the Lakers. Cousy had retired, Auerbach had stepped down as coach, and Russell had assumed the mantle of player/coach. Boston, finally, was showing its age, finishing as the No. 4 seed in the East.

The Lakers made a seismic move, acquiring Wilt Chamberlain from the Philadelphia Warriors, sending expectations soaring with a nucleus of Wilt, West, and Baylor.

Predictably, the Celtics and Lakers met again in the 1969 Finals. West scored 53 and 41 points to lead the heavily favored Lakers to a 2–0 series lead. Boston countered with wins in Games 3 and 4 (including a Sam Jones buzzer-beater). L.A.'s win in Game 5 was dampened when West hobbled off the floor after pulling a hamstring, and Boston tied the series 3–3 with a 99–90 Game 6 victory in which Russell held Chamberlain to 8 points.

Lakers owner Jack Kent Cooke stashed yellow and purple balloons high in the rafters to be released once his team broke the Celtics curse in Game 7. The premature gesture horrified West, but it was too late to remove them. Nor could he do anything about the flyers on each patron's seat that laid out the celebratory plans for the evening with the words, "When the Lakers win," not if the Lakers win.

An incensed Russell instructed his team to run the Lakers and a hobbled West on every play. L.A. was trailing by 9 with 5½ minutes to go when Chamberlain landed awkwardly and went to the bench clutching his knee. Mel Counts checked in, and the Lakers went on a run, cutting the deficit to 1. With just over 3 minutes left, Chamberlain informed coach Butch van Breda Kolff he could return to the game, to which the coach, who had clashed with Wilt all season, infamously replied, "We're doing fine without you."

West submitted 42 points, 13 rebounds, and 12 assists and was named the MVP of the Finals, but it was of no consolation to the man who witnessed Don Nelson's awkward, game-winning jumper bounce high toward the balloons, then come straight down through the basket, to pin yet another heartbreaking loss on the luckless Lakers.

WEST: When Wilt came to Los Angeles, I'll never forget an article in *Sport* magazine that said, "Will three superstars make a superteam?" Turned out it didn't at all. It was a flawed team because we didn't fit well around Wilt. We had played so long with Elgin and I having to score 30 a night that we had to change our game and we had to put other players around him. And Wilt was changing, too. I think he understood that him being the scorer that couldn't be stopped wasn't best for the team.

RYAN: Boston will never let the Lakers forget the balloon situation in 1969, when Jack Kent Cooke had the balloons in the ceiling and they were going to be released when they won the championship and, of course, the balloons are still sitting there in the old Forum.

SANDERS: The band was practicing outside, and Sam [Jones] went out and saw the balloons. During warm-ups, he told me, "Hey, man, they got balloons up there, they got people practicing dances and celebration stuff. Man, they really think they're gonna win." Russell got all pissed off, like, "Who the hell do they think they are? We're gonna stick a pin in those balloons."

RUSSELL: Before the game, Sam Jones brought me a program that said when the Lakers win the championship, the USC band will play "Happy Days Are Here Again," with 10,000 balloons up in the ceiling, and they were going to let them loose and they were going to take some chairs out on the court, and [Lakers announcer] Chick Hearn and Wilt and Jerry would have a discussion. And they had 10 cases of champagne in the Forum Club. In my pregame [speech], I said, "That champagne will have been aged another year because they don't have a chance tonight."

NELSON: We knew about the balloons before the game. Russell actually talked about it in his pregame speech.

RUSSELL: I told our guys, "This Lakers team is very good, in fact you might say they're excellent, except there are some things that will come into play tonight. First of all, they're primarily a half-court offense, and everybody will tell you that you can't fast-break during the playoffs because the other team won't let you. Well, the key to the fast break is defensive rebounds and outlet passing. I am the best that ever did that." By halftime, we were 17 points ahead because Jerry West had a pulled muscle and nobody else could run anyway.

NELSON: The Lakers come back from 22 down to down 1 in the second half, and it looked like all the momentum was going their way. We couldn't do anything right, and Havlicek got the ball swiped from behind.

HAVLICEK: Keith Erickson comes around and deflects the ball out of my hand, right to Nelson, for a perfect pass at the free throw line.

NELSON: I just happened to be running across the three-second area, and the ball came right to me. The 24-second clock was running down, so all I could do was catch and shoot. I shot it too quick, and it took a crazy bounce.

HAVLICEK: He takes the shot and it goes up, up, up . . .

NELSON: I shot it so poorly. It must have gone up 20 feet in the air and came down right through.

GAIL GOODRICH (Guard, Los Angeles Lakers; 5-Time NBA All-Star): The all-time worst for the Lakers was when they waived Don Nelson [in 1965], and Boston picked him up for $1,000, then he played for another 12 years or something like that.

HAVLICEK: It was incredible. We stayed up all night to celebrate.

RUSSELL: Jerry West is one of the best guys I ever knew. Fiercely, fiercely competitive. And he did have a pulled muscle that did slow him down, because he was as good a defensive player as he was on offense, which most people don't know about.

NELSON: That game had so many situations going on. Van Breda Kolff took Chamberlain out and never put him back in. The Lakers start coming back and coming back. We couldn't stop them and we couldn't score, and it was just one of those things where something's gotta happen here, and that's when I made a lucky shot. We won, and they fired Van Breda Kolff right away.

HAVLICEK: We were leaving the floor. I put my arm around Jerry West and I said, "You're such a great player, you deserve to win a championship, and I hope it's not against us, but if there's anyone that deserves one, it's you."

GOODRICH: Losing to the Celtics six times obviously had to be real tough for Jerry because he's so competitive. He's such a perfectionist. And if you make mistakes, if you're not perfect, then he has some issues. Well, Jerry, not everybody can be as good as you. We're gonna make mistakes. It's about accepting those mistakes or correcting those mistakes and moving on.

Game 7 of the 1969 Finals turned out to be the final game of Russell's and Sam Jones's illustrious careers. The Celtics dynasty had come to an end, and both Bill Sharman and K. C. Jones turned to coaching. To the surprise of many, they were hired by the Lakers in the summer of 1971, with Sharman as head coach.

Chamberlain flourished under the new regime, leading the league in rebounding (19.2 boards) that season. In a clinching Game 5 of the Finals against the New York Knicks, Wilt was immense, with 24 points, 29 rebounds, 8 blocks, and 8 assists in a 114–100 win.

Finally, Jerry West could exhale.

RILEY: I called Jerry West on the phone. I said, "How do you feel about Bill Sharman and K. C. Jones coming to coach you?" He hated both of 'em. All those years at Boston, and now they're gonna coach us?

COUSY: We're all creatures of habit, but Billy Sharman used to take it to another level. He'd have his hot water and tea at 4 o'clock on game day. He'd have to take a nap from 4:30 to 5:30. Before the game he'd be on the floor doing exercises. We used to say, "Willy, get your ass up before Arnold sees you and has us all doing that."

RILEY: When I met Bill Sharman, he was so brutally honest with me. He's the man that really taught me about a role. I was in his office [in 1972], and he looked me in the eye and said, "The only way you're gonna make this team is to be the best-conditioned athlete on the team. Otherwise, you're going to be useless to me." I think his honesty helped me become honest with myself, and it carried over for the rest of my career.

GOODRICH: Bill Sharman is the one who introduced the shootaround in the morning. We watched game films, which, at that time in the pros, nobody else did. He believed in getting players up and on their feet, rather than sleeping in late. We'd go to the gym on the road, at home, to help bring the team together.

RILEY: I became one of Sharman's guys, and in my third year he wasn't playing me and I cussed at him and he said, "What did you say to me?" He was taking his whistle off. I said, "I was talking to myself." He said, "You and I can go right outside, and you can say that to me again." I could see him steaming. You could just see him boil. He would then clench his teeth and talk about defending and toughness and knocking the hell out of somebody, and he would come over, "Get up Pat," and he'd grab me by the arm and he'd get down in a defensive stance and say, "That's what I want." His face was red, he wasn't throwing anything, but I learned that sometimes when you're coaching, temporary insanity comes, which is bad because you can't control it, so you have to plan your insanity.

GOODRICH: By [1972] the Lakers had lost to Boston seven times. Why? Because Boston had a better team. Simple. They had Bill Russell, who controlled and dominated the game like no one else. They had good personnel, they had a great coach in Red Auerbach, and they probably got in the heads of the Lakers.

RILEY: Nine games into the season, we're 6–3 and Sharman says, "This isn't good enough." He wanted to take Elgin Baylor out of the starting lineup, and he went to Elgin and said, "You have to come off the bench." Elgin said, "I'm not going to do that," and he retired.

GOODRICH: That helped the team in many ways, because now Jimmy McMillian, who was coming off the bench, moved into the starting role, and McMillian had a great year.

WEST: Frankly, that was one of the saddest days of my life when Elgin retired. Both of us had been through so many horrendous defeats, sitting in the locker room after a game feeling like you wanna jump off a bridge. The night he retired, we made one lineup change. Jimmy McMillian, who was certainly not Elgin Baylor, took his spot, and we won 33 straight games.

DAVE COWENS (Center, Boston Celtics; 1973 NBA MVP): We had no chance to beat the [1971–72 Lakers]. We couldn't match their firepower, we couldn't match their depth, and we couldn't beat Jerry West and Wilt Chamberlain.

WEST: It was a year that was filled with pleasure, because of the ease [with] which we won the games. We could win a brutal half-court game. We could win a really physical game. We certainly could win a high-scoring game.

GOODRICH: I led the team in scoring—just by a few percentage points over Jerry West. K. C. Jones would look at the stat sheet and say, "You're 7 for 10, you're hot, keep shooting." In another game when I'm 1 for 9 he'd say, "Gail, keep shooting, saturation method." That came from the Boston Celtics' philosophy, when they had Bill Russell and guys would come down and shoot and Russell was there to get the rebound.

WEST: We won the championship [over the Knicks]. It honestly didn't sink in for three days after we won. I was so used to losing and killing myself and wanting to go to some deserted island, never seeing anyone again.

BARRY: The end of the Celtics dynasty was absolutely great for basketball because it allowed other teams the opportunity to experience championships. It was great for the fans, and it was great for the development of the game. You had the [1970 and 1973] Knicks, the [1971] Bucks, the [1975] Warriors, our team, so it finally gave someone else a chance.

COUSY: The Celtics won 11 championships in 13 years. That's never been done before, and that's one of the records in sports that will never be broken, given free agency and everything that goes on now. There's so much player movement, you're never gonna keep people together that long. Someone from Chicago called me a few years ago when Michael [Jordan] and [Scottie] Pippen were playing, asking me, "Is this the best team ever?" They'd won twice at the time. I remember saying, "Hey, let a little history go by before you start comparing them to those Celtics teams, will you, please?"

WILT'S CENTURY MARK

There's some debate as to why only 4,124 fans showed up for the March 2, 1962, game between the Philadelphia Warriors and the New York Knicks. Perhaps it was because Hershey Sports Arena was adjacent to a candy factory, where the aroma of chocolate was initially pleasing but eventually nauseating. Maybe it was general indifference to an NBA product that was not yet "fantastic."

The fans weren't the only ones who stayed away. Not one member of the New York press corps showed up, either.

All of them missed Wilt Chamberlain scoring 100 points—a historic feat without footage, because the game was not televised.

It was Wilt's third season, and the night before the game, he was cavorting in New York City until the wee hours of the morning and nearly missed the train to Hershey.

First-year Warriors coach Frank McGuire's strategy was to get the ball to Wilt early and often. He also counseled Chamberlain, who struggled to shoot free throws, to try them underhanded. Using that technique, Wilt went 28 for 32 from the line.

Knicks starting center Phil Jordan was out with a "sickness," although his teammates revealed later he was hungover.

Philly jumped to a 19–3 lead, with Wilt scoring 13 points in the opening minutes. He showed no signs of slowing down at the half, having already racked up 41 points. "Half of Wilt's shots were dunks because he was in terrific shape," said Warriors teammate Joe Ruklick.

By the end of the third quarter, Wilt had 69, and announcer Dave Zinkoff began providing running point totals after each basket. As Chamberlain approached 100, the Knicks intentionally fouled other Warriors players to keep the ball from him. Philadelphia countered by fouling Knicks players to regain possession.

With 2:12 to play, Wilt had 94 points. Ruklick, who was enjoying watching from the bench, heard McGuire bark his name moments later. "I take my sweats off and I'm absolutely cold," Ruklick said. "There's 2 minutes left, and I don't have any business in this game."

In 1955, Ruklick had been chosen to play in the North-South Cage Classic in Murray, Kentucky, but Wilt, the most hotly recruited player in the country, had not. Both rosters were composed of all white players. Ruklick was named the nation's prep high school All-American center, and when he finally met Chamberlain, he expressed regret that Wilt had been snubbed because of the color of his skin.

"I told him, 'I want to apologize, because I stood in your place that day,'" Ruklick said. "He looked at me and put out his hand, which was the size of a catcher's mitt, and said, 'It's OK. You deserved it.' We were friends from that moment on."

Now, with 46 seconds left, Ruklick had the ball, and Wilt had 98 points.

"I'm wide-open from 12 feet away, nobody on me," Ruklick said. "I'm waiting, trying to figure out what to do. Then Wilt bumps a guy off with his hip. Somehow, he pirouetted open. I toss the pass to him."

Ruklick said it's a myth that Chamberlain dunked the 100th point. "He [had] too much class for that," said Ruklick. "He finger-rolled it in."

The game was stopped as the fans stormed the floor. For the remaining 45 seconds, Chamberlain stayed clear of the action, explaining afterward that he liked the sound of 100 better than 102.

Coverage of Chamberlain's performance was minimal, even though he set NBA records for field goals attempted, field goals made, free throws made, and points in a quarter. When asked about scoring 100 points, Chamberlain remarked, "It's pretty exhausting to think about it." The closest anyone has come to matching his output was when Kobe Bryant scored 81 points to much fanfare against the Toronto Raptors in 2006.

"Nowadays, if a guy scores 100 points, you'd be elected the mayor of Philadelphia, right?" Ruklick said. "But there was no television that night. The only truth is what our memories tell us."

WILT VS. RUSSELL: Friends, Rivals, and Champions

Wilton Norman Chamberlain was a basketball sensation, accumulating nicknames (Wilt the Stilt, the Big Dipper, Goliath) as deftly as he produced outrageous statistics. By the time he was a senior at Overbrook High School in Philadelphia, more than 200 colleges were vying for his services. Celtics coach Red Auerbach was so enamored with Wilt, he tried in vain to steer him to a New England school so the Celtics would be able to select him as a territorial pick.

Auerbach had to "settle" for one William Fenton Russell, whose early years of basketball were so awkward that he was nearly cut from his high school team and received only one scholarship offer—from the University of San Francisco.

Chamberlain's and Russell's divergent styles collided in the NBA, with Wilt establishing himself as the most dominant offensive force in the game and Russell revolutionizing the way the game was played on defense. Chamberlain averaged 30 points and 28 rebounds a game against Boston, but it was Russell's Celtics that won seven of eight playoff series (including four Game 7s) against Wilt during his career with the Philadelphia/San Francisco Warriors, Philadelphia 76ers, and Los Angeles Lakers. This ignited a hotly contested debate over the notion of the individual star versus the team player, an argument that rankled Chamberlain until his death in 1999.

JERRY COLANGELO: Wilt always seemed to be a man—never a young person.

LARRY BROWN (1988 Naismith College Coach of the Year; 2001 NBA Coach of the Year): Since Wilt was a young boy, he was expected to be the greatest. Overbrook High School beat Villanova's college team in a scrimmage when he was there. Wilt was so much bigger and more gifted than everyone. The expectations on Wilt would probably take [their] toll on anybody. Russell didn't have that.

BOB RYAN: Though Bill Russell was accomplished, not a whole lot of people east of the Rockies had seen him play. There was no television available for college basketball, ESPN was many years in the future, so there was a controversy about how good he really was, because he wasn't in the mold of the traditional center of the day. . . . But Red Auerbach had a vision.

BOB COUSY: In Russ's first game, we played on national television on a Sunday afternoon against St. Louis. I think Russ played 16, 17 minutes. I don't remember that he practiced with us. Arnold said, "This guy's gonna solve our rebounding problems." Russ didn't do anything spectacular, but we all went back to the locker room saying, "Jesus, we might have something more than we've been told."

JACK RAMSAY: There's never been a defensive force the equivalent of Bill Russell.

TOM "SATCH" SANDERS: When people talk about players touching the top of the board, the only player I knew who was able to do that was Wilt Chamberlain.

PETER VECSEY (Columnist, *New York Post*): Everything about Wilt was exaggerated. He wanted to win at everything, kind of like [Michael] Jordan did. Try to outdo you with the money, intimidate you with money, bet on anything. But even though Wilt had the stats, it's all about winning—and Russell came into the league with two national championships with San Francisco, an Olympic medal in '56, and then won 11 out of 13 championships.

COUSY: The Wilt-Russ thing was interesting for all of us. It got more play in the media than anything I ever remember. We sold out every single game when those two guys went after each other.

DOLPH SCHAYES (Center, Syracuse Nationals; 12-Time NBA All-Star; Died 2015): There was always the Russell-Wilt thing. In 1965, we played an exhibition game in North Carolina, and a headline came out that Wilt was [the] first $100,000 player. Russell blew his stack and said to Auerbach, "I win championships, I want more," and then the next day it says Russell gets $100,001. I spoke to Wilt. He said, "Dolph, don't believe it. I really get a lot more than $100,000, but rather than break the financial structure of the league, they didn't want to announce it."

BILL RUSSELL: Very simple logic. If you play, you win or you lose. Nothing else. So, if you're going to play, you play to win. There were times in Boston when somebody had a 15-point lead with a minute to go. The guy from the other team would be on a breakaway, and I'd run him down to block it. They said, "Why are you wasting energy?" That's the way I play.

SANDERS: Russ was a phenomenal athlete. Couldn't shoot. Six feet from the hoop, he'd turn around, look at that basket like it was a snake. But when he got closer, he could do a lot of damage.

RUSSELL: The only time I got a shot was when I got a rebound and didn't pass it out to the point guard and dribbled it up to the top of the key and shot a jump shot. I didn't care if I made it or not. I wanted everybody on our team to know I play the full game of basketball and I'm not going to limit myself to defensive rebounding.

BILL SIMMONS (Author, *The Book of Basketball*): Russell said Wilt was always changing who he was. Wilt had different incarnations as a basketball player. I'm gonna lead the league in assists. Oh, I'm gonna be a rebounder, blocked-shot guy. Russell always knew who he was.

RUSSELL: We get home from a road trip, and the next practice Red puts in a play for me. It was called the 6 play [after Russell's number]. Red says, "I'm going to call this play to reward you." He tells the guys to pass me the ball and says, "Is that what you want?" I said, "No. I want to go on the blocks. If this guy passes the ball to me and goes by, then this guy follows him, crisscross." The guys find out if they [passed] me the ball and went by and were ahead of their man, I'd drop it off to them. Gradually, everybody was calling my play because they were the first options. I was the third option of my own play.

LARRY "THE SCOUT" PEARLSTEIN (New York City Basketball Expert): As far as talent goes, Wilt was a better player, but Wilt didn't have the dedication that Russell had.

SIMMONS: Not only did Wilt not want it as much, but he criticized Russell. He said, "What, you want me to be like Russell? That guy's a crazy person. That guy's throwing up in the bathroom before games. I'm never gonna be like that."

MARV ALBERT: I was a ball boy, and in Wilt's earlier years he would ask me to go to the concession stand to have four or five hot dogs waiting for him at halftime. Can you imagine? And I don't think he hid it—he was doing this in front of the coach and everyone else.

DAVE BING (Point Guard, Detroit Pistons; 7-Time NBA All-Star): I'm playing in my first All-Star Game, and Alex Hannum is the coach. We're a half hour away from game time, Wilt wasn't there, so everybody's looking around. Wilt comes in maybe 20 minutes before the game with a corned beef sandwich. Alex went nuts.

SCHAYES: I think it was more of a moral issue. Wilt was considered the bad guy, and Russell was the good guy. Russell is the consummate team player, and Wilt is the consummate individual star that doesn't care about team. And that wasn't true.

RAMSAY: Wilt's focus was more on his personal accomplishments. I remember sitting at the scorer's table [during one] game. I was the GM in Philadelphia, and Wilt came out to start the second half. In those days, the stats were kept by an individual. As Wilt came out to warm up, he stopped at the table, picked up the stat sheet, and said, "You have me down for 6 assists. I had 9 assists at the half." The statistician just shrugged. Wilt said, "Nine. Write it down."

JOE RUKLICK (Power Forward, Philadelphia Warriors): When Bill Russell came into the league, there was no significant change in attendance. When Wilt came in, he gave me figures that said he saved the league. I checked them, and there was a substantial increase in attendance around the NBA. So he would talk about his statistics and his career, but mostly he'd talk about the bastards who wanted to hurt him.

VECSEY: Wilt was always the underdog. There's no question Russell had better teams. Russell was smart enough to know that he should be the role player on these teams.

OSCAR ROBERTSON (Point Guard, Cincinnati Royals/Milwaukee Bucks; 14-Time NBA All-Star; 1964 NBA MVP): Russell felt he could will his team to win. Bill didn't try to overshoot; he didn't shoot that much. He knew who to pass the ball to. He's not going to throw the ball to someone who can't score.

VECSEY: I always say Russell is the ultimate role player. The master of intimidation. He'd be playing someone great, and he'd block his shot three or four times. He didn't care if he goaltended or not; he was just going to let the guy know, "This is what you can expect."

BOB PETTIT: Bill would get a rebound, throw it to the Celtics on a fast break. All of [a] sudden they'd intercept it and he'd run back on defense, and here they come, two-on-one, with Bill being the one on defense, and they'd stop and take a jump shot from 15 feet because they knew they weren't going to get anything close to the basket.

RUKLICK: I don't think any of us thought that Russell was in any way better as a player—team player—than Wilt Chamberlain. If you can devise some sort of computerized program that shows how they rebounded, or if you could put them in a game scripted to test rebounding skills, you'd always bet on Chamberlain. If Wilt played for the Boston Celtics with those guys, Cousy and the rest, they never would have lost a game. Wilt was vastly superior to Russell.

ROBERTSON: Nobody is going to approach what Wilt did scoring and rebounding and blocking shots—no one. Wilt averaged 40-some points a game against the Celtics, didn't he? But that hurt the rest of the players. They had to get the ball to Wilt all the time. Auerbach was the opposite. He had a good starting unit, but he got all these veterans off his bench and that's how they won.

RUKLICK: The Warriors were not built for maximum productivity. They were built to highlight Wilt Chamberlain, and that's what [Warriors owner] Eddie Gottlieb accomplished. So, comparing those two teams, those two players, Wilt against Russell, isn't fair in the game of basketball, the most team-minded game there is.

RICK BARRY: Every time Wilt had really great players around him, he won championships.

COUSY: Wilt was Russell's greatest challenge, obviously. But Russ frightened Wilt as much as anyone who ever guarded him. Not with strength—with speed and quickness.

BING: Russ would psychologically beat Wilt. Most times, Wilt didn't have to worry about anybody blocking his shot, but then Russell would block a shot or two and get into his head.

COUSY: Arnold didn't want them shaking hands before the game. I was the same in camp. I didn't wanna play kissy poo with the opponent. I wanted to glare at them and hate them, but Russ claimed he would have clandestine dinners with Wilt when he was in Philly.

VECSEY: Russell was smart enough to make friends with Wilt—"Come to Boston, eat at my house"—and Wilt's friends would tell him, "He's playing you; don't do it." I think Jordan did the same thing with Charles Barkley. Take him out on the golf course, buy him a gift.... That was the way he got to him.

AL ATTLES (Point Guard/Head Coach, Philadelphia/Golden State Warriors, 1960–83): They were so close. When Boston would come to Philly, Russ would go to Wilt's house for dinner, sleep there, come to the game. Wilt used to tell Russ, "You come down from Boston, come to my house, eat my food, sleep in my bed, and then go to the game and beat us."

SANDERS: Russell would be blocking shots and disrupting all of our practices. Red had to pull him out so we could run plays without him blocking shots. A lot of the media looked at it and said, "Russell doesn't practice; he sits on the side." Well, we were glad, because then we could play.

BILL BRADLEY: Russell always used to say, "The Boston press would be on me because I didn't practice." He says, "I didn't practice once the season started, but that's Auerbach's genius. What was the one thing that was going to prevent us winning the championship? If I got run-down. And Auerbach knew that, so that was the key to our championship. I would come to practice and sit on the side and sip a cup of tea. And none of my teammates was upset because they saw me vomit every night before the game, and they saw how I played."

PETTIT: Wilt wasn't as defensively oriented as Bill Russell. Would Wilt block your shot? Wilt would block the shot and spike it, boom, out-of-bounds. Bill would flip it with his hands and block it to where Cousy or K. C. Jones or somebody could get it, and off they'd go on a fast break.

RUKLICK: I don't think you can block somebody's shot and make sure Cousy gets it, because he's on his way down. I don't think it's done.

HUBIE BROWN: Wilt is the most dominant figure we've ever had. You leave the game and have 50 records, for Christ's sake. But the lane was the key. It's 6 feet. Then, because of Wilt, they made it 12 feet, and then it's 16 feet. So you can't expect guys today, with a 16-foot lane, to give you the same kind of numbers that they had back then.

RAMSAY: Wilt was a stats collector. He predetermined before the season which stats he was going to focus on. He liked being the best scorer. He also liked the fact he was a good passer, so there was a season he determined that he was going to lead the league in assists—and he did.

There was a season he determined that he was going to lead the league in rebounding, and he did.

COUSY: In Russ's heart of hearts, he probably feels today like he won that battle. Russ didn't have the dribbling, passing, shooting skills, but he didn't need them. Eleven championships in 13 years.

RAMSAY: Bill Russell couldn't care less about statistics except for W's and L's, and he didn't want L's.

Racism permeated the game during Chamberlain's and Russell's formative years. During a preseason exhibition game in North Carolina in 1960, Russell and his African American teammates were placed in separate hotels from the rest of the team. The following season, the Celtics traveled to Lexington, Kentucky, for an exhibition game in honor of Celtics teammate Frank Ramsey, a University of Kentucky alumnus. But when a Lexington café refused to serve Sam Jones because he was African American, Russell convinced his black teammates to fly back to Boston without playing the game. It was a controversial—and heavily criticized—decision, the first of many stands Russell would take on behalf of racial equality.

RUSSELL: A year before, we played an exhibition in North Carolina, and the blacks and the whites stayed at different hotels. I said to Red Auerbach, "This will never happen again." So the next year we go to Lexington, Kentucky, and Sam Jones went down to eat his pregame meal in the hotel, and they wouldn't serve him. I was getting ready to go down there, and K. C. [Jones] says, "They won't serve you; they don't serve colored people." So I go back to the room and I call Eastern Airlines and I say, "When's your next flight out of here?" I call Red up and said, "Red, I'm going home." He said, "Yeah, it has been a grind. Our flight is tomorrow." I said, "No, I'm going tonight." He said, "What are you talking about?" I said, "Sam went downstairs to eat, and they wouldn't serve him. So I'm going home where I know I can get something to eat." Red says, "Wait a minute, wait a minute." Comes back and says, "You guys can go down in the café and eat, and they will never discriminate again." I said, "Red, I'm going home on a 7 o'clock flight. There is nothing you can say to change that." So we all left, Sam, K.C., myself, and Satch. When we landed in Boston, [Celtics owner] Walter Brown was at the airport. It's 1 o'clock in the morning, and Walter says, "I'm here to apologize that this kind of stuff happens to you." And the St. Louis paper wrote a column that said we should all be suspended for embarrassing the white players from Kentucky.

COUSY: Russ has been intense all his life. I don't blame him. They broke into his house in Reading, Massachusetts. Defecated on his bed and on his walls. When you are the number one man and you've already won five or six championships and they're breaking into your house doing these things . . . Wow, I'd have trouble making peace with that.

RYAN: Boston was very tribal, very clannish, very compartmentalized, and there weren't a lot of people of color. They were pretty much herded into a section called Roxbury and were not a prominent part of Boston life. This is the world that Russell walked into.

JOHN THOMPSON (Center, Boston Celtics; Head Coach, Georgetown Hoyas, 1972–99): [I've] said, "Bill Russell made me feel safe." I don't think Bill understood what I was saying. I think he put it in a physical connotation, but I wasn't afraid of anyone physically. It was knowing what he represented and what he stood for that gave me a tremendous feeling of comfort.

RUKLICK: Wilt dealt with racism all the time. We were playing in St. Louis, which is a bad town. You don't leave the hotel if you're black in St. Louis. I could clearly hear the racist crap that came from the stands. The N-word was common. In a book published about the NBA, Cal Ramsey says in the locker [room] before the game that Cliff Hagan, Bob Pettit, and Clyde Lovellette, the big troika of the St. Louis Hawks, got together and said, "Let's get Wilt." Before the game, Ramsey comes over to where we're warming up and talks to Wilt. He heard what those three guys said in the locker room. I didn't know he warned Wilt then. During the game, Wilt is scoring and the rest of us are enjoying it, and Wilt is running down the floor and Lovellette throws his fist back into

Wilt's face. So Wilt gets hit, the game ends, and a trainer in St. Louis looks at him and says everything is gonna be all right. Wilt didn't say anything public, didn't complain. Turns out two of his teeth pop out, and two more are driven up into his cranium. We travel to Detroit, then to New York for a game, and Wilt collapses after the game and is rushed to Bellevue Hospital. He has a massive infection in his mouth, and he's in bad shape. That infection was caused by a deliberate assault. What happened there was unthinkable, but the NBA does nothing. Eddie Gottlieb is quoted in the *Philadelphia Inquirer* saying Wilt missed a game or two because he has a bad ankle. What? We knew what happened, and we knew the reason.

LENNY WILKENS (Point Guard; 9-Time NBA All-Star; 1994 NBA Coach of the Year): Wilt wasn't afraid of anybody, you kidding me? I saw him lift three of us up one time, all together.

VECSEY: Russell never fought. He was an aristocrat—he was above the fray. He was above the pollution.

RUSSELL: [Knicks forward] Harry Gallatin always stepped on my shoes, pulled my shorts, gave me an elbow in the ribs, and had himself a fine day. I didn't mind that because everything he did, I catalogued. So you can't do that the next game, OK? You couldn't do the same thing twice to me unless you were Wilt, who was very, very, very good.

COUSY: Russ would try to push Wilt as far away as he could. I think that's why Wilt developed that little backboard fallaway. When you're 7'4", you just overwhelm people. But Wilt was ready to settle for the fallaway with Russ guarding him because of Russ's speed. Wilt's not gonna take it in on Russ, because Russ would slap it, steal it, interfere with it in some way. And he knew that, that was ingrained, so he went to the little fallaway.

RUSSELL: In order to play against another player, you have to figure his temperament. If you do something to him, will that deflate him or inflate him? Or make him play harder? Wilt was a big, strong guy, but

I figured he was top-heavy. I spent most of the evening trying to get him to play [from] side to side as much as I could, rather than trying to challenge him vertically. That way, I could neutralize some of the difference.... I'd play him on one side or the other. I had to change it every game. I had five different ways that I played him, and some nights I would encourage him to shoot unobstructed and he would get 40 points, just like that. But if I get him to get 45 points, the other four guys cannot develop a rhythm. Their production would go down. So, if he had 45 points and they ended up with 98, it was a real job.

RYAN: Statistically, Wilt dominated. He was the far better offensive threat and [an] equal rebounder. But Russell had some kind of mental edge. There were, if you buy into the story, times when Russell would be having a good game against Chamberlain and the Celtics would have the issue well decided by the end of the third quarter, and in the fourth Russell would back off and allow Wilt to get 15 or 18, and walk away feeling that he had won the battle and that this mattered more to Wilt than winning the game. Obviously, Wilt would always deny that.

RUSSELL: The year Wilt averaged 50, which is like Babe Ruth hitting 75 home runs, the players voted me MVP. No writer had a vote. And then NBA marketing turned the MVP over to the writers. I never finished any higher than third after that.

RYAN: May 5, 1969, was the last time Bill Russell suited up to play a basketball game. He had 21 rebounds at age 35 in a [Finals] Game 7 against the Lakers. Of course, it ended once again with a fantastic juxtaposition of their rivalry—Wilt coming out of the game with some sort of injury, then being unable to talk his way back in because Lakers coach Butch van Breda Kolff, who had a disdain for Wilt, clearly wouldn't let him. So Russell winds up having the last say.... The late, great Harvey Pollack, statistician of the 76ers, did the definitive breakdown of every game. Wilt and Russell played 142 times, not counting exhibitions. Now that's a rivalry. Magic [Johnson] and [Larry] Bird, by contrast, played each other 32 times as pros.

RUSSELL: I retired when I was no longer willing to do all the things that I did to make me successful. I found myself taking shortcuts, and I was the one most cheated. The fans didn't know I was cheating them, but I knew.

RYAN: Russell would never, ever risk any indignity by playing in an old-timers game, I can promise you that.

LARRY BROWN: I was coaching at UCLA, and Magic would come over with Byron Scott, Bernard King, James Worthy, Norm Nixon, to play pickup games. Wilt was 43, 44 years old and would play just for the hell of it. It's game point, and Magic takes one of his running hooks and Wilt blocks it. Magic says, "That's a goaltend, game over, next." Wilt says, "That wasn't goaltending." And he turns and says, "Coach, was that goaltending?" I said, "No, I don't think it was." Magic starts screaming and yelling, takes his ball, yells, "Next!" Wilt grabs the ball from him and says, "We're gonna play another game, and there'll be no more shots taken at this basket." And he proceeded to block everything.

RUSSELL: Wilt and I became lifelong friends. I used to tell him, "You know, I think I'm the only person on this planet that really knows how good you are."

BASKETBALL'S BATTLE FOR RACIAL EQUALITY

Dr. James Naismith's final student before he retired from the University of Kansas was John McLendon, the pioneer of fast-break basketball, the full-court press, and the four corners offense. Yet McLendon never received the credit he deserved, because the majority of his work was accomplished at historically black colleges and universities when basketball was still segregated in the United States.

Long before civil rights legislation began to rid America of the scourge of segregation, McLendon was utilizing basketball to break down racial barriers. In March 1944, McLendon orchestrated a "secret game" between his team, North Carolina College for Negroes (now North Carolina Central University), and a collection of white former college basketball stars from Duke University Medical School, who had handily beaten the Duke varsity team in a scrimmage. McLendon planned the game for a Sunday morning, when most people would be in church. The medical students borrowed cars from friends and drove a circuitous route to the school to avoid being detected, arriving with their jackets pulled over their heads. They hustled into a locked gym, where McLendon's Eagles trounced them 88–44. There were no spectators.

"Coach Mac" went on to mentor countless African American coaches, among them Southern University coach Ben Jobe, Clarence "Big House" Gaines (who led Winston-Salem State University to a Division II NCAA championship in 1967 on the strength of a young guard named Earl Monroe), and former Georgetown coach John Thompson, who became the first African American coach to win a Division I championship.

SONNY HILL: Coach McLendon didn't sit at the knee of Dr. Naismith to play basketball. He sat at the knee of Dr. Naismith because Coach McLendon's father wanted him to further his education. So he took him to Kansas, where Dr. Naismith was the athletic director.

BILLY PACKER (NCAA Basketball Broadcaster, 1974–2008; Guard, Wake Forest University Demon Deacons, 1959–62): He was the only student in the graduate school who was black. James Naismith orchestrated it so McLendon would not only be able to get his degree but move forward in regard to his coaching.

HILL: Coach McLendon was taking a physical education class at Kansas. He had a chance to go to the swimming pool. The whites thought that if he went in the swimming pool, it would turn black, so they drained the pool so the water wouldn't be contaminated.

BEN JOBE (Head Coach, Southern University Jaguars, 1986–96 and 2001–03; Died 2017): Coach Mac did a great job of selling basketball in the area and kept us out of trouble. Without basketball, I think a lot of us would've been in serious trouble. His philosophy was, "It takes a village." So, if your parents weren't up to par, you could always go to Coach. If you needed food, you could go to Coach.

HILL: The vision of rebounding, kicking the ball out to midcourt, and then taking it up—that was Coach McLendon. He was the father of fast-break basketball.

WAYNE EMBRY: He called his offense "jack in the box," which was the four corners. He took what he learned from Dr. Naismith and was able to apply his own creativity to it.

JOHN THOMPSON: His style of play, pressing and running, was considered to be undisciplined—until white coaches started doing it.

HILL: [University of North Carolina coach] Dean Smith used to sit with Coach McLendon and Coach Gaines, and they would have basketball conversations. And one of the things that came out of those conversations was the four corners. Dean Smith was able to implement the four corners, which caught on because he was a white coach with a national audience, even though it was something that was done regularly prior to that at the black colleges.

JOBE: Coach Mac told us the game should be played from baseline to baseline, offensively and defensively. I bought into it and some of the other [African American] coaches bought into it, but when we integrated, they wanted to coach like the guys they saw on TV to show that we were "civilized."

THOMPSON: People always ask why I don't sit at the end of the bench. It was because of Coach McLendon. He sat in the middle of the bench and coached. He was the assistant coach [of the 1968 Olympic team], and players were on both sides of him. They could hear him. From that day on, I sat in the middle of the bench because of my respect for him.

EMBRY: You think about the '50s, '60s, and it was unique for a team to dominate as his teams did, because most of the world was against you. He was able to persevere through that.

THOMPSON: When I was growing up, all I heard about was John McLendon and Big House Gaines. Most of the guys I played with on the playground went to those traditional black schools, Tennessee A&I or North Carolina Central. Those were places I aspired to go before I realized I could look at a broader range of schools. Black schools weren't on television; black schools didn't travel as much. You were in a better position to go to the NBA if you went to a school like Providence [College]. The other schools were discriminated against.

EARL MONROE: I played for Coach Gaines at Winston-Salem. People revered him not only as a great coach but as a great man. He helped turn the tide in terms of how people perceive black colleges and black coaches.

PACKER: By the time I was a sophomore at Wake Forest, our team was really good and I was getting a lot of credit along with the other guys. We'd be in the front page of the sports section, and on the third [page] would be Winston-Salem. I kept reading about this guy named Cleo Hill who would score 30 points. I had nothing to do one night, so I hitchhiked across town. I walk in, and there's 1,500 to 1,800 people in this arena, and Big House Gaines walks over to me. He knew who I was because I had notoriety from playing in the ACC [Atlantic Coast Conference], and he says, "Why don't you sit over here with me on the bench." The game starts, and Cleo Hill jumps center. He's about 6'1", and he outjumps a 6'10" guy. . . . Cleo makes a couple of right-handed hook shots, a couple of left-handed hook shots, traps the ball above the backboard, dunks a couple of times. And I'm saying, "There's no player in the ACC that's even in his league, much less can play against him."

MONROE: They didn't have much regard for black coaches—or black schools, for that matter. You had people like Coach Gaines who stayed at Winston-Salem for 47 years because there was no place else to go.

JOBE: I went to see Coach McLendon one day. I opened the door and there was a white guy with his back to him, and Coach McLendon said, "I'm a little busy right now, but go to the cafeteria. Give me about an hour." He had chalk in his hand. I couldn't see the face of the guy with his back to him. When I came back, I said, "Coach, who was that guy?" He got real quiet and said, "I'm goin' to tell you this, but you must never, never mention it." This was 1955. He said, "That was coach Adolph Rupp from [the University of] Kentucky. They're in town to play Vanderbilt, and he had some questions about my philosophy of the game. But he wouldn't want anybody to know he was getting this knowledge from a black coach, so don't you mention it."

THOMPSON: They were so careless with black coaches. They put Big House Gaines in the Hall of Fame, but they put the wrong name on his ring. They put "Smokey Gaines" instead of "Big House." I went to speak at his banquet when he was inducted [into] the Hall. He hit me with an elbow and said, "Boy, I'm gonna show you something." I looked at his ring and he said, "They didn't even know my name."

AL SHARPTON (Civil Rights Activist; 2004 Candidate for President): There are those who feel there is too much emphasis in the African American family about what sports means. But I think you have to have grown up and have direct knowledge of the African American experience to understand why this is so.

EMBRY: Basketball gave me a sense of confidence because in the 1940s and '50s, African Americans looked for acceptance. I grew up in the Jim Crow era and couldn't go to restaurants, couldn't go to a lot of public places. I was the only African American in my high school. So naturally, you want to be accepted. Basketball got me accepted.

SHARPTON: Sports was one of the first areas that we could break through in American life. Before we could be a CEO of a Fortune 500 company, or before we could be a senator or president of the United States, we could be Jackie Robinson, we could be Oscar Robertson or Bill Russell.

SPENCER HAYWOOD: When I was growing up in Mississippi, I never went to a bathroom because it was whites only. I never drank out of a water fountain because it was whites only. If you don't want to serve me, I'll go around back and you'll serve me, and I'll go in the bushes and eat. That's life.

LENNY WILKENS: A lot of pretty good black athletes from my neighborhood went to black schools. They did not go to North Carolina or Duke or Kentucky—they weren't recruited.

SATCH SANDERS: [Frank] McGuire comes up to NYC and wants to meet with me. He says, "You're a Negro. Negroes can't play at North Carolina, you gotta be kidding me." He said, "I'm gonna kill my scouts. They told me everything about you, but they never told me you were a Negro."

PACKER: I'll never forget my first weekend at Wake Forest. Five of us went to a movie. In Bethlehem, Pennsylvania, where I grew up, we always got our candy and sat in the back. We get the candy and start going back, and a guy says, "Where are you going? That's where the niggers sit."

MONROE: My parents came down to visit me at Winston-Salem one time. We went to a place on Trade Street called Dan's Diner, and when we went in there, someone said, "We don't serve your kind." That was really the first time I had heard anything like that, and they had to physically drag me out of the place.

SHARPTON: Some felt they had to hold [black] people back because if [blacks] competed, they would break down our whole social structure and start wanting to date our daughters and live in our neighborhoods. You've got to keep them closed out because they may invade the world as you know it. They're not just looking at "Can you play ball?" but "You're going to want to live in my neighborhood, you're gonna want to date my sister, you going to want everything that is in my sociocultural setting, and that is a no-no." And I think that is where the fear came from.

HAYWOOD: The whites would call us the young bucks, and as we grew bigger and faster, the idea was for them to lay a false charge on you so you would go to jail for one or two or three weeks, or even a year. Then you would drop out of school and be beholden to the farm. That was the indigenous slavery process they had going on. I was the next guy in line, so my mother says, "We gotta get you out of here because I want you to graduate high school." We scraped up enough money, I caught the bus out of Belzoni, Mississippi, and I escaped up Highway 61.

EMBRY: I grew up wanting to play for the University of Dayton because they were perennial NIT [National Invitation Tournament] contenders. I was recruited by many schools in Ohio, all but Dayton. I grew up 20 miles from there and couldn't understand it. I ended up selecting Miami University [of Ohio] after several visits to Ohio State and a couple of other colleges. After I made my decision, my high school coach told me that Dayton didn't recruit me because they had a number of games in the South scheduled years in advance, and the coach didn't want to expose me to the treatment I was likely to receive there.

WES UNSELD (Center, Baltimore/Washington Bullets; 1969 NBA MVP): I was the first black recruited by [the University of] Kentucky. Another school had contacted me, which forced Kentucky to do the same. At that time, Kentucky had a thought process where they couldn't recruit a black person because they couldn't stay in school, couldn't do the work. There was a very renowned columnist at the *[Louisville] Courier-Journal* by the name of Dean Eagle who espoused some of my plaudits as to my academics and my basketball, because I was at that time one of the most highly recruited players in the country. So Adolph Rupp had no excuse.

AHMAD RASHAD (Broadcaster, *NBA on NBC*): In the '60s, the country was going through a change. African American athletes were trying to bring it more to light, saying, "Listen, there's been inequality too long. There's got to be something we can do. We can't keep winning championships and gold medals and then come home and be second-class citizens."

UNSELD: I never met Rupp initially. I talked to the assistant freshman basketball coach. That's when I knew that Rupp wasn't serious about recruiting me. Later on, after much pressure, I met the assistant coach, Harry Lancaster. There came a time when it got kind of heated and Rupp wanted to meet me. It just so happened, the day he wanted to do it, I had a commitment at La Grange Reformatory to be a speaker at the basketball banquet. He knew this. He wanted to meet my parents at our home. On that day, I stayed at the house to meet Mr. Rupp, with the prison car that was going to drive me up to the reformatory. I told them I had to wait at least for the meeting between Mr. Rupp and my parents. I waited a long time. . . . Finally, I got in the car and went to the reformatory. Next day, Rupp put out that I didn't have the courtesy to stay and talk to him. It doesn't bother me—it's just these stories weren't true.

SANDERS: It always amazed me when people asked me, "How can you play in Boston?" I'd say, "How can I play in America? I have problems all over the place."

WILKENS: St. Louis was an interesting city. We bought a home in a neighborhood, and For Sale signs went up everywhere. Some people moved, some stayed, and when they saw we weren't going to burn the area down, they became friendlier. You protested in your own way. I wasn't going to let anyone believe that I condoned this. There was a guy that lived next door to me. I was married by then, and our little girl was just starting to walk. I was out front with her, and the guy pulled up in his driveway. We had carports, we didn't have garages, and he pulled up and opened the door to his car and [then] backed out so he wouldn't have to look at me. After that, I decided [that] at 6 o'clock every evening, I would stand out front so he would have to back out. My wife thought I was a little crazy, but honest to God, I did it.

SANDERS: My worst times were in Los Angeles with cops. One time, Sam Jones and I were returning from the grocery store, and the cops thought we shouldn't be in that particular neighborhood and they pulled guns on us. Another time in L.A., we were at a party, and the cops got angry that we were there and went for their guns. The hosts of the party had to jump on them and hold them down so we could find a way to get out of there.

RASHAD: My freshman year in college, 1969, the coach of the basketball team kicked me off the team because my Afro was too big. If I didn't cut it, I would have to leave the team. I refused to cut it.

JULIUS ERVING (Small Forward, New York Nets/Philadelphia 76ers; 3-Time ABA MVP; 1981 NBA MVP): I learned a lot about race relations during my trips to South Carolina in the '60s. There was always the crossing of the Mason-Dixon Line, and there would be a big sign when you got past Virginia and into North Carolina that said, "Welcome to Klan Country."

ISIAH THOMAS (Point Guard, Detroit Pistons; 12-Time NBA All-Star): My journey to high school in 1979 was about three hours. I would have to take three buses to the end of the line and the train to the end of the line, and then I would have to walk a mile and a half to school. During that walk, your [white] friends would be driving by with their parents, but they wouldn't stop. It's cold in Chicago, and by the time you got to school, you'd say, "Hey, man, didn't you see me? Why didn't you stop?" And they'd say, "Well, I'm not like that, but my mom and dad are from a different generation."

PATRICK EWING (Center, New York Knicks; 11-Time NBA All-Star): One of the first times I experienced racism was when I moved to Boston. A lot of racial things happened with my Cambridge Rindge and Latin team. Our bus got broken into, our tires got slit, and the names that they called us . . . I just used it to fuel myself to be better.

SHAQUILLE O'NEAL: My junior year, 1988, I'm a high school All-American, playing at a small high school in Texas. We're on the bus and we're going through this town, and we're undefeated and everybody's talking about who is this Shaq kid? As soon as we hit the town, it's "Beat Cole High School," "Beat Shaq," "Beat the Monkey," "Beat the Gorilla." Right before we get to the school there's a tree, and there's a black, 7-foot scarecrow hanging from the tree with my jersey on it. Boy, was I upset. I was so upset that my coach called a play and I said, "No, we're not doing that today. Give me the ball." I dunked so many times that by the end of the first quarter, the rim was bent halfway to the floor.

In the early 1950s, after Celtics owner Walter Brown broke the color barrier by drafting Chuck Cooper, there was an unspoken agreement that an NBA team could not have more than two black players on its roster. (Later, that number was expanded to three). Too many African Americans, the owners believed, were bad for business. When Cleo Hill became the first overall pick of the St. Louis Hawks in 1961, he led the team in preseason scoring but saw his role abruptly reduced. The Hawks determined they needed their top scorer to be white—so Cleo Hill was frozen out by his own team.

EMBRY: In the '50s, '60s, the perception was there was a quota system. If you had more than three [blacks], you had to trade somebody. As the teams became more inclusive, we'd look at each other and say, "Well, one of us is going to be traded." As the story goes, when the Boston

Celtics continued to win championships starting five African Americans, that expedited diversity.

OSCAR ROBERTSON: I was the No. 1 draft choice in 1960. We had three black guys on the team. When they had a room report, they'd put an asterisk next to the black guys' names.

THOMPSON: I have a very good friend that got cut from professional basketball because of the quota situation. I have another friend who was just psychologically destroyed because he was cut. And both of those guys were better than me. Not only did they have to suffer the embarrassment of being cut, but when they go home, they have to explain to black people, who have accepted how society does things, "Why weren't you as good as this one?" And those guys said, "Hey, I didn't make the count."

SANDERS: In the summers, I'm playing with all these outstanding players, a lot of Eastern League players. Most of them are black. I say, "I don't see anybody that can touch these guys." I'm watching the competition in the NBA, and I'm saying, "There's a problem here. The guys aren't getting their chance because they're black. There's a limitation to how many [black players each team can have]." All these angry players in the summer—there was no question they were as good [as] or better than the NBA players.

THOMPSON: They never said, "I have this quota because of your color." They had to make sure you had a deficiency they could justify to the public—to make sure you weren't fast enough, you weren't intelligent enough, you were too small. The mistake they made with Cleo Hill was letting him on television, so everybody could see that he could play. Then those players on St. Louis ostracized him from the team, and he went to the owner and even the coach, who got in trouble for trying to support him.

PACKER: The St. Louis Hawks were the NBA defending champions, but they didn't want any part of Cleo Hill as the leading scorer on that team. And Cleo couldn't handle that emotionally. He never really became a great NBA player. People say it wasn't racist. It *was* racist, and if it was today, Cleo would be known as one of the great guards to have played in the league.

THOMPSON: When you got with black guys, the question was never whether I was better than the white boy. The question always was, "How many of us will they keep?"

BILL RUSSELL: Every single team in the NBA had three black players. And I called them out. I said, "Is there a quota or is this an accident or what?" And I get a call from the commissioner, Walter Kennedy, who said, "What are you trying to do to us?" I said, "Listen, if you catch me in a lie, you should kick me out of the league. But as long as I'm telling the truth, you can go to hell."

JOE RUKLICK: I asked [Philadelphia Warriors owner] Eddie Gottlieb, "Why do you keep me on the team? Three years on the bench, why?" And Eddie said these words: "Fans won't buy tickets if you have too many Negroes." I went home to my wife, who was smart, and I said, "Do you wanna go to San Francisco?" I said, "They told me that 'cause I'm white, I'm valuable." And she said, "You mean you are on this team because you are white?" I said, "Yeah." And she said, "That's not fair." And I realized, "She's right." So I quit.

HILL: When the NBA began to allow black players in, there was Earl Lloyd, there was Nat "Sweetwater" Clifton, there was Chuck Cooper. Then they say, "Well, they can have a roommate." So now you can have two. That was the quota up to that point. The person that really broke that down was Red Auerbach.

RUSSELL: When Walter Brown drafted Chuck Cooper, one of the other owners asked him, "You know he's colored, right?" And Walter Brown said, "I don't care if he's polka-dot, we drafted him."

HILL: Red Auerbach was the first coach to put five black players on the floor as a starting unit. I remember a writer who wrote for the evening

Bulletin in Philadelphia walked past me and said, "Sonny, do you see what's on the basketball floor? They've got a full house." The full house was five black guys.

SANDERS: It might have been groundbreaking in the NBA when the Celtics started the black five, but it wasn't anything special to our team because it was just a basketball decision for us, nothing more.

HILL: Red Auerbach was ahead of his time. He didn't see color. He just saw winning.

SANDERS: I'm sure letters and protests were sent to Auerbach, but it was never transferred to the players. We just kept on playing.

EMBRY: I'm getting myself mentally prepared to play a lot of minutes [in Game 7 of the 1968 Eastern Division Finals], and so I'm fired up, ready to go. After warm-ups, I sit down on the bench, and one of the Philadelphia fans comes and hands me a banana and says, "Here you go, you big ape."

RASHAD: Basketball is such a wonderful game. It's the only sport where you see the beauty of passing and receiving the pass and setting picks and everybody playing together, which is the way society should be. If you say, "We want to do that stuff but don't want any black players to do it," then I don't have any use for you.

DAVID STERN (NBA Commissioner, 1984–2014): The NBA led the way, not by some artful purpose, but by the talent of our players and the exposure we were able to give them. They had [an] enormous impact on society. I remember thinking that the perfect thing was if a white kid would dunk and say, "I'm Dominique Wilkins," and a black kid steps back to take the three and says, "I'm Larry Bird."

In 1966, Texas Western coach Don Haskins started five African Americans in the NCAA championship game against an all-white Kentucky team coached by Adolph Rupp, who was notorious for his racial insensitivity. While Haskins insisted he was not trying to send a message with his lineup, he did instruct David Lattin to go to the hole on the game's first play and slam the ball through to set the tone. At halftime, with Kentucky trailing 34–31, Rupp berated his players for being outplayed by the "coons."

Texas Western's 72–65 win was a turning point in college basketball. The following year, Vanderbilt's Perry Wallace would become the first African American player in the SEC (Southeastern Conference).

Although Texas Western's victory became a source of great pride in the black community, not everyone was pleased with the outcome. Following the game, the Miners waited patiently for an invitation to appear on The Ed Sullivan Show, *the customary reward for the NCAA champion. The invitation never came. In the months after the shocking upset, Haskins received sacks of hate mail condemning him as a "nigger lover."*

Yet Texas Western players recall the Kentucky players as gracious in defeat. A heartbroken Pat Riley made a point to walk over and congratulate each of the Miners as he left the court that day.

His coach did not follow suit.

RASHAD: When Texas Western won, it's probably the way black folks felt when Obama became president. You never thought it would happen in your lifetime. My dad wasn't a big sports fan, but he was, "Yeah! Texas Western!" I said, "Dad, you don't even watch basketball?" But he said, "Did you see them black boys?"

WILLIE WORSLEY (Guard, 1966 NCAA Champion Texas Western Miners): I was raised in the South, and there were always signs—"Whites Only." I've been called nigger from when I'm 4 years old on up. Over time, I learned to pick and choose my battles. I learned that if I wanted to put a stop to [discrimination], I could score more points than they could. That did my speaking for me.

PACKER: It started with the national championship with Texas Western. All of a sudden you have five black guys playing against five white guys, and the black guys win. The acceptance had to come along.

WORSLEY: I don't think race ever crossed Coach Haskins's mind. He treated us all the same—bad. He didn't give a damn if you were the number 1 player or the number 15 player. . . . In the locker room before the game, Coach Haskins called Bobby Joe Hill and Orsten Artis as his guards, so I figure I'm not gonna start, 'cause everyone played two guards. Then he said, "Willie, you, too." We have two Willies, Willie Cager and Willie Worsley. So I said, "Go ahead, roomie," 'cause Willie Cager and I roomed together. And Haskins said, "No, you, little one." I thought the man was drunk, having me playing forward at 5-foot-whatever [Worsley was 5'6"]. I was a little surprised with that, but Bobby Joe and I talked about it [and] he said, "You're out there because you can shoot." . . . I don't think Coach Haskins really saw us as five blacks starting; he saw us as five players who were quick enough. Kentucky was a fast team. He wanted that speed to compensate for their speed. I don't think it had anything to do with the racial part. He never mentioned to me anything about "I'm gonna start five blacks."

UNSELD: I was a freshman at Louisville watching Texas Western and [the] University of Kentucky play. Now, how could they have five blacks playing at Texas Western and Kentucky not have one, if Rupp really wanted black players there?

WORSLEY: When I first came on the court, I felt like we were in a hostile situation. All the news reporters were white, the TV camera people were white, the cheerleaders were white, the first level was all white, the whole bench of the other team was white. The only colored person I was seeing was on my side.

JOBE: What Coach McLendon did, beating Duke by 40 points [in the '40s], got lost in history. But because Texas Western was black and Adolph Rupp had the reputation of being a racist, it was really, really big. There were even whites who were saying to me, "I'm so glad he lost."

THOMPSON: In all fairness to Adolph Rupp, during the era that he grew up, there was a comfort level in saying things like that to people. I go back to the fact that there were several whites who didn't agree with [how we were treated], but they would've lost their jobs, their family would've been fired, they would've been isolated [if they'd said anything]. . . . I saw when I grew up what happened to whites who took a position for blacks. I saw how they were labeled, how they were called things because they said, "This is wrong." It takes a strong person to say something when they have something to lose.

WORSLEY: I remember one thing Haskins said to me that was outstanding. He said, "Boys, you are champions, and no one can take that from you. I don't care what they say, what they do, you are a champ, so act like a champ."

PAT RILEY: Louie Dampier and myself were coming down from an elevator to see our family after the game, and Adolph was going up. He looked at us and said, "One day you guys will understand the significance of this game." Now I know what it meant: it was the watershed game that opened up integration of sports in the South.

WORSLEY: Do I think we were represented rightfully? I don't think so. Do I think they gave us full credit? I don't think so. People don't talk about us as a great team. They talk about us as a black team.

HAYWOOD: A year after that game, Adolph Rupp was going to bring me down to Kentucky. They worked a deal out, I guess, with [the University of] Tennessee. [Tennessee] said, "We'll let you have him because you just lost to them five blacks, those Texas Western guys, so you've got a chip on your shoulder." But Rupp kept putting all these restrictions on me. He's saying, "When I bring you down, you can't look at the white girls." You can't do this, you can't talk. And he would always refer to me as "boy nigger." He seemed like a really good man, but there was an edge about him, and because of that defeat to Texas Western, I figured I was going to catch hell if I went to Kentucky.

DAVE BING: I don't think anybody gave Texas Western a chance to win the championship. As you saw the tenacity and the smarts they played with, it made you feel really good. It changed collegiate sports. When a team with the whole starting five that's African American wins the national championship, I think a lot of coaches started to look at it and say, "You know what, we're going to have to recruit some of these kids because they can play."

Six years after Texas Western's win, John Thompson inherited a basketball program that had gone 3-23 the previous year. Over the next 27 years, the Georgetown Hoyas won at a 71 percent clip. They were a predominantly black team with a physical style spurred by an "us vs. them" mentality dubbed "Hoya Paranoia" by writer Mark Asher.

The program reached its heights with the signing of big man Patrick Ewing, who also was recruited by North Carolina—and who witnessed a Ku Klux Klan rally on his official visit to Chapel Hill. When he chose Georgetown, his home city of Boston viewed it as a snub of Boston College, and the remainder of his high school career was tainted by racial slurs, including a sign unfurled at one of his games that declared, "Patrick Can't Read." Thompson, a fearless advocate for African Americans, was fiercely protective of his players. He initiated discussions on Martin Luther King Jr., Malcolm X, and myriad social issues. He pledged loyalty and demanded it in return.

Together, Ewing and Thompson went to three Final Fours in four years— and nearly won all of them. In 1982, victory slipped away in the final seconds when Fred Brown mistook North Carolina forward James Worthy for a teammate and threw him the ball. After winning it all in 1984, Georgetown looked to repeat in 1985 but fell to Big East Conference rival Villanova, which played a near-perfect game, missing just one shot in the second half en route to one of the greatest upsets in basketball history.

THOMPSON: I saw Elgin Baylor play. I saw him get recognition, I saw him make money, so that's what you wanted to do. Now, had I seen a doctor or a lawyer, or had I seen someone else who looked like me accomplishing those things, then maybe I would have wanted to do those things, too.

EWING: John Thompson had a lot to do with why I chose Georgetown. Number one, yes, he is black. And the way that he carried himself, the way that he spoke, he was very articulate. He was a person that as a 17-, 18-year-old kid, you looked up to and said, "I would love to be able to carry myself that way."

THOMPSON: I don't know what people were afraid of. You'd have to ask them. People don't want to share. It's very hard for somebody to make somebody equal to them. It's harder to make somebody better. The biggest fallacy in America is equality. I don't know any man that wants to make another man equal to him.

EWING: We were a predominantly black team. We had a black coach who people probably thought was militant and outspoken. So, yeah, that was part of why people hated us.

THOMPSON: We won 6 of the first 10 Big East championships. What are they gonna call me, Sweet John? That's not gonna happen.

EWING: Hoya Paranoia was great. Georgetown *was* college basketball back then. We kicked butt, we took names, we were the villains. We were riding in on the black horses with the black hats. We were very close, and the fact that everybody else was against us made us even closer.

THOMPSON: When I won the national championship, guys said to me, "How do you feel about being the first African American to win one?" I told them, "If that implies I am the first with intelligence, I resent that, because there were many guys before me that were not provided with an opportunity." I was criticized for it by some writers: "His attitude was not grateful." I was not the grateful nigger to say, "I'm so happy about being the first."

NOLAN RICHARDSON (Head Coach, University of Arkansas Razorbacks, 1985–2002): We were once 37-0 in junior college, and this guy said, "How did you guys do this?" I was so proud. Then he said, "Man, can you imagine what Dean Smith would have been able to do with that team?" I said, "Thirty-seven and oh, what could he have done?"

EWING: There's still racism today. Everywhere.

THOMPSON: God knows that King James and all those guys are great, great basketball players, but they didn't have the burden of being a basketball player and a pathfinder at the same time. They didn't have the burden that Oscar or Russell had, because those guys never had the luxury of psychologically just focusing on basketball.

SHARPTON: When I was growing up, Jackie Robinson had to be superman because he was all we had. Today, it's almost like, "Don't embarrass us, we've got President Obama, we've got Colin Powell, we've got Oprah Winfrey. It's not all on you, but don't make us look bad. As long as you don't take us down, we no longer depend on you to lift us up." Every time Bill Russell was on that court, he was playing for a race. The whole race felt like we won or lost a game. LeBron and that crowd, that's not on them.

THOMPSON: People talk about equality. I don't want equality. I want an opportunity to be better than you.

THE BIG O'S QUEST FOR JUSTICE

Oscar Robertson wasn't daydreaming about a litany of "firsts" while growing up in a segregated housing project in Indianapolis; he was merely trying to get by. His family was so poor they couldn't afford to buy him a basketball, so he practiced by throwing rolled-up rags through the hoop.

His career flowered under the watchful eye of coach Ray Crowe at Crispus Attucks High School, where, in 1955, Robertson led the school's basketball team to a state championship, making it the first all-black high school in the country to achieve such a feat. Tradition called for the winning team to ride atop a fire engine to the city circle, where the players would be let off to celebrate with friends and family.

When Crispus Attucks won, the fire truck took them 100 blocks *outside* the city. "It was the biggest insult," Robertson said. "The year before, when Milan won, the predominantly [white crowd] went down to the circle and stayed there for I don't know how many hours. They called our principal and told them they didn't want all the blacks in town because they were going to tear up something. For them to do that to young kids, just because they're black, I'll never forgive them for that."

It was the beginning of a long and decorated career for Robertson, one lamentably permeated by racism.

The next season, Crispus Attucks went undefeated, won another state title, and was again transported outside the city circle to celebrate. Robertson was crowned Indiana's "Mr. Basketball."

He committed to the University of Cincinnati and won the national scoring title all three of his college seasons. When the Bearcats were invited to play in the Dixie Classic in North Carolina, Robertson received a letter from the Ku Klux Klan. "They said if I came down to Raleigh, they were gonna shoot me," he said.

Robertson went anyway, and was stunned to discover "colored" drinking fountains, separate bathrooms, and orders to stay in a local fraternity house because blacks were not allowed in town. His brother was banned from sitting in the arena, where fans threw debris at Robertson.

A road trip to Houston resulted in similar indignities. The team checked into the Shamrock Hilton, but within an hour, Robertson was asked to leave. "I called the coach up and said, 'You did this to me?'" Robertson said. "He said, 'Oscar, I didn't know anything about it.' I said, 'You know what, Coach? You're always talking to me about the team being together. I really believed you, but not anymore. I don't want to go to any more banquets. I'm not going to any more interviews.' He said, 'OK.' And I didn't."

Some tried to taint Robertson's transcendent versatility—in 1959, he tallied 45 points, 23 rebounds, and 10 assists against Indiana State—because he spoke out on racial issues, leaving him branded as "ungrateful" and "bitter."

"That's what they say about intelligent black people—they're bitter," said John Thompson. "If you're not grateful and put your hat in your hand and agree with everything a white man says, you're bitter."

The Big O's talent was undeniable. In 1961–62, he became the first NBA player in history to average a triple-double for the season, a feat unmatched until Oklahoma City star Russell Westbrook duplicated it 55 years later. Over his first five NBA seasons, Oscar *averaged* 30.3 points, 10.3 rebounds, and 10.3 assists.

"Oscar was the best ever because he controlled the game," said Dolph Schayes. "If you needed a point guard, he'd be the point guard. If you needed a scorer inside, he'd be a scorer inside. If you needed a rebounder, he'd be the rebounder. If you need somebody to play good defense, he'd be it. He could do everything."

In 1964, the Big O was named the NBA's MVP, the only player from 1960 to 1968 not named Russell or Chamberlain to earn that award. One of the persistent frustrations of his career was his inability to knock off the Celtics, who eliminated Robertson's teams in the 1963, 1964, and 1974 NBA playoffs.

Robertson cemented his legacy in 1970, when he engaged in a

landmark antitrust lawsuit against the NBA that paved the way for free agency, higher salaries, improved travel, and better medical personnel. "If we didn't have the Oscar Robertson rule, no one would make $20 million a year," Oscar said. "There would be no LeBron [James] or [Dwyane] Wade or [Chris] Bosh being able to go to Miami together. And you wouldn't be treating basketball players like movie stars."

Robertson's lawsuit came with a price. When his career ended, no team would hire him as a coach or general manager. "I always felt that that [lawsuit] was held against him," said Jerry West. "I'm shocked that he was never given an opportunity to be involved as an executive, because he would have brought a real presence to another team. I don't blame him for being bitter."

In 1970, Oscar was traded to Milwaukee, where Lew Alcindor [who later changed his name to Kareem Abdul-Jabbar] was emerging as one of the best big men in the game. Robertson also paired with Wayne Embry to form a textbook pick-and-roll combination. "Oscar had the unique ability to see the court the way no one else could," said Embry. "*He* knew we were open before we did."

Robertson was 33 years old by then and willingly acquiesced to Alcindor's considerable talents. The result was Oscar's first (and Milwaukee's only) championship, in 1971. "Oscar played a lesser role so Alcindor could have maximum freedom as a player and his team could win a championship," said Jack Ramsay. "That's who Oscar was."

Robertson doubts that today's players are aware of his role in their lucrative endeavors. "The game owes Oscar Robertson a great deal," said Embry, "and so do generations of great players."

BREAKING BARRIERS: Title IX and the Growth of the Women's Game

The first West Coast women's intercollegiate basketball game, when Stanford eked out a 2–1 win over UC Berkeley, was an understated affair. The year was 1896, and it's likely the score was so low because the women were preoccupied with guarding the doors and blocking the windows to ensure that no men witnessed them competing in their dresses. Teams lined up six to a side, with only three players eligible to cross half-court.

Eighty-eight years later, on December 2, 1984, West Virginia center Georgeann Wells took flight and slammed the ball through the net against a transfixed University of Charleston team, cementing her status as the first woman to dunk in college competition. In so doing, Wells squelched the notion that women were incapable of playing "above the rim." She dunked with a regulation ball, the same one used by the men, a significant accomplishment, because two years later the women's ball was reduced by one inch in circumference to make it easier to handle.

It took another decade for the University of North Carolina's Charlotte Smith to duplicate Wells's feat, but once Candace Parker and Brittney Griner started dunking with regularity, it was no longer a novelty.

The growth of the women's game boasted all the ingredients of a successful venture. It enjoyed seminal performances, such as Carol Blazejowski dropping a record-setting 52 points at Madison Square Garden in 1977 (including shooting 17 for 21 from the floor in the second half), Anne Donovan blocking 10 shots to lead Old Dominion past Tennessee in the 1980 AIAW (Association for Intercollegiate Athletics for Women) Final, and Lynette Woodard racking up 3,649 career points at Kansas without a three-point shot.

Its pioneers oozed personality, like Nancy Lieberman, the brash New Yorker who muscled her way into games at the legendary Rucker Park, and Cheryl Miller, the glib leader of two-time champion USC, who, along with her younger brother, Reggie, used to hustle unsuspecting ballers to play two-on-two at the parks in Riverside, California.

The sport also sprouted dedicated coaches who churned out dynasties, including Cathy Rush, who led tiny Immaculata College, a school of less than 600 students run by nuns, to three consecutive championships, and Pat Summitt, the gatekeeper of the women's game, the first female (or male) to reach 1,000 victories, whose passion and leadership transformed her into a basketball icon.

Yet the evolution of women's basketball was a slow, painful process, particularly before the enforcement of the landmark 1972 Title IX mandate, which required that women receive equal access to educational programs, activities, and federal financial assistance. Although it took decades for society to recognize women as athletes and competitors, the pioneers endured the lonely journey to acceptance for one simple reason: they couldn't live without the game they loved.

CATHY RUSH (Head Coach, Immaculata College Mighty Macs, 1972–77): I grew up in the '50s outside Atlantic City. My mom would open the door and say, "Don't come back till dinner." After everyone left, I was still shooting. I was what they called a tomboy. I didn't understand why other girls weren't playing.

LYNETTE WOODARD (Guard, University of Kansas Jayhawks; 4-Time NCAA All-American; 1984 Olympic Gold Medalist): My brother and I went to everyone's backyard. Girls really weren't allowed to play. I had my feelings hurt many times when guys would say, "You should go home, Lynette, and learn how to cook."

ANN MEYERS (Guard, UCLA Bruins; 4-Time NCAA All-American; Broadcaster, Phoenix Suns): At one point, I was acting so much like a guy, playing ball with my brother and his friends, he got frustrated and finally said to me, "Why don't you just try being a girl?"

CHERYL MILLER: I didn't like playing against the girls because girls didn't play hard. They didn't like to sweat, and they liked to kiss boys. They weren't about the jumper, the crossover, and that's what I was all about.

RUSH: I never pretended to be anybody. There were no female role models.

NANCY LIEBERMAN (Point Guard, Old Dominion University Lady Monarchs/Phoenix Mercury/Detroit Shock; 2-Time AIAW Champion; Assistant Coach, Sacramento Kings, 2015–17): Basketball changed my life because I didn't have anything else. My parents were getting divorced, my mother didn't have money to put food on the table, we were one grandparent away from food stamps. I can remember the day I was in the kitchen and the lights went out, and I looked at my brother and said, "What just happened?" And he goes, "We're poor." I said, "I ain't living like this. Something's gonna change in my life." I started playing basketball, and that was my way out.

VAL ACKERMAN (Commissioner, WNBA, 1996–2002; Commissioner, Big East Conference): When I was in junior high school, there wasn't a girls' team yet. You had to try out for the boys' team. I didn't feel comfortable doing it, so I tried out for the cheerleading team. My enduring memory was getting cut and being shattered. So things flowed for me from being a frustrated cheerleader.

RUSH: I was our county's scoring champion. The next year, they got rid of the girls' team. I was very close with the woman who coached us, and she wasn't even upset, which shocks me to this day.

MEYERS: Girls wore skirts and dresses. Because I was playing sports at recess and lunchtime, and before school and after school, I would always wear shorts under my skirts so I wouldn't feel embarrassed if someone knocked me over.

LIEBERMAN: I can remember dribbling around the house, and my mother would take a screwdriver and puncture my basketball. I'd go in the closet, get another ball, dribble around. She'd come back out of her room, like, "You gotta be kidding me." She punctured seven basketballs.

CAROL BLAZEJOWSKI: The boys had all the teams. The girls had nothing. I went to our athletic director, Mr. Martin, who was also the boys' basketball coach, and very respectfully said, "Mr. Martin, I'd like to talk to you about putting together a girls' basketball team." He looked at me and said, "Well, we really don't have the funds for that, Carol." And I said, "Well, Mr. Martin, you have a freshman boys' team, you have a JV boys' team, a varsity boys' team, and maybe if you took one of these teams out of the equation, we could get enough together for a girls' team." And he didn't like that. He said, "We'll see what we can do." I said, "Mr. Martin, I really appreciate your consideration, but if you don't have a girls' team, then just be prepared, I'm gonna try out for your team." I knew Mr. Martin didn't want a girl on his team. Sure enough, the following year we had a girls' varsity basketball team.

MILLER: I remember trying out for the boys' seventh-grade basketball team and not making it at first because the coach didn't like me for beating up on them when I was in elementary school. After practice he said, "If you can beat my son one-on-one, you can play on our team." I beat him 21–0, and he still wouldn't let me on.

LIEBERMAN: Everybody would talk about the greatest players in the world, including Dr. J and Lew Alcindor, and all these guys played at Rucker Park in Harlem. One day, I decided I'm going there. I told my mother, "I'll be at the park," so she thought it was the one across the street. I took a couple dollars out of her purse, and I took the A train by myself from Far Rockaway, got off at 155th, and walked into Rucker Park. I stuffed T-shirts in my jacket on the train so I looked big, and I would glare at people before they did it to me 'cause I was scared. I walked into Rucker Park, and I couldn't believe how tiny it was. These black guys start looking at me. "Little girl, are you lost?" I say, "No, are you?" I wanted to be the dog that bites. They say, "What are you doing here?" I say, "I wanna play." They're just looking at this crazy 11-year-old girl. I say to one kid, "Is your name Rucker?" He says, "No." I say, "Good. So it ain't your park, and I'm gonna play." After that, they embraced me.

DIANA TAURASI (Point Guard, University of Connecticut Huskies/Phoenix Mercury; 3-Time NCAA Champion; 4-Time Olympic Gold Medalist; 2009 WNBA MVP): I always took it as a compliment when people told me I played like a guy. When I was little, who were the best basketball players in the world? All men.

LISA LESLIE (Center, Los Angeles Sparks; 3-Time WNBA MVP): Our team went 7-0 in the seventh grade. I was already 6'1", and they would throw me the ball and I would turn around and make bank shots. We won and they gave me the smallest trophy known to man—and it was a little boy.

LIEBERMAN: It was hard. When you are from my generation and you're playing basketball in the '60s and '70s, it's lonely, it's scary, and there's a lot of "She'll stop playing with the boys at some point and act like a girl." It was "Play like a boy but act like a girl." I heard so many times "What's wrong with her?"

ACKERMAN: There was one scholarship for women's basketball at [the University of] Virginia in the fall of 1977. Title IX was five years in the books, but enforcement was slow. So I grabbed half the scholarship. Another teammate who was also from New Jersey came in at the same time, and she got the other half. I'm fond of saying I got tuition and fees, and she got room and board. I got to go to class, and she got to eat.

WOODARD: Title IX was the emancipation proclamation. It was freedom. It opened up a world I loved. Women could not only be included in sports but it was the law.

MEYERS: Because of Title IX, I got a scholarship to UCLA. If I didn't, I probably would have gone to some junior college. I would never have developed the kind of reputation I had or generated the kind of publicity I got.

MILLER: You think about what Title IX did, not just for women's basketball but for women's sports across the board, and now men are going to complain it's not fair? I mean, get out of here with that stuff!

MEYERS: Title IX opened up so many doors for us. It was huge. In the early days, 1 in 30 girls competed in sports. Now it is 1 in 3.

MILLER: I can't imagine how it was before Title IX. Did we close the gap completely? No. Did we bridge it? Absolutely. Do we still have room to grow? Undoubtedly. But without Title IX, there wouldn't be any of us.

———

Ann Meyers won 13 MVP awards in four different high school sports, earned multiple All-American honors at UCLA, and medaled in the Olympic Games. The fledgling Women's Professional Basketball League (WBL) made her the No. 1 overall pick in 1978, but she didn't sign, choosing instead to preserve her eligibility as an amateur for the 1980 Olympic Games.

One phone call dramatically altered her career path. Indiana Pacers owner Sam Nassi offered Meyers a one-year personal services contract worth $50,000 to try out for his team. Meyers was torn but ultimately attended the three-day tryouts for Pacers rookies and free agents at the famed Hinkle Fieldhouse.

Her decision unleashed a torrent of derision and criticism from both men and women, who viewed her tryout as a publicity stunt. When asked about Meyers, potential Pacers teammate Mike Bantom growled, "If I had a chance, I'd go right at her and make her look as bad as I could." The WBL accused her of making a "mockery" of the sport.

Meyers completed the tryout, withstanding the rugged play of men who were as much as 6 inches taller and 40 to 50 pounds heavier than her. Assistant coach Jack McCloskey lauded Meyers's skills, claiming her fundamentals were better than those of half the team's roster, but when camp ended, Meyers was cut. The Pacers offered her a job in the broadcasting booth, and though she didn't realize it at the time, her second career was born.

MEYERS: I get a call from Sam Nassi, who was the new owner of the Indiana Pacers, and I get this offer to try out for their team. It certainly was a marketing ploy, there's no question, but the fact that he asked and really wanted to pursue it got me interested. I also really want to go to the 1980 Olympics: to play for coach Sue Gunter, to wear the USA [logo] on my jersey. It was a very difficult decision, but I was struggling with USA Basketball a little bit, because I had heard that people there thought I was over-the-hill at age 24. I was thinking, "Wow, really?" I went out to [the Olympic trials in] Squaw Valley, went through a couple days of practice, and I went to the coaches, Sue and Pat Summitt. I was in tears because it was hard to leave, but I chose to try out with the Pacers. A lot of people were against it, but for me it was, "How do I pass this up?" ...

The Pacers had a press conference in Los Angeles. Slick Leonard, who was the Pacers coach, came to California to talk me out of playing. He went to the owner and said, "What are you doing?" Slick came from a generation where women needed to be in the home raising the family.

WOODARD: Ann Meyers was an inspiration to me because I was watching the news one day and I saw Ann trying out for the Indiana Pacers. I thought, "See? Women can play with men." And that cemented my dream of playing for the [Harlem] Globetrotters.

MEYERS: I was taken aback by how aggressive the media was and the negativity surrounding my tryout. . . . The criticism puts you in a no-win situation. If they block my shot—"Ah, it's only a girl." If I made a shot against them—"You let some girl beat you." The Pacers didn't end up taking me, but if I could do it over, I'd do exactly the same thing. Because it opened up so many doors for me and gave me a bigger forum to stand on. My tryout, for me, was not about publicity. I loved the game and I wanted to play the game, and I tried to take it to another level.

WOODARD: I had a cousin who played with the Globetrotters for 25 years, Hubert "Geese" Ausbie, so of course every time the team came through Wichita, Kansas, the family would get in the car and go. I was watching that wizardry, and I wanted to learn it. That was my team and that was my dream. . . . In 1985–86, I read in the newspaper that the Globetrotters would go coed for the 1985–86 season. I called and asked, "Is this really true?" They sent me a letter inviting me to a trial in Charlotte. We went for a week, and the numbers were cut down to 15 by the time we left. At the time, the McGee twins from USC, Pam and Paula, were trying out. They were beautiful, tall, talented, and with the grueling schedule of the Globetrotters, it would be easy to play Pam one night and Paula the other night, and no one would ever know the difference. But the Globetrotters decided to just choose one [woman]. They lined us up like it was a beauty pageant, and they called my name. It was the greatest day in my life. I had posters on my wall of the Globetrotters as a child. I took pride in becoming one of the ambassadors of the game and traveling all over the world. I wouldn't trade it for anything.

———

When the playing careers of these early female stars ended, many gravitated to coaching. Lieberman, the girl who hijacked Rucker Park, wanted in on that, but she was angling for a job in the men's game. In 2010, Dallas Mavericks general manager Donnie Nelson was searching for someone to run his NBA Development League team when he ran into Lieberman in a coffee shop. After a brief conversation, he realized that Lieberman—who had Dallas roots, knew the game, and exhibited a great passion for coaching—had all the qualities he was seeking. He named Lieberman coach of the Texas Legends, and she led them to their only playoff appearance. Lieberman reluctantly stepped aside to assume an assistant general manager's role the following year so she could spend more time supporting her son T. J. Cline in the last year of his high school basketball career.

Lieberman waited for the next opportunity she was certain would be coming along, but it didn't materialize. She had hoped to become the first female NBA assistant coach. Instead, on August 5, 2014, Becky Hammon earned that distinction when the San Antonio Spurs added her to their staff.

Hammon had spent the final eight seasons of her WNBA career playing for the San Antonio Stars, which led to numerous interactions with coach Gregg Popovich. When Hammon suffered a season-ending knee injury with the Stars in 2013 and stayed in the United States to rehab rather than go overseas to play in the off-season, Popovich invited her to attend practices and film sessions. Pop offered her the assistant coach position a year later. Hammon texted Lieberman two words: "I'm sorry."

Eleven and a half months later, Lieberman accepted a job with the Sacramento Kings as assistant coach under George Karl. Her text to Hammon: "I'm with you."

BECKY HAMMON (Point Guard, New York Liberty/San Antonio Stars; 6-Time WNBA All-Star; Assistant Coach, San Antonio Spurs): People ask me about being a trailblazer, but somebody already went through these weeds and cleared it all out. I'm just walking through it. Nancy Lieberman, Ann Meyers, Rebecca Lobo, Sheryl Swoopes, Cheryl Miller, Lisa Leslie—you can go down the list of these amazing athletes. It's been a long journey for women who weren't supposed to sweat and women who weren't supposed to play sports and women who were supposed to be submissive and sit back and not be active. Those are the women that really grinded it out. . . . I understand the importance and the weight that it carries to be the first. I don't really know why I was chosen. It was just the right mix, the right time—for me personally, but also for the Spurs. They saw a piece that fit. I don't really consider myself an emblem.

LIEBERMAN: Becky caught lightning in a bottle. If she doesn't tear her ACL and she goes back to Europe, Coach Popovich doesn't get a chance to see her IQ, to see her interpersonal skills with the players and the respect she commands. Pop had a long period of time to watch her and appreciate her qualities.

HAMMON: I'm not going to sit here and say there's not gender bias. There is. There's a reason why it's never been done before and a woman has never really been welcomed in this capacity. There's always been a line: you can come this far, but you can't cross [it]. To be able to go over that line and be appreciated for my mind and for my personhood and what I bring to the team, I'm just so thankful the Spurs thought I'd fit.

R. C. BUFORD (General Manager, San Antonio Spurs; 2-Time NBA Executive of the Year): Becky and the Stars had raised the level of basketball in San Antonio. They made a WNBA Finals appearance, and the relationships that she built with her fans in our community were all really important to our organization.

HAMMON: I definitely think there will be more women hired. Sometimes it just takes courage to pull the trigger, to be the first one to say, "Hey, this is the right thing to do." R. C. Buford and Pop had the courage to say, "Screw it. We like her as a person, we like her mind, we like her personality, we like her energy." . . . I know Pop had watched and observed me in my element as a player, being an extended coach on the floor. But our first one-on-one sit-down happened on a flight back from London. We didn't really talk about basketball at all. We talked about politics and society and the economy. One talking point was my playing in Russia and him taking Soviet studies at the Air Force Academy. . . .

The Spurs didn't say, "Hey, we're going be the first to hire a female." They would have done it a long time ago. And it was really never my intent to say, "Hey, I want to be the first female NBA assistant coach." It just came together.

BUFORD: At the time when coach [Mike] Budenholzer and Brett Brown left [the Spurs], Becky wasn't ready to quit playing, but she had already established a relationship with our coaches. She joined our group a year before she became an assistant coach and spent time as an intern.

HAMMON: I learned so much from the players. I watched Tim Duncan, and maybe he didn't even touch a basketball, but seeing him work in the weight room, seeing how he interacted with his teammates, there's so many things behind the scenes that made him special. I tried to soak it up. As a coach, just standing back, you see things that you don't see as a player. It might be something timing-wise, or the way somebody's defending a player, or footwork—it can be the smallest thing. Those are the little tidbits that you want to drop in their ear in the heat of the moment. But I never said anything to Timmy unless it was really, really good, 'cause he probably already knew it.

BUFORD: Becky gained the respect of our players, she gained the respect of our coaches, she came well prepared and well themed to our team, and when it was time for her to move to what's next, none of us wondered, "Should we be hiring a woman?"

HAMMON: If you follow the Spurs at all, the last thing they want is front-page news. We knew people would be interested in my hiring, but I don't think any of us really had an idea of how big of a deal it was.

BUFORD: The overriding theme was "We've got a really skilled and talented person in our organization who could help us get better. So why not?"

HAMMON: I don't want anybody to hire me because I'm a woman. I want to be hired because I'm the right person for the job.

THE MIGHTY MACS

Cathy Rush hatched a simple plan: get married, work for three years, have children, and retire. In 1970, after her nuptials to NBA referee Ed Rush, she accepted a coaching job at Pennsylvania's tiny Immaculata College for $450 a year. It was the perfect low-key job—a school with fewer than 500 students, run by nuns, with no gym (it had burned down) and no expectations.

But soon Rush was captivated by the talented, competitive athletes in her program. Center Theresa Shank had planned to play at St. Mary's [in Maryland], but when her family's house burned down, she commuted to Immaculata instead. She would go on to become a three-time All-American.

Rush went home and gushed to her husband, "I have Jerry West in a female body." He replied, "Yes, dear, what's for dinner?" Immaculata flourished in Rush's first season, going 8-0 before Shank broke her collarbone in an auto accident on the way to a game. The next season, 1971–72, Immaculata qualified for the AIAW tournament in Normal, Illinois. When the team, which had no travel budget, came up short in its fund-raising efforts, Rush was forced to leave 3 of her 11 players behind. "It was," Rush says, "the saddest moment of my life."

Her team wore outdated wool tunics with white blouses underneath, bloomers, high socks, and Chuck Taylor sneakers. Immaculata played four games in three days, requiring the players to wash their blouses in the sink between games. The wool tunics wouldn't dry in time for the next game, so they remained unwashed, drenched in sweat.

Immaculata shocked everyone by advancing to the title game against West Chester State College, a team that had thumped them by 32 points just two weeks earlier. When Immaculata pulled off an unimaginable upset to win the championship, more than 500 fans were waiting for them at the Philadelphia airport.

The 1971–72 championship was the first of three straight for Rush. With players like plucky point guard Marianne Crawford feeding Shank in the post, Immaculata posted the first undefeated season in women's college basketball history in 1972–73.

By then, a new gym had been constructed, but there were no bleachers, so the school set up folding chairs for spectators. Starter Rene Muth's dad owned a hardware store and brought metal buckets and wooden dowels to drum up some spirit. Soon the nuns were banging away, earning their own moniker: the Bucket Brigade.

In 1975, more than 12,000 fans watched the Immaculata women edge Queens College in a regular season game at Madison Square Garden. Ten thousand of them left when the women's game was done—while the men were warming up for the second half of the doubleheader.

Ironically, the advent of Title IX proved to be the death knell for Immaculata. Rush pleaded for scholarships but was rebuffed. Mississippi's Delta State University emerged as the new dynasty, winning three straight championships from 1975 to 1978 under coach Margaret Wade and with the gifted 6'3" Lusia Harris.

In 1977, Rush retired to raise her two young sons. "I thought I'd take a few years off and get back to it," she says, "but I never did."

Her players carried on her legacy. Theresa Shank Grentz coached 12 seasons at the University of Illinois and 18 seasons at Rutgers, where she led the Scarlet Knights to an AIAW championship in 1982.

Rene Muth Portland spent 27 seasons at Penn State and won 600 games, although her reputation was sullied following revelations that she had systematically rooted out and dismissed lesbian players in her program.

Marianne Crawford Stanley won three championships at Old Dominion, with Nancy Lieberman and Anne Donovan as her star players.

"We were a group of strong, competitive women who loved the game," Rush says. "It truly was a magical mystery tour."

GAMBLERS ENSNARE THE GAME

The City College of New York (CCNY) basketball team was in high spirits in the wee hours of February 19, 1951, as the train from Philadelphia rolled into Penn Station. They were defending NCAA and NIT champions, a feat that had never been accomplished by any other school. Having trounced Temple 95–71 hours earlier, Coach Nat Holman's boys appeared well on their way to another banner season—until the train screeched to a halt and members of the New York County District Attorney's office climbed aboard and took seven CCNY players into custody on charges of fixing basketball games.

So began a devastating college basketball scandal that ensnared some of the country's finest programs and most respected coaches in the game, including Long Island University (LIU) legend Clair Bee and Kentucky coach Adolph Rupp.

The DA's office was tipped off by Junius Kellogg, a center from Manhattan College, who was offered a $1,000 bribe by gamblers before a game against DePaul. The investigation led prosecutors to petty criminal Salvatore Sollazzo and LIU guard Eddie Gard, who, during a meeting at a resort in the Catskills, plotted their infiltration of the college ranks.

Thirty-two players from seven colleges, including NYU, Manhattan College, Bradley University, and the University of Toledo, would admit to taking bribes to shave points between 1947 and 1952. Among those players were LIU's Sherman White, who led the nation in scoring during the 1950–51 season, and Kentucky players Alex Groza and Ralph Beard.

The repercussions reverberated across the country. CCNY was dropped from Division I to Division III and slapped with a lifetime ban prohibiting it from playing at Madison Square Garden. LIU shut down its basketball program for six years. Neither school would ever return to national prominence. Kentucky disbanded its team for the 1952–53 season. Yet it was the integrity of the college game that incurred the most damage.

And then, 10 years later, it happened again.

The mastermind was former Columbia star Jack Molinas, who had been expelled from the NBA in 1954 for his gambling ties. He worked with book-maker Joe Hacken and underling Aaron Wagman to entice players to fix games.

The 1961 scandal devastated programs across the country, from St. John's to St. Joseph's to NC State to Bowling Green. Yet, in their zeal to stomp out il-licit gambling in college basketball, prosecutors also swept up a number of in-nocent players. Doug Moe of North Carolina and Tony Jackson of St. John's had been offered bribes and refused, but both were banned from the NBA for not reporting them. College basketball was embroiled in a gambling witch hunt, and many of the game's top players—including those who were never found guilty of any wrongdoing—paid the price.

HOWARD GARFINKEL (Founder, Five-Star Basketball Camp; Died 2016): The gam-bling scandals were a disaster. The 1961 scandal came within an inch of ending my basketball life, because I had sent three players to NC State, and they were all involved. It was a crushing blow to me that my kids would be involved in a thing like that.

CHARLEY ROSEN (NBA Journalist; Author, *The Wizard of Odds*): It all started in the Catskills. The owners of the resorts wanted to keep the customers there at night. They didn't want them to go into town and get drunk, spending their money somewhere else, so they organized basketball teams.

TOMMY HEINSOHN: They had summer league games for various Catskills hotels, and betting would go on among them.

ROSEN: They would import players as bellhops. Wilt Chamberlain was one. During the summer, it became the place to go if you wanted to stay in shape and compete against the best players around. It became dan-gerous, because all the good players were at five or six hotels, and the gamblers could approach them in an informal atmosphere.

LOU CARNESECCA (Head Coach, St. John's University Redmen, 1973–92): It was one of my biggest fears as a head coach—that some poor young men would be tempted. Guys throw $10,000 at these kids, when they've never seen that kind of money.

ROSEN: The kids saw the coaches driving Cadillacs and wearing fancy suits, and these kids were grubbing along in poverty. It made them susceptible to someone saying, "Here's a couple of bucks; miss a shot or throw a bad pass or something."

DONNIE WALSH (Indiana Pacers Front Office Adviser): Great coaches never see that coming. I know, from coaching myself, I never sat on the bench thinking someone did something on purpose, like throw the ball away. You think he made a mistake. It's a game of mistakes.

ROSEN: To say the coaches never knew is bullshit. How could a coach not know?

GARFINKEL: I still don't believe that my players shaved points. I just don't believe it, because they were clean-cut, the nicest straight-arrow kids in America. To this day, I don't know how it could have happened. But it did.

WALSH: So at some point somebody tells you, "They were dumping that game," and you say, "They were what?" It would crush you, particularly a guy like Clair Bee. It's a betrayal of everything he believes in.

JOE B. HALL (Head Coach, University of Kentucky Wildcats, 1972–85): Right before the accusations came out about the Kentucky players, it had already surfaced with other players in other schools. Coach Rupp said in a public statement that the gamblers "couldn't touch my players with a 10-foot pole."

ROSEN: Adolph Rupp's best friend was a bookie. After several games, he berated his players in games his team won because they screwed up the point spread and his buddy lost money.

BILLY PACKER: City College, LIU, and NYU were always big favorites. So, if they were a 15-point favorite, they'd win the game by 7 or 8 points but also be dumping. They got the idea in their heads they weren't doing anything wrong because their team still won.

BILLY CUNNINGHAM (Small Forward, Philadelphia 76ers; 4-Time NBA All-Star): The scandal was truly the downfall of New York basketball.

PACKER: It wasn't just happening in New York. It was all over the place.

HALL: We were playing Holy Cross in the Boston Garden, and a fight broke out and the police escorted us to the locker room. As we went in, a big guy with a long, dark overcoat shook hands with Alex Groza. When Groza got inside the locker room, he pulled out this wadded-up bill, opened it, and it was a $100 bill. Now, in 1948, a $100 bill was like a thousand today—or more. You could buy an automobile with three or four hundred dollars. That's the first contact that I think the gamblers made, and it was a gift.

ROSEN: At the height of it, guys were underneath the basket waving $20 bills, $50 bills, at the players.

CUNNINGHAM: The old Madison Square Garden had a line of about 20 phone booths. At halftime, man those things were packed 10 deep because everybody was calling their bookie.

ROSEN: The Baltimore Bullets were famous for dumping. The old New York Knicks were famous for dumping. The NBA had special undercover detectives who got the goods on everybody and told them, "If you don't retire at the end of the season, we're coming after you and we're going to arrest you." That was 1956. A bunch of guys retired at the height of their careers.

HEINSOHN: I remember playing in New York and throwing up a hook shot from half-court at the end of the game. It went in, and the place went bananas because it beat the spread.

ROSEN: Phil Jackson, his first game with the Knicks, he gets in for garbage time at the Garden, scores a basket at the buzzer, and everyone starts booing. He says, "What's going on here?" and he was told, "You screwed up the point spread."

CUNNINGHAM: I played a game in Madison Square Garden with the Philadelphia 76ers and Wilt Chamberlain. There's about 3 seconds left in the game, we're up 16 points. Wilt misses the first foul shot. The Garden goes crazy on this side. Wilt makes the next one, and the place goes crazy on the other side. The Knicks take the ball, throw it the length of the court, lay it in, and the place goes crazy. The spread is 15. We take it, throw it the length of the court, guy lays it in at the buzzer, now it's back to 17 and there's pandemonium. We were laughing so hard we were crying, because we didn't know until that point. All of a sudden you go, "Oh, we get it now."

HUBIE BROWN: If you talked to any of those guys who fixed games in the '50s, they would say, "Look, we were just shaving points. We were still winning but not by the point spread." But in the second fixes, the Jack Molinas fixes in the '60s, they were definitely dumping games.

PACKER: Jack Molinas was a bad guy. He was a great player but also a fixer.

ROSEN: Molinas was a guy that if he saw two flies on the window, he'd bet you which would fly off first.

GARFINKEL: NC State was playing Georgia, and Lee Terrell was an assistant. He calls me at 1 o'clock in the morning and says, "I have bad news for you. The game tonight wasn't on the up-and-up. Your guys were throwing the ball over the lot. [NC State head coach] Everett Case is gonna call the State Bureau of Investigation. He's calling them to look into this game and other games."

CUNNINGHAM: There was a guy named Lou Brown on the University of North Carolina team. Brown was the middleman between the bookies and the players. He would reach out to players to get them to shave points. He approached Doug Moe, who, if I'm not mistaken, told him, "No, and if you ever approach another player, I'll break your neck."

DOUG MOE (3-Time ABA All-Star; 1988 NBA Coach of the Year): I was offered a bribe. I didn't turn it in, and back in those days, you just were banned.

PACKER: Doug wasn't looking to throw games; he never took money from anybody. But, unfortunately in Doug's case, he was suspended from the University of North Carolina and never played there again because he didn't tell Frank McGuire about it. Doug would have been one of the great NBA players.

MOE: Lou Brown was my best friend. They brought me up to New York, and they had tapes of everything. I'm with a detective, and I'm scared stiff. I was young and dumb and didn't know anything. He said, "Look, they know you didn't do anything. They got all these tapes." And he's playing these tapes for me, and I hear my boy Lou say, "Ah, let me just keep working on him."

LARRY BROWN: Doug had every right to turn Lou Brown in, but knowing the kind of person Doug is, he would never even think about that.

WALSH: Doug's name got put in the paper with other people, and back then that meant you didn't get a chance to play in the NBA, even though he didn't do anything.

SATCH SANDERS: Everyone wanted to make the guys who did this out to be bad people, but we're talking about people who were extraordinarily needy. I would sit down with [NYU teammate] Ray Paprocky, and he'd say, "I'm married. I got a kid. I gotta find a way to work, to get a job afterwards." Practice would stand in the way of him working other jobs. We kept saying, "Ray, you're gonna be all right; you're gonna make the pros. Then you won't worry about it." And he'd say, "Yeah, but my kid's hungry now. So is my wife. I got rent, I got bills to pay."

Of all the players affected by the gambling scandals of the '60s, none paid a higher price than Connie Hawkins and Roger Brown. Hawkins was one of six siblings who grew up on welfare in the Bedford-Stuyvesant neighborhood of Brooklyn. He played for Boys High, while Brown starred for Brooklyn rival Wingate, and when the two met in the epic 1960 Public Schools Athletic League (PSAL) semifinals, the game became an instant classic, cementing the players' reputations as the finest high school players in the nation. Hawkins signed with Iowa, and Brown committed to Dayton, yet neither played a college game. Instead, they were expelled from their universities and banned from the NBA. Their crime: they knew Jack Molinas.

CONNIE HAWKINS (Small Forward, Phoenix Suns; 1968 ABA MVP; 4-Time NBA All-Star; Died 2017): No one's ever told me I was good at anything other than basketball.

LARRY BROWN: Connie Hawkins was Michael Jordan before Michael Jordan.

WALT FRAZIER (Point Guard, New York Knicks; 7-Time NBA All-Star; NBA Analyst, MSG Network): He was Dr. J before Dr. J, had the one-handed dunks coming into the paint.

WALSH: I remember playing with both Connie and Roger Brown and thinking to myself, "Uh-oh, guys like me aren't going to have an easy time," because these guys were off the charts. They were more athletic, they were bigger, they had all the skills that I did, but they were five inches bigger.

HAWKINS: Jack Molinas was a pretty good basketball player and he was a lawyer, and every time we'd see him he would give me a few dollars and say, "If you need anything, give me a call."

CUNNINGHAM: Jack Molinas would take Connie and Roger Brown down to Manhattan Beach. During the summer, that was the place to play against the best players in New York. I can still see them. I can't tell you the make of the car, but it was a red convertible. They would get out of the car with him, and we would play.

HAWKINS: A detective from New York came to Iowa and talked to my coach and told him they wanted to bring me in to interview me. That was the first time I had known anything about the scandal.

ROZ LITMAN (Antitrust Lawyer; Civil Liberties Activist; Died 2016): I always heard Connie refer to every coach he ever had as "Coach," but with respect. So the detective comes to Iowa, talks to coach Sharm Scheuerman, and Sharm tells Connie to go with him. It never occurred to Connie to think, "Do I have some other option?"

HAWKINS: When I got to New York, the first person I met there was a detective named Anthony Bernhard. He checked us into the hotel, and the next day we went down to the DA's office. They started asking me questions about being involved in a point-shaving scandal. They asked, did I get money? If they checked the records, they would have known in high school, we won all our games. I never played freshman [college] ball, so if they bothered to check, they would have known there was no way that I could have been involved in fixing a basketball game.

LITMAN: Bernhard was a tough New York detective. He was there to get Connie to implicate himself or somebody in this basketball scandal. He was a professional, and he knew how to lean on Connie.

HAWKINS: I was scared, I was bewildered, I was baffled, because at the time I knew I was innocent. I didn't do anything wrong. I had known Jack Molinas and Joseph Hacken, so they tried to link me to fixing games.

LITMAN: Connie went from Iowa to New York believing that he'd be back after the weekend. He didn't know what a grand jury was, he didn't understand anything about the investigation, but there was one thing he did know—black kids from the streets had to be afraid of the police, because police beat them up, police hurt them, police didn't like them.

HAWKINS: It's very safe to say I was not educated. Matter of fact, after I got home and explained to my parents what happened, we didn't have the intelligence or the smarts to get a lawyer. It never crossed nobody's mind.

LITMAN: They get to New York, and he says to the detective, "I'd like to call my mother," and the detective says, "No, you can't call your mother; we don't want you to." So he goes meekly with the detective to this hotel, where they have all these guys who had shaved points and fixed games boarded up in rooms. They put Connie in with two of them, and that's when Connie first hears about point shaving.

HAWKINS: Before they brought me to New York, I didn't even know what point shaving was.

LITMAN: They kept him in that hotel room and interrogated him every day for a week. They'd say, "You introduced players to Molinas, didn't you?" and Connie said, "No, I never introduced anybody to Molinas." Then it was, "You took money to help fix games," and Connie said, "No, I never did that." He kept insisting that for the first five, six days. They kept saying, "You know what perjury is—you'll go to jail for five years if you commit perjury," and he'd say, "I am telling you the truth." Finally, it got through to him that if he kept telling them the truth, they were not going to let him go.

PETER VECSEY: The kid was 19 years old, and they had him locked up for days.

LITMAN: Eventually, they took him into the grand jury room. The district attorney asks the questions, and the questions that he asked were totally, 100 percent leading questions. They weren't, "What is your name?" It was, "Your name is Connie Hawkins, isn't it?" And, "You knew Joe Hacken, didn't you?" Even with all of those leading questions, there was nothing in that transcript. It was so confusing and contradictory that at one point Connie said yes, he had introduced someone to Molinas. It was supposed to be Wilky Gilmore, who Connie never introduced to anybody. Wilky Gilmore tried to talk to the detectives to tell them, but they didn't want to hear [it].

HAWKINS: They used the good cop, bad cop, trying to convince me: "If you want to go home, tell us what you did." I said, "I didn't do anything." The DA probably wanted the names of top basketball players, and my name and Roger's were the two top guys coming out of high school.

LITMAN: My God, Connie Hawkins had no lawyer, no adviser, 19 years old, knowing nothing about his rights, being constantly hammered by the police, being put with all these other people who had participated, and finally [he] gave up and said he introduced a player to Molinas.

HAWKINS: I was never arrested. I was never indicted. They never handcuffed me, never took a mug shot.

LITMAN: Poor Connie believed that what he told the detectives in the grand jury room was all going [to] be secret, and when he found out his name had been released as part of this investigation, he was mortified.

HAWKINS: They kept me there for like a week and finally came out with this article in the paper, "Basketball Fixers." It had me, Roger Brown, and five other people on the cover. Once that happened, all hell broke loose.

LITMAN: They didn't care about Connie Hawkins, they didn't care whether his rights were violated, they didn't care whether he was coerced or pushed into saying something that wasn't true.

HAWKINS: There was nothing I could do about it. Power of the press— once you see something like that, everyone thinks you are guilty.

CUNNINGHAM: It was a scary time. This net was thrown over all of college basketball, and they were dragging everybody in.

HAWKINS: My college coach, Sharm Scheuerman, wrote me a letter and tried to explain that if it wasn't for what happened, I could have had a great career at the University of Iowa. He gave me the option of coming back to school, but I had to prove I was innocent.

LITMAN: Connie went back to Iowa thinking, "At least that's behind me. I didn't do anything wrong. I can go back to Iowa, and now I can play." Because, of course, when Iowa was trying to get him to go there, they had wined and dined and beguiled him in every way. He went back figuring everything would be fine. But Scheuerman told him he had to leave. When his coach told him that, Connie's whole world came crashing down.

HAWKINS: I was expelled from Iowa. It was shocking. You're thinking to yourself that this is going to take care of itself. Eventually, someone is going to see that I'm telling the truth, and the truth will set you free.

LITMAN: Connie was banned from the Eastern League when he was trying to make a living.

HAWKINS: I was a total outcast. I was blackballed.

MEL DANIELS (Center, Indiana Pacers; 2-Time ABA MVP; Died 2015): It was the most embarrassing thing to ever happen in pro sports. What they did to those poor guys is crazy. Insane. But they got away with it.

HAWKINS: It never occurred to me that my life was going to be screwed up until I started trying to play basketball. I couldn't even go out on the school yard. One summer, I went to the Rucker [Park] Tournament, and some of the guys up there wouldn't play because I was a fixer. I went the week after that, and Wilt Chamberlain was out there playing, and Wilt said he was going to play against me. Once he started playing against me, everybody else kind of jumped ship and started playing, but prior to that it was pretty tough.

DANIELS: They turned Roger and Connie into pariahs.

HAWKINS: I used to cry watching guys on TV playing. I developed an ulcer from worrying so much about the situation and how nothing was being done. It was a hopeless feeling. I was innocent. How could they not see that?

LITMAN: The first time I saw Connie, he was playing for the Pittsburgh Rens. They practiced in an old, dilapidated gym called Tree's gym. It was dusty, the seats were rickety, and here comes this kid—this amazing, tall, skinny, beautiful kid, with eyes that went all around to the side of his head. My brother-in-law owned the team, so we got to know Connie.

HAWKINS: I went to Pittsburgh to play for the Rens, and I had to get a letter to show that I was innocent before I could play. They got a letter from the DA stating that I hadn't done anything wrong, and then that's how I was able to play in the American Basketball League. Same thing later on with the ABA [American Basketball Association]. But the NBA was content with blackballing me. The commissioner [Walter Kennedy] said, "Hawkins will never play in the NBA, never."

LITMAN: When we first met Connie, we assumed he'd been involved in a point-shaving scandal. We didn't ask him about it. It seemed intrusive. But then my husband, David, had conversations with Connie and said to me, "You know, I think maybe he didn't do anything wrong. I think maybe he's innocent." We began to think there had been a terrible wrong done to him.

HAWKINS: Jack Molinas, Joseph Hacken, neither one of those guys never talked to me about fixing games. They talked about basketball and good players and things like that, but they never asked me about fixing games.

LITMAN: My husband came back from his meetings with Molinas and Hacken, and both told him they never asked Connie to do any of the things that he was accused of doing.

HAWKINS: I didn't know what [Molinas and Hacken] wanted from me, but growing up in Brooklyn, I couldn't care what they wanted from me. As long as they gave me $10 here and there, I was happy. If they had an ulterior motive, I didn't know what it was.

LITMAN: There was an incident where Connie borrowed $200 from Jack Molinas. When he was in his freshman year, he went home for Christmas and had his tuition money with him. It was the first time he'd ever had money in his pocket. He spent the money, and he didn't know what to do. He was afraid . . . then he remembered Molinas said to him a number of times, "If you ever need anything, let me know."

HAWKINS: A bright light went off in my head. My man, Jack Molinas, I can call him up and get this money back and pay my college tuition. So I told him I needed to borrow a couple hundred dollars. He met me and lent me the $200. I went back to Iowa and paid my tuition and sent him the $200. He got his money back.

LITMAN: I actually met Jack Molinas when my husband, David, and I started investigating the case. Molinas was in a jail in New York called the Tombs. David came home and said, "We're going to have dinner with Molinas tonight." I said, "Are we going to the Tombs?" and he said, "No, he's gonna meet us at a restaurant." I said, "How's he going to get there?" We go to the restaurant, we're sitting at the table, and in walks this guy, nicely dressed, not in prison garb, with a very attractive woman on his arm. These two gentlemen see him in and they leave. The guards from the Tombs had driven him to the restaurant, dropped him off, and then came back after dinner to pick him up.

HAWKINS: Back in the '60s, you couldn't become eligible for the NBA draft until your college class graduated. So I had to wait until 1964 before my lawyers filed an antitrust lawsuit against the NBA.

DON NELSON: Connie was banned from the NBA. One day, he says to me, "I have to go to court to prove that I'm good enough to play in the NBA, and right now everybody is telling me I'm not good enough, that's why I'm not in the league." I said, "That's ridiculous. You're probably the best player I've ever seen." So Connie said, "Would you say that in court?" And I said, "Absolutely." About two or three weeks later, we were starting the season in Boston, and Red Auerbach called me in and said, "You can't testify that Connie Hawkins is good enough to play in the NBA. The league wants to protect its position, and if you testify for Connie Hawkins, you are never gonna play in the NBA again." I'm going, "Whoa. That's unbelievable." I said, "Well, that's not right. All

I'm gonna testify is that he's good enough to play." And Red said, "I'm just telling you. Those are my instructions to you." I had to really think hard whether I was gonna do it or not. Connie called me up, and I said, "I'm still gonna do it. I've been threatened and everything, but it's the truth." [The case] was settled before I had to go through that situation. I'm glad I didn't have to, because my career was in jeopardy.

LITMAN: The NBA decided that they would not approve the contract of anyone who had testified in the grand jury. And the NBA, almost to the end, denied that they had made any decision to ban these players.

DAVID STERN: I didn't know Molinas, but as a young lawyer [with Proskauer Rose], I was involved with private detectives, sitting down with people who I didn't really feel comfortable with. I was in it because I was defending the NBA to the hilt—that's what lawyers do.

LITMAN: Once we brought the suit, the NBA began to realize it had a worry on their hands. They didn't think at the beginning there was any possibility that anyone could hold them accountable. They were above antitrust law and these little pip-squeak lawyers in Pittsburgh.

STERN: We were sued by Connie Hawkins, we were sued by Roger Brown, we were sued by Alphra Saunders, we were sued by a slew of players who were denied entrance into the NBA.

LITMAN: When I was doing the depositions, I'd ask the NBA owners, "Did you ever read the transcript of the Molinas trial? Did you ever see what Hawkins was accused of? Did you ever try to talk to Molinas to see what his story was? Did you ever try to talk to Wilky Gilmore to see what his story was?" And they all said, "No." Why didn't you do that? "Well, it never occurred to me." So they didn't do an investigation. They didn't do anything. All they had was this stupid piece of paper with these names on it and newspaper articles, and they didn't care if somebody got destroyed.

STERN: Ultimately, Peter Andreoli in the district attorney's office arranged for us, properly or not—I think it was proper—to see the grand jury minutes. And I read them, and I went in to George Gallantz, the partner at Proskauer, and said, "These people should be allowed to play in the NBA. We gotta make this right."

LITMAN: Somewhere along the line, someone in the Proskauer firm really started to look at the complaint. There was a huge institutional arrogance by the men who were running the NBA. They ran it their way. They had always run it their way. They didn't want anybody telling them how to do it or what rules they had to follow.

PACKER: It's amazing how it destroyed the lives of so many kids.

LITMAN: I was sitting in my office—we had gone through pretrial—and my phone rang, and on the other end was David Stern. He said, "Mr. Gallantz will be calling you Monday to discuss whether you would like to settle the case."

STERN: I just said, "I think we should talk." And they put down the phone and said, "Yaaayyyyy." I was the sacrificial lamb. And I was actually driving it from our side, saying, "This is an injustice that we have to correct."

LITMAN: I said, "Fine, I look forward to hearing from him Monday." I put down the phone, and I went screaming through the office: "Mr. Gallantz is gonna call me Monday to discuss whether we want to settle!"

STERN: By the time we settled, Connie Hawkins had lost five years.

LITMAN: When I was finally able to go in and tell Connie, "The NBA agreed to settle the case, and you're going to play for the Phoenix Suns," he was totally overwhelmed. This fountain of tears just kept pouring out.

CUNNINGHAM: I know there was a settlement with the NBA, but it was nickels and dimes compared to what it took away from them—the most important part of their lives.

DANIELS: The NBA sent Roger Brown a letter of apology and they paid him, but what about the years that he lost?

HAWKINS: The Suns were an expansion club. I had never heard of Phoenix. They won a coin flip to sign me. I was on a plane to go there to sign my contract. I've got a wool suit on, and the stewardess said, "Welcome to Phoenix, the temperature is 117 degrees." I said, "I'm not getting off this plane! One hundred seventeen degrees, are you kidding me?"

JERRY COLANGELO: We kind of missed the best of Hawk. And that's really a shame.

PACKER: I thought it would be a good idea to interview some of these guys 20 years later, because people were forgetting about the possibility of games being thrown. I had an opportunity to get back with Ray Paprocky. I'm paraphrasing, but he said, "The night we played against your team, Wake Forest, I couldn't miss a shot in warm-ups. I was playing so well that I forgot all about the consequences of what I was supposed to do. When the game ended and I got home, I got a phone call, and they told me that I would not be paid because the spread didn't turn out the way it was supposed to. The guy on the other end of the phone told me, 'Let's not ever have that happen again, or it will be a lot more than not getting paid.'"

ROSEN: It destroyed basketball during that time. The game has to be pure.

PACKER: You can imagine what a kid must think today: "Hey, wait a second, my school's getting a check for $15 or $20 million, and I'm the guy that's the star." Then some guy comes along [and] says, "How'd you like to make some money?" They tell these kids, "You don't have to lose the game, just don't play so well." So could it happen again? Of course.

THE WIZARD OF WESTWOOD

Before he made history and emerged as one of basketball's most beloved and revered icons, John Wooden was a quirky, bespectacled coach who preached repetition and fundamentals, yet couldn't implement them to defeat his in-state rival. Wooden came up short the final eight times he faced Cal Berkeley coach Pete Newell, who won an NCAA championship in 1959 and an Olympic gold medal in 1960. Newell abruptly retired following the Olympics, citing the stress of the job, and UCLA embarked on a 25-year winning streak against the Bears using a press similar to the one Newell introduced.

Wooden once confided to LSU coach Dale Brown, whom he mentored throughout his career, that he was not stellar when it came to X's and O's. What set him apart, Wooden believed, was his ability to mold players so they would fit together. "The best players don't always make the best teams," Wooden told Brown.

Wooden won titles with a small, quick lineup led by Walt Hazzard and Gail Goodrich (who once admitted that if Newell had stayed at Cal, he might have gone there). He won three championships with big man Lew Alcindor as the anchor. He won with a troika of Henry Bibby, Sidney Wicks, and Curtis Rowe, then again with Bill Walton, Keith Wilkes, and Greg Lee. Yet the most gratifying was his last championship, in 1975, when Richard Washington, Marques Johnson, and Dave Meyers eased him into retirement by upending Kentucky in Wooden's final game. That UCLA team, devoid of superstars, embodied Wooden's cherished Pyramid of Success: "Success is peace of mind, which is a direct result of self-satisfaction in knowing you made the effort to do your best to become the best you are capable of becoming."

DENNY CRUM (Assistant Coach, UCLA Bruins, 1963–71; Head Coach, University of Louisville Cardinals, 1971–2001): If you asked Coach Wooden what he did for a living, he'd tell you he was a teacher.

BILL WALTON: John Wooden never used the blackboard. We never watched film, we didn't have any plays, he never talked about the other team, he never called timeout. Before the game, we're so fired up we're ready to explode, and he is so calm. He looks at us and says, "Men, I've done my job. The rest is up to you."

GAIL GOODRICH: He could be very vocal, but he never cussed in the three years I played for him.

CRUM: His cuss words were "goodness gracious sakes alive."

DICK VITALE (NCAA Basketball Analyst, ESPN): To be able to win 10 national titles—there's no losses there. It's not like a best-of-seven NBA championship. On the collegiate level, you're going unblemished. That means 10 national championships, you've gone 50-0.

CRUM: Coach Wooden was so organized. We'd take a three-by-five card and put down what we needed to work on, and we'd bring those to practice and we'd stick to it by the minute. From 3:25 to 3:30, it was one thing. At 3:30, boom, we moved on to the next thing.

GOODRICH: His drills were impeccable. And he'd keep records. He could go back 10 years and tell you what he did at 4 o'clock in the afternoon on a certain date.

CRUM: Even the day before we won a national championship, we were running fundamental drills for half an hour in practice.

GOODRICH: I remember going behind my back as a sophomore on a three-on-one break instead of coming to the foul line and stopping. The ball goes out-of-bounds. At halftime, Coach Wooden let me have it. That was the last time I threw a behind-the-back pass at UCLA.

DALE BROWN: John Wooden said one time, "Why should a shot beyond the three-point line be worth 3 points? How about when the ball is passed around and a guy hits his teammate wide-open for a layup? That should be 3 points."

BILLY PACKER: Coach Wooden used to go to Campbell College in North Carolina to be a camp counselor. I'm thinking, "Hey, I'm going down to Campbell. I'm going to be a great coach because I'm going to pick his brain for a week." We get all the counselors together to decide who is going to do what. You're in a little gym, and it's hot as hell. I figure Coach Wooden does the film room and maybe occasionally says hello to the kids. We start getting assignments, and he raises his hand and says, "I would like to take a gym where I work on individual defense"— which is the last thing you'd ever want to do as a counselor! You've got these kids coming in and it's 100 degrees and you're going to be talking about defensive stamina? What is this guy, nuts? It made me really angry, to be quite honest with you. I'm thinking, "This guy is the biggest phony I've ever been around in my life."

CRUM: John Wooden had no ego at all. I would say to him, "Coach, if we force this guy to go this way, it might help us." I'd show him on a blackboard, and he'd say, "Interesting. Let's put it in tomorrow at practice, and if it works, we'll leave it in. If it doesn't, we'll throw it out."

GOODRICH: He believed in execution, execution, and execution. We had a drill where he'd say, "OK, we're gonna run the offense without a shot." Pass, cut, run, go through the whole thing. It was really detail- and spacing-oriented. We'd do it for 20 minutes without shooting.

PACKER: At night, the counselors [at Campbell College] would go out and gamble. I stayed back. I said, "Coach, this will be my first year of coaching, and there's some things I'd like to talk to you about." He said, "Yes, Billy, I've been watching you work in camp and you've got the right attitude and I'll be happy to do that. Just give me a second." He goes back in his room, and I figure he's going to come out with some drills or something, and he comes back with a pair of socks. He says, "Billy, you can never have a quality team if the team's feet aren't in great shape." He said, "Blisters will really hurt your ability to train your players." He takes his slippers off and starts to show me how to properly put on socks. I was so pissed off. I'm thinking, "How can he be that damn bad a guy that he won't divulge anything about how you play the game?" After he got through the first sock, somehow I was able to say, "Oh, Coach, I forgot . . ." I had to get out of there. I could not stand him. But as the years went on, I realized it was all about the fundamentals. If you've got a blister, you can't run, so let's not talk about running a drill until you know how to put on your socks right. I grew to respect him so much.

JERRY NORMAN (Assistant Coach, UCLA Bruins, 1957–68): When I first came on the staff, Wooden said to me, "You know, Pete Newell is doing something. I don't [know] what he's doing; maybe you can figure it out." Newell was creating a strategy to create the tempo of the game. If you could force somebody to play the way you want them to play and maybe it's not the way they want to play, that's an advantage.

CRUM: Cal was tough to beat. We didn't quite get over the hump against them. I think the greatest difference in their team was Darrall Imhoff, who was a really good center, great rebounder and shot blocker. And Pete Newell was a very good coach.

NORMAN: Had Pete Newell stayed in coaching longer, he would be considered maybe the greatest of all time in basketball. I'd watch us play Cal and try to decide which team had the best talent, and I couldn't tell any difference. But we'd lose by 12 or 13 points. I know Coach Wooden was a very good coach, but he's not winning these games, so there must be a reason. I'm sure it was frustrating for John—it would be for any coach.

GOODRICH: Jerry Norman was instrumental in selling his own press to Coach Wooden, which made our championship teams in '64 and '65. We were a small team, quicker than anyone else [on] the West Coast. Jerry didn't feel we could play a half-court game, so we wanted to extend the game 94 feet.

NORMAN: We needed to increase the tempo of the game because all our conference schools were what you'd call "walk the ball up" teams. One way to do that is to use a zone press and double-team, where they have to throw the ball down the floor. Anytime you pass the ball, it's faster than dribbling, so these were the conceptual principles we put together. . . . We had a center, Fred Slaughter, who was big, very smart, very strong, quick, and could run, so where are we gonna play Fred? I decided the best place was up front with Gail Goodrich. Those two would start off about the free throw line. We'd let the other team inbound and start dribbling. Gail's job was not to let the dribbler get down the sideline, always force him to the center of the court. Fred's job was to stay close enough to Gail so if he needed to help double-team, he could. We'd make the player give up the ball, and when they started giving up the ball, that increased the tempo.

GOODRICH: We introduced the press early in the season, and we played Michigan at the Sports Arena in Los Angeles during the Christmas tournament. Michigan was No. 1 at the time, and we blew them away.

NORMAN: Most of these coaches thought we were pressing them to get the ball. That wasn't the objective—it was to force the tempo. Sometimes they couldn't get the ball over the half-court line in under 10 seconds. Then, with time running out, the guy would make a desperation pass, which was the exact wrong thing to do.

GOODRICH: We'd run off 10, 11 points in a row, and the game would be over.

NORMAN: We had Walt Hazzard and Gail Goodrich, the best backcourt in the history of college basketball.

WALTON: Walt Hazzard showed up, and everything changed. He was a combination of Martin Luther King on the public stage, and on the court he was Magic Johnson before Magic.

GOODRICH: The ball belonged in Hazzard's hands. I'm not sure at the beginning I accepted that. But Coach Wooden came to me and said, "I want you to learn to play off the ball. You get open, and Walt will get the ball to you."

NORMAN: Over time, when they realized how they could play together, they were phenomenal.

GOODRICH: Going into the [1964 NCAA Final] against Duke, we're 29-0, and we're the underdogs, which was sort of interesting. At the beginning of the season, *Sports Illustrated* sent someone out to different schools. It was Frank Deford's first year as a writer, and he comes to UCLA and watches practice for a couple of days. The magazine comes out, and we're not in the top 20, but on the last page they list us as a "surprise package." When I get to Kansas City for the semis, I go up to Deford and I say, "Not bad for a surprise package."

NORMAN: In those days, the only games televised were the championship games. All the coaches can watch practice, and they come down and watch us and they say, "Jeez, we watched these other three teams, how'd you guys get here?" All they could see was size. Duke had two 6-10 guys, Michigan had Bill Buntin, and Kansas State had a 7-footer.

GOODRICH: Coach Wooden says in his pregame talk, "How many of you remember who finished second last year?" Silence. I knew, but I didn't raise my hand. And he says, "No one remembers who finishes second. Now go out and play the way you're capable of playing, and I think you'll be very happy with the results."

NORMAN: There were no three-point shots in those days, so unless someone was a phenomenal outside shooter, we just let 'em shoot. The advantage was, if they missed, which in those days the percentage from outside was probably 30, 35 percent, it's gonna be a longer rebound, and that's going to benefit players who are smaller [and] quicker, like our guys.

GOODRICH: Duke was ahead early, but eventually the press and the tempo got to them. They started missing shots, and I think they got a little tired.

PACKER: It took John 15 years to win his first championship. When he won his first, he said, "Nobody thought I would win my second one."

Phase Two of UCLA's dynasty arrived in 1966 in the form of Lew Alcindor, who immediately led the freshman team to a win over the varsity in a scrimmage. Alcindor then led UCLA to three straight championships from 1967 to 1969 and was named tournament MVP all three times.

Alcindor and rival Elvin Hayes served as the backdrop for the "Game of the Century," played between UCLA and the University of Houston at the Astrodome on January 20, 1968, in front of 52,693 fans. Wooden, originally squeamish about the spectacle of the event, finally acquiesced when organizers agreed to truck in the floor from the L.A. Sports Arena and allow young UCLA announcer Dick Enberg to do the game, which was broadcast in 120 markets. By halftime, television executive (and Chicago White Sox owner) Eddie Einhorn was feverishly selling 30-second spots for the second half from courtside.

Alcindor, who had suffered a scratched cornea the week before and struggled with blurry vision, was thoroughly outplayed by Hayes. UCLA had a chance to tie in the final seconds, but Mike Warren inadvertently deflected a pass meant for Lynn Shackelford out-of-bounds. Sports Illustrated ran a cover photo of Hayes scoring over Alcindor, which Alcindor kept taped in his locker for the remainder of the season as motivation.

Two months later, UCLA thumped Houston 101–69 in the national semifinals. The game was not without controversy. Houston point guard George Reynolds was ruled ineligible because there was a problem with his junior college transcript. Houston officials were convinced it was Wooden and UCLA that tipped off the NCAA.

GOODRICH: UCLA plays Houston in the Astrodome, over 50,000 people, marquee Lew Alcindor vs. Elvin Hayes. That changed the landscape for college basketball.

NORMAN: Lew Alcindor didn't show a lot of emotion, but he was a great team player.

CRUM: The Astrodome was a new stadium. [The game was played] out on an arranged floor in the middle of the baseball area with some chairs around it, but when you sat in the coaching chairs, you couldn't see the feet of any of the players. So, if they called traveling, you couldn't argue even if they were wrong.

PAT RILEY: What happened in the Astrodome was like a freak show. You had this little court in the middle of this huge dome, and you could hardly even see the players.

NORMAN: Houston doesn't believe Lew Alcindor is really hurt, but his eye is so bad he's seeing double. And Hayes had a phenomenal game. He had 29 points in the first half. Most *teams* never got 29 against us.

PACKER: That game, and what happened consequently in the NCAA tournament, when UCLA destroyed them in their next matchup, was the forerunner of putting together great national teams and putting them on television and making college basketball something extremely important.

ELVIN HAYES (Center, Baltimore/Washington Bullets; 12-Time NBA All-Star): My plan for that game was to get [Alcindor] in a one-on-one situation. His star was so high and so bright in the sky that he was held up as unbeatable. He was all-everything, and I wanted to take his star down and put mine up there. . . . Before that, we were friends, but after that Houston game, we never talked again. We could play on the same All-Star team and never talk to each other. When I played with Washington and he played with L.A., I never shook his hand. That game created such a competitive nature.

GOODRICH: That game was an eye-opener for UCLA. They had dominated everybody up to that point.

HAYES: Every time [Alcindor] went up to shoot, Ken Spain and I were coming over the top of the key and blocking his shot. Maybe that was hurting his eye, you know? I'm glad he played and I'm glad they gave him an excuse, but we still won the basketball game.

NORMAN: My thought [when we played them again] was, if we could do something to limit Hayes, the other players are not used to carrying the burden of scoring. So I designed this defense to try to keep him from getting the ball.

HAYES: UCLA's little press—our point guard George Reynolds would just dribble right through it. You couldn't stop him. But Coach told us the day before we were leaving for the national semifinals, "George won't be playing. They said he didn't take a class his freshman year [at Imperial Valley College] in California." Now we are playing a point guard [Vern Lewis], the coach's son, that hasn't played all year. Don Chaney fouled out, Theodis Lee fouled out, Ken Spain fouled out, so we have a football player out there. We had three football players on our team. . . . Even though UCLA beat us the next time, they didn't get redeemed because they lost history. They can't go back and get that game before 53,000 people, a national TV audience, when we broke their 47-game winning streak.

GOODRICH: Elvin Hayes stood around the elbow at the foul line. He wouldn't drive. He'd get the ball and take one dribble and shoot. So, in the second game, UCLA put Lynn Shackelford on Hayes and played him body to body, never left him. They didn't let him catch the ball, and he was ineffective.

HAYES: You only get one shot at history, and that game was history.

The next great Bruin, Bill Walton, aimed to duplicate Alcindor's three straight championships. Walton led UCLA to a title in 1972 over Florida State, and in 1973 he shook off persistent foul trouble to shoot 21 of 22 from the floor against Memphis State. His 44 points set a new NCAA record, surpassing a trio of familiar names: Princeton's Bill Bradley, Notre Dame's Austin Carr, and fellow Bruin Gail Goodrich.

Yet Walton's dream of three straight was squashed by high-flying NC State forward David Thompson, the first to perfect the alley-oop slam, who led his team to a thrilling double-overtime win against UCLA in the 1974 semifinals. The loss snapped an 88-game winning streak and deprived Wooden of the distinction of his eighth consecutive championship. Walton was immense, submitting 29 points and 18 rebounds in 50 minutes, but UCLA blew an 11-point lead with 10 minutes left in regulation, a collapse that haunts Walton to this day.

CRUM: I got a call from a UCLA graduate named Frank Cushing. He had helped our football team recruit Bruce Walton. Frank called me one day and asked if I had heard of Bill Walton, his brother. I hadn't heard anything about him. I went down [to San Diego] to see him. I had seen a lot of good ones, but Walton did special things. Bill was dominant in every aspect. He passed the ball, he took good shots, he rebounded and made the outlet pass. He did anything and everything you'd want a post player to do. His team won by an average of 50 points a game.

WALTON: Denny Crum was the first person that ever contacted me. I got a letter from him when I was a sophomore at Helix High School in San Diego, and the letter said, "Dear Billy, it's come to our attention that you're a good player, and we just wanted to let you know that we're interested in you for UCLA down the road, but we want you to be aware that UCLA is a very strict school academically, and we want you to make sure that you're prepared and qualified to get in." Academics was always the easiest part of my life, so I was ecstatic.

CRUM: Coach Wooden asked me, "How was the Walton kid?" I told him, "He's the best high school player I've ever seen." Coach got up, closed the door of the office, came back, and said, "Now, Denny, don't say stupid things like that. You're telling me there's a redheaded, freckle-faced kid in San Diego that's the best basketball player you've ever seen?" I said, "That's what I'm telling you." He said, "They've never even had a Division I player come out of San Diego, let alone the best you've ever seen." I said, "Coach, you didn't question me on these other players. Why are you questioning me on Walton? You need to come watch him play. His folks are both Cal Berkeley graduates, and if we don't get him, he'll be playing against us."

WALTON: I was UCLA's easiest recruit. We grew up in a household without a television set, for financial reasons at the beginning, and then later on my mom, who was the town's librarian, said, "There's nothing worthwhile watching on television so we're not going to have one." So I didn't see basketball on television until 1965. First game I watched was Gail Goodrich setting an NCAA championship record of 42 points, and I said that day to myself, "That's what I want to do. I want to go to UCLA, I want to play for John Wooden, and I want to be a champion."

CRUM: Coach Wooden and I jumped on an airplane to see Walton. Wooden didn't say a word. The next day he said, "I know this has to be eating at you because of our previous conversation, but I will tell you he's pretty good, isn't he?" Now that was an accolade from Coach.

WALTON: I was at a clinic where Billy Packer was interviewing John Wooden on the stage, and I was sitting in the back of the room, dreaming, thinking about something else, and all of a sudden Coach Wooden barked out from the front of the stage, "Walton, what are the three rules of rebounding?" I immediately snapped out of my zone and went into it: anticipate every shot will be missed, get your hands above your shoulders, and then go get that ball.

CRUM: Bill was so unselfish. He would rather give it to a teammate than shoot it himself. He shot a great percentage when nobody else was open, but we never started a game saying, "We gotta get the ball into Bill."

WALTON: My senior year at UCLA was one of the most disappointing periods of my life, because that was our best team. All the things that made us great those first two years, we couldn't get our hands on them. I broke my back that year, we had some personnel changes, and we lost a number of key guys who were part of the team.

DAVID THOMPSON (Shooting Guard, Denver Nuggets; 4-Time NBA All-Star): We played UCLA in a preseason game. These guys were like movie stars. We play in St. Louis, and prior to the game Bill Walton walks into the locker room. He comes in and says hello. I don't know why he did that. I guess he was trying to intimidate us. . . . With 10 minutes to go in the game, we were actually leading. Walton was in foul trouble, but he came back in the game and they go up. We kind of panicked a little bit because it was the first time we had been behind at the end of the game. They ran away with it from there.

WALTON: At UCLA, it wasn't about the winning. That was [a] given. It was how you played—and we played well. And then it fell apart.

THOMPSON: We knew we could play with UCLA, even though we lost that game. We knew we didn't play anywhere near up to our abilities, and we were in the game. We just wanted another chance. . . . So now we're in the [1974 NCAA tournament] semifinals, and we're down 7 points with a little over 2 minutes left. Coach [Norm] Sloan calls time-out. He comes over to the bench, saying, "Guys, you gotta make something happen." And he looks at me. He had us pick them up full court to trap them. Monte Towe drew some charges, Tom Burleson made a steal, and I made some buckets. And next thing you know, we're down 1 point and we have the ball with a little bit under a minute left. I have the ball at the top of the key, and I cross over and go baseline, then jump and hang in the air and bank it off the glass. We win.

WALTON: My career at UCLA, the way it ended, became one of disappointment, shame, embarrassment, and complete frustration. I let my team down, I let my coach down, I let my school down, I let the sport down. It was a stain and a stigma on my soul.

True to his word, John Wooden stepped away from coaching in 1975, but "Papa Wooden" maintained a presence on the UCLA campus. When Larry Brown took the job as head coach in 1980, he admitted he hesitated to call himself the UCLA basketball coach, "because there was really only one—and he had an office down the hall."

Yet Brown—and Wooden—had a problem. His name was Sam Gilbert, a millionaire contractor and UCLA booster who lavished cars, cash, and gifts on players and was known to entertain them poolside at his spacious home. Gilbert established these relationships while Wooden was coach and continued until the NCAA sanctioned UCLA and ordered the school to disassociate itself from Gilbert in 1981. Gilbert was later indicted in a drug money–laundering scheme, although he died before he could be prosecuted.

Former Long Beach State and UNLV coach Jerry Tarkanian scoffed at suggestions that Wooden was unaware of Gilbert's activities, claiming that "Sam bragged about it all the time." Even though none of the school's championships were vacated, Wooden's once-pristine legacy was tainted.

NORMAN: I didn't really know Sam Gilbert. He was starting to come around our program right when I was ready to leave. What normally happens is, alumni come to you and say, "Coach, is there any way I can help?" Well, maybe. A lot of kids want summer jobs. But Gilbert started going behind the coaches. Alcindor calls me one day in the spring. I ask him, "Where are you?" and he says, "I'm in Mr. Gilbert's office."

CRUM: I met Sam Gilbert, but I wouldn't say I knew him. I've been asked this question so many times over the years, and my answer is the same: I had no knowledge of anything that he ever did that was illegal.

BROWN: Several friends of mine would say to me, "Dale, why are you kissing John Wooden's ass? He's a cheating son of a bitch." I replied, "Why do you say that?" "Well, I recruited a guy, and Sam Gilbert did this shit." . . . I told my wife one [day], "I'm close to Coach. I've got to ask him about Sam Gilbert." "Dale," she said, "that's none of your business. You're his friend. That would be really, really rude." I put it off for a year or two. Finally, I went to John and said, "Do you know Sam Gilbert?" He said, "Yes, I do." And I said, "Why is Sam Gilbert's story always so shifty?" He said, "Dale, I'm gonna tell you, this is exactly what happened. I'd heard rumors that our assistants were taking players to see Sam Gilbert. I knew him, but not intimately. Nell and I are at a freshman game, and Curtis Rowe and Sidney Wicks are walking by, and they've got these beautiful leather gym bags and black leather pants and black long coats, and I know they didn't have that kind of money. I turned to my Nell and asked, 'What did Sam Gilbert give us for Christmas?' She says, 'He gave us all this leather.' " . . . Coach Wooden went to see J. D. Morgan, the athletic director, and said, "I believe this is something that should be looked into. I've heard also that the players are going up there, and I don't want to get UCLA or myself in any trouble." J. D. Morgan said, "John, I'll be the athletic director, you coach basketball. You don't worry about Sam Gilbert. All you have to do is coach. Turn it over to me."

NORMAN: I don't think Coach Wooden would have condoned anything Sam ever did. I really don't think that would be true. But somehow that didn't stop Gilbert, apparently.

BROWN: John said, "Dale, do I know of anything concrete? I do not. Now, most people won't believe that. They'll think I was negligent. Could I have done something else?" So Sam Gilbert was involved with the UCLA program. There's no question. But if John Wooden would have known, I'm telling you, he would have stopped it.

CRUM: You know the first thing I did when I took the Louisville job? Disbanded their booster club. Because I didn't want people around the program that might do something illegal and then get the program in trouble.

BROWN: I was invited to John Wooden's 98th birthday party at his little condominium in Encino. We're sitting there talking. There was a book that came out that was real critical of him. How that pompous, pious, self-righteous, hypocrite, phony, cheater . . . Sam Gilbert built the UCLA program, blah-blah-blah. . . . I said, "Coach, when you see all this criticism, you never strike back. Why?" John crossed his arms and said, "Dale, whenever you're in the public eye, you're going to receive a huge amount of unjustifiable criticism and a large amount of undeserved praise, and you should not be unduly affected by either. That's how I choose to live my life."

RELIEF OR JOY? NCAA Championship Coaches on the Feeling of Winning a Title

JIM BOEHEIM (Head Coach, Syracuse University Orange): Coaches always say, "If I don't win one, I'll be OK." I don't think that's true. I've never really thought that. I might have said it, but I didn't believe it. If you get close a couple times and you don't win, you're going to carry that the rest of your life. You need to win one. That one championship meant everything to me, and not just for me but for [the] players and fans. I get letters from fans who've been waiting for this their whole lives.

JOHN CALIPARI (Head Coach, University of Kentucky Wildcats): I never judged myself on winning a national title, but everybody else did. I was at UMass and Memphis, and the whole thing was, "[He's] never won." It's funny, I had a guy come up to me before the game and say, "How does it feel to be one of the best coaches to never win a championship?" That was before the game. You know what he asked me after? "How does it feel to be one of the worst coaches to ever win one?"

DENNY CRUM: My first feeling was relief. We'd [the University of Louisville Cardinals] already been to two Final Fours and hadn't won. *Can Crum win the big one?* Well, on that particular night, we did, and it was more relief than joy.

MIKE KRZYZEWSKI: It was all joy, winning the national championship. First of all, coaching should be a joy—the joy of winning, the joy of competing. We [the Duke University Blue Devils] had gone to four Final Fours before that, and there were people who wanted to say, "You can't win the big one." You know, this monkey on my back. [Actually], for a coach, the biggest game is the regional final. Once you win the regional final, the Final Four is a crowning achievement. 'Cause if you keep coming, you might actually win that darn thing. When we won the first one, it was all about joy: "You've just won the biggest prize. You better be darn happy about it." Relief is not why you should play, and I wasn't gonna let other people define our success.

NOLAN RICHARDSON: To me it was joy. I always liked to play the best. We [the University of Arkansas Razorbacks] played Duke three or four times and Duke had beaten us, and now we're gonna play Duke in their backyard. I was fired up to play not only one of the greatest coaches of all time but also having the opportunity to play him in North Carolina. I love those kind of challenges. This is the time to show who you are.

RICK PITINO (2-Time NCAA Champion Coach): We [the University of Kentucky Wildcats] had one of the greatest teams in college basketball history [in 1996]. The pressure was enormous. I knew we could only beat our-selves, so when we finally won, it was a relief. Tremendous inner joy, tremendous relief. I remember going into the locker room, and Antoine Walker was disappointed because he didn't play well in that game. I said, "Antoine, you accomplished an amazing feat right now. I know you didn't play great, but you're gonna go on to the pros. If you don't go out and celebrate with your teammates, if you don't have this moment, you're going to regret it for the rest of your life. Forget your individual performance, understand the team's season, and go out and celebrate." He left that locker room and went out and went crazy, and we all felt that way.

LARRY BROWN: When we [the University of Kansas Jayhawks] ended up winning, I was blown away. It was like I was just on this ride. Some-times it's fate—you just know it's gonna happen, and it did. I don't think anything could have been better than that. I remember one thing Chuck Daly said—that you won't really appreciate it until one day, you'll just be driving around, and you'll think back and you'll have a big-ass smile on your face, and someone will look at you in the car and think, "What's this crazy man laughing about?"

FROM UNBEATABLE TO THE UNTHINKABLE:
Team USA and the Olympics, 1956–72

The United States dominated international competition in basketball in the 1950s and '60s, posting undefeated records and earning gold medals in the 1956, '60, '64, and '68 Olympics. But the national team's success disguised underlying tensions within USA Basketball. Some of the best American players of the era declined invitations to the Olympic tryouts in protest of widespread racial inequality and the United States' involvement in the Vietnam War. A quota system that required the team to be made up of amateur players from the NCAA, AAU (Amateur Athletic Union), and U.S. military meant that Hall of Famers like Rick Barry and Pete Maravich never got a chance to represent their country. And at a time when transformational players such as Oscar Robertson, Jerry West, Earl Monroe, and Bill Walton were inspiring a faster, looser, more improvisational style of basketball, the national team program remained controlled by coaches from an older generation who insisted on slowing down and controlling the game.

1956

BILL RUSSELL: [Patriotism] was a thing they would throw around, but before the Olympic team went to Australia, we had some exhibition games here in the United States, and in a couple of places we [black players] couldn't stay in the same hotel as the rest of the team. Treat guys like that, and then they tell you to be a superpatriot. I don't think so.

1960

OSCAR ROBERTSON: In 1960, it was a very good basketball team. Had a good coach in Pete Newell. We had myself, [Jerry] West, [Jerry] Lucas, [Walt] Bellamy. Years later, when I was out of pro ball, I felt very fortunate when I realized that not everyone gets an opportunity to play [in the Olympics].

JERRY WEST: I've always said that probably my greatest thrill as an athlete was winning a gold medal. [I] was a young kid from small-town West Virginia getting involved with AAU players and seven collegiate players and going over there when something big was at stake. It was the cold war—us against the communist countries. I said to myself, "My God, we can't fail. We cannot fail."

ROBERTSON: Hell, I didn't know that much about patriotism, but we didn't want to lose to the Russians, which is all they were preaching in those times.

WEST: The game that was most meaningful was against the Russian team. It was physical, it was dirty. And only two of us got to receive the gold medal then—Oscar Robertson and myself. We were co-captains. They gave gold medals to everyone, but two of you went up and accepted it. And when they played the national anthem, it was the proudest I ever felt.

ROBERTSON: The '60 Olympics—I think we [are] sort of misplaced by the Olympic committee, by the ESPNs, the HBOs, and all those others, when they start talking about great teams. The Dream Team [1992] had future Hall of Famers. So did this team. I don't understand how they say that the Dream Team were the greatest ever. All they did was play one-on-one basketball. There wasn't even any resistance in a lot of the games they played. They wouldn't beat us.

1964

LARRY BROWN: When I made the Olympic team in '64, there was an eight-team tournament at St. John's. There were three NCAA teams with unbelievable players; there were two—I think—armed services teams; there were two AAU teams; and then there was an NAIA [National Association of Intercollegiate Athletics] team.

GAIL GOODRICH: In 1964, after we won the [NCAA championship], we go to the Olympic trials as a team. Wooden was the coach, we had five guys from UCLA, and then we picked up some other all-stars from the NCAA.

RICK BARRY: It was so unfair back in those days. They already pre-picked the team. They knew they wanted Mel Counts; John Thompson never had a chance. Hank Iba was the coach, and they had a quota system. They had to take guys from the AAU, the NAIA, military—it was ridiculous.

GOODRICH: At that time, the AAU and the NCAA were fighting for power as to who controlled amateur basketball. So there were six players from the AAU and six from the NCAA. They may have had one or two from the military as well, so maybe the AAU only had four, whatever.

BROWN: When you say they had to take certain AAU guys, I think they had to take more white guys. I think that was something—that there were seven white players and five blacks. I may be speaking out of turn, but I kind of got that feeling.

GOODRICH: We played three games. The first we lost by 5 or 6 points to an AAU team that ultimately won the tournament. Larry Brown was on that team. And then the next two games we won against college all-star teams.

BARRY: I thought I played really well. I was proud—I actually did a good job defensively—but there was no way I was going to make the team. And afterward, the great Joe Lapchick [former center for the original, barnstorming Celtics in the 1920s] came up and said, "Young man, you're not going to be on the Olympic team, but I want to tell you one thing: you're going to be a great pro basketball player." And it was kind of like, "That's really nice, but how do you know I'm not making the Olympics?"

BROWN: After Game 2 of the tournament, I guess the Olympic committee had meetings to discuss the players, and my AAU coach came to me and said, "Larry, I think you made the team." I just let it slide, but then when we won the third game, the next morning you had to come in and see the list to see who made it. And that was one of the most exciting things that ever happened to me. I saw my name as one of the 12 guys.

GOODRICH: I was an alternate. At that time, alternate didn't mean a lot. You don't play, you don't practice with the team. If someone gets hurt, then you play, but what's the chance of that? It was probably one of the most disappointing times individually that I had playing basketball.

BARRY: I always wanted to be an Olympian. It's probably the one thing that I miss more than anything. And to this day, it's a really contentious point with me. It was not right. They didn't take the best players—they really, truly didn't—and that's not the way it should be in life. It should be based upon your merit and your performance. If you look back in the trials, Bill Bradley did not play well. Based on the trials, Bill Bradley should not have been [on] the Olympic team.

GOODRICH: There were a number of great players that didn't make that team.

BROWN: I remember Billy Cunningham didn't make it. Willis [Reed] didn't make it. A lot of great players . . . Jerry Sloan.

GOODRICH: Iba was the coach, and he went with bigger guards. Hazzard, who was on that team and should've been on that team, he was a point guard. Joe Caldwell was 6'4". They went with size. I was still small—6'1", weighed 150 pounds. The international game was a lot more physical, though I never had any problems with that later, as a pro. In hindsight, it probably was pretty good for me not to make the team, because it made me tougher.

BARRY: It would have been nice to have been able to stand on the podium, representing the country, because one of the biggest thrills I had in basketball was an exhibition game in Indianapolis against the Soviet team. When I stood there, wearing a USA uniform, and the national anthem played, it was the most meaningful national anthem that I'd ever heard, because I was representing my country. I was just thinking, "Wow, if I could be on the Olympic team, how cool would that be?"

GOODRICH: Coach Wooden was upset with that whole process. They said they were gonna pick the team based on performance at the trials, and they didn't. And one thing about Coach Wooden is that you gotta be truthful. So he was very upset. You know, he never coached an Olympic team. He refused. Now flash forward [to] 1968: Alcindor, Lucius Allen, Mike Warren—they all refused to play in the Olympics. Not because of Wooden telling them not to play, but for other reasons.

1968

EARL MONROE: The '67 Pan American trials—I went out for the college division team. Anyway, we won the tournament out there. We played against the AAU teams, the NCAA college division teams with Elvin Hayes and all those guys, and we beat all [of] them. I was actually leading scorer and leading assist in that tournament, and I'm the only guy on my team that didn't get picked to go to the Pan American Games. They told me that my game was too black.

CALVIN MURPHY: In '68 when I went out for the Olympics, we were going through an era of "Say it loud, I'm black and I'm proud." And everybody wanted to boycott the games, and I got some threats 'cause I announced I was going down there. I wanted to play for this country. I'm a very proud black man, but I'm also a very proud basketball player.

NELSON GEORGE (Author, *Elevating the Game: Black Men & Basketball*): There was a lot of ferment from the black nationalist wing, as well as the mainstream civil rights movement. As black people, this is a time to use our leverage to put our grievances against the U.S. government on the national stage. And when you play in the Olympics, you wear the flag. You are an embodiment of the American Dream. So, for these players, it was a question of "Am I gonna go out in the middle of rioting, the struggle for equal rights, police brutality, government repression—am I gonna go out and wear the American flag for a country that's been very slow in acknowledging my demand for equal opportunity?" Some of the greatest athletes of the era got together and said, "No. We're not gonna be part of this."

CHARLIE SCOTT (Shooting Guard, Phoenix Suns/Boston Celtics; 3-Time NBA All-Star): Remember, that was the year when Elvin Hayes was graduating, Wes Unseld was graduating. And Kareem and Lucius Allen and Mike Warren turned down invitations to go to the trials because of people out in California, from San Jose State—the professor up there, Harry Edwards, who was talking about, you know, they shouldn't go to the Olympics.

WES UNSELD: I played with the World University Games that year, the Pan American Games before that, and the truth was I just didn't like the way they treated people. The only people that got treated well were the track-and-field people. I remember I went to Japan in the World University Games, and we spent 30 days over there, and we got two dollars a day per diem. That was it. We stayed in the compound for the entire length of time except when we were playing and one time when they took us to the ambassador's house or something like that, and I just got tired of it. I did not get caught up in the boycott, but I wasn't surprised by it.

SPENCER HAYWOOD: Because of the black boycott that was taking place in America, we were considered Uncle Toms because we played. Well, I knew what an Uncle Tom was, and I knew I wasn't *that*. I know what it is to be an American. I know what freedom is. All of the people that were complaining—all of the problems—I lived these problems.

GEORGE: The idea of [an] Uncle Tom is a guy who doesn't care about black people, who's gonna do whatever the white man tells him. And so, beginning in '68, black nationalism has really come forth. It's not peace, love, and all get together. It's black power. There's arguments to be made on both sides. I don't know what side I would have [been on] . . . but in '68 it was a very bold thing to go [to the Olympics]. It was a very bold thing to not go. Whether you went to the Olympics or not, you were making a statement.

MURPHY: Leading up to the Olympic tryouts, there were some people up around western New York that came to meet with me. They came up to me in the student center in Niagara University, and they were members of the Black Panther movement. They asked me to be a true black man and stand up against the injustices in this country and not represent this country in the Olympic Games. My attitude then was, number one, I don't even know if I'm gonna make the team, but I'm going to try out. And of course they said some things that weren't very nice, and they said, "You better not." And I said, "After I come off the Olympic gold medal, then we can discuss it. That's the best thing I can tell you." There is nobody that is more of a proud African American than myself. But when I was looking at basketball, I wasn't looking at race. I was looking at a sport, I was looking at a country that I was proud of. I didn't want anybody else to be ahead of us, and I wanted to do my part. I don't know if that's patriotic, I don't know if that's corny, but that's the way I felt.

SCOTT: Coach [Dean] Smith had made a very poignant point to me. He told me I went to [the University of] North Carolina to integrate, and if I wouldn't go to the Olympics, it would be tearing down all the things that I was trying to do at North Carolina. I would be boycotting the circumstances that I was trying to integrate.

HAYWOOD: You got Harry Edwards: "You're not doing anything but picking cotton for The Man." And then I extend my silly question: "Did you ever pick cotton?" Because I *was* a cotton picker, and he's 6-foot-8, he's a big old man—maybe he picked in the fields over from us. So I asked him, "Were you in the fields or anything? Because you keep talking about this cotton field." I mean, what they thought we were is on them. But I knew what we were. We were Americans, and we were there to save our country's honor.

SCOTT: At the Olympic trials, they put us on teams, and I was playing with Calvin Murphy. That was the year that Calvin was averaging 30, Pete Maravich was averaging 40, and Rick Mount was averaging 30, and all these guys went to the Olympic trials. The funny thing about it was Calvin was my roommate, and when we were in the room I said to Calvin, "Listen, everybody knows you can score. You know you have 30-some points a game, that's not a question. You should prove that you can pass and play defense." And I ended up being the leading scorer in the tournament. Calvin never let me forget that one.

MURPHY: First of all, nobody listens to Charlie Scott. If you room with Charlie, you'd understand. I've had players work my head for years, and he's not even in the top 100.

HAYWOOD: When I got there, I was MVP of the junior college ranks, averaging 26 points and 26 rebounds a game. If I would have went to Michigan or Michigan State, or if I would have went to the University of Tennessee as I had my eyes on doing, I [would have been] ineligible because we didn't allow NCAA players to try out for the Olympics as freshmen.

MURPHY: I had a very good tryout, but of course Hank Iba was coaching, and he played the 15-passes, slow-down type of basketball. I could have played that style if I was picked, but my style was get off the glass [and] go.

HAYWOOD: Hank Iba cut "Pistol Pete" Maravich, Calvin Murphy, Tom Boerwinkle. He was cutting guys like crazy.

SCOTT: The reason that we were chosen was because of our defensive ability, not because of offensive ability, and we won all of our games because we were a great defensive team.

MURPHY: The style of ball during that era—United States basketball—was exciting, off the glass, movement and go. But the team was coached by Hank Iba, [so] they walked it down, then dropped it down low, that type of thing.

SCOTT: We were a team of speed, and we really didn't get an opportunity to play it. Coach Iba was like all coaches at that time—dictatorial. We went up to practice in Colorado, where the altitude was like 7,200 feet, to get used to the altitude that would be in Mexico City. For about three weeks, all we did was practice defense. For me, my only relationship that I had with a white coach was Coach Smith. And then my next relationship with a white coach was Coach Iba, which was the two extremes of the spectrum. There was a rigidity to [Iba] that didn't make me feel comfortable. I think [assistant] coach [John] McLendon was there to make the black players feel comfortable. I don't really think they allowed him to have as much input as he should've.

HAYWOOD: I was trying out for the team to get me some gear. I just wanted to get some gear with "U.S. Olympics" on it and take it back to Detroit and say, "Hey, I tried out." And all of a sudden, [Iba] looks over and says, "This is the guy that's gonna lead us to the gold medal right here." I was like, "He can't be talking about me."

MURPHY: And, of course, Spencer was the one that won the Olympic gold medal for the U.S.

HAYWOOD: I didn't even have a passport when I made the team. So the Olympic team says, "We need to get him a passport." They came to me and said, "Where is your birth certificate?" I didn't have a birth certificate. I was born by a midwife, on my mother and daddy's bed where I was conceived! So they call my mother in Silver City [Mississippi], and she answered, "Yes, I got the birth certificate. His name is written right here in the Bible under John 21, and he was born on April 22." So they had to fly me to Jackson, Mississippi, with the head—not the head of the Olympics committee but of statistics and so on. But it's my mother, you know? You gotta come down to the Delta and eat some food! So they had to go by the *Jackson Daily News*, bring a photographer, he takes the picture of the written document in the Bible, go back to Jackson, and they created my birth certificate. I get the birth certificate, and I look at the name and I'm like, "Wait a minute—that's not my name. That's Spensie!" But that's how the midwife spelled the name, and so they made a quick change of it. But I remember Jo Jo White, Charlie Scott, Mike Silliman, Bill Hosket, and Jim King was like, "Spensie! Spensie! Spensie!" They was like, "This dude is so country! Is he real?"

Once the Mexico City Olympics began, Team USA cruised to the gold medal, winning all its games by double-digit margins. Off the court, however, the players remained split over the issues of the day. Some, like Charlie Scott, felt conflicted over representing the United States just one year after racial unrest swept the nation in the long, hot summer of 1967. Others, like 19-year-old Spencer Haywood, remained more focused on the competition than on social issues back home.

HAYWOOD: When I made the team in 1968, we had our first meeting, and the conversation was always about we cannot lose this Olympics. *Sports Illustrated* and all the major media outlets were saying, "This is the first time America is going to lose, because we don't have Kareem, we don't have Elvin Hayes, Wes Unseld, Bob Lanier, Calvin Murphy, Pistol Pete, Rick Mount." And so Iba was like, "We cannot lose to the commie Russian bastards." It was drilled in our heads, and so we wrapped ourselves in the flag, in defending America. For me, it was a great thing. I was a Mississippi cotton kid, and all of a sudden Howard Cosell and everybody was looking at me like, "You are gonna save America." *And I had got a passport with my name spelled correctly.*

SCOTT: After [medal winners] Tommie Smith and John Carlos [gave the black power salute on the podium], we said that we were going to make some type of statement. They called the Olympic team together and brought in Jesse Owens to speak to us. He was trying to tell us this is not the time, not the place, to make a political statement. And we disrespected the man. We felt like [International Olympic Committee president] Avery Brundage sent him, and that was the last person we were gonna listen to. We booed Jesse Owens, and that was one thing I really regret, understanding what he had gone through.

HAYWOOD: Once I won the gold medal, it was a big issue: We were such Uncle Toms, [so] how are we gonna go back to Detroit? And how would they receive me? Would I have to come in at night and go home, put my medal away? But when we landed in Detroit, black people were out at the airport to honor me. I was so proud.

SCOTT: For us, school was in, 'cause the [competition] was in September. So, right after the championship game, I was on a plane going home. And after what they had done to Tommie and John, we were a little bit frightened that they would not give me my ticket home, that I would be left down in Mexico City. So we end up not doing anything [to protest racial injustice]. The only thing I did, which I regret to this day, is that after the game was over, I took my Olympic uniform off and I threw it on the ground and left it. I just left it there and got dressed and went to the airport to go back to North Carolina. And I wish I never had done that.

HAYWOOD: The Olympics were pretty cool. All you gotta do is go to practice and go to the matches and come back and eat. I was growing and all I wanted to do was eat, and when I got to the Olympics I found a running buddy that loved to eat as much as I did: George Foreman. We became buddy-buddy, dog-tight because we had two things in common: food, and we were young and dumb.

SCOTT: Before the '72 Olympic team went to Munich, they had an exhibition against the '68 team. And I'm at the airport in Chicago, and a little guy comes up to me and said, "Mr. Scott, I really enjoy watching you play. I made the '72 Olympic team, and I'm so proud. I go to a little school called Illinois State, and nobody knows about me." It was Doug Collins.

1972

The problems roiling beneath the surface of the national team program came to a head at the 1972 Olympics—with help from the most controversial finish

*in basketball history. But even before that infamous championship match,
the Munich games were marked by turmoil. Shortly after being named to the
Olympic roster, forward Mike Bantom was quoted in the New York Times
as saying, "I'm no patriot. I'm going to Munich because my family can use
whatever I get out of it. . . . There's no glory in Munich for the people of
North Philadelphia. The Olympics can't mean much to ghetto people."*

DOUG COLLINS (Shooting Guard, Philadelphia 76ers; 1972 Olympic Silver Medalist; Head Coach, Chicago Bulls/Detroit Pistons): Representing my country is
why I didn't leave college. I wanted that opportunity, and I believed in
myself.

BOBBY CREMINS (Head Coach, Georgia Tech Yellow Jackets, 1981–2000): In
1972, I had finished playing at South Carolina, but I was playing AAU
basketball, and they liked to bring a couple AAU players to try out. The
tryouts were in Colorado Springs at the Air Force Academy. Doug Collins was my roommate, and Doug drove me crazy every night. All he
talked about was, "How did I play?" He never asked how I played, and
finally after the third night he said, "Well, do you think I'll make it?" I
said, "Yeah. What about me? Do you think I'll make it?" And he looked
at me dumbfounded, like I had no shot.

MIKE BANTOM (Power Forward, 1972 U.S. Men's National Team): Coming from a
small school and not being that recognized nationally, I really didn't see
it as an opportunity to make the team. I thought that I was just gonna
go out there and spend the summer practicing against the best players
in the country. And I surprised myself and probably some other people
by actually being one of the 12 guys selected.

LEN ELMORE (Center, Indiana Pacers/New Jersey Nets; President, National Basketball Retired Players Association): I could've been on the '72 team. At
first, I wasn't invited, and then I guess Lefty [Driesell, Elmore's coach
at Maryland] went crazy and tried to get me invited. But I said, "I'm
not doing that. We're in a war in Vietnam that I don't believe in. I don't
think I can wear the colors."

BANTOM: A reporter called me one night and asked some very pointed questions about my motivation for representing my country. And, you know, I answered honestly. I was living in a ghetto. The Olympics was not a commonly known thing where I was. In fact, when I made the team, there was no fanfare in my neighborhood. Hardly anybody knew what it meant. So I stated that I was doing this because I was trying to move up the ladder in terms of being a recognized basketball player. The feeling of patriotism came after I actually went to the Olympics and saw what it meant to have all these countries there and everybody vying for the honor of winning a gold medal.

BILL WALTON: I told the Olympic team in 1972 that I would play, but, since I had already made the team in 1970, that I didn't feel I needed to try out again. And all the things that went wrong in the 1970 World Championship in Yugoslavia—I told the Olympic team that I wasn't gonna be part of that nonsense. The endless exhibition tours, three weeks of tryouts with a hundred guys to try to figure out how you're gonna get a 12-man team. Please, I had already made the team once, and I was playing for UCLA and I had work to do there. So I told them under what conditions I would play, and they said no.

BANTOM: There was some very good players at the trials that didn't make the team. Marvin Barnes comes to mind. And you may have found a guy here or there who you might have picked over somebody on that team, but when you think about the system that we were gonna play, and how you needed guys that could defend and run and pass and be unselfish, I thought they picked well.

TOM McMILLEN (Center, Atlanta Hawks/Washington Bullets; 1972 Olympic Silver Medalist; U.S. Representative, 1987–93): We were in our 20s and didn't know much about international basketball. We were brought together and we had a short few weeks to train, and we had coaches who were pretty conservative. I'm not sure that was the right coaching mix for the players, because [we] were used to more of a fast game than a slow-down game, but it was very disciplined.

COLLINS: In '72, I don't think Iba really wanted to coach the team. I think he did it because the Olympic committee went to him and said we need you to do this one more year. But once he was in, he was all in. Obviously, the huge criticism is "Why are you playing a 50-point game when you have these thoroughbred athletes who can run and shoot and score? Why are you playing the other team's game?" But that's who Coach Iba was. At his heart, he was a defensive-minded coach.

BANTOM: [You're] talking about putting together a team in a short period of time, and you've got guys from all over the country, never having played together, never having played international basketball. So you gotta learn all this stuff, and you got maybe a month to do it. So you can run plays with all kinds of options and reads if you want, but I think you're asking for trouble, especially when you're playing against the disciplined, mature teams that we faced in those Olympics.

McMILLEN: My brother had played for a coach at Maryland who was an Iba disciple. It was a very rigid style, very focused on defense. Offense was very structured—you literally had to pass three times before you took a shot. And I never ever played basketball where I thought about passing three times before a shot. You took a shot when you had a shot. So that was difficult to absorb, and yet that's how we had to play. I often wondered, what if Coach Wooden or Dean Smith had coached, with a more modern view of the game?

BANTOM: We had a system; we played within that system. It didn't maximize all our talents, but it made us a pretty good team. Before we got to that Russian game, we were beating everybody handily. It's easy to look back and say, "Coulda, shoulda, woulda."

COLLINS: Am I protective of Coach Iba? I am. Because he loved me as a player and he gave me a good opportunity and he helped make me better. When he gets criticism about the way we played, I hurt for him. Especially once you've been a coach, you understand the criticism that goes with it, and I say to this day: had our free throws stood up and we won, it would have been so great for Coach. But he had to deal with that the rest of his life—being the first to lose in the Olympics.

McMILLEN: It's easy to make a retrospective judgment, but Iba had great success. His career was very notable. The irony is that we won that game. We should have been awarded at least a dual medal, and we weren't, but I don't blame that on Coach Iba.

COLLINS: Coach Iba was an intense competitor. He was gonna reach into the deepest part of you and find out what you had—whether or not he could trust you when it counted. In fact, I've told this story before, but we flew to Pearl Harbor to train. Everybody thought we were going to [the beach]. We were on the naval base. All 12 slept in the same room until after a week, then we got some individual rooms and slept on these navy cots. Practiced three times a day. It was the hardest 21 days of my life as an athlete. I've never been through something like this ever. And Coach Iba used to say every single day, "We're gonna see the Russians in that gold medal game. We're gonna see the Russians."

BANTOM: I would probably quit if they asked me to do it again. We were living like enlisted men: Wake up at six in the morning with reveille. Go to bed at "Taps." We lived in the barracks. And the gym was not air-conditioned. It was hot and humid every day, and we worked like madmen—nonstop, going at each other. I never experienced anything like it, but I figured that at the end I was gonna be so much stronger. I never worked that hard before, but they were telling us, "This is what it's gonna take to beat those Russians." I think it bonded us. When you're going through misery with 12 other guys, you get closer.

McMILLEN: One of the athletes, Swen Nater from UCLA, quit the team because it was just too rugged.

COLLINS: He was the leading scorer in the Olympic trials, got to Hawaii, practiced three days, and said he wasn't eating properly or whatever, and left the team.

WALTON: Swen quickly realized that this had nothing to do with players. It was all about bureaucrats and coaches and executives and administrators, which was the antithesis of the world we knew and lived in and loved.

McMILLEN: This was a proxy cold war. We might as well have just had [Soviet leader Leonid] Brezhnev and [President Richard] Nixon arm wrestle.

COLLINS: As we were getting ready to practice, Coach Iba wrote the number 50 up on the blackboard and underlined it. And in his gravelly voice he goes, "You boys know what that number stands for? We're gonna play the Russians in the gold medal game, and they're not gonna score 50 against us." Well, had my free throws stood, the score of that game would've been 50–49. We would have won, and we would have held them under 50.

Tragedy struck during the final week of the competition in Munich, when Palestinian terrorists stormed the Olympic Village, took 11 Israeli athletes hostage, and eventually killed them. Less than a week later, the Soviet Union defeated the United States 51–50 to win the gold medal in basketball, and the American team, believing they were cheated, refused to accept silver—a protest that endures to this day.

COLLINS: I don't think I ever realized how much being a part of the United States Olympic team meant until we got to [the] Munich opening ceremonies and everybody's dressed in their red, white, and blue. Walking out and hearing thousands of people chanting "U-S-A, U-S-A," it washed over me, like, "Wow, this is the United States, man. I'm representing our country."

McMILLEN: Five days before [the gold medal game], the Israeli athletes were murdered. That was such a sobering incident throughout the Olympic Village. You couldn't get it out of your mind. This was before "terrorism" was even a word that most people knew. We had to rise above that, go out there, and play. You're going to practice, and just a couple days ago, your fellow athletes were murdered. There was a feeling that the games should have been canceled. I think it would have been a mistake, in retrospect, because it would have been succumbing to this terrorist activity.

COLLINS: We had one tough game [before the final]. I think it was one of my better games, where Coach sort of let us break the pattern, and we had to rely a little bit on our individual ability. That really was our only tough game going into the semis, and between that [and the final] is when they had the terrorists.

McMILLEN: We were at a point in time where international basketball had become much better. This was no longer America's game. There were countries and teams who had taken so much of our innovation that they could compete. The Italians, the Brazilians, the Cubans— they were all very good—and, of course, the Soviets were as good as anyone. We were playing against a very experienced Soviet team that was probably, on average, 8 to 10 years older than us, who had been through many Olympics before.

BANTOM: Those same guys playing for their national team were already playing in pro leagues in Europe. But according to the rules, they were still amateurs, so they were eligible to play in the Olympics. So we were playing basically against the pros of the world, and at the time our basketball was so much farther advanced that we had managed to win. But you could tell that it was starting to catch up to us. Sending immature 19- and 20-year-olds who didn't have time to gel as a team, [it] was going to be difficult to beat a Russian team where a guy was playing in his third Olympics, and the team had hundreds of games together, and the guys were probably 28, 29, 30 years old.

COLLINS: Back then, you didn't have any tape, so when we played the Soviet Union, there was a scouting report on paper, but you didn't have the breakdown of film and the plays they did. It wasn't that sophisticated. Now, Sergei and Alexander Belov were really good. Had they wanted to be in the NBA, I thought they were both NBA players.

BANTOM: I remember us struggling to get our rhythm going. We were a little bit taken aback by how disciplined and how strong they were. Because just like today's USA team, our team was based on disrupting you, putting pressure on you with our defense. Turning you over and running on you. And we had a hard time disrupting them. Sergei Belov was a Hall of Fame player. We didn't know it at the time because we were all kids, but he was one of the best players in Europe, and as their point guard, he kept their team under control and managed the tempo of the game.

McMILLEN: They were playing a better brand of Iba basketball than we were. They were very structured and disciplined. Very strong on defense—that very mechanistic approach to basketball. As the game wore on and we were down, the American team came out of its structure and played a little more freely and loosely, and that's how we came back.

BANTOM: We had some misfortune in the game. To me, it was another sign of the shenanigans going on out there. They had a player that they inserted into the game, who hadn't played in any of their former games, and he got into a mix-up with our starting center, Dwight Jones. They just locked arms or did some pushing and shoving underneath the basket. No elbows were thrown, no punches were thrown. The referee turned around and threw them both out of the game. So they lose their 15th guy, we lose our starting center. Another thing happened to Jim Brewer, [who was] probably our best big guy defensively. There's a jump ball, the ball goes up, Jim goes to jump, and their guy, instead of jumping, goes under him. Low-bridges him. [Jim] flips over, hits his head on the floor, has a concussion. He leaves the game, and he can't play. So I'm the only big guy who has been getting regular minutes, and now I'm playing the whole game. I got some fouls that I shouldn't have gotten because I was playing a very tough offensive player, Alexander Belov. I remember going for a couple of his head fakes. Normally that wouldn't have mattered because I was playing limited minutes, but given that I ended up playing 30 or 35 minutes that game, it ended up costing us, because I fouled out and wasn't in there at the end.

McMILLEN: Give the Soviets credit. They were a pretty good basketball team. World basketball had changed. We couldn't send 18-year-old kids anymore. The United States hegemony in basketball was no longer unchallenged.

BANTOM: At some point in the second half, we said to ourselves, "OK, we gotta get going. We gotta turn this up." We started turning them over, running on them, and you could see 'em get nervous. They started throwing the ball all over the place, and we're picking them off and here we come. As the clock ticked down, we were continuing to shave that lead, and eventually, with a little before 3 seconds left, we get the steal that eventually takes us to a chance to go ahead.

McMILLEN: That climactic ending with Doug Collins getting fouled and hitting two amazingly pressurized free throws—it was just incredible. I think back at him getting up after having fallen to the floor—he gets up and hits those free throws. They had to be two of the biggest free throws in basketball history.

COLLINS: After I had been knocked down—I had fallen on my head; I slid under the basket; I was unconscious for a short period of time—I had a knot under my eye, and I was at the free throw line and I was trying to get myself composed, and Coach Iba and Coach [Don] Haskins and Coach [Johnny] Bach were about 10 feet from me. They were talking, and Bach or Haskins said, "We gotta find somebody who's gonna shoot these free throws." I'll never forget it to this day. Coach Iba said, "If Doug can walk, he's shootin' 'em." All I could think about was, "I can't disappoint Coach. I can't disappoint him—he believes in me." And fortunately, I was able to make the two free throws. He trusted me at the most important time of the game.

McMILLEN: We had a lot of confidence [in Collins]. He looked like he was locked in. He was the go-to guy, and he just had that—oh, what's the word I'm looking for? He made things happen. He was very kinetic. The last thing you wanna do is take your most kinetic player and say, "Don't shoot those free throws," 'cause there's no way on this planet that was gonna happen.

COLLINS: You go back to your training. I was at the free throw line, and people say, "What were you thinking?" Probably, I wasn't thinking. I had the same routine every free throw I ever shot: three dribbles, spin the ball, shoot it. I guess the thing that probably saved me was I didn't think of the consequences. Like, "Wow, what are you going to do if you miss these?" All those days of playing Jerry West in my backyard, shooting free throws, never losing. All the experience—you just go with what you've known, and that's what I had to do and I made them.

BANTOM: Doug Collins, God bless him, knocks down two of the most pressure free throws ever. And our comeback is complete. All we have to do is defend for 3 seconds on a desperation play, and the gold medal was ours. And we did! Unfortunately, it didn't turn out the way it should have, but we made our comeback. In that moment when we had won the game, it was just this great feeling of having gone through this marathon of trials and tribulations, and it all being worth it because here we are, on top. It was a great feeling of relief and joy. And then, all of a sudden, we start to hear the rumbles that—wait a second—there's something going on at the table. We had to go back and replay those last 3 seconds.

COLLINS: As you look back on the last 3 seconds, as I'm getting ready to shoot my second free throw, a horn blows. They're trying to get a time-out, but once the ball has been handed to me, there [can] be no timeout. In international play, you hit a button, a red light goes up, and in the next stoppage of play you get a timeout. I got the ball, the horn goes off, I shoot it, make the free throw. I'm guarding Sergei Belov. They throw the ball to him, and I'm thinking, "Great, they haven't thrown it long. If I can just stay in front of him for a couple dribbles, the game is over." And with 1 second to go the whistle blew, and it was right in front of the Russian bench and the game was stopped. To this day, we have no idea [why it] was stopped. They should have never stopped the game. So now they give them the ball with 1 second to go, but here's the problem: back then, the clock wasn't one of those clocks you could just reset. You had to run it all the way back, and so I think it was on 50 seconds, and they started the game. It was 50 [and] it went to 49. They threw the ball, we intercepted it, we won the game. They had their 1 second. Now Bill Jones from Great Britain comes down; he's the [head] of FIBA. He says that wasn't fair, you gotta put 3 more seconds on the clock. Why did they get 2 more seconds when the game was stopped with 1? To this day, [we've] never understood that.

McMILLEN: Literally, they had three different times to score the last point. The first time could have been a technical mistake. There's no question about it. The coach was trying to get a timeout. Whether he was too late or whether the button was not working remains to be seen, but there would be some question mark about that. But we did start that play over, so that really wasn't the point in contention. It's really the last play, where the clock was reset. That was the one Jones dictated. Some coaches retrospectively said [we] should have just walked off the court. Remember, Dr. Jones came from out of the stands. It would be like the commissioner of the NBA coming down and saying, "Reset the clock." It was a dictum from the top, and there wasn't much the officials were gonna do about it.

BANTOM: The officials, they've gone on record in some of the documentaries: this wasn't their call, and they didn't agree with it. Bill Jones instructed them to replay this game, and the referees were like, "What do you mean? We can't replay the game." The [head] of FIBA decided that this was something that he wanted done, so they followed instructions.

COLLINS: [On the last play], there was no timeout, so you couldn't substitute. There was no strategy. You had two referees who did not speak the same language, and to this day one of 'em has still not signed the scorebook to make it an official game. So they gave them the ball, Tom [McMillen] was on the ball, and the referee went like this [waves his hand], and when he did, Tom backed up to the free throw line. When he did that, he was in no-man's-land, guarding no one. He should have stayed on the ball. All the ref was saying was, "You can't break the plane."

McMILLEN: He kept putting his hand up. I think he was Romanian. He didn't speak English, so that's very complicated. My theory was [he] meant, "You better back off," or he'll call a technical. The truth of the matter is, the rules of international sport are as long as he had room to go back, I didn't need to move. But he was clearly telling me to do something, and he keeps motioning at my feet. I backed up, but when you back up, it's like you're almost no use at all. The pass is thrown, and I really didn't see a lot because I was running back.

COLLINS: We had Jimmy Forbes in the game, who's like 6'7", and we had Kevin Joyce. You could probably throw that same pass 100 times and it wouldn't get through, but it went over the top of Jimmy Forbes, Alexander Belov caught the ball, and Kevin sorta fell.

McMILLEN: Belov catches it, knocks down one of our players, and scores a layup. That's when the chaos really began. We were stunned. I mean, is this really happening? There were always stories about Jones and his relationship to communist nations. This was clearly an attempt to stop the United States from winning, and how high it went up and how far-reaching it was, who knows? You just don't do what Jones did.

COLLINS: With Coach Iba in the locker room after the game, I think he was shell-shocked, like we all were. Our center Jim Brewer had a concussion, so here's Jim in the locker room and he's looking at us like, "What happened?"

McMILLEN: At the end of the game, when all the chaos emerged, Iba had all the fans around him, and he got pickpocketed. It was a crazy night for Coach Hank Iba.

COLLINS: We went to the locker room and they were setting up the medal ceremonies, and we all just said, "We're not gonna go out there for those medals."

McMILLEN: We went in and talked about it. The team was very adamant. I think it was the right decision. We got robbed. If we had accepted the medals, this would have been buried in history. What we did as a team, which was not to take the silver medal, [was right], because it basically would have ended our argument at why this was wrong.

COLLINS: Johnny Bach said, "I'll write up a protest." It was submitted the next day, and we were back in our dorm waiting to get the results. They came back and said we lost, we gotta go get our silver medals, and we all just said we didn't win a silver. A lot of people think we were bad sports, but if we would have lost the game, we would have gone and taken the silver medal.

BANTOM: We were told to take a silver, and we weren't interested in it. We're still not interested.

COLLINS: We had our 40th-year anniversary in 2012. We had never all 12 been in the same room at the same time. ESPN filmed it. We had a roundtable, and we start talking about the gold medal, because Tom McMillen is in politics and he's been trying to get a duplicate gold medal.

McMILLEN: What I proposed is, the Soviets agree to give us a dual gold medal and we agree to give those [silver] medals to a Russian charity. We monetize that with corporate contributions, and we raise $20 million for kids, as opposed to having those medals sit in a vault in Switzerland. I didn't get very far with my teammates on that.

COLLINS: When Tom Burleson and [Tom] McMillen started wavering about getting the medals, Kevin Joyce let it be known, "Under no circumstances." Kevin was like, "No way." And I don't have to tell you, he's as tough as there is—that Irish in him started coming out. He was not a happy man. So we said the only way we would accept a duplicate gold is if they said we won the game, because there has to be a winner. We have a couple guys—Kenny Davis has it in his will—that under no circumstances will he ever accept a silver medal.

BANTOM: Some of my teammates have actually put it in their will that their kids are not allowed to take it. I've never given them specific instructions, but my kids are familiar with the history, and I don't think any of them would take it. They know.

IN THE BEGINNING, THERE WAS A HOOP

Basketball's hold on a player's heart can start in the cradle, and young people from all walks of life have found themselves seduced by the sport. From learning the game in big-city playgrounds and school yards to launching thousands of jumpers on a basket nailed to the side of an Indiana barn, players have always found a way to get their basketball fix. It doesn't matter if you're Bill Bradley, the son of a Missouri bank president, or Spencer Haywood, the son of Mississippi sharecroppers—the game will find you, captivate you, and become part of you.

BERNARD KING: I would play in the after-school center, go home and do my homework, then I would go back to the night center and play. I practiced every day. It was self-satisfaction derived from developing your talent and being able to perform against other players. There was a tremendous drive that I had, a focus and discipline to be one of the best, and the only way you can do that is to practice every single day. I don't care whether there was snow on the ground, I would move the snow and play, whether it was winter, whether it was raining, I would always play.

MAGIC JOHNSON: I used to have names for the ball. I would give it a girlfriend name. This ball was my girlfriend 'cause I carried her everywhere. I used to sleep with the ball. My mother would say, "Go to the store and get some milk." So I'd go, and I'd be dribbling left-handed all the way there, get what she wanted, and I'd dribble back right-handed. The neighbors hated me. They'd say, "Johnson, quit dribbling that basketball!"

SONNY HILL: It all goes back to Guy Rodgers. I was about 12 years old, in North Philadelphia, where we both lived. He was the first black in the city of Philadelphia to play in the white neighborhood in the northeast. He played for a guy named Bob Custard, who had an independent team, and I used to go to the rec centers with Guy Rodgers's bag in my hand. I'm so proud to say I used to carry Guy Rodgers's bag. Guy turned everybody on with all of his razzle and dazzle and the fabulous things he could do. Guy was most responsible for motivating me, stimulating me, and also reaching out and saying, "You can play."

MIKE BANTOM: I grew up in the projects, and when I was coming up, there were no rec leagues, no youth basketball. It was pretty rough. But then around fifth or sixth grade my mom moved us to a different neighborhood, but I didn't really start playing organized basketball until eleventh grade. Up until then I was just playing on the playground. Once I made the junior varsity, I dedicated myself to be as good as I can, kinda out of reaction to people laughing at me and thinking I was terrible.

WES UNSELD: Basketball allowed me to do things that I never thought about until much later—things that would seem silly or mundane today. I got to take a shower. And you think that sounds weird, but until I was at the high school gym, I never took a shower. Where I grew up, we had tubs. To this day, I take the longest [showers]. My son even had a specially built shower [installed] in my house because he knows I just love the shower.

WAYNE EMBRY: My dad played semipro baseball, and many thought that he was probably good enough to play in the majors had times been different. That was before Jackie Robinson. I wanted to be a baseball player, and so we had a game against a pitcher that we knew was pretty proficient in throwing a curveball. I asked my dad, "How do you hit a curveball?" and he said, "Just dig in and wait for it to break and hit it." So I followed instructions: I dug in, waited, and it didn't break. Caught me in the back of the head, and I said, "That's it for baseball." I started playing basketball, and even though I had size, I was slow and not very agile. I was clumsy but started falling more in love with the game as I started getting better. I jumped rope, started playing basketball every day. My dad took me to see the Harlem Globetrotters, so naturally I wanted to be Goose Tatum, 'cause I was able to palm the ball like Goose. I shot the hook like Goose Tatum and made passes with one hand like Goose did, got rebounds with one hand like Goose did.

DALE BROWN: Outside of a phenomenal mother, basketball was the one source that gave me confidence, taught me teamwork, taught me discipline, and gave me hope. No father—he abandoned my mother and I and my two older sisters two days before I was born. People would say, "Where's your father?" I would say, "He's deceased." We had nothing. I had an inferiority complex. They were having a fifth-grade tryout. My clothes smelled of mothballs—my mother bought them at a rummage sale. But [after] making the team, the coach came up to me, kinda patted me on the neck, and said, "Dale Brown, you could be a good athlete, young man. I think you've got some future." No teacher ever told me that.

LARRY BROWN: My dad died when I was young, and we happened to live across the street from a park. My mom worked, so rather than her worrying about me, I would cross the street and play. I didn't mind being by myself, and there wasn't a day that went by that I didn't dream about making a last-second shot—either on the court by myself or taking a hanger, cutting a sock, and making it the net and rolling up some white sweat socks as balls. That's why I think this sport is so special—you can be there by yourself.

LYNETTE WOODARD: I fell in love with the game very early. My brother, he's a couple years older, we played this game called sock ball. He would roll his socks together, and we had the entry to the bedroom door and the adjacent closet as hoops—the little crack over the top. He would write down the names of different players, and we would pretend we were dribbling and then we would shoot, and whoever dropped it in the slot, that was a score.

SPENCER HAYWOOD: I remember we were playing over at Peewee Boss's backyard. His name was Peewee because of his head being rather small.

So we was playing in his backyard, and I had been beaten down so bad by my brother Andrew. I guess I was like 13, and I had fun because I could whup my brother Floyd—he was a chump, so I could take him. But Andrew was really tough. He put me on his team, and he started yelling and screaming, and so I got so angry. The ball came off the backboard—I grabbed the ball and went back up and dunked it. Boom! And everybody was like, "Wait a minute! What?" My brother Floyd fell over backward—and my mother always told him, "Don't put your money in your mouth." He's like choking and gagging, so Andrew walked over, hit him in the back, and money falls out of his mouth.

NOLAN RICHARDSON: I was born in El Paso [Texas], and during those days there was segregation, so I spent most of my time at a school called Douglass. It was all blacks, and there was projects right across the street that had basketball courts. I would go over and play basketball every single day. On Saturdays I would probably leave at 8 in the morning and I didn't get back home till 10 that night, just playing basketball. Sometimes I never ate—I never even thought about it.

BEN JOBE: When we came off the plantation, 1945, I was around 11 years old. I really didn't know anything about basketball. And by the way, slavery ended in 1945, let me make that clear. Most people think it was 1865. Oh, no, [it was] 1945, when the federal government finally put some teeth into it and arrested some of the slave owners who are now plantation owners. When we came off the plantation, we saw kids with baskets hanging on trees and on the side of buildings, and it looked interesting. My parents were never into that type of thing, of course. With 15 children, everybody had to work, but being the last child, I had an opportunity to do some things that my older brothers and sisters didn't. So I started playing, [and] John McLendon came to town, and he was everything. He had that philosophy, "It takes a village." We always could depend on the coaches in the area, mainly because of him. If you need food, you can go to the coach. His house was always full—kids on the porch, out in the grass. When he walked out the door, you just want to be around him. He was that kind of guy. So all of us who had those great ideas that we were going to be doctors or lawyers—a lot of us gave that up and want to be like John McLendon, be a coach.

JERRY COLANGELO: We talk about basketball being this urban game, which it is. But when you go into the heartlands—downstate Illinois, Indiana, Kentucky—you could put a hoop up on the side of a barn and learn to play. You could do it alone, you could do it with one other player. Basketball was a way of life.

HUBIE BROWN: We had a court, a little basket, and it wasn't even a rim, it was a pail. Back then, there were no rubber basketballs. You had an old beat-up leather ball, and you would shoot because there was no cement—you were shooting on the mud. You would shoot before school, then you would practice, and you'd still come back and shoot at night. Your fingers, because of the cold, would split.

VAL ACKERMAN: My dad was a high school athletic director. He loved basketball, he played it, he was a referee. I have the fondest of memories of playing with him on our driveway basket, shooting into the night. I had a lamp that I would attach to the dogwood tree next to the driveway so I could shoot after the sun went down.

GEORGE McGINNIS (Power Forward, Indiana Pacers/Philadelphia 76ers; 1975 ABA MVP; 3-Time NBA All-Star): Growing up in Indiana—well, basketball and Indiana go hand in hand. It was easy to gravitate toward the game. I started watching it at 5 years old and playing at about 10, and I always had a ball in my hand, dribbling, throwing it against the wall.

DON NELSON: I was a farm kid, went to a one-room schoolhouse, so we didn't have a team or anything. My uncle put a basket up in the chicken yard, and that's where I started playing. He put the basket up too high—11 feet—but it was fun to see the ball go in every once in a while.

BILL BRADLEY: [There were] 96 [students] in my high school graduating class in Missouri. I actually went out into the countryside to recruit kids from farms to come in so we would have enough [kids] to play in the state tournament.

PHIL FORD (Point Guard, University of North Carolina Tar Heels, 1974–78; 1979 NBA Rookie of the Year): I would go in the house and steal cookies so I [could] bribe my friends for one more game.

BECKY HAMMON: My parents had pictures of me when I'm 2 years old with a basketball. I lived in South Dakota and we had a basket on the front of our house, and I remember trying to go around the world, playing H-O-R-S-E at a very young age. I don't know how to explain it other than I don't remember a time that I didn't love basketball.

PHIL JACKSON (2-Time NBA Champion Player; 11-Time NBA Champion Head Coach): The story my mother used to tell was that she used to check my sleep patterns in the night—and I was just a 3-year-old kid—and she said, "The strangest thing is, you are always making motions [like] catching a ball in your sleep." When I moved to Williston, North Dakota, at 12, the people that had this concrete basketball court kept the basketball warm for me if I came over and it was really cold, so I'd have a warm ball and be able to shoot.

BOB PETTIT: I got cut as a sophomore from the high school team. I went home, my parents put a goal in the backyard, and I started practicing two or three hours every night. I put lamps in the windows that would shine out, so I could practice after homework and just shoot and shoot and shoot. It's tough, a very emotional thing when you get cut and you want it so badly—more than anything. My ambition in high school was to win a letter. That's all I wanted, to wear that letter sweater. And once I got my coordination and started having some success, that encouraged me more. My goals ratcheted up, and 10 years later I wanted to be the greatest player in the world.

THE RENEGADE LEAGUE

From 1967 to 1976, the American Basketball Association rose to challenge the NBA's status as the world's premier professional basketball league. The ABA lacked access to major markets, its teams often played in near-empty arenas, and it became as well-known for its fistfights as its superstars. Yet the upstart ABA managed to shape much of what fans today associate with NBA basketball. It launched the careers of Hall of Famers Julius "Dr. J" Erving, George "the Iceman" Gervin, and David "Skywalker" Thompson, and saved the careers of players such as Connie Hawkins, Roger Brown, and Doug Moe, whose unproven connections to gambling scandals left them unjustly banned from the NBA. The ABA popularized the three-point shot; it experimented with new forms of in-arena entertainment, from dance teams to halftime cow-milking contests; and it held the first slam dunk competition. The league's up-tempo style highlighted the grace and athleticism of African American players in an era when the NBA was still believed to abide by quotas restricting the number of black players who could suit up for a given team. By highlighting the brilliance of players like Dr. J, Artis Gilmore, and George McGinnis, the ABA not only pushed the NBA toward adopting a faster-paced game, but it also nudged the NBA toward full integration.

PETER VECSEY: What made the ABA special was that everybody was in the same situation. We were all trying to make it. We were all looked down upon, and I'm talking for myself as a writer at that time, talking about players and coaches [who] were only there because they were no longer in the NBA.

ROD THORN (Guard, St. Louis Hawks/Seattle Supersonics; 2002 NBA Executive of the Year): You were always on the verge of extinction, so there was this closeness that came to be among people in the league. It seemed like every other day some team was on the verge of bankruptcy, and so the feeling among coaches and players was something that I've never felt in the NBA.

MICHAEL GOLDBERG (General Counsel, ABA; Executive Director, National Basketball Coaches Association; Died 2017): The league was modeled on the old AFL, the American Football League. It was very difficult to get a franchise in the NFL, so somebody thought, "We'll form our own league, we'll get our own star players, and eventually we'll merge. Instead of paying a big entry fee, we'll wind up with an NFL franchise at half the price." The ABA was modeled after that: "We'll come up with our own league; we'll go in markets and compete with some NBA teams, [while other teams] will go to untested markets in smaller cities where basketball is popular; we'll come up with a red, white, and blue ball, which we'll get a patent on and sell billions of these balls around the world; and we'll come up with the three-point play. We're gonna differentiate ourselves, and at some point we will be embraced by the NBA and be part of that club."

TERRY PLUTO (Author, *Loose Balls: The Short, Wild Life of the American Basketball Association*): Owners tended to be local guys that were schemers and dreamers. They were men who wanted to be in the game, whatever the game is. They thought we could come up with enough franchises in the first few years [that] the NBA will get tired of us and they'll let us in.

GOLDBERG: The [price] range for an ABA franchise was low seven figures—a million to a million and a half dollars. But in reality, if you had a hundred grand [and] put up the letter of credit, we grabbed you by the lapel and pulled you into the room. We had guys that came out of the woodwork. We had a dentist that owned a team in San Diego. We had a cable TV operator that was just starting in Utah. They didn't have the deep pockets to stick with the program and fight the NBA and finally get a merger.

PLUTO: These were guys that felt, "I know a little about basketball, I know a little about business, and I could scrape together fifty to a hundred grand from other people." And bingo! You're in, especially if you could put yourself in a city that looks like it might be decent to have a team. But sometimes they weren't even sure where to put the team, so they had regional teams. The Carolina Cougars played in Charlotte, Raleigh, Greensboro. Gene Littles, who played on that team, said, "We played everywhere, we played nowhere. All we ever did was pass through the airport."

JULIUS ERVING: We [the Virginia Squires] had four [home courts]: the Norfolk Scope [Arena], the Hampton Coliseum, the Richmond Coliseum, and the Roanoke Arena. We played half of our games between Hampton and Norfolk and about a third up in Richmond, and then a few games over in Roanoke. And you have to take a plane over to Roanoke, 'cause it's all the way at the other end of the state. So we had a home game where you had to take a flight.

PLUTO: To figure out where to put franchises, you started with 12 NBA teams. The NBA had the big ones—New York, Chicago, Boston, Los Angeles. So the ABA [was thinking], "Do we go into the big markets, or do we find other markets?" The reason Cleveland, Buffalo, and Portland all received NBA franchises in 1970 was the ABA. The NBA was scared to death that the [ABA was] gonna go into these cities which didn't have pro basketball.

GOLDBERG: We were always looking to hit the NBA with a torpedo that would weaken them and [make them] say, "OK, join us, we can't stand fighting you anymore." We even went after some of the best referees in the NBA. We can see the commissioner pulling his hair out: "Referees? What's next? Our peanut salesmen?" We fought them at every level. Our total strategy was to bring the NBA to the table to merge with the ABA by making it economically unfeasible to continue this battle.

DAVID STERN: When it began, the ABA was a serious threat to the NBA. They had a spunky group of owners, they were willing to duke it out, and I was at one point on the front lines of these litigations. Rick Barry was going back and forth, Billy Cunningham. We were litigating all over, and it was a battle. The NBA was much stronger and held itself out as *the* major league of basketball, but there were not the deep pockets that there are now. The NBA was vulnerable to losing players to the ABA, and there was literally an all-star team of Hall of Fame basketball players who were ready to go. Look at Moses Malone, Artis Gilmore, Maurice Lucas, not to mention Dr. J. Their problem was, they couldn't get any television coverage.

GOLDBERG: We thought that when we formed this league, TV networks would come storming in for content, but the NBA was having difficulty on television. In the early years of the ABA, the NBA playoffs were on tape delay at night. So we didn't have TV. When that goes out the window, it's guerrilla warfare. You have to try everything you can imagine to showcase this league and its talent.

PLUTO: The ABA was really the last line of opportunity. Many of the early black players felt there was a quota system [in the NBA]: three, no more than four, on the court at once. The ABA didn't care; they needed players. The ABA would say, "We're going to try the red, white, and blue ball. We're going to try the three-point line. Let's play faster. Let's have younger coaches. Let's take the Rucker League, let's take the playgrounds, and put it in more of a structure setting."

GOLDBERG: There was a lot of talent out there that was rejected by the NBA or banned for various infractions. Our approach was, "We're not going to let these beautiful players just linger." Connie Hawkins, Doug Moe, Roger Brown—these were great players, and we felt they belonged on the basketball court. We weren't gonna let youthful mistakes stand in the way of our league surviving. The ABA: "Bring us your tired, your hungry, your poor"—as long as they could play basketball.

PLUTO: When you consider who was banned from the NBA, they felt like pariahs. I didn't spend a ton of time trying to investigate exactly what the connection was to gambling, but clearly it was iffy, 'cause Connie Hawkins sued the NBA and was admitted. Roger Brown also won his suit. He took a financial settlement instead, because Roger Brown loved playing in Indiana. This is another thing to [the ABA's] credit: they didn't care where these guys were before.

GOLDBERG: We were always differentiating ourselves from the NBA. We tried everything—dancing girls, three-point plays, free tickets—and we just couldn't get traction. To some degree, I think that was a racial situation. The league was very African American in those days. The Afro was a big statement of the ABA. There was a certain swagger. This wasn't *Hoosiers*, if you follow what I mean. This was freedom of movement, freedom of expression, and even our coaches bought into [it]. The talent was so rich, there was no holding these guys back.

SPENCER HAYWOOD: We had the loud clothes and the wild colors and the big old Afros and long mullet haircuts. You know, white guys had mullets, beards, and shit. But in the NBA you couldn't wear that stuff. They were corporate, and we were the new guys, the renegades.

PLUTO: The remarkable thing was they thought, "We need a team in Minneapolis [because] we want George Mikan to be commissioner." Before there was Kareem and Wilt and Russell, there was George Mikan, considered the greatest NBA player of the first 50 years of the 20th century. He is living in Minneapolis, owns a travel agency. So they decide, "We want Mikan to be commissioner," and they want Mikan to move to New York, and he goes, "I'm not moving. I got my travel agency here." So they decide [to] put a team in Minneapolis so at least there's a team where the commissioner is.

GOLDBERG: You want to have a commissioner that's instantly recognizable, brings credibility, and has the patina of an honest gentleman about him. And that was George Mikan.

PLUTO: So they go to Mikan, give him fifty grand to be commissioner, and all of a sudden, Mikan comes up with, "I want a red, white, and blue ball." Remember, Mikan wears glasses, had bad eyes. The black-

and-white TV, it's grainy, [and] George can't see the ball. So they want a red, white, and blue ball, and Mikan, his big line was "When they see our ball, everybody'll salute." Mikan would say these strange things that didn't really resonate with anybody else besides George Mikan, but it was genius marketing because it gave the league a stamp.

CONNIE HAWKINS: When the ball came out, all the guys would have turnovers because when they threw you the ball, [it] would rotate and you couldn't tell if the ball was far or close, so it took us about two months to get used to the ball.

HAYWOOD: Once you shoot, you know everything that you done wrong with your shot because [of] the rotation in the red, white, and blue. If it spins wrong, you just know it.

DOUG MOE: It wasn't made of the best material. It was slick. You'd have to rub 'em down and dirty to have it to where it was all right.

RICK BARRY: That ball sucked! It had hard edges; it would get slick at times. It was a great gimmick, but quality-wise the ball was horrible.

PLUTO: This is classic ABA: They come up with the red, white, and blue ball, but they patent the ball with the ABA logo instead of the color scheme. So, for example, the red, white, and blue balls that my mother bought me were just made by whoever. Just don't put the "ABA" on it, and you could make it yourself.

GOLDBERG: The courts found that making a ball red, white, and blue was not different enough to warrant a patent, so that was a big source of revenue out the window.

PLUTO: They didn't have the ball manufactured [in time for] the first Indiana Pacers preseason game. Here's what you learn: Don't take a brown ball and paint it red, white, and blue. It would be like throwing a greased pig. They painted these balls in this exhibition game, and they're throwing the balls all over the place. It's slick, the paint's starting to run off as the guys are sweating. Later, they learned to put dye in the ball.

One of the ABA's most ambitious attempts to pressure the NBA into a merger came before the 1969–70 season, when both leagues competed to sign Lew Alcindor out of UCLA.

PLUTO: Project Alcindor: the ABA thought, "If we do this we could force a merger." They spent $10,000 to have somebody work up a psychological profile on Alcindor, and they talked to people around him to find out, "How can we get him to sign with the ABA?" 'Cause the draft rights to him went to Milwaukee in the NBA, they thought, "This guy's from New York, he played [college basketball] in Los Angeles, he doesn't want to play in Milwaukee. We'll let him play in New York— frankly, name your team." Their research showed, number one, that Alcindor was going to make his own decision; two, [that] he did not like negotiating back and forth; and three, he said it himself, "I'm going to take one offer from one team and one from another." So they planned to hand him a million-dollar check right there, ask him, "Where do you want to play?" Mikan's gonna be the front man with Arthur Brown, who owned the franchise in the New York area. This is where the stories conflict. The Indiana group behind the million-dollar check and the research believed Mikan just flat out forgot to take the check. Mikan said he was holding it back for a second round of negotiations. So they went into what they thought was a preliminary meeting, or they treated it as such, and Alcindor became disillusioned. He felt like these guys didn't have their act together, and they lost him to Milwaukee. The Indiana [group] and the ABA people believed—and I tend to agree with them—that had they gotten Alcindor, this merger comes quick. But they messed it up.

The ABA may have botched its attempt to sign Alcindor, but over the years, the league managed to attract veterans from the Eastern League and other

regional and commercial leagues that preceded the ABA; college underclass-
men who chose not to wait four years to enter the NBA and signed with ABA
teams under the "hardship" rule instead; and NBA players who jumped
leagues. The NBA may not have been willing to admit it, but a legitimate
rivalry was beginning to take form.

LARRY BROWN: [When] the ABA started, they were trying to find players wherever they could. So Doug [Moe] got a call, and basically Doug said, "The only way I'll sign is if they take Larry with me." So Doug and I get invited to New Orleans. I get a call from Marty Blake, who was GM of the St. Louis Hawks, saying, "Larry, this league's not gonna go over. You could try out for us, and if you don't make it, you could be an assistant coach." And I said, "I wanna play." So Doug and I fly down, and we go to the building where the New Orleans Buccaneers offices were. We look at the directory, and there's no New Orleans Buccaneers. But we see Sean Morton Downey Jr., president of some company. And Doug and I go to his office, and he's sitting there, chain-smoker, and he turns this plaque around and it says, "President, New Orleans Buccaneers."

MOE: First year ABA—that's when Morton Downey Jr. was the GM for us. He was a trip. This was before he was famous for his show and smoke. After we signed, he told us, "I woulda given you guys anything."

LARRY BROWN: Doug and Sean start a dialogue, and I'm just there. Sean says, "Doug, we want you to be our first guy. We not only think you're a great player, you're like all-world." He talked about all the great things Doug did and how we're gonna have a great situation here. Doug says, "Well, what are you gonna pay me?" And [Downey] just jumped with a number: $20,000. Doug said, "I want more than one year." He said, "All right, we'll give you 22 the second year." And before he agreed, he said, "What about Larry?" I don't think they were that excited about me, but if it was gonna mean getting Doug, you might as well think about taking Larry. So he said, "I'll give him $12,500." That seemed pretty great, and then Doug said, "What if he starts? If he starts he deserves more than $12,500." He said, "I'll give him a $2,500 bonus if he starts." I said, "Sounds good to me." So that was basically the way my contract was made. I'm sitting there, knowing I made a hell of a score. Then Doug says [to me], "I'm not so sure this league's gonna go over. We ought to get some money in advance." I didn't even think about that. So Doug got a $5,000 advance, and I got $2,500. I said, "Doug, when we walk out of here, this [check] will probably self-destruct or something." And we just giggled about it, and that's how I ended up in the ABA.

GOLDBERG: Larry Brown and Doug Moe, I remember them telling me they had never heard of money like this to play basketball. So they signed immediately and were joined by players like "Jumping Joe" Caldwell and Billy Cunningham, who were in the NBA and got a whiff that there was a league out there drunk with money.

PLUTO: From the beginning, the NBA didn't even consider the ABA the junior varsity. The classic Alex Hannum line: "That ball belongs on the nose of a seal." You know, the red, white, and blue ball. The irony is that a couple years later, Alex Hannum ends up coaching that ball [with the Oakland Oaks]. [The NBA's attitude] was very dismissive, Red Auerbach saying, "Julius Erving, he's a nice player. He might be able to come off the bench in our league." The ABA was rebelling against the big empire, and they wanted to win a little warfare here, there, and everywhere. The ABA fought them on players, having Rick Barry and Billy Cunningham and Zelmo Beaty jump; [on] referees, having people like Earl Strom and Jack Madden come; and they fought them for franchises.

EARL MONROE: Players in the NBA really perceived the ABA as a wild league. We had more respect for it as the years went on. I can remember Connie Hawkins playing in it, then Doc [Dr. J] and George Gervin and Charlie Scott. We realized that those guys were great players. After my second year in Baltimore, I was approached by the owner of the Pittsburgh team to come play in the ABA, and I flirted with that idea because he was talking about paying so much more than I was getting at that time. The determining factor was that they wanted to spread my payment out till 2060, and that wouldn't work.

CALVIN MURPHY: They came after me in my junior year. I was approached to leave early and come into the ABA. I spoke to my mother, and she said, "There's nothing doing. First of all, the money's not guaranteed. And Calvin's dream has always been the NBA, so we're gonna let him finish college and then go from there."

GAIL GOODRICH: I never considered the ABA. I guess it was in its beginning stages. I always felt that while the ABA did end up having a lot of individual stars, the NBA was the top league.

WAYNE EMBRY: I thought the ABA [players] were vagabonds.

PLUTO: Drafting in the ABA was not exactly like the NBA. The ABA had a very socialistic view—they just wanted to hurt the NBA if they could get a college player. Suppose you were drafting before Indiana, but Rick Mount, star at Purdue, is in the draft. Guess what? Indiana got his draft rights. Different players were assigned to different areas. But some of the guys who did these early drafts were not exactly the most astute, and sometimes the teams were cheap. For example, in their first draft, the Dallas [Chaparrals] didn't have enough money to send their coach or general manager. The owner went himself, and they made a draft list [of whom to pick]. But for whatever reason, the list is in alphabetical order, so if you look at how Dallas drafted that year and you line up all the names, they're in alphabetical order.

BOBBY "SLICK" LEONARD (Head Coach, Indiana Pacers): We were the underdogs, there's no question about that. The NBA hated the ABA because we changed the salary structure. Guys could barter, whether they were going into the NBA or the ABA, so it really did up the salaries for everybody.

BILLY CUNNINGHAM: The reason I made a decision to go to the ABA was simple: money. I was going to go from $45,000 to $300,000 a year.

PLUTO: Ron Grinker, who was an agent back then, worked both sides. He was able to go to NBA owners and say, "I got this offer from the ABA;

they're offering three hundred grand over three years." Of course, it was actually $30,000 a year for three years, and then it was deferred. Seventy, 80 percent of [ABA] contracts were deferred out [until] basically the only thing you're paying for is the guy's funeral. But Grinker said he was able to use this on the NBA, who then started saying, "We'll give 'em three hundred grand, and we'll actually do it within three years." So these deferred contracts on the ABA side led to real contracts on the NBA side, which jacked up their budget. The ABA [thought] this was great because they were inflicting more pain on the senior league.

DAVID THOMPSON: I went to the ABA because I thought the best young players were in the ABA at the time. They played more above the rim. It was an up-and-down type of ball that was more pleasing to the players. And Denver wined and dined me. They brought me out, picked me up in a limo, took me out to eat these big steaks. They took me to a playoff game where they introduced me to the crowd, and they gave me a standing ovation. And I meet [the] Atlanta [Hawks] in a McDonald's. I chose the Nuggets, and it worked out great. Also, I knew the leagues were gonna merge at some point. My lawyer had me sign a five-year guaranteed contract with a player opt-out after three. In case the leagues didn't merge, I could go to an NBA team.

LEN ELMORE: I was drafted by the Washington Bullets, first-round pick, and it would have been great to stay in the neighborhood. But this is the NBA, and [there was] a little bit of arrogance. The general manager offered me a three-year deal, but only two guaranteed. The Pacers offered me a six-year deal, all guaranteed, with annual money that surpassed what the Bullets offered. How could I not go? And I did some research. The Pacers were the strongest team, financially, out of all the teams in the ABA. If there were to be some kind of merger, the Pacers would have to be in the forefront.

ABA teams would try anything to stoke interest in the league, and in the process they ushered in the three-point shot and an up-tempo style that changed professional basketball forever.

HAWKINS: We had no fans. We couldn't get nobody to come watch us play. The only place that drew a crowd was Indiana. Every time we played in Indiana, they would pack the place—15,000, 18,000 people. Everybody would enjoy playing against Indiana because they knew there was going to be a crowd.

MOE: There were times when you could count the people in the stands. The best places as far as crowds were Denver, Kentucky, Indiana, and San Antonio. They were the teams that helped carry the ABA, because some of the other teams—the crowds were awful. We're talking maybe hundreds.

PLUTO: It was always hard to get crowds. No team really had this motto, but if they had a second motto, it's "A good seat's always available."

BARRY: I remember playing a game in Houston. There were more people sitting at the scorer's table and on the benches than in the stands.

PLUTO: They wanted to draw, but remember, the point wasn't just to make money. Everything was designed to force the merger. They wanted to make life as uncomfortable as they could for the NBA.

MARK CUBAN (Owner, Dallas Mavericks): Fifth grade, sixth grade—somebody who lived around the corner from us worked for the Pittsburgh Pipers. So I would get tickets and be one of the 17 people in the stands.

PLUTO: What we now call dance teams in the NBA, the ABA took no pretense: nobody's really dancing; this is cheerleaders in bikinis jiggling. The Miami Floridians take credit for that. They couldn't get anybody to come to games, [but] the girls came out and jiggled, they handed the officials a towel and some water, and they just wandered around the empty stands. The Indiana Pacers take credit for having the first cow-milking contest at halftime. Billy Keller, a little guard for the Pacers, was one of the great cow-milkers in the league, and proud of it.

MOE: A lot of arenas we played in didn't have showers. You carried your own bag. You'd get dressed at the hotel, put on your uniform, play the game, come back, and shower at the hotel.

GEORGE McGINNIS: We smoked cigarettes in the locker room. Half the league smoked, and it was not that big of a deal. When I started with the Pacers, people would smoke right in the arena, in the front row. I remember walking out and seeing the lights filled with smoke.

GOLDBERG: ABA arenas lacked certain amenities. Some of them didn't have heat. Some of them had limited restrooms. Some of them, the department of health might have issues with those concession stands.

LARRY BROWN: They were trying to save money and cut costs. One of our players was our trainer, Mel Peterson, 'cause he had some phys ed experience. Generally, trainers didn't travel. You'd go on the road, and there'd be a guy that'd show up to tape you. One day, a guy was taping me, and he was a poultry farmer. I didn't want to embarrass the guy, so I went into the shower, cut the tape off, and taped myself.

AL ATTLES: The ABA played in Oakland, and we [the San Francisco Warriors] used the same facilities. We used to practice at a recreation center, so we go there the first day, and I'm the coach, and they tell us we can't practice. They say, "Aren't you the guy from the ABA?" And we say, "No, we're from the NBA." They say, "Oh, it's the ABA that owes us money." So they let us practice.

GOLDBERG: Money was not our strong suit. In fact, the league office money, which came from the annual assessments of teams, was often slow in coming. I remember once calling up the owner of the San Diego team, the dentist, with the drilling noise in the background, and I said, "We need money." He kept saying, "What? I can't hear you." We eventually got it, but I would say [rob] Peter to [pay] Paul was the way we operated.

CUNNINGHAM: [For] three-quarters of the league, you didn't know if you were going to get your check on the 1st and 15th. Guys were running to the bank to be the first to get their checks cashed. But I absolutely loved it, and the level of talent that emerged, from the George Gervins, the Julius Ervings—George McGinnis, Roger Brown—oh my goodness, it was absolutely great.

Dr. James Naismith, the Canadian physical educator who invented basketball at the Springfield, Massachusetts, YMCA in 1891. *Kenneth Spencer, University of Kansas Libraries*

LIU star Leroy Smith, flanked by a pair of detectives, is booked for bribery charges at New York's Elizabeth Street police station, one of scores of college players across the country who were ensnared in the infamous 1950–51 point-shaving scandal. *Bettmann/Getty Images*

At 6'10", George Mikan, of the Minneapolis Lakers, was the NBA's first great big man. Later he would become the first commissioner of the ABA. *Seymour Wally/*New York Daily News*/Getty Images*

Jack Molinas, the former NBA player turned game-fixer who was at the center of the 1961 point-shaving scandal that led to the unjust blacklisting of Connie Hawkins, Roger Brown, and Doug Moe. *Bettmann/Getty Images*

Attorney Roz Litman's dogged pursuit of the NBA for blackballing Connie Hawkins finally freed Hawkins to display his considerable talents for the Phoenix Suns. *Roz Litman*

Coach John McClendon, the father of fast-break basketball and the four corners offense, with his players at Tennessee A&I in the late-1950s. *Tennessee State University*

Adolph Rupp, head coach of the University of Kentucky Wildcats from 1930–72.
Lee Balterman/ Sports Illustrated Classic/Getty Images

Bob Cousy kicks back to savor a Celtics win, while Boston forward Jim Loscutoff enjoys a cigar.
Bettmann/Getty Images

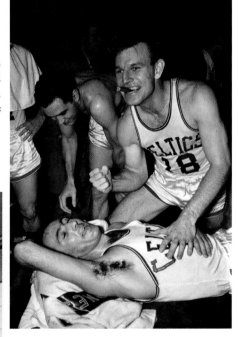

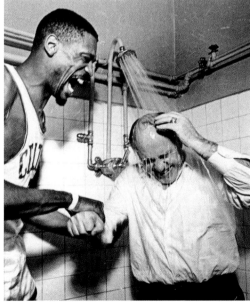

Boston Celtics center Bill Russell celebrating with head coach Red Auerbach.
Associated Press Photo

Although they were fierce rivals on the basketball court, Wilt Chamberlain (left) and Bill Russell remained friends and confidants until Chamberlain's death in 1999. *Herb Scharfman/ Sports Imagery/Getty Images Sport Classic/Getty Images*

Laker greats Jerry West (right) and Elgin Baylor reached the NBA Finals seven times in the 1960s and early '70s, yet they never managed to win a championship together. West's first title came in 1972, after Baylor had retired earlier that season. *George Long/Sports Illustrated Classic/Getty Images*

Oscar Robertson faced racism and discrimination at every level of his career, and "The Big O" overcame these conditions to have a brilliant, Hall-of-Fame career. He was the first player to average a triple-double, he won the NBA's MVP award in 1964, helped steer the Milwaukee Bucks to a championship in 1971, and he led the Players' Association's lawsuit to force the NBA to adopt free agency. *Bettmann/Getty Images*

Coach Frank McGuire taking a victory lap on the shoulders of his UNC Tar Heel players. *Associated Press Photo/William P. Straeter*

Guard Charlie Scott was the first African American scholarship player at the University of North Carolina, playing under coach Dean Smith from 1967–70. News & Observer

Spencer Haywood's landmark antitrust suit against the NBA in 1971 struck down regulations that a player couldn't be drafted until he waited four years after graduating high school. *Associated Press Photo*

Old Dominion All-American Nancy Lieberman honed her skills by mixing it up with the boys in New York City's famed Rucker Park. *Bettmann/Getty Images*

UCLA Coach John Wooden's obsession with fundamentals convinced Gail Goodrich to stick to the basics. *Associated Students UCLA*

A shirtless Doug Collins in the locker room with other members of the 1972 US National Team. *Rich Clarkson/ Clarkson Creative*

Elvin Hayes claims after his Houston team upset Lew Alcindor's UCLA Bruins in the "Game of the Century" at the Astrodome on January 20, 1968, that the two never spoke to each other again. *Neil Leifer*/Sports Illustrated/*Getty Images*

In addition to leading UCLA to consecutive NCAA championships in 1972 and '73, free-spirited center Bill Walton made plenty of time for student activism. *Los Angeles Times Photographic Archive. Department of Special Collections, Charles E. Young Research Library, UCLA*

David Thompson, one of the greatest leapers in basketball history, after a violent fall in the 1974 NCAA tournament. Thompson had jumped to block a shot, but flipped and landed on his head after his feet grazed a teammate's head. *James Drake*/Sports Illustrated/ *Getty Images*

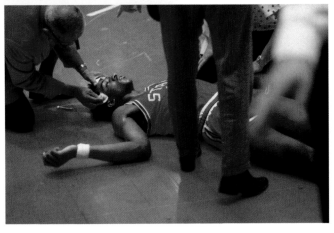

Coach Cathy Rush with the 1974 national champion Mighty Macs of Immaculata University.
Immaculata University

In 1978, Montclair State forward Carol "The Blaze" Blazejowski dropped 52 points on Queens College to set the (male and female) scoring record at Madison Square Garden—without a three-point shot.
Manny Millan/Sports Illustrated/*Getty Images*

Dr. J—and his signature afro—became the face of the ABA after he took flight during its slam dunk competition.
Dick Raphael/National Basketball Association/Getty Images

PLUTO: The three-point shot came from the old American Basketball League [ABL]. At one point, the ABA even talked about making a four-point shot from beyond half-court. Remember, in the ABA, if you have an idea, don't be afraid to double down—the wilder the better.

HUBIE BROWN: We were running two-on-one full-court drills. Louie Dampier coming down on the break, [and] I'd never seen this before—he drifts over to the corner, they throw him the ball, and he shoots a three. I stop practice: "Whoa, wait a second. We got a two-on-one, I want a layup. I do not want a three-point shot from the corner. [If you do take a three], you better make that every time. You don't, you're getting fined." Well, he was the best three-point shooter in the league. He could run to the spot without even looking at the line. You had to change how you coached against the three-ball, and then it had to become part of your offense.

PLUTO: The three-point shot was an adjustment. Other than a couple years in the ABL, nobody coached with it. It also opened the door for some strange guys to get in the league, because if you could make long shots, maybe you're useful. Back then, many ABA players came from the industrial leagues—the Akron Goodyear [Wingfoots], the Phillips 66ers. There was a guy named Les Selvage who played a little bit of industrial ball, and he also was working at an airline counter at LAX. He saw there was going to be a team in Anaheim, so he went and tried out, made the team. His first year in the ABA, he shot 42 percent from three-point range, 32 percent from two-point range, and took more three-pointers than any team in the league except Pittsburgh. Les did not win the assist title.

HAYWOOD: I'm an inside guy. My first game, I was running back on defense, and I stopped at the free throw line. We had two guys coming on the wing and a guy bringing it up, and he shot a three-pointer and I was like, "What kind of basketball is this?" They didn't take the layup, they went outside. I was like, "This is gonna be fun."

PLUTO: The NBA had a sameness to it. You're stuck in one way of doing things—walking the ball up, throwing inside to Wilt or Russell or Walt

Bellamy. Hubie Brown and Larry Brown and Doug Moe, rather than just walk the ball up the floor and pound it inside, [they coached] more wide-open games. They were in this basketball laboratory. I mean, if you're coaching in Kentucky or Utah or wherever Virginia or Carolina is playing this week, you're not under a ton of media scrutiny. If you try some crazy half-court trap that doesn't work, it's not like you're being skewered. . . . It's hard to get NBA players to admit this, but I'm sure some of them wished that they could have played under that coaching in the ABA, because they would have not just averaged more points but had more fun.

In its time, the ABA was the fun, chaotic, innovative alternative to the NBA, but as much as anything else, the league was known for fisticuffs and enforcers such as John Brisker, Warren Jabali, and Wendell Ladner.

GOLDBERG: One of my early assignments was to enlist the services of the FBI to find Marvin Barnes, who one day disappeared, and there was rumors that he was either kidnapped by rival teams or got in trouble with criminals.

BARRY: There were a couple of guys on my teams that used to pack a little iron. I remember being at an All-Star Game, and the owner and the coach got in a fight and were ripping sleeves off their jackets.

MEL DANIELS: I had no problem fighting anybody—none. I was out of control. First game I played as a pro, against Kentucky, and they sent a hitter in. He knocked the shit out of me, and then I popped him in the face and knocked him down. Then I didn't have any trouble. Back then, if you were weak, you had no shot. You should start selling stuffed animals, 'cause you aren't gonna work in this league.

GEORGE KARL: I was the only guy that ever got into a fight with Pete Maravich. That was in an exhibition game. I wasn't a great player, but I was pesky, and at that time you could chuck guys. Pete got fed up and he elbowed me. He opened it up—I have a scar—and I saw blood and I just went at him and wrestled.

VECSEY: Neil Johnson, from New York. People probably never even heard of him, but the guy was the toughest ABA player ever. You did not want him angry at you. There were times when there'd be a fight in the game, then there'd be a fight in the locker room, and then Neil would go on the team bus and try to finish the fight.

ARTIS GILMORE (Center, Chicago Bulls/San Antonio Spurs; 6-Time NBA All-Star; 1972 ABA MVP): I remember Maurice Lucas—something happened and I started chasing him across the floor, and he just stopped and let one go. Apparently, I didn't see it coming, and he caught me flush. It was a good one, put me down for the count.

LEONARD: John Brisker, Warren Jabali—you didn't wanna mess with them, [and] guys knew that.

PLUTO: When you talk about Brisker or Jabali, the two toughest guys, the interesting thing is, they never fought each other. Maybe they were smart enough. Jabali stomped [a] guy's head, and actually, later in life, Jabali became a very good community guy down in Florida, but at that point he was a very angry guy.

KARL: I was always afraid he was gonna kill me.

GEORGE GERVIN: He'd come down the middle kicking, and everybody'd get out of his way. You talk about matador [defense], players were like, "Go ahead and lay it up."

LARRY BROWN: When I met Warren, Doug [Moe] and I came to Oakland, and we used to play Henry Logan and Warren two-on-two. Warren was 6'3", strong, one of the most gifted guys I've ever played with. And I didn't think he liked white guys very much, but he respected us on the court. Even though he might not have felt comfortable around you off the court, on the court you were his teammate. And he was an incredible, unbelievable competitor. Had enormous hands, could shoot it outside, could dunk in a crowd. Guards couldn't guard him—he was simply too strong. Big guys couldn't guard him 'cause he's too good off the dribble. He was as tough as anybody.

BARRY: I heard that one time, Brisker had to have three or four policemen subdue him outside of one of the stadiums in Pittsburgh. Brisker was nuts. I don't know how true it is, but I heard he went off and became a mercenary overseas and got killed.

DONNIE WALSH: There was one story about Brisker where he got in a fight, they kicked him out. He came back on the court, they kicked him out again. And then he was seen crawling, trying to get back on the court again!

VECSEY: I saw Brisker stomp on a little guard with the Nets. Almost put his head through the floor.

PLUTO: Brisker always had a gun in his bag. He was scary. John Brisker was terrorizing the ABA, elbowing guys in the head. They weren't real good at suspensions in the ABA, and they also knew he had a gun somewhere, but frankly, even without the gun, he was just flat out frightening. Tom Nissalke was coaching in Dallas at the time. He's tired of Brisker beating up on his players, so he says, "I got a $500 check for whoever can take Brisker out tonight." Len Chappell, one of these journeymen guys, at the opening of the game, the jump ball goes up and Len just decks Brisker right in the jaw. Down goes Brisker. For a sneak attack, it was ingenious. In fact, Len wasn't even supposed to start the game. He went up to Nissalke, "Just start me, don't worry about it, I got an idea." Nissalke said, "I gave him $500, and we won the game."

GERVIN: John Brisker had a reputation that defies everybody. Talkin' about guns. You didn't mess with him. John Brisker died strangely, that's how bad he was.

PLUTO: Brisker disappeared. He played a little in the NBA, and then he goes over to Uganda with Idi Amin. Basically, he gets caught up in the criminal underworld. He's smuggling diamonds and sort of disappears. Nobody knows exactly what happened to him. Is he still in some remote village? Did someone take him out and just dump him where we'd never see him again?

ELMORE: Those guys took no prisoners. They were as mean as you want to be. That's part of the ABA mentality. At the drop of a hat, guys like Brisker, Jabali, Ladner were ready to throw down. I kinda liked that. I wasn't a fighter per se, but I wasn't backing down from anybody.

PLUTO: The ABA was the last significant sports venture that had mystery about it. There's a ton of stories, and some of them are even true. I spent three years of my life interviewing all these people and going through the tapes, digging up things written about the league. Most of the time, I didn't know what was the truth. Bob Costas said it so well. He talked about how the ABA, before cable TV, it was like the Wild West. Do we really know what Billy the Kid did? Do we really know how many banks he robbed? Do we really know that Warren Jabali got mad at this player who was wearing cotton briefs and told him to take them off, because "Don't you know slaves picked those briefs, and you should wear silk—you're a pro now"? I don't know—a couple of players told me the story.

After being expelled from the University of Iowa in 1961 and subsequently blackballed by the NBA, Connie Hawkins spent the next six years scratching out a living with the Harlem Globetrotters and the Pittsburgh Rens of the American Basketball League. When the ABA launched in 1967, Hawkins joined the Pittsburgh Pipers, and the league revived the career of one of the greatest talents the sport has ever produced.

LARRY BROWN: I grew up with Connie. As a junior in high school, he might've been as good as any player in the country. The Hawk could do anything. If you wanted him to score 40, he'd score 40. If you wanted him to get 20 rebounds, he'd get 20 rebounds. He's just what basketball should have been all about.

ERVING: Junior year of high school, I heard about the Hawk from my freshman basketball coach. He referred to me as "Little Hawk" one day, and I was like, "Whatcha called me?" He said, "Well, there's this guy named Connie Hawkins, and he picks the ball up with one hand the way you just did, so I called you Little Hawk." I didn't see him play until he was with the Pittsburgh Pipers, and I was like, "Wow, he's smooth." And I started hoping that one day I'd grow to be 6'8" because he was 6'8".

MOE: Connie Hawkins was one of the nicest guys you ever wanna meet. He had such a smooth game, was the first guy that really had the Dr. J stuff.

HAWKINS: My lawyers get a call from the ABA saying they wanted me to play with the Pittsburgh Pipers. I had to get a clearance letter that [said] I wasn't guilty of any wrongdoing, and once they got the letter, I signed with the Pipers.

PLUTO: Connie Hawkins, with his huge paw and the red, white, and blue ball, waving it around and dumping off passes, it was the flair of the ABA.

HAWKINS: Pittsburgh, to me, was a steel city, a workingman's town, and when I got there, I was so happy to be playing basketball and making a few dollars. I loved the ABA. It was a lifesaver, an opportunity for me to play a game that I love and get paid for it. That first year, we had a 17-game winning streak [in the regular season], and we couldn't draw any fans. Then the Finals were three games apiece, seventh game in Pittsburgh. I walk in, and the place was packed. They had 17,500 in there, and that gave us a jolt. We won the championship, and we thought we were the best team in the world. You couldn't tell us that we didn't win the NBA championship. Everybody in the locker room was crying, pouring champagne on each other.

Until 1971, professional basketball players had to play four years in college or wait until their graduating class was four years removed from high school to enter the NBA draft. That changed because Spencer Haywood, then a 20-year-old center who left the University of Detroit after his sophomore year, challenged the NBA's rule and played the first year of his professional career with the ABA's Denver Rockets before jumping to the NBA. Since then, every player who has left college early to enter the draft, has gone straight from high school to the pros, or has taken advantage of the NBA's one-and-done rule owes a debt of gratitude to Haywood.

GOLDBERG: The ABA looked at the scene, and desperate measures were required. Why not take young kids? Why do we have to have four years of college eligibility for these kids? They have talent, why should they be denied the right to earn a living?

HAYWOOD: The draft came up, and the ABA assumed they were going to get Kareem Abdul-Jabbar, and Kareem signed with the Milwaukee Bucks, so they say, "Let's go after this young guy Spencer Haywood." They say to me: "We're going to make you an ABA player. We're going to pay you what you would be paid in the NBA, and you don't have to sit out."

GOLDBERG: Renegade league looking for renegade answers. Spencer Haywood got in through a hardship exception. Remember the antitrust laws in those days, [and] this was before collective bargaining agreements. Forcing him to stay in school, preventing him from making a living. America is a land of opportunity. You don't say you can't have an opportunity until you're 21 and finished college. We spotted a great talent in Spencer Haywood, but we needed somehow to dress up our effort [so it] wouldn't look like we were ruining a guy's life by enticing him out of college. So the concept of a hardship exception came up. This young man, like a lot of young men, came from a very tough background, and the ABA was gonna lay a nice slice of money on him.

HAYWOOD: I was not afraid of the decision. I knew I could play, because David Bing would bring the Detroit Pistons to practice against us in high school. And when I was in college and the Olympics, I had played with and against pros. To keep the NCAA and the NBA off of our back, the ABA came up with this propaganda that they were trying to help the sons of former slaves. They were going to give reparations in the form of an opportunity for Spencer Haywood to play. I was like, "Damn, that sounds pretty cool." Then the University of Detroit claimed I was violating the contract to play, even though I was not supposed to be paid. They were suing me over lost revenues, which is crazy. But you have the number one player leaving, and we had scheduled like 12 games with NBC.

PLUTO: The ABA loved to have little nicknames to make what they wanted to do sound like it wasn't as bad. They came up with the idea "Why do we have to wait for these guys to be seniors? 'Cause the NBA does it? We don't have to do it. Besides, if we get these players before the NBA . . ." Remember, everything is about getting the merger. Spencer Haywood, Olympic hero, star at the University of Detroit—they give him this contract to play in Denver. It looks really good until you read the contract, and like half of the money's deferred.

HAYWOOD: The draft pool was not spitting out players in four-year cycles. Julius Erving, all of us guys, were like where do I go? UMass got [Erving] playing like a stiff; Eastern Michigan, they were treating George Gervin bad; George McGinnis's father had fell off of a ladder while [George] was at Indiana. Guys wanted to make some revenue. So the ABA says, "See what we did for Haywood? Sign under this ruling here, and we will bring you in the ABA." So those guys were signing in the ABA, and the NBA was getting ready to lose out.

McGINNIS: I was the second hardship player to go pro behind Spencer Haywood. The NBA was not open, although the Philadelphia 76ers drafted me. If a team drafted you even though you wasn't eligible [yet], they held your rights for life.

DOUG COLLINS: I did not want to come in with [the] label "hardship," because I thought that reflected on my family. I did not want to make it look like my mom and dad didn't provide for me. If you would have said "early entry"? Whatever. But I just didn't like "hardship."

GOLDBERG: Moses Malone was the first player to come out of high school and go directly into the pros, much to the chagrin of Lefty Driesell, who was to be his coach at the University of Maryland. I remember getting a telegram from Lefty, and it said, "How dare the league take advantage of this young man and his future education." In fact, my second day on the job, Moses was drafted by the Utah Stars, and there was a press conference here in New York. He looked like a very large pencil, tall and thin, very shy and quiet. And I said, "My goodness, we're taking a player like this? He looks like he belongs in school and that his mother should be bringing him in the morning." Lo and behold, he had a fantastic career.

THORN: Moses, when he went to Utah, I was with [the] New York [Nets]. We played them early in the season, and after the game Kevin Loughery and I said, "This guy's going to be terrific." He went after every rebound at both ends of the court, he loved contact, and he was quick off his feet. In those days, he probably weighed 210 pounds, but you could not deter him. You could try to beat him up, but it just didn't work. He had no offense—his offense was offensive rebounds or maybe fall into a layup some way. But his toughness and his ability to see where the ball was coming and go get it were unparalleled.

ERVING: There was no drafting of underclassmen [in the NBA] at this time. You had to be a senior or your class had to graduate. This was '71, my class is graduating in '72, and in '72 when my class graduated, I signed with the [Atlanta] Hawks, but the Milwaukee Bucks drafted me. We tried to influence the decision based on my preference to go to the Hawks. They had three Hall of Famers: Walt Bellamy, Pete

Maravich, and Lou Hudson. I wanted to play with those guys, and I wanted to live in Atlanta. So I go to training camp, and we play a couple of exhibitions—scored like 160 two games in a row. And Milwaukee complains, "The NBA says you got an illegal player. You gotta sit him; otherwise we start fining you." After a week of sitting, my agent and I decided we better go back to [the ABA]. I was 21, and the whole NBA thing was put off five years.

GOLDBERG: The ABA had a great star in Spencer Haywood, who came out of college after one year and joined the Denver Rockets. Spencer was a unique player, [Olympic] gold medal in '68, a hero, first year in the ABA he's MVP of the league.

HAYWOOD: That year, I averaged 30 points per game, 20 rebounds. I was Rookie of the Year, leading scorer, leading rebounder, MVP. There's only two players in the history of professional basketball who recorded those numbers in a rookie year: Wilt Chamberlain and myself.

GERVIN: I couldn't get in the NBA. Nineteen when I withdrew from school—hardship. That's how I got into the ABA. Spencer was the first.

HAYWOOD: Prior to that, you had to [wait] four years after your high school class had graduated. And the ABA says, "We are going to go after the young guys and bring them into the ABA, and we're going to put the NBA out of business. And we're gonna give Spencer Haywood the highest-paid contract in professional basketball history." They made this announcement, $1.9 million, the highest-paid athlete in sports. The fine print says $400,000, because they put $10,000 per year into the stock market and said, "When you get to be age 50 to 70 is when you can draw out $1.5 [million]." Which never was gonna happen, but it looked good on paper and I signed it. I was 20 years old. We doing something special, but they gave me a fraudulent contract.

PLUTO: Spencer Haywood's contract was a beautiful thing to behold if you happened to be an owner. It's three years, $450,000, big money. Here's the problem: he started getting $20,000 a year 10 years after he signed. So more than half of it was put out from basically the time he'd be 33 on.

HAYWOOD: I knew it was a fraudulent contract because that summer I went to Panama with a group of NBA players—Emmette Bryant, Nate Bowman, Dave Stallworth, Sonny Dove—and they were like, "What are you doing with that phony contract? We're in the NBA being paid real dollars." Well, I came back and I was like, "You guys need to renegotiate this thing and give me the dollar amount." The [Denver Rockets'] owner was Don Ringsby, and he was an old trucker, so he believed in scheming, doing whatever. And they were like, "We got you to a contract. You can't go to the NBA, you can't go back to college. Where are you gonna go?"

GOLDBERG: That was the environment in those days. For every bit of fantastic basketball on the court, there was drama and lawsuits off the court.

HAYWOOD: I found this young lawyer named Al Ross who wanted to make a name for himself. He asked the owners [to] create a contract that would be legal and binding, and they told him and me, "You get your Jew ass out of here and take this nigger with you. We ain't doing nothing." So we let it be known that we were unhappy with the contract, and the NBA was like, "We can't touch you." So Jerry Colangelo, the owner of the Phoenix Suns, who had taken Connie Hawkins a year before, he became interested, and Sam Schulman, who was owner of the Seattle SuperSonics. They were like, "We're going to do something about this. Sign this contract with us, sit out for your senior year in college, we will pay you to do nothing, [and] play next year." And I was like, "I want to play." Schulman says, "Sign with me and I'll make sure you play. We will fight this thing all the way."

GOLDBERG: So Spencer eventually took his talents to a more stable organization, the NBA, and wound up in Seattle, but not before a Supreme Court case, his reputation being damaged, and the ABA losing a great star.

HAYWOOD: We went to the Supreme Court and won that case on the Sherman Antitrust Act. You cannot stop a person in America from making a living. The case is written up as *Haywood v. National Basketball Assn.* The NBA says, "We're not going to give him that credit, like *Roe v. Wade* or *Brown v. Board of Education*. It's gonna be called the hardship rule, because you gotta show that your family was in desperate need." Then you could come into the NBA. And I think when Alvan Adams left Oklahoma to come to the Phoenix Suns, his daddy was an oilman. This was a white guy coming in, so it wasn't just black players. You had Rex Chapman and other guys coming in under this ruling, but it ain't hardship. It's, "I played three years in college [and] I'm ready to ball." So they changed [the name] again and called it early entry. Never the name of the person who won the case.

SONNY HILL: Most people understand that players are now able to enter the NBA through whatever rule they wanna call it. It's really the Spencer Haywood rule.

HAYWOOD: During this period, I am like this pariah in the league. Even players walked in like, "You're a troublemaker." That's my tag. These are guys who would come in under my ruling. And they would say, "I can't be seen talking to you out on this floor." To this day, I can be at an NCAA Final game, sitting there with all the greats, and I'm a bad person for the NCAA. "He's the one who broke that ruling, and that's why we don't have these guys for four years." And the NBA, they said, "We can't have nobody lifted up that sued the NBA." People who were lawyers on that case became commissioners—it was all so big for everybody but me. I'm still the guy that's being oppressed.

Among the first and loudest shots across the bow in the ABA's attack on the NBA was the signing of Rick Barry to the Oakland Oaks. Barry was the NBA's leading scorer in the 1966–67 season, then decided to leave the San Francisco Warriors to play for a rival franchise in the brand-new ABA. It was among the first of many advances in the tug-of-war between the ABA and NBA, as well as a lesson for Barry that things in the ABA rarely worked out as expected.

CUNNINGHAM: Rick Barry was the first player of major notoriety that jumped to the ABA.

BARRY: The first year of the Oakland Oaks, my father-in-law, Bruce Hale, was the coach, and the owner was the famous singer Pat Boone.

PLUTO: The Oaks were picked up by Pat Boone. He got hustled by some of these other guys. "Don't you want to be an owner, Pat? You love to play. Come on, shoot around with these guys afterwards, it's great! We can have Rick Barry!" OPM—other people's money—that's how most of these guys are. So Boone buys into the league, and he hands one of these other owners a blank check to cover bills. It's very unclear to me why he would do this, but it's his story. Well, by the time this guy gets done with the bills, it's $1.3 million! They win a title, and [Boone] said, "They gave me this championship ring. It looks really nice." Later on, he found out the ring was glass. It doesn't cost $1.3 million to win an ABA title and a glass ring.

GOLDBERG: Pat was a basketball nut. He would love to play, probably would have suited up, and I think he may have one or two games. They had enticed the great Rick Barry into the ABA.

BARRY: I was vilified [for leaving the NBA]—traitor, all this other stuff. The press was brutal. I gave the Warriors every opportunity. I said, "Give me your best offer. I'm going to get an offer from them, an offer from you, and that's it." And the [Warriors] gave me a lowball offer. They basically opened the door for me to go.

PLUTO: Rick Barry, with the San Francisco Warriors, was a big-time player. From a distance, I always thought, "He jumped for the money," but I remember sitting down with Rick one night and he said, "How would you like it if they hired your father-in-law to coach at this competing newspaper? When your father-in-law approaches you about coming to work for him?" The father-in-law was Bruce Hale. Hale had coached Rick in college, and that's where Rick met his wife. So the Oakland Oaks hire Hale to coach, he convinces Rick to jump for family harmony.

BARRY: It was tough [to leave the Warriors]. I literally cried when I left and told [Warriors owner] Franklin Mieuli that I respected him and he was great to me and I loved the experience I had there.

PLUTO: So the NBA sues, Rick has to sit a full season, Bruce Hale coaches the Oakland Oaks, they're terrible. Now Barry's eligible to play, but Pat Boone and these other people didn't think Hale could coach, so they go out and get Alex Hannum, which is big, because they stole him from the NBA.

BARRY: I was looking forward to go because I thought my father-in-law was going to be the coach. Then they wind up hiring Alex Hannum, which was fine because I had played for Alex and liked him.

MOE: Rick Barry's one of the great players that doesn't get as much recognition as he should. Great shooter, great driver, just great all-around player.

CHARLEY ROSEN: Rick Barry was a *great* player. He could pass, shoot, run, finish, but there was nothing fancy about him. None of this under-the-leg, behind-the-back pass. He'd throw the right pass at the right time.

BARRY: We had some very good players. Doug Moe was on that team, Larry Brown—they were exceptional. Doug was still healthy, always a tough defender, and could score, shoot with the right and left hand. Larry: two-hand set shot; great playmaker; you know he's going to get the ball to you. Warren Armstrong, who became Warren Jabali, was another great player. We had a guy by the name of Henry Logan. Man, he was one of the best ball handlers I'd ever seen.

Barry, known in both the NBA and ABA for his perfectionist streak, could rub teammates the wrong way, but he also commanded their respect.

GILMORE: Rick Barry was very competitive, and he was not hesitant about voicing his opinion. Probably some of the comments made people frustrated, but, you know, that was Rick.

VECSEY: Rick, he snaps easily. He's the first to admit it, but then he'll come back and apologize. He would ignite some inner feelings from people. I saw him in Seattle once—I think it was after an All-Star Game—and some kid asks him for his autograph. He signs the autograph, and the kid crumpled it up and threw it at Rick.

ROSEN: I got "Rick the Prick" stories. When he joined the Nets, he [told] his teammates, "This is a fucking bullshit league. I'll tell you what I'll do: I'll play each of you. One-on-one, one right after the other, in whatever order you want. We'll bet $200 on every game. If one of you beats me, it's all your money." And he beat 'em all.

BARRY: I was only 23. I was still a baby. I used to laugh when people would say, "You're immature." Then when you get to be 30, you realize.

The ABA lasted for nine seasons, and the Indiana Pacers went to the Finals in five of them, claiming three championships along the way. Their front line of Mel Daniels, George McGinnis, and Roger Brown was considered to be one of the finest in the history of the sport. The Pacers were the ABA's version of a dynasty.

PLUTO: The closest there was to the Boston Celtics in the ABA were the [Indiana] Pacers. The league was around for nine years. Five times they go to the Finals; they win it three times. And they basically have the same coach, the same core players. Back then, if you were coaching in the ABA, you were also in effect general manager. Slick Leonard was the guy that was getting George McGinnis to come, the guy that was saying, "Billy Keller [can] do more than milk cows. He can shoot three-pointers." He was finding Mel Daniels down at New Mexico, putting together these players and making sure they didn't jump to the NBA or get traded to some other franchise.

GOLDBERG: Indiana was probably our flagship franchise. The Pacers played in Indianapolis, the heartland of basketball. It was a sport that had thrived in Indiana over the years, coached by a great former player, Slick Leonard. They were well run by businessmen from the Midwest, who I would say were the real McCoy as opposed to the hundred-grand guys that we pulled in.

PLUTO: What helped the Pacers is they did have a fanatical fan base, so they weren't always broke. As they say, a well-run ABA franchise is one that is almost broke; the rest are completely broke.

DANIELS: When I came, they were Roger Brown, Bob Netolicky, Fred Lewis. We had a coach by the name of Larry Staverman, and when he relinquished his job to Slick Leonard, all the pieces fell into place, and that created three championships.

VECSEY: Slick had one form of communication, which was cursing at you. But the players could take it because Mel Daniels took it.

LEONARD: I coached them, but they were my buddies off the floor. We'd go in a bar and drink together. They knew I cared about them. The funny thing about coaching—you can try and fool a player for a week, two weeks, a month, but if you're not honest with them and they find you out, you might as well quit.

McGINNIS: Off the court, he was a buddy. On the court, he'd eat you alive.

DANIELS: He set the tone early. I was shooting jump shots, and he came to me [and] said, "You put your ass on the block, and if you shoot beyond the 15', I'm gonna punch you in your goddamn nose." It was no bullshit about him.

McGINNIS: Bob Netolicky, [Slick] went after him with a hockey stick. He pulled Netolicky out of a game, and Netolicky started complaining: "I'm not givin' up any playing time. You're screwing me." There's fans behind the bench, and they're starting to hear this little commotion, so Slick walks by him and says, "Cool it," and then [Netolicky] gets louder and louder. Slick completely shut down, never said another word. So we're walking in at halftime, and we shared locker rooms next to a minor league hockey team, and I saw Slick goin' in there. All of a sudden I hear things rambling around, he comes out with a big hockey stick, and he's lookin' for Netolicky. He says, "Now what did you say?" And wham! He misses, and Neto says, "I'm sorry! Please, I'm sorry!" And I'll tell you what, Neto never loudmouthed on that bench again.

LEONARD: It was a group of guys that you had to pull together and make them understand that winning was what the game was all about. I broke it down very quickly. I said, "I don't care if you're black, white, or yellow. If you're good enough to play, you're gonna play." I didn't wanna hear any of this racial thing, and we never had it. We built a family atmosphere.

ELMORE: Slick knew how to work crowds, how to play with your psyche, and he had a story for everybody. I'll never forget one time, we are in a slump, and we fly into Buffalo. There's a snowstorm, and it's gonna be hard to get to practice, so Slick says, "We're not gonna practice. We'll have a meeting in the ballroom." We got to the ballroom and he pulled a curtain back and there's a huge bar. He says, "All right. Everybody get drunk."

DANIELS: Slick Leonard was a legitimate tough guy. He had our backs. And when there was a fight, he was the first one on the floor. He didn't mind dropping people at all.

LEONARD: In all the years I've been in basketball, there's been some good front lines. For example, when Boston had Robert Parish and Larry

Bird and Kevin McHale. When we had Mel Daniels, Roger Brown, and George McGinnis, this front line could compete with any of them.

DANIELS: I believe we were as good as Boston or any front line that played basketball.

PLUTO: Mel Daniels, for his time, was a monster. And McGinnis, until his knees went bad, was virtually unstoppable.

LEONARD: Nobody really knows how good Roger Brown was 'cause he didn't get the exposure. Roger could do it all. He had moves where guys guarding him would fall on the floor. He could hit the three-pointer, he could pass. He was Bob Cousy at a forward spot in the ABA.

DANIELS: We knew the deal. At the end, if the game was close, Slick would call timeout: "Rog, put 'em to sleep." What [Brown] did to people . . . I heard grown men scream, "Help! Help! Help!" And Roger's beaten them so bad he's almost missed the layup from laughing.

LEONARD: They tried to tie Roger and Doug Moe and Connie Hawkins to Jack Molinas in New York, and it was not the truth. And they beat it, they won the lawsuit. But it cost them four or five years out of their career.

McGINNIS: You gotta figure they lost, what? Five? Six? Seven years to this mess? Roger didn't laugh a lot; he always had a serious look on his face. After I found out his story, it all made sense. He held a lot of stuff within him for a long time and then, one day, it was my fifth or sixth year in the league, he told me the whole story. It was unbelievable, just the fact that he was able to get through that—work in a factory in Dayton, Ohio, and he figured that was gonna be his life. Then, all of a sudden, this ABA starts. He was past his prime, but he was still so good that he was one of the all-time greats.

HAWKINS: Big Mel Daniels. He was strong as dirt.

McGINNIS: Mel was intense. Emotional, blue-collar guy, wore his heart on his sleeve. If a guy was a lot bigger, like Artis Gilmore, he'd battle him just for position on the block.

DANIELS: Georgie [McGinnis]—great athlete, magnificent use of body, 6'8", could run, jump, handle, shoot, pass.

ELMORE: George was one of the best all-around players I ever played with. He was LeBron before LeBron. With that body, the quickness, he could've played any sport he wanted.

The Indiana Pacers may have been the ABA's most consistently excellent franchise, but this was still the ABA, and along with their Finals appearances and championships, the team spun off its share of outrageous stories.

CHARLIE SCOTT: Mike Maloy and Mel Daniels got in a tussle. [Virginia Squires coach] Al Bianchi had a rule: if you didn't fight, you were fined. So we all got into it, and I saw a guy grab Coach Bianchi by the throat, so I grab the guy off of Al, and we threw him down. Then, during the game, Freddie Lewis tells me, "Charlie, you better get out of here. They're gonna lock you up at the end of the game." I said, "Nah, it was a fight. It happens." Well, Indiana, we call it the home of the KKK, so it wasn't like a liberal bastion. And the guy who grabbed Al Bianchi was an off-duty policeman. [He] felt insulted that he was thrown down by these basketball players, and his father was a lawyer, so at the end of the game, the police came in the locker room and locked us up.

McGINNIS: Mel, he had a fight every other night. There was a game . . . Wilt Chamberlain had just retired from the NBA and there was a team out in San Diego. Wilt coached that team for a year. We went out to play them, and we were all looking forward to seeing Wilt on the bench. Well, he shows up in the second quarter. Mel gets into it with one of their players. And Slick, he had a rule that if we get to fighting with the other team, if our guy is winning, you don't go and break it up. But if our guy's losing, then you gotta get in there and help him out. So Mel's got this little guard, and he's just pounding him. All of a sudden, Wilt gets up and he walks in the middle of it. He just like parts the Red Sea. He goes, "OK, get over here, Mel." Well, Mel was still trying to go to the guy and take [a] swing over Wilt's shoulder, so Wilt turns around and just looks him up, 6'9", 250. Then Wilt lifts [Mel] in the air and says, "Big fella, can you settle down?" And he takes two steps and sits Mel down. Mel goes, "C'mon, guys, let's get Wilt!" We go, "You gotta be crazy! We're not gonna mess with the Dipper!"

LEONARD: I remember Earl "the Pearl" Monroe became a free agent. We had him come to Indianapolis, and he went to the locker room to meet the guys, and we had three guys that were putting their guns on top of their lockers and it scared him to death. I heard that back in New York he said, "I'm not going there. That place is crazy."

ELMORE: They were all honorary Marion County sheriffs. They had their badges, and they had the little visors on their cars. They could park anywhere and go anywhere. Shows you the value of being a champion in Indianapolis.

PLUTO: They went through, as they called it, their "cowboy period." They rode horses and wore cowboy hats and had six-shooters, and they would bring 'em into the locker room. There was no shooting. I mean, they were nice guys—they were young, testosterone's flowing, they wanna watch *Rawhide* or whatever. It added to their mystique.

DANIELS: At halftime, George would light up, Rog would light up, and Slick would light up and grab a beer. That was part of the program. We didn't have Gatorade. We had to have a brew.

Of all the Hall of Fame players who passed through the ABA, none captured the imagination of fans like Julius Erving and George Gervin, teammates for one season on the Virginia Squires before Gervin moved on to the San

Antonio Spurs and Erving became the most famous player outside the NBA, with the New York Nets.

MIKE VACCARO (Sports Columnist, *New York Post*): I grew up about 10 minutes away from Nassau Coliseum. Obviously, Julius Erving was amazing to behold. One of my earliest recollections is a commercial of him dunking a basketball backwards, and it was the first time I had ever seen that. It seemed otherworldly, like something a martian would do. Then I remember watching him a couple weeks later in person, doing the same thing, and thinking to myself, "I don't know if I could ever do that, but I could watch that all day."

PLUTO: When Julius Erving came into the ABA, nobody had a clue who he was. Johnny Kerr was general manager of the Virginia Squires. They just were another vagabond team. Julius was playing for UMass, and remember, this was before websites and ESPN, and most of the scouting would be done in postseason all-star games. Somehow, a friend sent Kerr and Al Bianchi this grainy black-and-white tape of Julius Erving. He said you saw the ball go up and you just saw hands—these hands and this Afro rising above everyone else. They didn't know who he was, nobody knew. So he comes and they're having their first scrimmage, and the first time somebody misses a long shot, the big hands go up and you see this slam. They swear he was 12 feet off the ground, tomahawking it through the rim, and Johnny Kerr said everybody just stopped and stared.

SCOTT: After my [first] year, they had rookie camp in Richmond, Virginia. I drove down to see the rookies play, and that was my first introduction to Julius. After watching him at rookie camp, I'll never forget, I told Julius, "Whatever [Squires owner] Earl Foreman [is] paying you, that ain't enough."

ELMORE: I actually played against Julius at Jack Donohue's camp. Donohue was the coach of Lew Alcindor at Power Memorial [Academy], and he had a basketball camp up in New Hampshire. I think I was a junior in high school, and Julius was a freshman at UMass. He and I jumped center, and I'm expecting him to be a center, stand in the post and everything, [not] running up and down the floor, playing outside, driving to the basket. It was real difficult to stay with him.

GILMORE: My first experience with Julius Erving, it was right after the NCAA tournament [in 1971], and we had this all-star game in Schenectady, New York. Julius was on the team, and I was observing Julius in the corner, lacing up his shoes. I was not quite aware of Julius, so I introduced myself, and once the game started, I watched him go up to dunk the ball. He had his knees up on the top of [future Knicks center] Harthorne Wingo's head and he slammed the ball, and I said, "Who did you say you're playing for?"

ERVING: After my third year in UMass, we go to the NIT, lose to North Carolina by like 40. I get a call from an agent, and he says [the] ABA and NBA are gonna merge within two years, and contracts are gonna change. He said a couple of years ago, Wilt and Russell negotiated $100,000-a-year contracts. Now a team's gonna offer you a hundred twenty-five to come out of school. They probably gonna set up a deferred payment, where they pay you for four years' work over seven years. It comes out to like $71,000. My parents' total income is like $11,000, [and] they're talking $150,000. I called home, told my mother what the offer was, and she said you just have to promise you gonna finish school. I said I promise, but I think I better take this contract, and I became a Virginia Squire that day.

BARRY: With his jumping and the way he can control the ball, he had the ability to do things most humans can't. I always prayed that I never got stuck under the basket if he was on a breakaway, because I didn't want to be a poster child.

VECSEY: Julius could slither around. I remember some woman at the Rucker calling him the sensuous superstar. He'd do stuff up there. He'd shimmy and—I can't describe it, I wish I could, but it was unbelievable. It was a joy to see that stuff.

HAWKINS: Me and Julius Erving used to argue about who had the biggest hands, and every time we'd see each other, we'd measure. Our hands are exactly the same size. We'd get a ball and we'd palm it and we'd try to pull it out of each other's hands and we couldn't do it. It was a stalemate.

VECSEY: My line on Julius was that his hands were big enough to palm Sunday.

HUBIE BROWN: People say Dr. J was great in the NBA. Listen, in the ABA, that's where he did his stuff. On the break, he did things that were amazing. But the big thing was the love of Doc. No player would blindside Doc into the stanchion. If you did, your own players would whup your ass. That's how much respect the Doc had.

PLUTO: That Virginia team, which was coached by Al Bianchi, had Julius Erving, George Gervin, and Charlie Scott, and no one cared. [Fans] didn't go to the games. It just fizzled.

THOMPSON: I didn't know this about Charlie Scott. He had the highest-scoring season in the history of the ABA. He [averaged] 35 points one season for the Virginia Squires.

ERVING: Charlie and I really had a ball that first year in Virginia. He was the lead scorer, a star in college, so I deferred to him. It was young, foot-loose and fancy-free, take on all comers, we want the best in the league.

GERVIN: Dr. J still calls me "Rook." He took me under his wing, fell in love with me my first day. I'm 19, so after practice, me and him used to play one-on-one. He built up my confidence, helped me understand that I belong in professional basketball. That's what he meant to me. I'm 66, he's 68, [and] today he's still, "That's my rookie." And I'm proud of it.

PLUTO: I think a player kind of lost in time for his ABA career was George Gervin. While Julius was the leaper, Gervin was the master of finesse. He had more finger rolls and spin shots, and it seemed like his arms were always rising above everybody else. San Antonio didn't know how good Gervin was going to be. The reason Erving became so well-known is, he ended up in New York, so the media got a look at him.

MOE: If he was in New York, Gervin would be as big as any player there ever was, as far as I'm concerned. He was unbelievably good.

MURPHY: He invented cool. He weighed about a hundred and three pounds, he was 6-9, but his game was so smooth that he would give you 50 and you don't know he scored that. He had all the shots. We talk about pure shooters, George was one of the originals. We played in an era where there was a lot of bumping and holding and pushing, and they still couldn't stop him.

DANIELS: The Iceman, he was Miles Davis on the floor. That guy was a joke with some of the shit he did. I've seen him go underneath the basket and flip it up and hit the backboard and spin it, and it go in. He'll come at you. You would put your hand up, and he would take the ball and move it around your head and flip it in the air. Or switch hands, switch back again, and then flip it in. He wasn't a great athlete, but he understood how to get the ball to do what he wanted it to do when it needed to be done. I've never seen anybody do it like him.

VACCARO: I went to the last ABA game ever played, Game 6 of the Nets and the Nuggets [in 1976]. David Thompson was incredible that night. [The Nuggets] were up 20 points in the third quarter, and then Julius brought [the Nets] back, but that mano a mano, even in my 9-year-old brain, was something I realized I want to remember for the rest of my life. That night, the Nets won the last ABA championship.

As the ABA began its final season in 1975, both the NBA and ABA had been weakened by nearly a decade of competition. The ABA was struggling to field enough teams to maintain its legitimacy, while the NBA finally started to recognize that the league could no longer afford to look down on the dazzling, open-court style of ABA basketball, typified by Julius Erving and rookie sen-

sation David Thompson, fresh off a college national championship at North Carolina State. At the 1976 ABA All-Star Game in Denver, Erving and Thompson squared off in the finals of the first-ever slam dunk competition, an event that showcased the ABA's electrifying talent and set the stage for the battling leagues to finally strike a deal.

GOLDBERG: The 1975–76 season, we had run out of owners. We were down to six teams at the end of the season [and] needed 10 to be legit. We had to do something and do it now. The other thing was David Thompson. The ABA wanted to get Thompson to play with Denver and have a huge rivalry with Julius Erving and the Nets. Carl Scheer, the owner of the Nuggets, got on a conference call with the other teams and gave what I would consider the Gettysburg Address: "We have to have this guy; we have to be united; we have to do this." American flags were being waved, tears were being shed, and the other five teams agreed to guarantee Thompson's contract with Denver. It was the only way David Thompson was coming to the ABA.

McGINNIS: Boy, when [David Thompson] jumped. One time I was under the rim and he went up to get a rebound, and I looked at the bottom of his tennis shoes. I couldn't believe it.

PLUTO: The slam dunk contest was a classic ABA creation, which means "We've got a problem here." The problem was [the league] had seven teams and an All-Star Game in Denver. It's not feasible to break [the players] into two teams. Also, we don't know if people will come. So let's have Denver, which was leading the league in the regular season, play All-Stars from six other teams.

THOMPSON: The game was in Denver, so our team played the All-Stars. We had a sold-out crowd. Denver was one of the franchises that was doing well. We led all of basketball in attendance that year in the ABA.

PLUTO: Now, to do something else to get people in here—what do people like about the ABA? Dunks. The red, white, and blue ball slammed through the rim. [ABA marketing director] Jim Bukata says, "Let's have a slam dunk contest!" and they said, "Great!" And then there was silence. "How do you do it?" So they made up rules.

THOMPSON: They decided to have the slam dunk competition at halftime of the All-Star Game. All the players that competed were All-Stars: Larry Kenon, Artis Gilmore, Dr. J, George Gervin, and myself. It was spur-of-the-moment, no one really knew what they were doing. They said, "You go over there and dunk from here and then dunk from there."

ERVING: This idea of a slam dunk contest originated from the Denver organization, and I felt good about it 'cause I used to do slam dunk exhibitions after my Converse clinics. I used to put on a little show, finish with a dunk from the foul line, and then run out the door. I knew David was an awesome dunker—you don't call a guy "Sky" for nothing. I figured he had to be the favorite [because] we were in Denver.

GILMORE: I was the first guy to go, so I'm the first creator, trying to think of something to do. They gave me two basketballs, and I end up taking both, dunking the two balls.

ERVING: They said there are five requirements. You have to dunk one from the corner; you have to dunk standing beneath the basket; you have to dunk from an angle; and then you have to dunk from straight on. And you had a free dunk. So you gotta have at least five dunks in your bag. That dunk underneath, I dunked two balls. Took 'em up and boom, boom. Artis did the same thing—he did his facing, [and] I did mine backwards.

THOMPSON: Artis started off, [then] George Gervin comes up and does some pretty good dunks. Larry Kenon comes [next], and now it's my time. I take off from the 12-foot line and do a tomahawk windmill. The crowd went crazy. My next dunk, I went up and put my ball to the rim, brought it down to my knees, and dunked it over my shoulders. The crowd went wild. Then, my specialty: I did a 360-degree dunk looking away. That was the first recorded 360. They brought that to light, and the crowd really went wild. I said to myself, "I might win this." But now it's Dr. J's turn.

ERVING: From the corner, I came out and did like a reverse windmill. From the angle, I did a tap on the board and then a dunk backwards. And then the freestyle was tossing it and catching it and throwing it in. They had a hash mark about two feet inside the foul line—they said we have to dunk from outside of there. That's when David did the 360, and it came down to me and him in the final.

GERVIN: We was excited because we get to see two of the best dunkers in the league, Doc and DT. Did I realize I was seeing history? I couldn't think this far ahead, that this was going to be as significant as it was.

ERVING: [David] came out of the corner and he was doing that pirouette, and the ball got away and hit the back of the rim. It was his home crowd, so it took all the air out [of] the building. Prior to that, he was perfect. He was doing dunks that, I'm looking at it, I'm like, "This little guy, he's a bad man." And once he missed, I went to the other end of the court.

PLUTO: It was always legend that Erving could take off at the foul line and dunk. So that's really the underlying thing that the first dunk contest was about.

ERVING: Doug Moe and some guys wanted to place bets. They had heard about this foul line dunk, and they were like, "Nah, you can't do that. Nobody can dunk from the foul line. David can't even dunk from the foul line." So we got this little side action going.

THOMPSON: We're dunking on this end, and Dr. J takes off way from that end. He's marking his steps, and back then everyone wore those short shorts and big Afros, and Dr. J picked up the ball like it was a volleyball or an orange or something. He took off running and his Afro was blowing in the wind, and he took off from the free throw line.

ERVING: [I] ran the distance of the court and jumped. I stepped on the foul line, floated in, and dunked, and [the crowd] went crazy. I ended up winning a gift certificate for 50 bucks.

RICK WELTS (President, Golden State Warriors; Executive Vice President and Chief Marketing Officer, NBA, 1996–99): Julius Erving did something that no one had ever seen before: run to one end of the court, pick up a basketball, run the full length of the court, take off from the free throw line, and dunk.

PLUTO: What the dunk contest did, it got them on TV, on the news. You had these two young stars doing this dunk thing. People were riveted. And when it came to the end of the season, the NBA discussing, "Let's bring these guys in," they wanted Thompson.

GOLDBERG: The [ABA] was waffling. We were bankrupt, and it was a tough situation. The original plan failed, but in the end we got in there on the sheer talent of the players. We had hit a vein of huge basketball improvisation—a balletic form of the sport that no one had ever seen. San Antonio had the Iceman, but Dr. J was our nuclear missile, so to speak. No one had ever seen anything like that before. Up-tempo, creativity, moves to the basket—stuff that people's jaws dropped when they saw it.

HILL: Julius Erving forced the NBA to say, "How can we align ourselves with the ABA? We need this guy, because he can sell tickets and he [can] open the door [for] TV."

PLUTO: Both leagues had been pounding on each other for so long. They realized by 1976, "This can't go on. We're stealing each other's players, guys are jumping from league to league, [and] fans are becoming disenchanted because you can't grab on to your franchise for long." The NBA wants Julius Erving, so the NBA decides, "Let's cut a deal."

GOLDBERG: There was always talk of [a] merger, and overtures were made. This battle of attrition was economically weakening the NBA and torturing the ABA. This was life or death: if the NBA didn't take us in some form of merger, we were going out of business. One of the turning points was the NBA's agreeing to play exhibition games with the ABA, and I think that was based on demand. Fans wanted to see Dr. J: "Are these guys BS-ing us, or can they really hold their own?" When the [ABA] did well on the court, that was very important—it gave huge credibility to the ABA.

HUBIE BROWN: We were all in the same basket: "Hey, we could beat those Knicks! We could beat those Chicago Bulls!" Well, in '75 and '76 we were winning those exhibition games. We would go anyplace to play an NBA team. We wanted to show how good we were. Ask any ABA coach during that time, we were all pulling for one another to beat those teams.

HAWKINS: There was a distinct difference between the ABA and the NBA, and the guys that were ABA players thought that they were better than the NBA players and probably vice versa.

MONROE: It was that looseness of how they played—the aura of the big hair and all the rest of this stuff flying through. I admired those guys. You knew that they were just as good [as the NBA players].

GOLDBERG: In the exhibition games, once you got on the floor, the competitive juices took over. The ABA players were playing for their livelihood and their future, and they gave it their all. Some people say the NBA [players] didn't really knock themselves out. Not true. When you put 10 basketball players of that caliber on the court, guys are giving 100 percent.

CUNNINGHAM: We would play the NBA teams in exhibition games, and in most cases we would win, but it was a different atmosphere for the ABA. Putting myself in that position, the NBA, yeah, they liked to win, but it's an exhibition and [they were thinking], "We'll never see these guys again." [For ABA players], it was "We're putting you on notice: we can play and compete against you anytime." I could feel that when

I went to the ABA and played against the Knicks. It became more than an exhibition game.

When it came time to finalize the ABA's absorption into the NBA, multiple deals needed to be made: the NBA's 1976–77 expansion, which included four former ABA franchises (San Antonio Spurs, Denver Nuggets, New York Nets, and Indiana Pacers); a buyout of the Kentucky Colonels; and, in the case of the ABA Spirits of St. Louis, one of the most lucrative arrangements in the history of professional sports.

PLUTO: The NBA is finally open to a deal, but the [ABA] needed a guy to cut the deal. Remember the first commissioner of the ABA? George Mikan: NBA connections, the hope being that Mikan could broker a deal with the NBA. Several commissioners later, they're coming back to the same idea. Dave DeBusschere: background in business, former NBA player, knows how to do business with those guys. So he sits down with [NBA commissioner] Larry O'Brien and a younger lawyer named David Stern.

STERN: I was a lawyer for the NBA when we tried to get [a] congressional exemption to merge with the ABA. We were moving around the country doing depositions, and there were these litigations going simultaneously. I got to know the ABA guys as well as the NBA owners. It was fun—if you're a lawyer.

GOLDBERG: DeBusschere was hired for basically one reason: he was an iconic figure, a New York hero and a basketball hero, and [he] would keep the credibility of the league going. No one thought he would have the skills to run the league as well as he did, nor the business acumen to sit down with Larry O'Brien, but Dave held his own. One of the great attributes that he brought was that everyone loved him. Even if you had the guile or the thought about putting one over on Dave, you couldn't do it.

STERN: The NBA owners announced, "We're settling this, but we will not make a deal with the ABA. There's no such thing as a merger." End of story.

GOLDBERG: A lot of people think there was a merger, but actually it was an expansion. The ABA had to buy their way in. Imagine how much crow you have to swallow to pay your way into a league after you've struggled for years to get a merger of equals. The price was $3.2 million per team to get in, and the NBA indicated they were only going to take four teams. They had no interest in St. Louis [because] no one had gone to the games for the two or three years they were in existence, and they were not going to take Kentucky because Louisville was too small of a market.

PLUTO: They say, "We'll take four teams," almost like, "We don't care which four. You guys figure it out." The teams that agreed to go were Denver, Indianapolis, the Nets, and San Antonio—the four hotbeds of the ABA. Now you gotta settle with [the] other teams. The Virginia Squires just faded out. The Kentucky Colonels, who I always thought should be part of the settlement—they were a really good team, and they had a good base. But [Colonels owner] John Y. Brown says, "You give me $3 million, I'll drop out." They say fine—they're thinking this is good. [But] John Y. Brown has an idea. He realizes the Buffalo Braves are for sale for $1.5 million; he thinks he made the deal of the century.

GOLDBERG: John Y. Brown went to the four ABA teams and made a deal that he would sell the Kentucky Colonels for $3.6 million. He then took the $3.6 million and bought half of the Buffalo Braves, a team in the NBA, and then shortly thereafter swapped an interest on another team and wound up owning half of the Boston Celtics. So now the four ABA teams have to get approval, and John Y. Brown, a guy who used to be in the ABA, is on the committee approving the merger. Only in America and only in the ABA. He winds up owning the Boston Celtics and driving Red Auerbach completely crazy.

PLUTO: John Y. Brown figures, "I end up with the Celtics. I make a million five. I'm a genius." No, he was smart. The geniuses were the Silna brothers.

GOLDBERG: The [Spirits of] St. Louis were owned by two gentlemen from New Jersey, the Silnas [Ozzie and Daniel], with a very smart lawyer by the name of Donald Schupak. Now visualize the Silnas: young men who loved basketball when they were kids, have every basketball card of everybody that ever played. The Spirits of St. Louis hung on for these couple of years and wound up being at the party when they received the news that no one wanted to dance with them. It was up to the other four teams to buy them out, and there came one of the most unusual deals in the history of business.

STERN: St. Louis didn't wanna be bought out. They wanted to come [to the NBA]. And if they weren't gonna come in, they wanted to have an interest in a franchise. I actually argued unsuccessfully that we should take in the fifth team, St. Louis. That would've saved the [NBA from the] famed Spirits of St. Louis deal.

GOLDBERG: There was no amount of money that St. Louis would take to go away—at least no amount that these four teams could afford. But the lawyer, Schupak, said, "I'm gonna make a deal with you. We're gonna go in for very little, but we would like one-seventh of the television rights of the four teams going into the NBA"—and here's the phrase—"in perpetuity."

PLUTO: Which means forever. At this point, TV didn't seem like a big deal. These owners just want into the NBA. They actually figure, "Finally! We won!" But as TV grew, the piece of this money from each franchise keeps growing and growing. The Silnas owned the Spirits for two crummy years! They won one playoff round! They're loaded! This is the world's greatest IRA.

VACCARO: "In perpetuity." If I were those guys, I would have that on my welcome mat, on the side of my house, on the license plate of my car.

GOLDBERG: Why would anyone agree to "in perpetuity"? The ABA side was exhausted. The four teams' attorneys said, "There are no television rights. They're minuscule. The NBA doesn't have any television rights, practically." No one envisioned cable television, satellite television, viewing on your iPhone or your iPad, international rights.

STERN: At that time, the NBA's television revenue was, I think, $22 million, which the ABA teams weren't even gonna share in for a period of years. So against that background, it was "OK, we'll do what we have to do." Little did anyone know that was gonna turn into hundreds of millions of dollars.

PLUTO: You'd need a battery of accountants to count all the money for these two guys. I tried to get them to talk about this for [my] book. It was kind of like, "The deal is so good, I don't want to explain it because it might go away."

GOLDBERG: You can imagine, every time one of the four teams—Indiana, San Antonio, Denver, or the Nets—walk onto a basketball court and the cameras go on, one-seventh of the TV revenue from that game goes right into the coffers of the former owners of the [Spirits of] St. Louis. That is one of the richest deals ever in sports. The Silnas and their lawyer probably walked away for close to a billion dollars without ever having to worry about an arena, contract disputes, free agency, drug problems, domestic violence. Since 1976, they just have gotten the checks.

STERN: Each time I negotiated a new TV deal, the Spirits of St. Louis would send me a case of wine, because it just kept going up.

GOLDBERG: The NBA and the Silnas made an arrangement [in 2014 for them] to be bought out. Even though "in perpetuity" is in perpetuity, nothing lasts forever.

While the first order of business was to get the two leagues to agree on how to add four ABA franchises to the NBA, there was still the matter of the remaining players on the Kentucky Colonels and Spirits of St. Louis, who were added to NBA teams via a dispersal draft.

PLUTO: You've got four teams going in, but you also have very good players from other teams.

STERN: We called it a dispersal draft. They were on teams that had been bought out or folded. If you looked at the players that were drafted— Artis Gilmore went to Chicago, Maurice Lucas went to Portland, [Moses] Malone went to Portland—there were great players up and down the line.

JACK RAMSAY: When I was coach at Portland, the ABA expansion allowed the Blazers to select Moses Malone. We had Bill Walton. We also had Lloyd Neal, who could play big forward or center. We didn't especially need Moses, but I thought, "He's a guy we need to keep." I remember going into a meeting after Malone had been acquired and saying, "Wow, Moses Malone." I said, "That's really a good choice." And the owner, Larry Weinberg, [said], "No. We got him to trade him because we can't afford to keep him."

PLUTO: Louie Dampier went to San Antonio, but by then his career was over. It's a shame—players like Dampier, Roger Brown, Ron Boone, Mack Calvin, were so good in the ABA, [but] by the time they got a chance in the NBA, the knees were aching. And remember, half the time in the ABA they didn't even travel with a trainer.

GOLDBERG: During the negotiations, a key piece of the puzzle was who's gonna get Julius Erving. Roy Boe, who owned the Nets, knew he would have to give Julius up to an NBA team. As I recall, Julius was offered to the Knicks, and the Knicks' bean counters did their homework and said no.

PLUTO: The Knicks get a $4.8 million indemnity fee from the New York Nets [for playing in the Knicks' territory], which busts the Nets, who can't pay Erving. All the Knicks had to do was say, "Give us Julius Erving." The two leagues are merging, you're making up the rules as you go, nobody is gonna say, "No, we don't want Julius Erving in New York." They would have loved to have him play for the Knicks. So the next move is Pat Williams, general manager of the Philadelphia 76ers. He knows the Nets are broke, so he swoops in, bails them out, takes Julius to Philadelphia.

GOLDBERG: Who knows what the history of the Knicks would have been if they had gotten Julius Erving.

THOMPSON: The whole ABA was excited to play in the NBA. Everybody looked down on the ABA, but we were determined to prove the ABA had good teams. We took our whole team in, but they didn't let us have any draft picks that year, and we won 50 games and the Midwest Division title. In that first [post-ABA] All-Star Game, I think 9 or 10 of the 24 guys had played in the ABA the year before. The fact that three of us made All-NBA that year—I made first team, and Julius and Gervin made second team—that made us very proud.

LARRY BROWN: Two of our teams—San Antonio and Denver—won division titles in the first year. Two of the four division championships were won by ABA teams.

RUSS GRANIK (Deputy Commissioner, NBA, 1990–2006): My impression was that the ABA people always felt they had been looked down upon by the old basketball establishment. There was a very interesting dynamic in those first few years, particularly in the adoption of the three-point shot. A lot of NBA people did not want the three. They thought it was not good for the game and had some resentment to the idea that the ABA had something special that the NBA needed to adopt. It was a very contested issue until it ultimately got put into place [in the 1979–80 season].

KARL: The Red Auerbachs and the NBA didn't want anything to do with the three-point shot.

LEONARD: After the merger, I was representing the Pacers [on] the board of governors, and I made a presentation on the three-point line. I said, "The fans in New York, Chicago, Los Angeles, Detroit, are no different than the fans in San Antonio, Indiana, Denver, and New Jersey." Before the three-point line, if you had a 10-point lead with 2 minutes to play, fans walked out. Not with the three.

MOE: When the ABA and NBA merged, we saw what it was like, and it was like they should have merged with us. Not because we had better players, but the atmosphere. The NBA was unfriendly, boring—I can't explain it. The whole feeling was off. The NBA was slow. The ABA changed it to a faster game.

BILL SIMMONS: You watch those tapes of the NBA from '71 to '76, it's a very white sport. It's slow; it's played a certain way. The speed and dunker guys were all in the ABA. Then they came over and there's the speed athletes, but you also have the old-school guys, and they're all trying to figure out how to play with each other.

KARL: Basketball was lifted up by the ABA. All of a sudden another hundred players had an opportunity to develop their careers. The '70s might have been bad for basketball because of the drugs and all the craziness that went on, but that was the time the game got more integrated. We got the athlete into the game more. It just seemed like the NBA wasn't taking the chances that the ABA was taking. And because of the chances that the ABA took, the game got better.

NELSON GEORGE: That whole period was the most radical change in basketball that I'd ever seen. The NBA game basically became old-fashioned in a three-year period. It's unbelievable how quick it happened. In the ABA, the three-point shot [was] opening the floor, and these above-the-rim players were changing the game completely. Everyone feels like it happened with Magic and Bird, [but] it was happening all along.

DANIELS: The American Basketball Association put a bright light on basketball in general. At one time, bowling was more popular than professional basketball. We brought a different thinking to the game—more up-tempo, more flashy, something that young fellas could relate to on the playgrounds.

JERRY COLANGELO: The ABA was in show business before the NBA. As a league, we learned from them. I think the NBA front office recognized this marriage between entertainment and sports and took it to a whole new level.

THOMPSON: The NBA now is similar to what the ABA was. You have the three-point shot, the All-Star Weekend with the slam dunk—that stuff started in the ABA.

PLUTO: The NBA basically bought everything from the ABA except the red, white, and blue ball.

GOLDBERG: What do I take away from that experience? You could talk about the ABA as a microcosm of race relations in this country. We could talk about tremendous athleticism. We could talk about shenanigans and people pulling fast ones on one another. A league that was alive with smoke and mirrors. But I think that the ABA gathered the energy. It had an oil strike of fantastic talent, primarily African American basketball players that were not an integral part of NBA basketball [before the ABA]. ABA basketball infused the NBA to provide the fans a sport that really has turned into an art. It has made the NBA what it is today—a beautiful sport for television [that has] lit up the global fan. When they saw players like Dr. J, Magic Johnson, Larry Bird, Michael Jordan, LeBron James—this was ABA basketball in the 1970s.

ELMORE: The ABA, it was some of the most fun you could ever have.

UNC: The Family That Frank and Dean Built

Before Michael Jordan, James Worthy, and Sam Perkins; before Rasheed Wallace, Jerry Stackhouse, and Jeff McInnis; before Vince Carter, Antawn Jamison, and Shammond Williams; and before Raymond Felton, Sean May, and Rashad McCants, there were head coaches Frank McGuire and Dean Smith. McGuire, a dashing Irish-Catholic New Yorker, came to the University of North Carolina at Chapel Hill in 1952 after coaching basketball and baseball at St. John's University. He and Smith, his assistant coach, who took over the head job in 1961, built the Tar Heels into one of the most successful basketball programs in the sport's history. That process began with McGuire and his "underground railroad" of New York City recruits, who came to the South, left their mark on the Atlantic Coast Conference (ACC), and put Carolina on the college basketball map.

ROY WILLIAMS (Head Coach, University of North Carolina Tar Heels): In the South, football is dominant, but not in North Carolina. There's a passion about college basketball at North Carolina, at North Carolina State, at Duke, at Wake Forest. The proximity of those schools, the tradition of these programs, has stood the test of time. Kids grow up realizing how important basketball is. They go to games or watch on TV with their mothers, fathers, grandfathers, grandmothers. It's been here a long time, and it'll always be important here.

TOMMY KEARNS: The University of North Carolina is now very much a basketball school, and that started with our winning [the 1957 NCAA championship]. We were five kids from New York playing basketball, and we got lucky and won a game in triple overtime.

BILLY PACKER: Frank McGuire was a Northerner that had come to the University of North Carolina and won a national championship with New York City kids.

DICK VITALE: Frank was a great salesman. He had that class about him. I don't think it even comes down to whether you're Catholic, Jewish, whatever—you're a basketball player, that was the common denominator. And kids would go to Carolina and see the basketball hysteria in that state, and he would bring these kids in and blend them as a unit.

DONNIE WALSH: Frank McGuire knew every high school coach in New York. Some of them played for him and ended up having great players. Lou Carnesecca played baseball for Frank, [legendary Archbishop Molloy High School coach] Jack Curran played baseball for Frank—he had tentacles everywhere. Once he zeroed in on "I want that guy," he was one of the greatest closers of all time. He was very magnetic, well dressed, but a real New York guy. When you got in front of him, you just wanted to play for this guy.

BILLY CUNNINGHAM: I ended up at North Carolina because I used to deliver a newspaper in my neighborhood, and one of the people I used to deliver to happened to be Frank McGuire's sister. When Frank came to visit, he walked in the house, walked right by me, and sat down with my mother and father. They had a cup of coffee, a little Danish. Then they got up, [he] left, [and] my father announces, "Bill, you're either going to a Catholic university or you're going to play for Uncle Frank." End of discussion.

KEARNS: I had a lot of schools interested, and Coach McGuire had come to St. Ann's to watch one of our players when I was a sophomore. He caught half of my game and got interested in me. Mother and Father were concerned about a Catholic boy going to Baptist country in North Carolina, and Coach McGuire assured them we would convert the state to Catholicism.

JOE QUIGG (Center, University of North Carolina Tar Heels, 1955–58): I would have stayed in New York, but Frank McGuire left [St. John's], and he was the one that recruited me. McGuire was impeccably dressed. His appearance, his confidence—he was a man's man. He came to the house, charmed my mother and my dad. He would start with stories about his childhood and where he came up. He was one of 10 children. I think his dad was a cop, and he would tell stories and not even talk to me, just Mom and Dad. And when he left, they said, "Boy, you need to follow him."

WALSH: Frank McGuire made it clear that he wanted to bring New York players down there. He liked the fact they could play freelance, and he understood them and they understood him.

BOBBY CREMINS: He would walk in dressed to the tens. He really believed in image, cleanliness, and always looked perfect. His hair, his suit, his ties, his cuff links. He loved his cuff links, and his shoes would be absolutely shined. The suits were the best suits from New York. He was impressive, and he would tell parents, "I will look after your son and make him do the right things."

QUIGG: First time I was on an airplane was when I did a visit to North Carolina. The first day walking around campus, the Southern accents, everybody says "hi." In New York, you say "hi," a guy will look at you like you're out of your mind.

KEARNS: There's no question, we were strangers in a strange land.

WALSH: They had Tommy Kearns, Bobby Cunningham, Lennie Rosenbluth from Brooklyn, Joe Quigg, and Pete Brennan—all New York kids.

QUIGG: Lennie was probably the greatest shooter I've ever seen. Tommy was a drive guy. That season there were a couple games where he came through on the foul line and won for us. Bobby was not a good shooter, but a defensive man. There were five games that year that Lennie, we could have left him on the bus; he just had horrible games. And every one of those games, Cunningham came in and scored and added that extra touch.

KEARNS: Lennie Rosenbluth was a senior when we were juniors and just a great player. I think he averaged 27.5 points per game senior year.

Lennie could pop them in anyplace. If there was a three-point line, he probably would have averaged 35 a game, that's how good he was.

QUIGG: My game progressed from a typical center to a forward. Lennie Rosenbluth was an All-American, a great shooter, and Lennie played wherever he wanted to. So I stopped being a center. I didn't post up; I went out to the corner. The other thing during that year—I saw Wilt Chamberlain. He was this colossus. There were stories that he could jump from one side of the basket and go over the top of the basket and drop it down. One of his teammates said he did see him touch the top of the [backboard] with his hand. I figured I was no longer gonna be taking hook shots [against defenders that big], so I started practicing a jump shot, and my role became as an outside force.

KEARNS: The rivalries in the ACC at the time were North Carolina–North Carolina State, and Wake Forest with Bones McKinney and Coach McGuire. Bones was a great coach, but there was a lot of personality differences. Frank, he could get his tongue pretty sharp when it needed to be. He voiced his feelings to Bones on several occasions. Everett Case's style was completely different than Coach McGuire's. He was a run-and-gun guy, had a lot of really great shooters at North Carolina State. Coach McGuire liked to control [the] tempo, and that came from [assistant coach] Buck Freeman. Control the game and you're going to win.

WALSH: Frank was a very outspoken guy and didn't take criticism too well, so that kinda got under the skin of rival schools.

QUIGG: McGuire didn't give a damn about technique. He was a motivator. It was us against them: "They're out to get you, and you're gonna get 'em first." And he told such great stories. One time, we're playing Virginia. It's our championship season, Virginia's in last place, [and] we're down at halftime. He comes in, gets on Pete Brennan: "Brennan, I got the wrong damn guy. I shoulda got your father. He's got two jobs. He's got 10 kids. He's got more balls than you'll ever have." So Brennan goes out there, grabs every rebound, and we beat 'em by 20.

KEARNS: He accused me of needing one ball and the other four guys another one! I went through a big transition after my freshman season. I didn't play as much as I thought I should in sophomore year, and that was because Coach McGuire was teaching me a lesson. And the lesson was that I became All-ACC for two years and All-American, so he was right on. Without that, I would have been a different guy.

LARRY BROWN: Players want to know you care about 'em. You care about a kid by getting on his ass, but the only way he's gonna accept that is if he knows you care. Coach McGuire, he would say things—it would rip your heart out. But two seconds later he's embracing you. He cared.

KEARNS: The common thread with the old-line coaches was they demanded excellence and they would settle for nothing less. They would work and work and work on the same things until you got them down.

QUIGG: Freshman year, we had four Catholics on the team, and when we got fouled, we would make the sign of the cross before we took the foul shots. One day, McGuire told us he heard from the bishop: "You guys gotta stop doing the sign of the cross or improve your foul shooting." He didn't want us making the cross and then missing our foul shots—gives the Church a bad name.

In 1956–57, Rosenbluth, Kearns, and Quigg led Carolina through an undefeated regular season, then defeated Wake Forest in the ACC tournament final to earn an NCAA berth and a chance at the national championship. To finish the perfect 32-0 season, however, McGuire and his team would have to go through Wilt Chamberlain and the University of Kansas Jayhawks.

QUIGG: We felt we could beat anybody that we played. We knew what to do at the right time, and especially that year, with five overtime games, we were good but we were also lucky.

KEARNS: At the time, you had to win the ACC tournament to get into the NCAAs. We played Wake Forest in the final—we had beaten them three times during the season, [and] the biggest margin, I think, was 5 points. In the ACC final, tie game, 12 seconds to go, and we get the ball to Lennie. He throws up a hook shot, gets fouled, and we won 61–59.

QUIGG: The year before, we were 18-5 and finished the season with a horrible loss in the ACC tournament. That was the game that won the national championship for us, because we knew how [losing] felt. That got us ready for the next year.

KEARNS: So now we're going to the NCAAs. After beating Yale, we went the next weekend to the Palestra in Philadelphia and played Canisius [College] in the first game and Syracuse in the second—won both and on to Kansas City. This is 1957, and San Francisco was coming off back-to-back wins with [Bill Russell]. They were in the Final Four again, and they played Kansas and we played Michigan State.

QUIGG: I scored 2 points and fouled out early in the second half. Lennie took 40 shots and was 10 for 40. [Michigan State forward] Johnny Green was this tremendous leaper, and we kept telling Lennie to fake. Lennie says, "I don't fake." So he took 40 shots.

KEARNS: Michigan State had "Jumping" Johnny Green. We played them in triple overtime. In the second overtime, Johnny Green is on the foul line in a one-and-one. We're down two, and this little guy comes over to me, he says, "30 and 1." At the time, we've won 30 games. Johnny Green misses the front end. Pete Brennan gets the ball, dribbles down the court, and hits a jumper with 2 seconds to go, and we go into the third overtime and win.

QUIGG: Triple overtime in the semis on Friday night. Now we're back Saturday night, ready to go.

KEARNS: We played the next night in the national championship, and Kansas City did not have a locker room, so we had to dress in a hotel and walk over to the War Memorial Coliseum in our uniforms. Buck's on the bench, along with the governor of North Carolina, Luther Hodges. The governor wanted to assume a position next to Coach McGuire, and McGuire said, "No, that's not going to work, you're gonna go down to the end." He wasn't too happy, but that's the way it goes.

QUIGG: Coach McGuire said, "Kansas can't beat you, but Chamberlain can." Anytime you played Chamberlain, you were an underdog, even though we were No. 1 and they were No. 2 in the rankings.

KEARNS: There was a fellow who covered college basketball for *Sports Illustrated*, Jerry Tax, and we sat in the lobby of the hotel having a cup of coffee and he was saying, "There's no way you're gonna beat these guys, they've got too much firepower." I said, "Mr. Tax, I really think you're wrong." We had been through so many games that we could have lost or should have lost, and Wilt was not going to stand in our way.

QUIGG: Wilt Chamberlain was imposing just to look at. He's listed at 7 feet, but I believe he's 7'2". He had a tremendous body and was a great athlete. He could race up and down the court like nobody I've seen. Against Chamberlain, we played zone, with everybody on Chamberlain. Anywhere he went, we had a man in front and a man behind him. My role was behind him, and everyone else was in front.

KEARNS: The perception we had of Wilt was not awe, but a high level of respect for his ability. We all played in the Catskills against Wilt in the summer, so we knew what we were up against, and that gave us an edge going into the final.

QUIGG: During the [pregame] meeting, McGuire says to [5'11"] Tommy, "Kearns, you scared of Chamberlain?" Tommy says hell no. McGuire says, "Good, you're gonna jump against him." So we went out, the four of us go all the way back in a zone and leave Tommy out there with Wilt. And Wilt's looking around like, "What's happening?"

KEARNS: I have a great picture with Wilt having his hands on his hips, looking down, and saying, "What the hell are you doing?" I think the strategy was to play with Wilt's and the Kansas team's head.

QUIGG: Sometimes you just feel good when you go out on the basketball court, and that was one of those games I felt really good. They opened in a box-and-one on Rosenbluth and left us alone in the corners. I hit 2 baskets, Pete Brennan was fouled on a drive and made 2 free throws, and then I hit 2 jump shots from the corner. We built a lead, and they came out of the box-and-one. Chamberlain played me. I ran around outside and he was following me, and that left it open for Lennie inside. We were up something like 29–22, and we shot 60 percent in that first half.

KEARNS: Second half, they came back and went up by a point or so. When Kansas came back, they slowed it down, and I thought they made a major mistake. They should've gotten a lot more aggressive with us defensively. When you see the game film, there is no question they got Wilt laying back, guarding the hoop, and if they get aggressive with us, they probably would have won, but they let us control the pace of the game.

QUIGG: Once they got the lead, they slowed the ball down. We don't know why—it was crazy. We had so many fouls, and they played into exactly what we wanted to do. If I would have been the coach, I would have gone right at us, with that many fouls on key players. And Chamberlain—you can't do anything but foul him.

KEARNS: We didn't let the game get away from us. We tied it and went into three overtimes. One of the overtimes, there was no scoring, and a couple times I'd try to go in for shots, and Wilt just blew it up into the balcony someplace.

QUIGG: The first or second overtime, they held the ball. I had four fouls, Brennan had four fouls, somebody else had four fouls, and we were saying, "Wonderful, let's just rest." They tried a last-second shot, it didn't go in, and we went to another overtime.

KEARNS: The last 25 seconds, we're down a point. There's a timeout, and I drive to the hoop and get it blocked.

QUIGG: Tommy drives to the basket, beats his man, but Chamberlain comes from the other side and just slammed it away. We're down to about 16 seconds, and Cunningham takes it out, throws it underneath the basket to Bob Young. Bob gives it to me at the foul line. We've got 10 seconds, Chamberlain's in front of me, and I know I can't go up for a shot. The only thing I can do is drive, hope to get fouled, maybe throw something up [and hope] it goes in. So I drive, Chamberlain blocks the shot, whistle blows, foul called. Whistle is on Maurice King, the guy that came over to help. So I've got 2 foul shots with 6 seconds to go.

KEARNS: Joe gets it and goes back to the hoop and gets fouled. We have a timeout first, and Coach McGuire says, "After Joe makes these 2, here's what we're gonna do . . ."

QUIGG: I did not know it at the time and I didn't hear it, but after I left, Coach McGuire got ahold of Cunningham and said, "If Joe misses, foul Chamberlain." So I went to the foul line, took the first one—net. And after the first went in, the next one was easy. Net again. Six seconds to go. They take it out and I think threw it to half-court, called timeout. Five seconds to go, Danny Lotz is in the game, and I said, "You get behind Chamberlain. I'm gonna front him." We set up, and the next thing I know Danny is guarding the guy in the corner. I'm yelling, "Danny! Get over here!" I don't know if he did or not, 'cause they passed to the top of the key, guy gets the ball, throws to Chamberlain. That was a scary moment because the guy who passed it could have thrown another four feet over my hand, and Chamberlain could have gotten that. But I was able to knock it away—it's probably the highest I've ever jumped in my life. Tommy got [the loose ball] and threw it up to the ceiling. National championship winners.

KEARNS: When we came back from Kansas City, we were overnight rock stars. Fifteen thousand people greeted us at the airport. Pilot couldn't land the plane—he had to circle a couple times to get people off the runway.

QUIGG: We were conquering heroes. I had a date, picked the girl up, went to the movies, and everybody in the theater stood and clapped. The next Monday I had class, and Wednesday we had a big biology test. We had a really mean professor, and he says: "Students, in honor of Mr. Quigg, your test has been put off till Friday."

KEARNS: I've always felt that it's interesting we won by 1 point. One point changed my life. It propelled me to a whole other level. I was in the financial business in North Carolina. People knew me, and it gave my career a huge start. Whoever [said], "Winning and losing doesn't make a difference"—well, in our case it made a hell of a big difference.

McGuire and Smith, the two coaches responsible for creating North Carolina's culture of dedication, loyalty, and excellence, couldn't have been more different in their personalities and approaches to the game.

BROWN: I was lucky. I had two of the greatest college coaches in the history of the game—Coach McGuire and Coach Smith. Coach McGuire, he's as much of a people person as there is. And then Coach Smith, he's the most decent person I've ever met.

KEARNS: I met Dean Smith when he was the first assistant in 1959. One was the antithesis of the other. Coach McGuire's family were New York policemen, and Coach Smith, his father was a professor. Dean was a mathematician, which goes to [the] four corners [offense] and some of the things he did in his career.

DOUG MOE: Coach Smith was very detailed—everything precise. Coach McGuire was the opposite. He's very loose, lets you play. When I think of Coach McGuire, we played NC State and it was tie score with about 10 seconds left. It was [a] timeout, and Coach McGuire said, "Take a look down there at that sly old fox Everett Case. He's telling them what we're gonna do, what I'm gonna do. I don't give a blankety-blank what we do. Moe, throw it to [Lee] Shaffer; Shaffer, throw it to [York]

Larese; someone put the ball in the basket, and let's get the heck out of this place." Just like that, and all I remember is Shaffer laying the ball in and the buzzer goes off and we got out of there.

BROWN: Coach McGuire would humiliate Dean—just in fun. He puts me in, and Dean starts talking about how we're gonna break the press. Frank says, "No, just give it to him; that's why we recruited him. If he don't break the press, we should've gotten somebody better."

CREMINS: Dean Smith was a genius. His game preparation, his organization, was incredible. Coach McGuire was not that organized. He became a genius when the game started. He knew how to work officials. Putting the ball in the right player's hands was crucial to him. I'll never forget one game [after McGuire had moved on to coach at the University of South Carolina in 1964]. They were double-teaming John Roche and I was wide-open, and I went over to Coach McGuire and I said, "Coach, I got a wide-open shot, should I take it?" He fixed his cuff links, did his necktie, and said, "If you get a layup, go ahead and take it." In other words: "Get the ball to John Roche."

BROWN: We [played] Duke in the finals, and I dove for a loose ball and called timeout as I was falling. Coach Smith jumped up: "Great call!" Frank took him and threw him down on the bench. He said, "I call all the fucking timeouts." Then he grabbed me by the shirt and said, "You hear what I said?" Then, when nobody was around, he came up and said, "Hell of a play."

WALSH: Frank McGuire was a guy that would go out to practice, you go through warm-up drills, and then he would scrimmage. He put you into what he called sets. He believed you can't tell players every move to make, that you put them into position and let them play off one another. In scrimmages, he would stop it when he saw something he didn't like. Over the season, more and more you came together and understood this is the way we have to play to win. Dean, on the other hand, broke things down into drills, and then he put the drills together and made the offense and defense out of those drills. So there were defensive stances for like two minutes, and then you go to fast-break defense, then you go to the shell drill, and it would all be timed. At the end, he would scrimmage, but nowhere near the way Frank scrimmaged.

CREMINS: It was difficult, 'cause Dean came to North Carolina because of Frank McGuire, and then once Frank went to South Carolina, they had to go against each other. That had to be real tough on Dean, because Frank, his big thing was loyalty. If he went to New York recruiting a kid, the last thing he expected was for Dean to come in and recruit that same kid. He expected Dean to back off, but Dean could not do that. So it started a great rivalry.

KEARNS: One of the things Coach Smith learned from Frank McGuire was recruiting. He was introduced to the New York market by Coach McGuire, and he recruited some players up here. Not a lot, but he learned the ins and outs from Frank.

CREMINS: The Frank McGuire–Dean Smith rivalry all came to a head after I left [South Carolina]. Frank McGuire was building a new dynasty, winning the recruiting wars again. Dean Smith was starting to build his dynasty. And back then there was no Big East. The ACC was *the* thing. It really heated up—Frank McGuire and Dean Smith were going head-to-head, and it caused a lot of friction. It was tough, because at the end of the day they loved each other.

Dean Smith inherited a wounded program when he took over as head coach at North Carolina in 1961. NC State had been implicated in the same point-shaving scandal that cost players like Connie Hawkins, Doug Moe, and Roger Brown many of the best years of their careers, and because UNC was part of the same state university system, the NCAA put the Tar Heels on probation. Despite the difficult start, Smith rebuilt the program, eventually coaching UNC to 11 Final Fours and winning national championships in 1982 and 1993. Smith recruited some of the most talented rosters ever in college basketball, but he didn't just roll the balls out and tell the guys to play. Smith's teams were known for their precision, preparation, and patience, and their signature offense before the adoption of the shot clock in 1985 was the four corners.

BROWN: Coach McGuire left after the 1961 season, and that was the year of the scandal. And because we were part of the greater University of North Carolina, we got punished along with NC State. [As part of the NCAA's punishment], Coach Smith inherited a 16-game schedule, losing two of our best players. With a team that was really shorthanded, I think we went 8-8. The second year, one of our better players tears his ankle up, we go 15-5. Dean's third year, they go 14-14. The [next] year, they go 15-9, [and] now people are really furious with Coach Smith.

KEARNS: Dean had a tough start—he was hung in effigy and almost got fired—but chancellor Bill Aycock kept him on and he got a couple of really great players, and the rest is history.

CUNNINGHAM: I tore that [effigy] down. It was infuriating. It wasn't the coaches' fault—Carolina, at that time, was on probation. The only recruiting you were allowed to do was in-state. In most cases, the players were walk-ons. They were great guys, played their hearts out. We had a great time playing together. But the quality of play? Come on. Looking back, seeing what we were able to achieve, even to get to .500, Dean Smith did a phenomenal job.

BROWN: Chancellor Aycock said, "This is the most decent, well-respected person I know. He's gonna be my coach no matter what." Think about this: if you didn't have a chancellor or president like Aycock, Dean's gone.

GEORGE KARL: He didn't like to show he's competitive, but he's a competitive SOB. He was mean in a way that he never would show. He very seldom showed anger in a way that you were fearful, but he always showed toughness in a way that you loved to be in the gym with him. To this day, I still can't remember him swearing. He had some cockiness to his gig, too. He had a belief that he could outwork, outcoach people.

BROWN: I remember, he picks me up in his blue Cadillac when I visited North Carolina, and the porter at the airport, he gives the guy a 20. He'd go into a restaurant, give the maître d' a 20. And when I became a young coach, he told me, "I want you to remember why I did that. You might have a recruit sometime, and he'll think the way they treat this coach, he must be some pretty special guy. You go into a restaurant, the way they give me the best seat—it makes the recruit think, 'Wow, this is somebody I want to be around.'"

PHIL FORD: My mom and dad were public school teachers. My mom wasn't a big sports fan and my dad was, but he didn't play growing up—he had to work on the farm, being a sharecropper's son. And the first time that Coach Smith came to visit my home, my mom thought he was the dean of a school—she didn't know that was his first name. She never sat in on the recruiting visits, but when Coach Smith came, she wanted to sit in. The first 30 minutes, we just talked about being a good student, being a good citizen, race relations. We got into basketball, and he mentioned that I may have to play junior varsity. I think that's when my mom really fell in love with Coach Smith, because other coaches were promising that I was going to start and how much I would play. After Coach Smith left, my mom said she thinks we can trust Coach Smith. She said if I go to North Carolina and work hard my freshman year and don't get to play; work hard my sophomore year and get a chance to play a little; work hard my junior year and get a chance to play more; then by the time I was a senior, if I was going to have an opportunity to start, he wouldn't be out promising another high school All-American my position.

CHRISTIAN LAETTNER (Forward, Duke University Blue Devils, 1988–92; 1997 NBA All-Star): When I made my decision to go to Duke, I told my mother and she started crying. I was like, "Why are you crying?" And she said, "Because I love Dean Smith."

FORD: The thing that made Coach Smith special is how he paid attention to detail. On a last-second shot, sometimes we'd have a guy setting a screen for someone to get the rebound if the [shooter] happens to miss.

In the pregame layup line, there's a manager keeping [track of] whether you make or miss—even in warm-ups!

WALSH: Dean Smith was also a genius at peer pressure. You'd come in as a freshman, and he'll tell you, "We're gonna run sprints and time them." Well, he knew that if you were a freshman, you are gonna run the fastest you ever ran in those sprints. Then that would be your time for the rest of the time you were at Carolina. The other thing he did, if you made a mistake and you kept making it, he would just say, "Make that mistake again and you all run." You make the whole team run two or three times, and the guys are saying, "You better get it straight, man."

KEARNS: Dean Smith's greatest strength was situation basketball. I look at games now and I see where you get down to the last 20 to 30 seconds, and teams don't know exactly what they're doing. Coach Smith was fantastic about that.

FORD: We were prepared for everything. There wasn't anything that could go on in a basketball game that we hadn't practiced.

KEARNS: You could talk to Coach Smith about "Do you remember playing at Clemson and we're down 4 with 37 seconds?" and he would describe the whole situation to you.

PACKER: The thing I admired, seeing hundreds of his practices, he always thought out of the box as to how to utilize his talent. The four corners using Charlie Scott, Larry Miller, Phil Ford—putting that as part of his arsenal and changing how the game was played.

WALSH: Dean was very innovative. Sometimes he'd go to a game and see a coach doing something, and he'd say, "I'm gonna try that." That four [corners], he got that from [John McLendon] and just added the right player—let's say Phil Ford.

CREMINS: The four corners was tough to defend. Their best ball handler would be the point, and his job was to penetrate. And anytime anybody helped from the wings, he would pass the ball to the wing and go get it back. His ideal was one of two things: to penetrate and get an uncontested layup, or to penetrate and dish to one of the big men, where they would lay it up.

KARL: It was basically a delay game, structured to score layups. You have a lead, and you're holding the ball and making the defense come out to get you, which stretches the defense into a situation where layups are easier to attain. You were using the clock to create a defensive mistake that gave you the easiest shot in basketball. And if you didn't stretch out, we were just gonna hold the ball.

VITALE: As soon as they took a lead, they spread that court and the party was over. You couldn't defend that four corners, especially with Phil Ford, who was as good as it gets in college.

WILLIAMS: Phil Ford, the four corners fit him better than anybody. There was no shot clock—you couldn't take it away from him. He could get baskets on his own, or the backdoor cuts, and if you fouled him, he made the free throws.

FORD: I always say I get too much credit for four corners. For four corners to work, you have to have five very good ball handlers, because at some point everybody is going to handle. You have to have five very good free throw shooters, because at some point you're going to have to make a free throw. You have to have five pretty cool players, to stay patient. And you also have to have five pretty good defenders, because most times, after running a little time off the clock and scoring, the other team would take a quick shot out of frustration.

KARL: I thought it was a much more aggressive offense than people gave it credit for, because of the fear of the scoreboard saying you gotta do *something*. We scored more often than people [remember]. You got fouls and layups, which at that time were the two best shots in the game. Basically, it was saying, "We're not gonna shoot anything except fouls or layups."

CHARLIE SCOTT: The four corners was never meant to be a stalling tactic. Four corners was a matchup tactic. Coach Smith felt like his best athlete could beat the other athlete, and that matchup would be in favor of whoever was in the middle of the four corners. If I could beat my man, then someone will have to help and that would give other guys open shots. The idea was not to take the first opportunity, but to lull the team into a belief that it was a stall tactic, lull them into the idea that you never really wanted to shoot. Then, when you made that move, they wouldn't react as fast as they would if they thought you were trying to score every time you went to the basket.

FORD: I was cognizant that the opponents would get frustrated in the four corners. That's what we wanted to do. We wanted to get them out of what they normally do defensively, wanted them to make mistakes.

KENNY SMITH (Point Guard, Sacramento Kings/Houston Rockets; NBA Studio Analyst, TNT): Teams didn't like it because it was humiliating: "We're trying to steal a ball to get back in the game, and you're turning down shots?" It was fun to put [the ball] out there, then we'd go back in and out, and then we'd lay it in. It was a dog chasing its tail—never going to catch us. It was the worst feeling in the world as a basketball player, and we made you feel that way.

The Atlantic Coast Conference was established in 1953, and for the first 12 years of its existence, ACC basketball remained segregated. While historically black colleges and universities like Winston-Salem State nurtured the careers of future NBA players like Earl Monroe and Cleo Hill, there was not a single black player on the varsity teams of nearby ACC schools Duke, NC State, Wake Forest, or North Carolina. That changed on December 1, 1965, when Maryland guard Billy Jones broke the league's color barrier. Two years later, Charlie Scott suited up in Tar Heel blue and became UNC's first African American scholarship athlete. Scott paved the way for future Carolina greats like Phil Ford, Bob McAdoo, and Michael Jordan. Dean Smith's efforts to integrate college basketball remain among his greatest contributions to the sport.

CUNNINGHAM: The first time I left New York was when I went to North Carolina. First time I got on a plane was when I went to school. I still remember getting off the plane, I had to go to the men's room, and [I saw] "Whites Only." [I thought], "What does this mean?" It was like going to another country. I saw sit-ins. I saw terrible things which were disgraceful. You just wanted to cry. Especially coming from an environment where you didn't even realize . . . You [lived] in Brooklyn. People don't understand—you didn't have television till you were maybe 15, 16 years old. You had a couple daily newspapers that covered your borough. You lived in your little pocket, and that was it.

PACKER: I arrived in the South having lived my entire time in the North. It's not like today. In the 1950s, if you grew up in the North, at least where I was, the black-white situation was not something you were even aware of.

CUNNINGHAM: I'll never forget being at practice when I first got there, and I say to a guy, "How come there's no black players?" He said, "There's segregation. There are no black players in the conference." I said, "You're kidding me." That's how naïve I was. There were several hundred black students at the university, but no athletes. And Chapel Hill was a little oasis where anybody could go to any restaurant or the movies, but don't go a mile outside of Chapel Hill if you were a minority.

SONNY HILL: How many black basketball players were at white universities in the '40s? Very few. How many were at white universities in the '50s? A few more. Then in the '60s, it's like, "Let's bring these black basketball players into Division I, and they can become a big part of what's going on." If you remember, Charlie Scott was the first black to play [at North Carolina]. That was Dean Smith.

WILLIAMS: His most significant contribution really started outside the game, and that was with the civil rights movement and the African American athlete playing basketball in the South.

SCOTT: My choice came down to being rebellious. Everyone said a black couldn't do well academically, couldn't do well athletically, and the best way to earn [respect] was to prove people wrong.

CUNNINGHAM: The step that Charlie made—what a courageous man. He could have gone to any other university in the country, had a wonderful career, gone on to the pros, et cetera. And here he was—it was almost a Jackie Robinson situation. He knew what to expect. He's gonna go into arenas, he's gonna be called every name conceivable. Even some people in Chapel Hill probably don't like what's occurring. And he's ready for it. Not only ready, but he performs at such a wonderful level. Winning games, taking the team to the Final Four.

SCOTT: After I visited schools, a lot of them would send letters—they're still recruiting. Well, what I got from Villanova was newspaper clippings of lynchings in the South. I guess they knew I was interested in going to a school in the South, so they wanted to give me an insight [into] what I would have to deal with.

WILLIAMS: When Charlie was a junior, I was a freshman. That was the most amazing season I had ever seen any basketball player have. So many games down the stretch, [he] made every shot. Made his last 9 shots against Duke in the final of the ACC tournament. Made the shot to beat Davidson in the eastern regionals and go to the Final Four.

SCOTT: I remember we played Davidson and I hit a shot to win the game, and a reporter went to the barbershops in the South and a guy said, "Charlie Scott for president. Charlie Scott is God." The next week, we played Purdue in the NCAA semifinals and we got beat, and the reporter went back to that same barbershop and the guy said, "Told you niggers fold under pressure."

WILLIAMS: I'm sure he did face a lot of things. Most of them I did not see and would not have seen, but Charlie tried to represent the University of North Carolina basketball program. He tried to set an example that others would be successful coming behind him.

SCOTT: I understood the responsibility of the times. I understood changes were only going to be made by people who were willing to do the things to make it possible. I heard taunts, I heard threats. I'm pretty sure Coach Smith went through my fan mail and never gave me letters that were threatening. Coach Smith understood there were things he could control and things he couldn't. They played "Dixie" at Carolina, so what Coach Smith would do, right before game time, he would take the team back into the locker room at the precise moment that the band was ready. So I would not have to be on the court and listen to people stand and cheer for "Dixie."

KARL: We played many a game that didn't have a lot of black players on the court. We were actually at the beginning of the integration of the game in the '70s. The [black] players on our team felt the pressure more. Those guys went through more difficulties than I could feel, but it was there.

SCOTT: Coach Smith never talked to me about being the first black. He treated me as if I were any other player. He never felt like that was a conversation he needed to have, because that's not how he looked at me. He knew he could not change how society looked at me, but he never wanted me to think that was part of the reason he recruited me. Coach Smith always told me that I wasn't the [first] black player he recruited; I was the first black athlete to accept a scholarship offer from him. . . . I was in the cocoon of the basketball program. The guys I was playing with accepted me, so I was able to feel like basketball was the family.

CUNNINGHAM: Dean Smith—there was a restaurant where we would eat pregame meals. It was called The Pines, and we all looked forward to it because we'd get a steak. And he and his minister took this black gentleman to The Pines for dinner, and initially they were questioned why they were doing this. Dean Smith explained that if you didn't accept and change your ways, we would never eat another meal in The Pines. That helped segregation just outside of Chapel Hill and helped change the world.

SCOTT: There was only one time I felt like Coach Smith made a decision that had to do with race. It was when we played in the Far West Classic my sophomore year. Against Utah, down 16 at halftime, we came back and won, and I had scored 20 points and played a great game. Then we played Oregon in the championship. We were up like 15 at halftime, and because the game was basically over, the reporters voted for Most Valuable Player of the tournament at halftime. I had won the vote, [and] Coach Smith pulled me aside at the end of the game and said, "When you get back to North Carolina, you're going to hear that you were voted the Most Valuable Player at halftime. I went to the reporters and told them they should rethink it." He did, and they named [Tar Heels guard] Larry Miller Most Valuable Player. Second half, we went into our four corners, and Larry had the ball in the middle. They had to foul him, so he kept going to the free throw line. Coach Smith said to me, "I did it because I feel like seniors should get their rewards, and when you're a senior these things will come upon you." I was crushed. I felt like it was just as important to blacks to see me win that award my first year at North Carolina. But as I got older, I understood Coach Smith. If you wanted to bring dissension among the team, to have a black guy come in and win MVP from a guy who was first-team All-America might have caused a fracture in that early part of my career.

FORD: Growing up, I was a North Carolina fan because of Charlie Scott. I was going to an all–African American school when Charlie Scott started playing at the University of North Carolina. A lot of us wanted to be Charlie Scott.

Dean Smith will be remembered for his national championships and Final Fours, for his strategic innovations, and for his role in pushing forward racial progress. But perhaps his greatest legacy will be the tight-knit culture he built at North Carolina and the uncommon bonds Tar Heels players share across generations. When you played for Frank McGuire or Dean Smith, you became more than a college basketball player. You became family.

JIM CALHOUN (Head Coach, University of Connecticut Huskies, 1986–2012): The first family I saw basketball-wise was Dean Smith and his assistants

Bill Guthridge, Roy Williams, and Eddie Fogler. I discovered a program, not a team. And that program was a family, everything about it.

PACKER: Coach Smith never allowed you in his family if you weren't in his family. One reason he probably is the best who ever coached the game, on and off the floor: whether you were Michael Jordan or the lowliest manager, he would know who you are, and it would be important to him what happened to you. He would know your wife's name, he would know that you have three children, he would know about your success or lack of success. He would be available to help you in any way he could. I have had Coach Smith come up to me and say, "How are Barbara, Mark, and Liz doing?" I didn't even know he knew I had kids!

FORD: In practice, former players will come back, and as a former player you're allowed to sit on the court. But if you aren't [a former player], you have to sit up above the rail where you can't hear. The reason he asks non–family members, per se, to sit up there, is sometimes he may get on a player, and he may not want to embarrass that player.

CUNNINGHAM: Dean Smith had a way about him. It's hard to put it in words how he could pull people together. It didn't matter what your political view was, your color, your creed—he had this ability, almost like a magnet drawing you to him. He treated every player number one, if you were the number one player or the last player on the team.

SMITH: Dean Smith, the only man I've ever met who can treat every single person the exact same. That's a unique quality. My mother and father don't treat my brothers [and me] the same! If you closed your eyes during practice, you couldn't tell who was the best player and who was the worst player by what he said or the tone that he said it.

SCOTT: I've been around a long time. I've seen a lot of coaches, a lot of players, a lot of general managers. Played for Jerry Colangelo, [Johnny] "Red" Kerr—they all were great people. But the moral standing of Coach Smith and his loyalty to his players is unmatched.

PACKER: For Coach Smith, [winning] the individual game was not as important as the program. I think if he had more of the mind-set of Bobby Knight, he would have won many more championships. The reason I say that is he would never abandon the approach of his program to win a game. People say, "If I had had the talent Dean Smith had, I would have won more championships." But here's what Dean Smith was able to do: he put a team on the floor in an unbelievably competitive league, year after year, and there were no down periods. He did that by always having his program be more important than an individual game or an individual player.

CUNNINGHAM: The thing that always impressed me about him was that he would recruit these great players—Jordan, Worthy, Carter, Stackhouse—and they always had a commitment to Dean. If they went out of school early to turn pro, which he would push them [to do] if he thought it was time, they would come back and get their degrees. That always amazed me—the loyalty he demanded and the respect he had from his players. These young men were making millions of dollars, and during the summer they'd go back, or somehow they would find a way to get their degree, because that was the commitment they made to him.

FORD: The common denominator is Coach Smith. The fact that Coach Smith was there for 36 years—so many of us played for Coach Smith and everybody went through a lot of the same things. There's so much commonality that we all feel like brothers.

KARL: In August or September, we always had a retreat with Coach Smith and Roy Williams, and Roy would bring Larry Brown. There would be these incredibly good coaches hanging out in Chapel Hill for three or four days, talking hoops.

WILLIAMS: Things that Coach Smith was the first to do: You can watch every level of basketball, whether it's junior high, high school, college, NBA, or WNBA, and you still see people pointing at the passer to thank him for the assist. You still see teams huddling at the free throw line. People play four corners at every level. The shot clock has changed some of that, but Coach Smith was one of the leading advocates of the shot clock. His influence on the game was incredible.

PACKER: You see guys today pointing when a guy makes a good defensive play or a good pass or a nice rebound; you see a kid on the bench stand up and applaud—that's North Carolina.

KARL: Coach Smith always said he's a better teacher of men than of basketball. And I wasn't an easy guy. Going to North Carolina, I had to be broken a little bit—being told I couldn't shoot; point guards here don't do this and don't do that. But he had a spirit that you gravitated toward. You gravitated toward his information, toward his stories, toward being loyal. Everything was based on team, playing hard, playing together.

MOE: Dean Smith was like a second father to me. I have no clue where I'd be today if it wasn't for Coach Smith, and I was always the kind of clown. I'd call him El Deano, Smitty, Coach Smith. We were close friends, but I could never get myself to call him Dean. Coach Smith saved my life the day he called me and said, "Dougie, you got to go back to school. You got an appointment at Elon College. Wear a coat and tie and be on time."

FORD: Coach Smith would get on me; he would get on everyone. But I can say [that] when I went to North Carolina as a freshman and when I left as a senior, I was a completely different player. I was so much better that it was not even close, and that's what happens. All the players that played for Coach Smith, we got better each year. That's all you can ask for.

SCOTT: I owe all that I am to Coach Smith—my persona as an individual, my moral standing, my belief in family, my belief in loyalty. I give all the credit to Coach Smith. He showed me true loyalty.

COACH K: From Bobby Knight's Protégé to the One-and-Done Era

He played for a coach who implored him not to shoot.

Perhaps that's why, once Mike Krzyzewski became entrusted with the Duke University basketball program in 1980 at 32 years old, he encouraged his players to freelance offensively—and he actually *meant* it. When Bobby Hurley manned the point on back-to-back national championship teams in 1991 and 1992, Coach K crafted a motion offense enabling Hurley to push the ball, make reads, and rely on his instincts to create. "If there were 50 times that I drew up a play in a timeout," said Krzyzewski, "there were 45 times Bobby didn't run it—but we were still successful because he saw something."

Coach K established trust with his players by delivering unvarnished truths directly, eye to eye, with conviction. "I wanted them to understand," he said, "that when I say something, I'll do it."

It isn't difficult to trace the influence of that notion. As a cadet at West Point, Krzyzewski played for Bobby Knight, a stern disciplinarian who preached defense above all and demanded that Krzyzewski concentrate on that end of the floor.

Knight built a dominant Indiana University program instilling fundamentals and respect for the game. Krzyzewski enjoyed a courtside view from the bench as a graduate assistant on the 1974–75 Hoosiers team, which was undefeated and on its way to an NCAA title before Scott May broke his arm. Knight won three national championships, including a 1975–76 team that was a perfect 32-0, but he was stubborn, inflexible, and he paid dearly for his obstinacy. It cost him his job at Indiana and nearly ruined his relationship with the young protégé who would eventually surpass him in both career wins and championships. As Coach K rose to prominence, his relationship with Knight became strained over subtle slights, jealousy, and misunderstandings. It fractured following the 1992 Duke Final Four victory over Indiana, when Knight dismissed Krzyzewski with a terse postgame handshake. Nearly 10 years passed before the breach was repaired, when Krzyzewski chose Knight to present him for his induction into the Naismith Memorial Basketball Hall of Fame.

In spite of their differences, Krzyzewski made Knight's relentless defensive philosophy the core of his basketball outlook. Nine Duke players have won national Defensive Player of the Year honors under his watch, more than any other program.

Like so many before him, Coach K had to endure his share of hardships before winning kicked in. In his first three seasons at Duke, his record was a pedestrian 38-47 (including a dismal 11-17 in year three), and some alumni called for his replacement.

"I watched Mike lose a lot early on," said former Georgia Tech coach Bobby Cremins. "It was tough on him, but learning to deal with that made him a great coach. If you handle losing in the correct way, it's a tremendous asset down the road. If you handle it the wrong way, it could ruin your career. Out of all the coaches I've watched lose, I think Coach K kept it in perspective better than anybody I've seen."

Coach K's first championship came in 1991 with a nucleus of Hurley, Christian Laettner, and Grant Hill. That trio returned in 1992 to win it again, but not before they accounted for one of the most dramatic moments in college basketball history.

With Duke trailing Kentucky 103–102 with 2.1 seconds left in overtime of an Elite Eight game, Hill hurled a fastball the length of the court to Laettner at the foul line. Laettner turned and stuck the jumper just as time expired. Coach K never saw what was later dubbed "The Shot" because his players and assistants leaped into the air and obscured his view.

With the acerbic Laettner and the publicly austere Krzyzewski emerging as the face of Duke basketball, the Blue Devils became the team everyone loved to hate, much like the New York Yankees and the New England Patriots. "There started to be some kickback," Laettner acknowledged. "Coach K talked to us about it. He said, 'Sometimes people get tired of success.'"

It would be nine years before Duke would win another championship, this time in 2001 behind the cerebral forward Shane Battier and electric point guard Jay Williams. The Blue Devils experienced yet another nine-year drought before the trio of Jon Scheyer, Kyle Singler, and Nolan Smith captured the 2010 championship. It was a roster devoid of superstars, and when Coach K led the postgame team prayer, he exalted them as the epitome of "team." Duke won another title in 2015 thanks to three one-and-done stars—Jahlil Okafor, Justise Winslow, and Tyus Jones.

Krzyzewski stands alone with five titles in the college coaching ranks, trailing only John Wooden, yet he still laments the ones that got away, particularly his 1986 team that won 37 games but was beaten in the championship by Louisville and 18-year-old freshman "Never Nervous Pervis" Ellison. Duke's starting lineup included seniors Johnny Dawkins, Mark Alarie, Jay Bilas, and David Henderson, who played on that 11-17 team in 1982–83. "They were the most deserving team of winning the championship," Krzyzewski said. "I loved that team as much as any I've ever coached."

Coach K's iconic status was cemented when he was tapped to be head coach of the U.S. Men's National Team in 2006, after many years of service to USA Basketball, including an assistant's role on the 1992 Dream Team. He's won three Olympic gold medals coaching NBA pros, a transition that was seamless, according to Larry Bird, "because [Krzyzewski] is believable."

Coach K is now in his 70s, and the 50-something contemporaries who challenge him today include Kansas coach Bill Self, who won in 2008; Kentucky's John Calipari, who won in 2012; and Villanova's Jay Wright, who won in 2016 and 2018.

Krzyzewski's primary task is no longer earning his players' respect. That's inherent. Now he must guard against his Hall of Fame résumé being so intimidating that players deem him unapproachable. "I want to make sure," Coach K explained, "that the guy playing for me doesn't think I'm a statue."

LARRY AND MAGIC: NBA Renaissance Men

Earvin "Magic" Johnson assumed he and Larry Bird were friends.

They were, after all, teammates on a 1978 summer all-star team representing the United States at the World Invitational Tournament. Magic and Bird anchored a second unit that delighted in decimating coach Joe B. Hall's starting lineup, which mostly consisted of Hall's own University of Kentucky players. After the tournament ended, Bird gushed to his brother Mark, "Magic Johnson is the best basketball player I've ever seen."

One year later, Magic and his Michigan State team met Larry and his Indiana State team for the 1979 NCAA national championship. Johnson approached Bird at the pregame press conference expecting a hug or at the very least a hearty handshake. Instead, Bird looked straight through him.

Bird's icy response was twofold: Magic was the opponent, which in Bird's mind meant he was the enemy. And Bird was irked that Michigan State had two players on the dais—Magic and Greg Kelser—while Bird was up there alone, without teammate Carl Nicks.

Magic left that afternoon wounded and angry. "I thought Larry was a good guy," he told Kelser. "Guess I was wrong."

Michigan State went on to throttle Indiana State 75–64 in what remains the most watched college championship game in television history.

Later that year, Magic migrated to the NBA as the No. 1 overall pick in the 1979 draft, landing with the Los Angeles Lakers, and Bird officially signed with the Boston Celtics. (Celtics president Red Auerbach had shrewdly drafted Bird the previous season as a junior-eligible player.) Their joint arrival in the league ignited a renaissance for pro basketball. In 1980, Bird won Rookie of the Year honors while Magic (again) won a championship, leading the Lakers, who were without the injured Kareem Abdul-Jabbar, past Julius Erving and the Philadelphia 76ers by playing all five positions. Bird seethed as he watched the game on tape delay at a local watering hole in French Lick, Indiana.

Bird earned his ring the next season against the Houston Rockets, with Magic stewing in Los Angeles as his nemesis hoisted the trophy.

It was inevitable that they would meet again in a championship game, and they did—in 1984, 1985, and 1987. Along the way, their battles became one of the most compelling story lines in basketball history.

DONNIE WALSH: Whether you want to say they saved or rejuvenated the NBA, Magic and Larry brought it to another level, because they both came in with such backing from colleges that drew interest. One was on the East Coast, one was on the West Coast, and you could tell that both wanted to specifically beat the other guy.

ARN TELLEM (Vice Chairman, Detroit Pistons; NBA Player Agent, 1981–2015): There's never been anyone like Magic before or after him. He played with such passion and a smile. He put the team first. He was one of those monumental players at the right time.

PETER VECSEY: I remember calling Magic the blank in the Scrabble set, because he played every position against the Sixers in the [1980] Finals as a rookie.

MAGIC JOHNSON: It worked out great that America said, "Man, we gotta tune in and see what's gonna happen tonight with these two guys." We were both Midwest boys, we grew up poor, but we loved the game, and we would do anything to win.

BILL SIMMONS: I'm a die-hard Celtics fan. We have season tickets, and Game 6 of the 1981 Finals is on tape delay at 11:30 p.m. I'm 11 years old, and my dad says, "What should we do? Do you want to listen on the radio?" We decide to go to bed, he wakes me up at 11:30, and we watch the game. Could you imagine that now? It's insane. So you can't say enough about how things changed in the '80s because of those two guys.

ROBERT PARISH (Center, Boston Celtics; 9-Time NBA All-Star): You have to ponder not only what Magic and Larry did for basketball and the NBA, but what they did for race relations. Larry and Magic did not care about the color of each other's skin. They respected one another, and over time that respect grew into love.

STEPHEN A. SMITH (Host, *First Take*, ESPN): When you look at Bird, it's a different kind of brilliance, but it's tinged with courage, because Larry Bird wasn't just the white dude playing the sport. He was the white dude willing to go up against the brothers and make them feel like he was one of them. And when he performed, you had brothers saying, "Damn! He's better than us!" Not only that, but he talks smack like us, he comes at it like us, he challenges us like we challenge him, he doesn't back down, nor is he trying to be different. He's just trying to win.

JOHNSON: We understood some people [saw it as black versus white], but we didn't buy into it.

SMITH: The thing about Magic Johnson that made him even more profound and allowed him to resonate even more than Bird was that smile. Because you saw black folks, whether it be in the '50s and the '60s, suffering. You saw them in the late '60s and early '70s trying to overcome adversity and the lack of recognition as it pertains to their civil rights. If Magic was braggadocio and in-your-face and disrespectful and snubbing his nose at people, if he were Allen Iverson—if he were somebody who came across as rebellious—it never would have worked. You needed Magic to be Magic for America to embrace it.

LARRY BIRD (Small Forward, Boston Celtics; 3-Time NBA MVP): I think the NBA was in a better place after we got here, but I don't think we saved anything. David Stern had a lot to do with the changes when he took over in 1984.

SIMMONS: I think what made Bird and Magic special was how they actually changed how their teammates played. If you look at video from the mid-'80s, Kevin McHale is a black hole on any other basketball team. He's just a guy trying to score in the low post. He became a good passer just from playing with Bird, because the more you play with somebody who's seeing angles and who's unselfish and makes the extra pass, you start doing it. I don't think James Worthy would have been a good passer if he didn't play with Magic.

QUINN BUCKNER (Point Guard, Milwaukee Bucks/Boston Celtics; 1976 Olympic Gold Medalist): Nobody thought Larry Bird could play in the pros, but Red Auerbach drafts him as a junior-eligible. Then Red gets Dennis Johnson—DJ's in the Hall of Fame!—for Rick Robey. Red gets Kevin McHale and Robert Parish in the same trade. One of my old business partners calls it "See the future, be there waiting." Red did that.

BILL WALTON: Red had the ability to create a culture where the players would sacrifice everything for the team. We loved that guy.

BIRD: Red was at every practice, every home game. He'd pull you aside and tell you a few things. He would tell me how Russell did things, how John Havlicek went about his business, so you'd pick up on a lot of stuff.

HUBIE BROWN: Red was so far ahead of everybody. They took for granted what he did with the Bird thing. How many guys would give up a pick like that and take a guy that's not even going to play for a year?

JOHNSON: The Celtics were the smartest team I ever played against because they didn't make mistakes. You had to beat them; they were not going to beat themselves.

NATE "TINY" ARCHIBALD (Point Guard, Boston Celtics; 6-Time NBA All-Star): I didn't have a great feel for Larry until we had some exhibition games. Everybody thinks they have a book on you: guy can't jump, can't run, can't shoot. People are thinking, "Typical white guy." Wrong, y'all, because that's not the guy I'm playing with, OK?

SIMMONS: Bird could go 5 for 22 and be the best guy on the court. Magic could score 2 points, he'd be the best guy on the court.

AHMAD RASHAD: Magic's smile would be something that would trick you. Because Magic was a killer.

JOHNSON: I knew everybody frontward and backward. I knew where Byron Scott was going to be before he even got there. I knew what James Worthy was gonna do before he committed to his move. I knew when Kareem was really ready to play. When he had those goggles on down low and he put that hand up, I'd say, "He's ready. James, you not gonna get shots tonight; you neither, Byron Scott."

RASHAD: There are many guys that got hit in the face with one of Magic's passes. You had to be looking at him at all times, because you were getting stuff when you weren't ready for it.

VECSEY: I remember being in L.A. and somebody on the team did something wrong, and the fast break was going the other way, and Magic stayed behind and was chewing out the guy. I talked to [Lakers Coach Pat] Riley afterwards, and he said, "You can't coach this. It has to be someone on your team saying this."

PARISH: Both Magic and Larry were great leaders. When you think about it, the two teams had great leadership, top to bottom. We had Red, they had Jerry West. We had K. C. Jones, they had Pat Riley.

SIMMONS: Pat Riley got the job 'cause the head coach [Jack McKinney] crashed his bike, and the other guy [Paul Westhead] took over for a year and then decided, "Hey, guys, I'm gonna change the offense. I'm gonna take the ball out of Magic's hands. We're gonna slow it up and just feed Kareem." What? You have Magic Johnson.

GAIL GOODRICH: Pat Riley was an average player. An overachiever, competitive. Did I ever think Pat would be the coach he turned out to be? I don't think anybody did. Pat's strength was he was able to communicate and understand players. And he was tough.

JERRY WEST: Every practice with Pat [when he was a player] was like a war. I said, "Don't guard me today; I'm sore and tired. Go guard Goodrich for a while." He said, "I have to defend the best player," and I said, "Well, I have to score and lead this team." He was so smart and tenacious, and he took that to his coaching career.

RASHAD: Pat Riley is one of the five greatest coaches in any sport, in any era. It's not easy to deal with superstars. Normally, in situations like that, you can't have three-hour practices. You got two stars—Magic and Kareem—that stand up and go, "Hey, we aren't doing it," but instead, they follow the guy and say, "We need three-hour practices." That's a sign of greatness.

JOHNSON: There's two coaches that created small ball—Don Nelson and Pat Riley. Golden State today? That already started with the Lakers. Pat said, "Man, I got all these greyhounds, why don't I use to it to my advantage? I'm going to come up with this one-three-one trap, because I got five guys who can run all over the court." Trap you, get back, help. We used that against the Sixers in the [1980 Finals] and coach [Billy] Cunningham went crazy. We bottled them up so bad.

ARCHIBALD: Our styles were different. They wanted to get out and run. We rolled with the best frontcourt of all time.

BOB RYAN: Kevin McHale retired in 1993 as the best low-post forward the game had ever seen. Kevin set a standard of competence down there, a range of versatility where he could go on the right box, the left box, he could turn to the middle, he could turn to either side, he had the jump hook, he had the up-and-under, he had a fadeaway with some pretty good range. He's still the only person in the league who shot 60 percent from the floor and 80 percent from the line in the same season.

ARCHIBALD: Kevin McHale was 6'11". I don't think Kevin jumped that high, but Kevin would fake guys out so bad in the post. Kevin called it his torture chamber. And then you talk about Robert Parish. Chief didn't get the headlines, but he did whatever we asked.

BIRD: Robert was a guy who didn't care about numbers. He only cared about winning, and his sacrifice allowed us to win even more.

JOHNSON: It's something that you can't describe, being in a Lakers-Celtics rivalry. It's the most intense rivalry I ever been in in my life.

The long-awaited duel between the Celtics and Lakers in the 1984 Finals tilted in L.A.'s favor in Game 1. The Lakers nearly took Game 2 at the Boston Garden as well, but Celtics guard Gerald Henderson picked off an errant James Worthy pass, and Magic Johnson inexplicably dribbled out the clock as time expired.

The Lakers recovered in Game 3 with a 33-point beatdown of Boston, prompting Bird to call his teammates "sissies." In Game 4, the tenor of the series turned when Kevin McHale clotheslined Kurt Rambis on a fast break. Tempers flared as Bird and Abdul-Jabbar had to be separated in that game, and when Worthy missed a critical free throw, Boston forward Cedric Maxwell flashed him the choke sign. Boston prevailed in overtime, 129–125, then went on to win the championship behind Maxwell's 24 points in Game 7. As Maxwell explained afterward, "Before Kevin McHale hit Rambis, the Lakers were running across the street whenever they wanted. Now they stop at the corner, push the button, wait for the light, and look both ways."

RYAN: It was the perfect alignment in '84. You had Bird and Magic as rivals, and Riley with the slicked-back hair. The players didn't like each other, and it really took on a whole other dimension once McHale brought down Rambis in Game 4.

PARISH: When Kevin clotheslined Rambis, that was the turning point. Not only did it ignite our play, it shocked the Lakers.

BIRD: The funny thing is, I don't think Kevin even meant to do it.

PARISH: The Lakers fell apart after that. Magic had a couple of turnovers, and Max [Cedric Maxwell] and M. L. [Carr] started calling him "Tragic Magic."

RYAN: The Celtics basically out-toughed them in 1984, and I maintain Riley said, "I'm never going to get out-toughed again."

BUCKNER: When we won the championship in '84, I was prepared for a night of celebration. I go by Larry's house, and his [now wife] tells me,

"Larry's out running again." Because he was already thinking about next season.

Magic Johnson was trapped, forced to witness Celtics fans celebrating the 1984 championship in the streets of Boston from high above in his hotel room. "Remember this feeling," he told himself as the crowd below taunted, "Fakers!" The next season, the Lakers won 62 games and averaged 118 points. Bird took home his second consecutive league MVP, and Magic and his teammates took aim at the bull's-eye on his back.

In Game 1 at the Boston Garden, famously dubbed the Memorial Day Massacre, the Celtics crushed the Lakers 148–114 by shooting 60 percent from the floor, including a perfect 11 for 11 by reserve Scott Wedman. A sluggish Kareem was held to 12 points and was outhustled by younger adversaries McHale and Parish. The pundits declared the game the death knell for Kareem—and, perhaps, the Lakers.

SIMMONS: The sky hook is the greatest shot in the history of basketball. Nothing's close—most automatic 2 points ever—but it wasn't fun to go see Kareem play. There was a wall between him and the fans, and then he started wearing the goggles, and it literally became a wall. You couldn't connect with him. He seemed like such an angry, sullen guy.

PAT RILEY: Kareem was probably one of the most intelligent, intrinsically motivated players that I've ever been around, and also one of the most controversial and hard to figure out. So I never tried. I just tried to embrace whatever he brought to me, because I knew he was at this level of peace and quiet and tranquility that would enable him to compete and also to get through life.

SIMMONS: All the great black basketball players from the '50s and '60s were damaged in some way. They saw stuff that just wasn't right, and they were treated in ways that weren't right, and none of them really bounced out of it. I think Kareem was really damaged by some of the stuff that happened to him.

WALTON: I had to play my absolute best to have any sort of impact on the game at all against Kareem. His left leg was the power. Most big guys in basketball are two-legged jumpers. Kareem was a one-legged jumper. Kareem was like Scottie Pippen and Dr. J except in a 7-2 body with power and strength and length and range and all the different things that you dream about.

PARISH: Kareem's left leg should be in the Hall of Fame.

WALTON: No one fought harder for offensive position than Kareem Abdul-Jabbar. Kevin McHale was second. No one had better footwork than Kareem. McHale was second. Here was a guy that would get that ball and say, "I'm going to tell you what I'm going to do, right here, right in your face." And there was nothing anyone could do about it.

RILEY: I was worried about Kareem after the Memorial Day Massacre. There are four days between Game 1 and Game 2, and he was getting killed in the media: he was too old, he was too slow, McHale and Parish were kicking his butt, he's embarrassing the Lakers, and he should have quit a long time ago.

PARISH: I actually felt bad for Kareem. We all had games like that. The only reason everyone gave him so much crap was because of his age. I understand athleticism is a perishable skill, but Kareem was long from finished.

RILEY: Kareem was 37 years old, and he had a bad day. For four days, he focused on film and practice and said, "I want you to beat the hell out of me—get me ready." I believe to this day that Game 2 of the 1985 Finals was the most important game in the history of our team. If we would have lost Game 2, we probably would have lost the series.

RASHAD: Before Game 2, Riley lets Kareem's father ride on the bus. Great coach's decision. He was going to get the best out of Kareem for that. If he said no, he would have lost him.

RILEY: Kareem was about to be late. The bus is going to leave at 6, and I don't want to slam the door on him. I'm looking out the window, and I finally see Kareem running. I said, "OK, he's gonna be on time," and then I see another guy running with him. It is his father, "Big Al." Kareem was polite about it. He didn't assume anything. He got on the bus, looked me in the face, and he said, "Can my dad go to the game with me?" I'm thinking all the players in the back of the bus are going, "We've got a rule about this. No outsiders." Well, there's no rules—these are covenants. Rules are tacit agreements, whereby you come to a place with your players about how you're gonna conduct business and how you're gonna get through the season. When he looked at me and said, "I need him; I'd like to have him with me," I said, "Absolutely. Get on the bus."

PARISH: Kareem came out and had a monster game. Old man? Hell no. He played like he was in the peak of his career.

RILEY: Kareem was playing one of the most significant games in his life—for his pride, for who he was as a man. He gets 30 points, 17 rebounds, 8 assists, and we win going away. They stick a microphone in his face and say, "What do you attribute this performance to?" Kareem looked at [them] and said, "Contrary to public opinion, the demise of Kareem Abdul-Jabbar was highly exaggerated."

PARISH: Kareem stole the series from us. After that, you could feel the confidence of the Lakers surging.

RILEY: If we had not won in '85, I would have probably gotten fired, because we won in '82, lost in '83, choked in '84, and '85 was the last year of my contract. I had to win, and my wife, Chris, knew it, too. When we won it in Game 6 at the Boston Garden, I was going into the locker room, and there's only one person I was looking for. . . . I couldn't find her. Champagne all over the place, and [finally] there she was.

———

The most important transaction prior to the 1985–86 season was Boston's acquisition of Bill Walton, the brilliant but oft-injured big man. Walton's first move after landing at Boston's Logan Airport was to drive to Robert Parish's home. "I'm not here to steal your spot," he assured Parish. "I'm just here to help the team."

Boston lost just one home game during the 1985–86 season. The Celtics were poetry in motion, and they eagerly anticipated a Finals rematch with Magic and the Lakers. Instead, to the dismay of fans on both coasts, the Houston Rockets, with their Twin Towers of Hakeem Olajuwon and Ralph Sampson, dispatched the Lakers in the Western Conference Finals.

RICK CARLISLE (Guard, Boston Celtics; Head Coach, Dallas Mavericks): After we lost to the Lakers [in '85], we knew we had to make a move. Max got traded to the [Los Angeles] Clippers for Bill Walton. We got this guy that was the quintessential Boston Celtic—big, smart, highly skilled, great rebounder, great grasp of the game, made others better. The question was his health.

BIRD: When Red asked me about Bill, I said, "Get him if you can." When Bill was healthy, he was incredible. I knew after two days of training camp, if we stayed healthy, nobody was gonna beat us.

CARLISLE: The irony was, in 1985–86 Bill Walton played 80 out of 82 games. We won the championship in six games against the Houston Rockets, and he was the difference maker.

SIMMONS: The best game Bird ever played was Game 6 of the 1986 Finals in Boston. Ralph Sampson had punched Jerry Sichting in the game before. Bird was really mad. Sampson comes out, and the crowd is ready to almost charge the court, they are so angry. Bird missed a lot of open shots, but he's everywhere on the court. He's like a free safety—running around, stealing, deflecting balls. His passing and his force of will [were] incredible. And the best thing was when he smelled blood at the end. He didn't shoot that many threes, but he shot them for effect. And that's what he did in that game.

BIRD: Of course you're happy when you win the championship, but we all wanted the Lakers in the Finals.

Magic Johnson spent the summer of '86 honing his jump shot, sharpening his outlet passes, and refining yet another new wrinkle—the "junior, junior hook," his version of Kareem's most potent scoring weapon.

Before the season, Riley informed his point guard he would be the primary offensive option going forward, not Kareem. Johnson embraced his new role by averaging 23.9 points, 12.2 assists, and 6.3 rebounds, leading the Lakers to 65 wins and picking up his first league MVP award.

The Celtics, who should have been riding high after the 1986 championship, instead mourned the loss of No. 2 overall pick Len Bias, who died of a cocaine overdose the night he was drafted. Walton reinjured his foot and played in only 10 games that season. More injuries plagued Boston during the postseason, with McHale hobbling on a broken foot, Bird struggling with back and elbow injuries, and Parish and Danny Ainge playing on sprained ankles. Yet the Celtics managed to stagger past Detroit to meet the Lakers in the Finals—again. "It's what the people want," Riley noted.

The turning point was Game 4, with the Lakers ahead 2–1 in the series. After Bird drilled a three-pointer, L.A. was down 1 with 7 seconds left at the Garden. Magic drove to the hoop, where Bird, Parish, and McHale all converged on him. He unleashed the junior, junior hook high above the best front line in the game and dropped it through. Bird's final attempt was a spinning jumper from the corner that bounced off the rim as time expired. The Lakers, whose transition basketball was as lethal as it was breathtaking, went on to win the series in six games.

PARISH: Larry was great when the occasion called for him to be great. He was going to step forward—you could count on that. But Magic was the same way.

BIRD: When you've got control of the ball and control of the game and everybody's looking at you and you can't make it happen, for that little bit of time you feel like a failure.

PARISH: I have to say, I have profound respect for what Kevin and Larry endured in the '87 Finals, pain-wise. Neither one took a [cortisone] shot. Either one could have said, "I can't go," but they never did.

BIRD: We'll never know because of the injuries, but I felt that our 1987 team was one of our strongest groups in terms of playing together.

RYAN: The Lakers of that time may have had the best collection of finishers that one team has ever had. James Worthy was phenomenal, a greyhound up and down the floor at 6'9". He could finish, Michael Cooper could finish, and of course Magic was probably as good an end-to-end threat as the game has ever known, taking the ball off the glass and taking it all the way himself.

RASHAD: The Lakers *were* Showtime. It was the best ticket in town, and if you could get in the Forum Club, you were the coolest guy in the city. After games, the players would come through, every starlet in Hollywood would come through, it'd stay open till 2, 3 o'clock in the morning, and it was *the spot*.

JOHNSON: Your competitor can make you better. Larry Bird made me a better basketball player. And I think I made him a better player and a better man. That's what a real rival can do for you. Even when we weren't playing against each other, I was stat watching. "What'd Larry do tonight? He had a triple-double? Oh, I gotta get a triple-double tonight."

BIRD: There's a lot of nights I didn't get any sleep at all, anticipating the next game [against L.A.].

JOHNSON: When you got done playing, you were mentally, physically exhausted. I had to go to sleep for two weeks. We would have the parade, the next day I would go home, kiss my parents, say hello, then I would get on another plane and go to the Bahamas and sleep for a week straight. I wouldn't even leave the room. Just room service, go back to sleep. My body was fatigued, my mind was fatigued. That's what it took to play in a Celtics-Lakers series.

SIMMONS: The '86 Celtics were the best team ever, and they were about to add Len Bias. Then he dies. We don't talk about that one enough. If you removed Scottie Pippen from the Bulls, how many titles do they win? The Celtics had already won 3, and they were adding Len Bias. They really could have won 10.

BIRD: My problem is I always remember the big misses and the bad plays or shots I should have taken that I didn't. I have a tendency to remember the losses more than I do the good times.

PARISH: Even if we were healthy in '87, the Lakers had more firepower. They were just better. We lost Len Bias and Walton. It was my fault. We were playing one-on-one, and Bill broke a finger. After that, he stepped on my foot and aggravated it. If only Bill had stayed healthy. There were days in practice when he just hijacked our scrimmages. Then there were days he could barely move. God has a strange sense of humor.

Incredibly, 1987 was the last time Magic and Bird met in the Finals. Devastating injuries, including bone spurs in both heels and, later, debilitating back problems that would eventually require fusion surgery, cut short Bird's career, forcing him to retire in 1992. He later asserted he should have retired three years earlier. Detroit's "Bad Boys," Isiah Thomas, Dennis Rodman, and Bill Laimbeer, supplanted Boston and assumed the Eastern Conference mantle of physical, bruising play.

The Lakers followed their '87 title with a repeat in '88, and it seemed as though nothing could stop Magic and his Showtime teammates—until November 7, 1991, when Johnson stunned the world by announcing he was HIV positive. That news brought his Hall of Fame career to an abrupt halt and left the NBA reeling.

DAVID STERN: I learned about Magic the night before the announcement. Nothing else dawned on me, honestly, until an owner called and suggested I do some polling. The most recent news involved a young kid named Ryan White in Indiana, who had been barred from going to school because he had become HIV positive as a result of a transfusion because he was a hemophiliac. So America was really gripped by horrendous fear, some would say a panic, and we didn't know what to do with it. But he was Magic, he was one of us, and we were going to stand by him.

WEST: That was probably one of the worst days of my life. I didn't even care about basketball because I cared about Magic so much. I thought, "My God, we have this magnificent player, a really good guy, and we may not have him very long."

RILEY: Magic's HIV diagnosis was one of those "Where were you?" moments. I was in my office at Madison Square Garden [as Knicks coach], preparing for a shootaround, and [agent] Lon Rosen called me and just said, "Pat, Earvin's got HIV." I didn't really know [much] about it, other than it was a death sentence.

JOHNSON: When they told me I had HIV, first, you're stunned, you're in disbelief. Then, after I let that soak in, my first concern was my wife, Cookie, and our baby. She was pregnant with our son, EJ, at that time. You experience a lot of emotions: "Oh, man, I hope she doesn't have it. I hope the baby's gonna be OK. How can I tell her I have HIV?"

RILEY: It was a very sad day because everybody worried about Magic, but it was probably one of the greatest days ever, because of how Earvin approached it. He said, "I'm the one that God gave it to, because I'm the one who can do the most to help people."

JOHNSON: You're thinking basketball will be the toughest thing you had to do—play against Michael [Jordan], Larry. But the toughest thing was to tell my wife I had HIV. We prayed about it, and she said, "I'm gonna stay with you; we're gonna beat this together." And, thank God, the following week we got the good news that she was OK and the baby was OK. Telling my parents was difficult as well. That was the first time I ever heard my father cry.

PARISH: When Magic made the announcement about his HIV diagnosis, you would have thought Larry's mother had passed. That's how hard Larry took it.

BIRD: It was the first time in my life I didn't feel like playing basketball.

STERN: It was going to be quite a journey for the NBA, because we realized this was an existential threat to us. We weren't going to say, "Everyone has to get tested, and anyone who's HIV positive is out of the NBA." That would've been ludicrous. We hired the best doctor—his name was David Rogers—and every night, even though it didn't appear in the press or public, we would meet in the office and ask, "What are we going to do?"

JOHNSON: I never thought I was going to die. I'd have tough days, of course, because at that time they only had one drug, so you're taking 15 pills three times a day, and you have these mood swings. For the first month or two, it was really messing with me. I was throwing up a lot, my head was hurting, but I kept working out. That was the saving grace. I was still going to that basketball court and shooting by myself. My doctors said, "Have you played basketball?" I said, "I haven't." They said, "Man, get out there." I went to the court and started playing again, and I tell you, it was the therapy that I needed.

STERN: When Magic came back and Karl Malone announced he wasn't going to play with Magic, it's, "Oh my God." We had to be armed with information, and we learned that you cannot get AIDS, you cannot contract the HIV virus, by the transmission of sweat. We had infection-control procedures, we knew about the T-cell count and that Magic was down close to zero, and we knew, because we were so experienced in the world, that Magic was going to die, OK? Now, previously, we had David Ho, who was Magic Johnson's doctor, visit with our team docs. Our doctors had grave concerns, because they're awash in blood, and they often get pinpricks and everything else, and so they were on the front lines of contracting HIV. So this had many different components to it.

SIMMONS: A lot of those guys like Karl Malone got crucified after the fact for not wanting to play against Magic, but I can't totally blame them. They were uneducated [about HIV]. I don't think it was a mean-spirited thing. It was more, "Wait a second. What if I get blood on me?"

STERN: Linda Ellerbee did a show on Nickelodeon with Magic dabbing the eye of a young girl who was HIV positive and didn't want to be ostracized from her social group. I daresay that Magic and HIV was one of the largest impacts that we had on a vital issue to our society, where we helped people become a nation of understanders rather than a nation of haters.

JOHNSON: The thing that really helped me was playing in the [1992] All-Star Game. I still gotta thank David Stern for allowing me to play, the fans for voting me in, and Tim Hardaway for letting me start [in his place]. If not, I don't know where I would be right now.

STERN: Magic started in that All-Star Game in Orlando, and he hit the last shot, got the MVP, and I had the opportunity to hug this big, sweaty, HIV-infected African American, which I thought was important in what we were doing.

RILEY: Magic's strength after learning the news—how he presented himself to the public, how he admitted everything and then became an advocate—was incredible. The research and the drugs had come along at the right time, and through exercise and diet and just the attitude that Earvin had, he believed he could beat it. Now it's 20-something years later, and he's healthy and thriving.

BIRD: I'm glad he's doing well, but now I'm stuck with him. First thing everyone still asks me is, "How's Magic?" We're connected forever.

BIRD STEALS THE BALL—AND DETROIT'S TRIP TO THE FINALS

Isiah Thomas surveyed his Detroit teammates celebrating on the famed Boston Garden parquet floor. "We finally got 'em," he exulted.

With 5 seconds left in Game 5 of the 1987 Eastern Conference Finals, Dennis Rodman had just swatted away Larry Bird's shot. Pistons' ball. The Bad Boys were about to take a 3–2 series lead back to Detroit, where they had drubbed the Celtics by an average of nearly 22 points per game.

Thomas had been brilliant, submitting 36 points, 12 rebounds, and 9 assists and scoring the go-ahead jumper just seconds earlier. But in a heartbeat, those numbers were forgotten.

As referee Jess Kersey began the 5-second count to get the ball inbounds, Thomas spotted Bill Laimbeer, who was an excellent free throw shooter, on the baseline. Pistons coach Chuck Daly frantically signaled for a timeout, but Thomas lofted the ball toward his trusted teammate. "If I can get the ball to Laimbeer, he gets to the line, he makes the free throws, and we win," said Thomas.

At that moment, Bird feigned as though he was running up the court. "I was on someone else, but I could see out of the corner of my eye [Laimbeer] was open, so I knew they were going to throw it there," said Bird.

Bird wheeled around and leaped in front of Isiah's floating pass. "I don't know where Larry Bird came from. I don't know where he was lurking," Thomas said. "All I know is when the ball was in the air, it was like, 'Oh shit.'"

Bird grabbed the ball, teetered for a split second, then hit a streaking Dennis Johnson. "He catches it, and I'm thinking, 'He's gonna go out-of-bounds,'" Thomas said. "But he stops almost like he was a ballerina. He's on his toes, and if you look, you'll see the baseline underneath his heels."

DJ expertly finished off the layup—and the Pistons. Boston won the game and the series in an emotional Game 7 back at the Garden.

Following that loss, which included a violent head-to-head collision between teammates Vinnie "the Microwave" Johnson and Adrian Dantley that left Johnson ineffective and Dantley carted off on a stretcher, Rodman claimed Bird won three MVPs because he was white and was "very overrated." Thomas concurred, adding, "Larry Bird is a very, very good basketball player. But if he were black, he'd be just another guy."

The firestorm that ensued was so charged that Bird appeared in an extraordinary press conference alongside Thomas during the Finals to defuse the controversy. But the damage was already done. Thomas, with his dazzling smile, was viewed as calculating and insincere. Add the sneering Laimbeer, the mercurial Rodman, and the bruising Rick Mahorn, and the Bad Boys became the NBA's public enemy number one.

"I think Isiah wanted to be viewed in the same category as Bird and Magic and Michael, and it just wasn't going to happen," said longtime *Boston Globe* columnist Bob Ryan. "He had to get that out of his head before he could calm down and be the player that he should've been."

Thomas takes umbrage with insinuations that Laimbeer was a dirty player who delivered hits after the whistle. "Bill Laimbeer played the way the Celtics played, the 76ers played, the Bucks played," said Thomas. "At that time, physical basketball was the norm, and Laimbeer was getting beat up. Now, did he use his body? Absolutely. Did everyone else use their body? Absolutely.

"I remember playing the Bucks, and Bob Lanier turned around and punched Bill right in the face. So why are you calling Laimbeer a thug? Why were the negative labels attached to our team, but not to the others?"

Detroit finally dispatched the Celtics in the 1988 Eastern Conference Finals, then lost to the Lakers in a series that featured Thomas exploding for 25 third-quarter points on a badly sprained ankle in Game 6.

The Pistons vanquished the Lakers in the 1989 Finals, then won again at the expense of Clyde Drexler and the Portland Trail Blazers in 1990. By then, Detroit was thriving as the men in the black hats.

"When you are discriminated against, and the stereotypes and the labels are heaped upon you, you get to a point where the only way you can fight back is to embrace the stereotype," Thomas said.

The ultimate indignity came when Thomas was pointedly left off the 1992 Dream Team—with Daly as its coach.

The Pistons should be remembered, Thomas says, as the first small-market team to slay the big-market dragons, and who packed upward of 60,000 fans into the Pontiac Silverdome. "We kept crashing the party," Thomas said.

"They like to say the league took off with Magic and Bird," he continued. "OK, that's true. But there was another thing happening in Detroit that made the league take off. The people who were outcasts, the displaced of America, bought into our team because we were very diverse."

THE CITY GAME

No city has left as large an imprint on the history of basketball as New York, and growing up in one of the sport's true hotbeds helped launch the careers of many of the greatest players and coaches of all time.

BOBBY CREMINS: My parents were Irish immigrants. They settled in the South Bronx, and right across the street was a New York City school yard. The rest is history.

MARK JACKSON (Point Guard, New York Knicks/Indiana Pacers; NBA Analyst, ESPN): My family moved from Brooklyn to Queens when I was about 7 years old, and I tried out for a team. My first year, I had 1 point. I scored 1 foul shot the entire year, and I remember it as if it was yesterday. But I fell in love sitting on the sideline, cheering and clapping. I fell in love practicing. I fell in love with dreaming to one day be good. I fell in love knocking that free throw down and looking at my mom and dad jumping up and down. I fell in love watching Earl Monroe with the New York Knicks—the incredible talent that can carry a team as an individual now all of a sudden has to fit into a team concept.

BOB COUSY: I was fabricated in a small farming village in northeastern France, and I was in my mother's stomach when we went through Ellis Island. I was born 6 months later. We lived the first 12 years on 80th [Street] and East End Avenue, right on the East River. And the first 12 years of my life I never saw basketball. It took my father that long to save 500 bucks to get us out to St. Albans [Queens], where the local high school had already won a city championship and every kid in town wanted to make the team. I was thrown into this milieu and became completely consumed with basketball. O'Connell Playground every weekend, every day after school in the school yard, we played three-on-three. When it snowed, you shoveled so you'd have space to shoot.

NANCY LIEBERMAN: I was about 8, throwing out the trash in Far Rockaway, and on the back of the newspapers, it said the New York Knicks beat the Milwaukee Bucks 119–110. I started watching the Knicks, and it was instantaneous—I fell in love with the game.

LENNY WILKENS: In Brooklyn we played all kinds of ball—stickball, handball, stoopball, baseball, box ball, punchball. But I started to go down to the playgrounds and really liked basketball. The two best players would choose teams, and I never got picked in the first group. I would wait for my "next" and pick three guys because we played four-on-four, and when the game started, those guys wouldn't pass me the ball. I got pissed. When I got the ball, I just threw it up, and they started to call me a heaver. I realized I needed to learn [more], but I liked the game because it was competitive, physical, aggressive.

CHARLIE SCOTT: Growing up in Harlem, in poverty, having someone cheer for you is something that I never experienced. Going to the park, especially by yourself, you were in control all the time. Once you hit that basket, [you feel] the imaginary roar of the crowd, the admiration that every individual looks for. I was like the Harlem Globetrotters against the Washington Generals—I never lost.

CHRIS MULLIN (Shooting Guard, Golden State Warriors/Indiana Pacers; 5-Time NBA All-Star): I was 10 or 11 years old when I first fell in love with basketball in Brooklyn. My dad put a basket in the backyard, and I'd be out there for hours. I'd count the clock down, act like I was at the Garden, until I made that last shot. My dad put a light in the back, so I would shoot at night and always try to be better than the day before. If I made 70 out of 100, the next day I wanted to make 75 or 80.

DOLPH SCHAYES: In the Bronx, [basketball] was a school-yard game. We played almost every day. Probably what helped is, the day I was born, I was tall. A group of my friends, we formed a club called the

Amerks, short for Americans, and we would play teams from all over. The churches in the Bronx had tournaments, and we'd enter and win most. We played the pure game—a lot of figure eights, great spacing, we would pass—everything that made basketball such a wonderful sport to play.

CHARLEY ROSEN: I was 13 years old, living in the Bronx on Fulton Avenue. I was walking by the public pool in the middle of winter, and I heard a ball bouncing. I walked in, and there were 10 black guys playing basketball. They had two portable baskets up, and they were in the locker room with all the benches and everything cleared [out]. I was a big, clumsy kid, and they welcomed me with open arms. They played every Saturday and Sunday morning, and it was tough games. If you called a foul, you were a punk. No blood, no foul. There had to be a lot of blood—it had to be an artery—to call a foul. One of the guys was rumored to be an ex-Globetrotter, and he says, "Big as you're gonna be, you're gonna be a player." They encouraged me, supported me. There was such a good feeling there. I said, "Wow, this is a place for me."

ADAM SILVER: My father and I bonded over basketball. I grew up in Rye, New York. My dad moved back to New York City when my parents separated, and I loved the Knicks. I used to take the train into the city, and we would take the subway down to Madison Square Garden. Walking into the Garden—that big cloud of smoke around the JumboTron . . . And my dad, who was a pretty quiet guy, would show an enormous amount of emotion during a Knicks game. I spent as much time watching him as the game.

BILLY DONOVAN (Head Coach, Oklahoma City Thunder): I remember taking the Long Island Rail Road, and Penn Station ran right into Madison Square Garden. Walking up the steps with my buddies, we'd buy a $5 ticket in the rafters and see if we can meander our way close to the court to watch those guys play.

KENNY SMITH: I was the kid that would chase guys down outside of Madison Square Garden for autographs, and my whole closet door was posters and pictures of NBA players. But my first love affair came listening to the radio—Marv Albert. When I was 7, 8 years old, I would cry when the Knicks would lose. When Marv would say, "It's 32 seconds to go and the Knicks are down 9," I would start crying.

DAVID STERN: I came of age in New York City when you could get a ticket at the Garden for 50 cents. My dad and I would walk from the delicatessen on 23rd Street up to the old Garden on 49th, and he'd make some arrangement with an usher that got us closer than we might otherwise have gotten. I was hooked.

MULLIN: That Knicks team—Walt Frazier, Willis Reed, Dave DeBusschere— the way they played had a huge impact on New York basketball. I wanted to be Walt Frazier. He was the coolest guy in town, no doubt about it.

SMITH: Clyde Frazier was my guy—his whole aura. I remember that Sunday paper when they did a spread on him going to the game on the subway in a fur coat. They showed his house—he had this circular bed, mirrors all around, and he had a Rolls-Royce. I was like, "I want to be Clyde."

BERNARD KING: I would pretend I was Dave DeBusschere. I loved rebounding, so he was my favorite player. In high school I wasn't a great scorer, but I averaged 28 rebounds. Other guys would emulate Earl "the Pearl" Monroe with the spin move, Walt Frazier with his quick hands and ability to get to the basket, or Willis Reed with his dominance on the low block. All of us young players tended to emulate the Knicks.

Before Walt Frazier was "Clyde," before Willis Reed hobbled onto the court for Game 7, before Phil Jackson and Bill Bradley, Earl "the Pearl," and the only two championships in the New York Knicks' 72-year history, New York had Madison Square Garden, "The World's Most Famous Arena," and some of the most passionate and knowledgeable basketball fans on the planet. In the late 1960s and early '70s, when New York rosters featured 5 of the NBA's 50 greatest players, the Garden crowd watched the Knicks lift the sport to dazzling heights.

MULLIN: The Garden's got that feel, like you're stepping onstage. And it's New York, so everything you do there gets covered times 10.

ELVIN HAYES: If you play well in New York, you made it. I remember going into the Garden for the first time: I've seen this on television, and now here I am playing against Willis Reed, Walt Frazier, Dave DeBusschere, Bill Bradley, Cazzie Russell, Dave Stallworth, Phil Jackson, Mike Riordan. I know I gotta play well when I go in there, and I light it up. I had 39, 15 or something rebounds. My mind kept flashing back to my backyard, watching these great players, and now I'm one of them.

BOB PETTIT: The arena was smoky and old, but it had 18,000 people there. And it had great basketball fans and wonderful stories. I remember once, I think everybody in the Garden had a bet on the game, and we're playing the Knicks. We're up 6, and a guy on our team makes a basket [at the buzzer] to put us up 8. The place goes crazy—well, the point spread was 7.

BILL BRADLEY: Madison Square Garden is a special place to play, and what makes it that is the audience. It knew the game. It appreciated the nuances: the pass that leads to the pass that leads to the basket; movement without the ball.

MARV ALBERT: There was a guy who played for the Knicks in the '50s, his name was Art Spoelstra. He was on the team because he set very good picks. And you know what's great about Madison Square Garden? They appreciated a good screen. Where else do you see that? They'd be applauding for someone screening.

BILL SIMMONS: I would say the Knicks fans are still probably the best day-to-day game fans.

WALT FRAZIER: New York was instrumental in bringing in the "De-fense" chant. "De-fense" is embedded on the side of our [championship] ring because that was the catalyst for us. Whenever the game was close, the crowd just started instinctively yelling, "De-fense, de-fense, de-fense," and that became a hallmark of New York.

BRADLEY: The crowd probably took us up a level or two. It wasn't that we were doing anything differently, just adrenaline rush. We felt that there was a larger force with us in these moments, on this hardwood floor, under these lights.

MULLIN: When I was a kid, we went to the Garden with a CYO [Catholic Youth Organization] group. I remember sitting up in the blues, looking down at the floor and how shiny it was, wanting to get down there and just touch it, and knowing I never could. You could never get near the floor. It was a sacred place. At that time, the Knicks were everything.

SONNY HILL: If you think about those great Knicks teams, how that ball would be moving, and then the jump shot. Maybe a little dribble, but it was all about movement of ball.

MARK JACKSON: You can't tell me that '69 Knicks team and that '73 Knicks team wasn't a thing of beauty. The way they moved the ball, the way they were united, the way they orchestrated victories, the way they needed each other, the way they followed a great leader in Red Holzman. It's a thing of beauty when done the right way, at its purest form.

The coach who led those New York teams didn't want the job. Red Holzman endured an unsuccessful stint as head coach of the St. Louis Hawks in the 1950s before spending a decade as a scout in the Knicks front office. He neither expected nor desired to return to coaching, but when Dick McGuire was fired in 1967, Holzman, whose "Hit the open man" motto spurred the ball movement that made those Knicks legendary, stepped into the head job, and the rest was history.

PETTIT: Red was a great guy and a really good coach. He had an impossible situation with us in St. Louis. We just didn't have the team, and

Ben Kerner was a volatile owner. If you didn't produce, he got rid of you. He fired Red, and Red went back to the Knicks as a scout.

JERRY COLANGELO: Red Holzman and I traveled together, scouting, until we were in Huntington, West Virginia, at the Marshall Invitational tournament, when the Knicks had really gone bad. As the game is coming to an end, we're going to an airport—Red back to New York, me to Chicago. We're gonna meet in Portland for the Far West Classic a day or two after Christmas. Red said, "I'll see ya there." I said, "I don't think so. You're gonna be coaching the Knicks before the week's out." "Yeah, I'll never do it, blah-blah-blah . . ." As the story goes, I go to Portland; Red's a no-show. I see on TV he'd been named coach, and back in those days, I had to send a telegram to him saying, "Told you so."

BRADLEY: Red knew he was coaching men, not boys. He had three rules: hit the open man on offense, help out on defense, and the hotel bar belongs to Red.

FRAZIER: If you're on the 1st floor, he's on the 10th. He treated you as a man. He goes, "Hey, I'm not gonna put curfews on you. You know why you're here, so if you don't perform, you're gone."

EARL MONROE: Red talks the language. I think his real skill was communication. A lot of times there's a barrier between player, coach, management, but he seemed to melt that barrier. He didn't show you up, he didn't talk about you in the papers, and he was a player himself so he understood being a jock and being in the locker room. He was a guy that you wanted to play for, and his relationship with players, top to bottom, was always very even.

FRAZIER: The main thing about Red, he had respect for the players. He didn't see color; he didn't have favorites. One set of rules. If you played hard, you got in the game.

MONROE: Red would say the things you want to hear that'll make you successful. I remember him coming up to me after the '74 season, and he said, "Earl, you've lost your ego. You know how you used to play against us? That ego you had? In order to be great, get your ego back."

FRAZIER: When I was a rookie, I used to take losing hard. I'd be sitting there, and Holzman would be like, "Come on, Clyde, the sun's gonna come up tomorrow. Gotta go get my scotch now." That's what I liked about Holzman. When things went awry, he's not yelling and screaming. If the coach isn't panicking, then you're going to remain calm.

BRADLEY: He wasn't the coach who masterminded every move or conveyed to the public that he did. He gave broad, general rules that he insisted upon and then gave players flexibility within those rules. We would often come to the bench, and Red wouldn't call plays. *We'd* call plays and look at each other, and Red would say, "Good idea, do that."

Holzman's first season as Knicks head coach gained a few degrees of difficulty and tons more media hype when it was announced that Bill Bradley, the former NCAA national Player of the Year, who had been a sensation at Princeton, would be returning to basketball after a two-year hiatus to pursue a Rhodes scholarship in Europe. Bradley joined the team in December 1967 but struggled to adjust to the NBA.

RICK BARRY: I wanted to be a Knick. I grew up in New Jersey. Nineteen sixty-five, that year, the two worst teams flipped a coin, and the winner got first and fourth, the loser second and third. The Knicks won. They took Bill Bradley knowing that he was going to be a Rhodes scholar and wouldn't be available. The Knicks had a chance to get me and they passed because Ned Irish, the [team president], said I was too skinny and flaky. I never forgot that. I loved to play against the Knicks and had a bunch of 50-point games against them.

BRADLEY: I didn't think I was going to play pro when I went to Oxford. Then I had that epiphany. I played in Italy for a year, we won the European [Champions] Cup, and then I didn't play anymore. That was April

1966. I went about a year without playing, and then one afternoon I went down to the Oxford gym. I was shooting, dribbling, and I began to go through my routine. I was going through all those moves, and I realized that I missed the game. To not play would be to deny a part of myself probably more fundamental than any other.

ROSEN: The Knicks attracted national and even international media attention, and a lot of that had to do with Bill Bradley's presence. He was a Rhodes scholar, Princeton, the son of a rich father who [was president of] a bank.

ALBERT: When [Bradley] first came into the league, the general manager, Eddie Donovan, would have [him]—before he would get into uniform—watch the games. It might have been 10, 12, 15 games. He wanted him to see NBA basketball.

BRADLEY: I didn't join the team until December, and this was a gigantic PR thing. I was going to come in and transform the team. My first game in the Garden, it was a standing ovation. I came in with the crowd applauding every time I touched the ball. I didn't realize I was not quick enough to play guard, and then, four games in, I got hit by a car. On 57th Street—it was raining and I ran across, having looked to see if there were any cars coming. Didn't think I saw one. Here came this little MG, and it leaped up and to the left and landed on my hip. I hobbled down to St. Clare's Hospital, had an X-ray. It wasn't broken, but it sure was sore.

ALBERT: Bradley, when he first came into the league, was out of position. When he was playing as a guard, he was really out of place. The first game was against Detroit, and Eddie Miles had a pretty easy time with him. Bill would get off some jump shots, but he was out of place, and he stayed like that until he was at small forward.

BRADLEY: I came back, and it became pretty clear I was too slow to play guard. I remember Wayne Embry setting picks at half-court, with me trying to keep up on defense and crashing into the brick wall. The crowd realized [it], too, and suddenly it turned on me. You exited the Garden through a ramp with people above you. They would spit on me, throw coins at me, shout everything at me. People would curse me in the street, cabdrivers would say derogatory things, and I realized, "Whoa, this is something I hadn't quite expected." I had to reach deep within myself.

Bradley was not the only Knicks rookie to experience growing pains in the 1967–68 season. Walt Frazier, New York's first pick in the previous off-season's NBA draft, arrived to a team stacked with experienced guards and languished on the bench behind starting point guard Howard Komives. It took two events to transform the Knicks into championship contenders: a December 1968 trade that sent Komives and Walt Bellamy to the Detroit Pistons for power forward Dave DeBusschere, and, one month later, a broken ankle suffered by starting small forward Cazzie Russell. The departure of Komives and Bellamy allowed Frazier to move into the starting lineup and Reed to shift to his natural position at center. Russell's injury opened a frontcourt opportunity for Bradley to move over from the guard spot. In Frazier, Dick Barnett, Bradley, DeBusschere, and Reed, the Knicks had found the starting five that would deliver the franchise's first championship.

FRAZIER: The team was in disarray. I didn't like my teammates, they didn't like each other, nobody played defense, they were very selfish, I was just lost. In the biggest city in the world, I was lost, lonely, and unhappy, and that showed on the court. I thanked God that I had signed a three-year contract, so the Knicks couldn't get rid of me for a while. That gave me time to adjust. I found New York very cold. People didn't have time for you, everybody hustle and bustle. When I'd go home at night, I used to see someone lying on the ground, and I don't know whether they're dead or not, and people are walking all over them. It was a tremendous transition I had to make, coming from Atlanta, then to Southern Illinois [University], then to the largest city in the world. When Wilt Chamberlain [first] spoke to me, I called everybody—my uncle, my mother. I said, "Wilt Chamberlain knows my name!" When I was a rookie, I saw Elgin Baylor walking down the street in New York, and I followed him to his hotel. I was walking in his footsteps, and I was too shy to talk to him.

ALBERT: Clyde's actually a very shy, quiet guy. He was well liked, but he stayed to himself.

FRAZIER: I never thought the Knicks would draft me, because Bill Bradley was coming, they had Cazzie Russell, Dick Barnett, all these backcourt guys. Phil Jackson was the second-round pick. We became like the odd couple—a black guy from Atlanta and a white guy from North Dakota, and now they're both in New York City. Phil was my roommate, and whenever we went to L.A., Chicago, Detroit, we'd just go sightseeing. When we did play, we were in for our defensive prowess. He had the long arms, so when the Knicks fell behind, we'd come in pressing and trapping to get us back into the game.

LARRY PEARLSTEIN: The thing that made this team was the trade for DeBusschere. Dick McGuire had coached Detroit, and Red offered Walt Bellamy for DeBusschere. Detroit also wants Howie Komives. Komives was doing a good job as a defensive player. Red didn't want to give up Komives, but Dick told him to do it.

FRAZIER: We traded the bad seeds. Walt Bellamy, very talented player but a bad example for me as a rookie. He was lazy, didn't like to work on his game. Howard Komives was another—very moody guy. He hated Cazzie, and they would not pass to each other. So we traded those guys and acquired Dave DeBusschere. That was the galvanizing of the team toward winning a championship, and that also catapulted me into a starting position.

BRADLEY: I came back my second year and I was better, but I was still not quite making it. Then Cazzie Russell, who was [a] forward, broke his ankle, and I moved into that position. When Cazzie broke his ankle, we had five players—Barnett, Frazier, DeBusschere, Reed, and me. We played 42 minutes a game for probably 38 games, and by the end of that time we gelled.

FRAZIER: We lost to the Celtics in the playoffs, but we knew we were on par with them, so when we came to training camp the next year, we were talking championship. Lucky for us, Bill Russell retired, so we were like, "This is it; this is our year."

The Knicks began the 1969–70 season on a historic 23-1 tear that remained an NBA record until 2015, when the 73-9 Golden State Warriors broke it. The Knicks' on-court chemistry was impeccable, but behind the scenes, animosity simmered between Russell and Bradley. Their rivalry went back to their college careers, when Bradley was the 1965 national Player of the Year, Russell won the award in 1966, and Russell's University of Michigan Wolverines defeated Bradley and Princeton in the 1965 Final Four. With the Knicks, Russell's injury forced him out of the starting lineup, and he accepted a sixth-man role behind Bradley, but not without some bitterness.

ALBERT: There was a possibility of success. You could feel it prior to '69–'70, once DeBusschere was with the team. And then you got the celebrities coming out—Robert Redford would be at games, Dustin Hoffman. People became interested in the Knicks. They became magazine covers, top stories in newspapers. And then they opened the '69–'70 season at 23-1. When does that ever happen to the New York Knicks?

BRADLEY: I had this competition with Cazzie Russell. He was the forward, I was the guard. He broke his ankle, [then] I moved in [and] we gelled. Next year, I'm in the unit of five and he isn't. Every practice is a war, 'cause he thinks he should start, and I think I should start. There was deep respect, but this tension was always there. I get in cabs and people say, "You bum—Cazz should start." It divided the city.

PHIL JACKSON: So much went into their relationship. They played against each other in a historic [national semifinal] game, and they both had NCAA Player of the Year in successive years, and then they ended up on the same team. It was like, "How did this happen?"

———

There was a racial element to the competition between Bradley and Russell. For years, the media had treated Bradley as basketball's white savior during an era when black athletes were rising to the forefront of the sport. Bradley rejected the notion, but his background—son of a bank president, Rhodes scholar, one of the best basketball players in the world, and white—fed the media's fascination with him. Russell had defeated Bradley twice when they went head-to-head in college, had beaten him out for the starting small forward spot, but now, due to an injury, he found himself back in the shadow of a white player who many believed was less talented than him. The intensity of their competition occasionally boiled over in practice, but thanks to the leadership of Holzman and Reed, the Knicks' team chemistry overcame racial tensions and personal rivalries.

BRADLEY: The crime of racism was imprinted on me. I grew up in Missouri. Our Little League team was integrated, and we'd play in a regional championship and be staying in a fleabag hotel. I'd say, "Why are we in this hotel?" and they'd say, "This is the only place that our African American teammates will be accepted with us." Or we walk into a restaurant, and they wouldn't serve our black catcher and we'd leave. Then, in this odd fate, I was turned into the white hope by the white press. It bothered me, but what was I going to do? I had to simply know my teammates, love my teammates, learn the game, play the game, and that's what I did. I learned more playing with my teammates—the majority of whom are African American—than they ever learned from me. I learned how much I could never know what it means to be black in America. I was white in a black world, and I was reminded about how much I didn't see.

FRAZIER: We had harmony because Red Holzman demanded that. Red was color-blind. That's how he conducted himself, and that's why he had the respect of his team.

BRADLEY: Once, we were playing in Detroit, and Cazzie's late to practice the day before the game. That's an automatic fine in the Holzman world. In the course of practice, there is a white player guarding Cazzie, and they have [a] little tiff. Willis steps in and says, "We'll have none of this," and Cazzie looks at Willis and says, "You Uncle Tom." Willis says, "You do that again, this Uncle Tom is going to whip some ass." I never quite saw Cazzie like that. Later, I discovered that on his way to practice, he was stopped by the police, shaken down. He had the experience of "driving while black." . . . Part of my role was, if a white player came on the team who had the wrong attitude, it was my job to bring him up to how the team was. I'd say, "You can't exist on this team if you even *think* what you just said. So you better change or you're not going to succeed, and not only that—we won't like you."

PHIL JACKSON: Willis was good at defining roles. It was Willis's team, and Willis always deferred, in a way, to give the support that was necessary. [Bradley and Russell] coexisted in a strange way. It created a bit of tension, yet it was still good. It was OK because they both produced, and they both supported each other.

BRADLEY: Flash forward 40 years, and we have a reunion. I walk into the room, there's Cazzie and his wife, and some way or another there is still that tension. I think to myself, "What's going on here?" The next day, we get to the Garden to meet the new Knicks, and Cazzie says, "Bill, could I see you?" And he said, "I'm a Christian preacher now, and I cannot preach my best sermon if there's anything heavy on my heart. So if I said or did anything to you in those years, would you forgive me?" And I said, "Sure. If I ever said or did anything in those years that offended you, would you forgive me?" He said yes, we hugged, and 40 years of tension disappeared. It was one of those beautiful moments, one of the best moments of my life.

FRAZIER: Willis Reed was my idol, man. The professionalism that he showed, how he intermingled with fans—he was the backbone of our team. When I first came to New York, he picked me up at the airport. He's driving this convertible, and he [says], "Hey, Frazier, put your bags in." I hop in the car, he's speeding down the highway, a cop stops him. He started arguing, and coming from the South, I started sliding down in the seat. I remember [thinking], "I can't believe I'm going to watch this guy get shot." But he talked the cop out of the ticket!

SATCH SANDERS: Willis Reed was one of the reasons I spent an awful lot of time on weight machines, trying to work on my body. You're talking about 240 pounds of 6'8" left-hander. The problem I had with Willis was on the boards. He'd bring that body and not go over me, but he would reach and use the other hand to hook around the neck, pull the defender down, and then step in to take the rebound and lay it back up. I was reluctant to do what I had to do against Willis Reed. I told the guys I was not going to be able to get any rebounds, because I'm gonna face Willis. When he would come to the boards, I would face him with the arms up, and he used to complain to the referees, saying, "This isn't football. This is basketball." But that was the only way I could keep him off the boards. I had to take a whipping every time against him.

The '70s Knicks were not just a great team. They played beautiful basketball, featuring lineups where all five players could shoot from long range, drive to the basket, and create shots for teammates with their passing. They were the forerunners of the modern NBA and the versatile skill sets possessed by stars like LeBron James, Kevin Durant, and Anthony Davis. And the Reed-Frazier Knicks remain the yardstick by which great passing teams—from Larry Bird's Boston Celtics to Gregg Popovich's San Antonio Spurs to Stephen Curry's Golden State Warriors—are measured.

LARRY BROWN: I really did coin the phrase "Play the right way." And aside from [Bill] Russell's teams, you look at a team that played the right way, [it was] the Knicks from '70 to '73. Frazier, Monroe, Barnett, DeBusschere, Bradley, Willis Reed, and Coach Holzman. They all had a role, they all sacrificed for one another, and they were just remarkable.

DAVE COWENS: Probably the highlight of my career is playing against those guys, even though we didn't win a championship until 1974, when Reed was hurt and we finally figured them out. Everybody matched up equally—Bradley and [John] Havlicek, [Paul] Silas and DeBusschere, me and Reed, Jo Jo [White] and Frazier. It was like us playing against us, and those are the toughest ones to beat. They were a unique team, more than us, because their bigs had better range than their guards.

When they had [Jerry] Lucas, it was insane. He was out there, easy three-point range. They had so many weapons.

BRADLEY: That was by far the most enjoyable time of playing basketball in my life, and that's where I realized I could give myself to the joy and feel the moment where everything was going to work. Where I had the man slightly the way I wanted him, so I knew that if I motioned my head, Frazier would go backdoor, and it was going to be an easy basket, perfect pass. Lucas and I used to speak the unknown language. We had a play where I had to come off the pick, but I had to make my man think I was going over the pick, so Lucas and I would speak the unknown language. Lucas would say [gibberish] and I would say [gibberish], and the guy guarding me would go, "Huh?" By that time, I was tucked behind the screen and had the shot.

FRAZIER: Dick Barnett was nine years older than me, and I admired him. Definitely underrated. He's the last guy you're going to mention, but he was an integral part. Bradley gave us perpetual motion. Barnett gave us a guy with the lethal shot. You couldn't double me and leave him open.

BRADLEY: We had a play—it's not really a play. It was a dialogue between Frazier and me. I'd be on the side, he'd throw the ball to me and start walking toward me, and I'd move down. That's where I would see an opening for a backdoor play, and he would suddenly make the cut, and I would drop the bounce pass. He'd take it and make the basket. That makes it all worthwhile. In the kaleidoscope of the game, there were those moments where I could see what was happening on the floor before it actually happened.

GAIL GOODRICH: Very rarely did you see forwards with the ability to create at that time. Bradley and DeBusschere presented some really tough matchups. The ability to pass and move was the whole concept, and at the forward positions, you couldn't match that kind of movement and ball penetration.

ALBERT: Bradley was with the perfect team. You'd see Bradley running and running. I don't know how many miles he did a game, but that puts pressure on the defense. He's running baseline, he's running to get screens. Bill would find picks and get the jumper off, but it was because of running.

BRADLEY: Moving without the ball is not some great skill; it's something you learn. You have to be able to see when the opening comes to take the shot or make the pass. I did that, but it wasn't some signature thing. Havlicek did it. We would run each other constantly. If there was someone bigger or slower than I was, I would just run 'em. There were a couple times where—I won't mention who—said, "Hey, Bill, don't run so much; take it easy." Of course, that told me to run some more.

JOHN HAVLICEK: Bradley and I had the same type of game. We knew what each other was trying to do, and he was a good competitor and a clean player.

FRAZIER: Havlicek—I never saw the guy get tired. He could run all day.

ALBERT: When I was young, doing radio at courtside, I would see the Knicks take the floor, and Bradley had excellent eyes. When he'd come out for warm-ups, he'd always check both baskets, and he could tell if it was infinitesimally off. And he would go over to the official and say, "The basket to my left, it's off a little." They'd measure, and he was always right. His best bit of gamesmanship was he always wanted to get a feel of the game ball. And he could tell that it was either too deflated or too inflated. Sometimes the officials would not pay attention to him, and he'd get ahold of the game ball and take a little pin out of his jersey, and according to what he felt would be right, he would either put air in or take air out. Sometimes they'd huddle around him so the officials would not see.

BRADLEY: That was a subtle felony—falling when you're not really hit, using your hands to hold, bumping at the right time, understanding how to hit the elbow of the guy shooting where people don't see. I always thought those were fine because the referees were there to call the fouls. If they caught it, great. If they didn't, move on. So I like a softer ball.

Before every game, usually home games, I would ask to see the ball from the referee. He'd throw me the ball, and the trainer would have a little pin, and if I thought it was too hard, I'd take it over, [deflate it], and throw it back to the referee. They never knew.

These days, the championship Knicks teams are remembered for the beauty and elegance of their offense. But it's unlikely they would have delivered any titles to New York without an elite defense, anchored by the inside play of DeBusschere and Reed and fronted by Frazier, one of the best defensive guards in NBA history.

ALBERT: Clyde had this cool style on the court. If he were knocked down, he would take his time getting up, even if someone knocked him down overaggressively.

FRAZIER: I had a poker face. I found that if I'm guarding guys—like if I'm guarding the Pearl and he's slapping my hand away, then I got him. If he's doing that, then he's not thinking about scoring, he's not thinking about penetrating. If I don't show any emotion, then the guy doesn't know what I'm thinking. The game is on the line, and I'm looking like the game just started. Then everybody is panicking, and I come up with the key steal or I make the key basket to win the game, and I just run off the court. No hoopla or pageantry, and I'd never really sweat. I never perspired like that, so people were like, "This guy doesn't even sweat!"

ALBERT: He's noted for being a terrific defensive player, and he was, but he had help. They were an excellent help-defense team with Willis and DeBusschere back there, and Barnett was an underrated defensive player, so [Clyde] could take chances.

FRAZIER: Basketball's like life. Everything has a rhythm, so players, when they're dribbling, they have a cadence. I mastered the cadence of dribble, getting into the passing lane, guys not protecting the ball with their body. I was the first to [be known for] taking the ball from a guy while he was dribbling. They weren't used to seeing a professional player get stripped like that.

SIMMONS: There's nothing scarier than dribbling up court against some-body who can do that. It is the single most terrifying thing, when you're dribbling and you're like, "Oh God, that's the guy."

FRAZIER: When I played, my guy rarely brought the ball up. They'd pass it to somebody else, run plays on the opposite side of the court from me, 'cause they know I have the ability to steal the ball. I was blessed with quick hands and anticipation. You don't have to be a high jumper, a fast player. The main thing is pride, not wanting to allow people to score on you. When Earl [Monroe], Oscar Robertson, Jerry [West], [Pete] Maravich, came to New York, the team was looking at Clyde to hold these guys down. That was my pride, trying to contain these guys.

ALBERT: He would not go for steals early in the game. He'd set players up and wait for critical moments, and many of his big steals came in the fourth quarter, where it was least suspected.

FRAZIER: Early in the game, I could make a steal, but it wouldn't have the impact that it does late. So I wait. Now he's comfortable. He's been doing it the entire game. He sees nothing wrong with it. I steal the ball, go down and score, and now the crowd becomes in a frenzy. Many of my steals came that way, unless [opponents] were blatantly ignoring me and making such a stupid pass that I had to steal the ball. . . . I used to make a lot of steals [when] guys start looking for the 24-second clock, which used to be [on the floor] in the corners. The other thing—in those days the basketball courts were old. I knew every dead spot in Madison Square Garden, so when you're dribbling, I'd force you into a certain area where I know the ball is not coming up. Savvy plays a big part. A lot of times, after I make a steal and a basket, the guy I stole the ball from takes it out-of-bounds, and I know he's distraught and he'll make a stupid pass. So I'll make another steal and score because his focus is gone. Some guys, especially big guys, they get a rebound, they don't look, they just pass it out. I'd call their name, and they'd throw the ball to me. I always capitalize on their folly.

After finishing the regular season 60-22 and defeating the Baltimore Bullets and Milwaukee Bucks in the Eastern Division playoffs, the Knicks faced the Los Angeles Lakers, with Wilt Chamberlain, Jerry West, and Elgin Baylor, in the 1970 NBA Finals. The series remains a fixture in NBA lore, largely thanks to the severe ankle sprain Reed suffered in the first half of Game 5. Even though New York rallied to win the game and take a 3–2 series advantage, the Knicks had lost their only player capable of matching up with Chamberlain, and the Lakers appeared to be on their way to a championship. Then, minutes before Game 7, while the Knicks warmed up on the Garden floor, Reed hobbled onto the court, in uniform. He started the game, drilling two jumpers and giving the Knicks an emotional lift that propelled New York to its first NBA title.

ALBERT: I still had in my head the idea that something's gonna happen. Something did! That was the Willis Reed injury in Game 5.

BRADLEY: We were playing the fifth game of the '70 Finals against Los Angeles, and Willis was injured. We had to devise a zone offense at halftime. I talk about how the game is a matter of selflessness and imagination and discipline, and those are all present in that locker room at that moment. We had to imagine a whole new offense, we had to have the discipline to go out there and execute it, and it had to be totally selfless to work. And it worked! The shot from the top of the key that put us up for the first time since Willis went down, that's etched in my mind.

ALBERT: Game 5, Willis got hurt and did not play the whole game. Game 6, Willis sat out. Game 7, the capper, all you hear about is Willis playing hurt, but Clyde had one of the great games in the history of playoff basketball.

FRAZIER: We were all concerned about Willis, whether he would play. We were just hoping he could give us 10 minutes, 5 minutes, whatever, to catapult the team. When we left the locker room, no one knew what Willis would do. We were as flabbergasted as everybody else when he came onto the floor. I'll never forget, three of the greatest to ever play—Chamberlain, Baylor, West—they were mesmerized. They stopped what they were doing. They were standing there, staring at Willis, and for some strange reason, I said to myself, "We got these guys."

JERRY WEST: We played the worst game I've ever seen a team play. That's the first time I walked out saying to myself, "How can I have been so bad? How could Wilt have been so bad?" We had an advantage, and we screwed it up.

FRAZIER: I had a favorite steal in that game. Jerry West was coming up the court and I was going the other way, and I don't know how, but I reached my hand in there and stole the ball.

GOODRICH: In '70, I was in Phoenix. I watched that game. I was not with the Lakers. Willis comes on and hits the basket, but Frazier was phenomenal. I think that was one of the reasons the Lakers traded for me [the next season]. Jerry was the off guard, and they didn't have anybody to bring the ball up against Frazier.

ALBERT: Clyde was not afraid of the moment. He made big plays, clutch shots.

FRAZIER: I like pressure. When the game is on the line, I'm percolating inside. The fans are yelling and chanting, and you feel omnipotent. Game 7, when Willis limped onto the court, I had the greatest game of my career: 36 points, 19 assists, 7 rebounds, 4 steals. I felt I could do anything in front of the roar of the crowd that night. I still get goose bumps talking about it. That was the Knicks' first championship.

New York, one of the country's oldest and most fertile basketball cities, had finally won an NBA championship, but the 1970 Knicks were also beloved for what they meant to the city and how they reflected it. There was Reed's understated leadership, Jackson's embrace of the late-'60s counterculture, and Bradley's professorial nature. But most of all, the city embraced Frazier's cool—the loud suits, flashy hats, and custom Rolls-Royce that screamed New York swagger.

COUSY: As a general statement, if you're in any league—bocce or basketball or whatever—you want your New York franchise to be successful. And certainly basketball. If the Knicks are competitive, that helps everyone.

FRAZIER: I wasn't cognizant of the impact I had on New York City. I didn't know the Knicks had been a doormat for so long, they'd never had a guard like myself, so I was naïve about what I was doing.

ALBERT: What did Walt Frazier mean to New York City? He was part of the cultural phenomenon of the Knicks. The whole *Bonnie and Clyde* aspect, with the popularity of that movie, somehow rang a bell to Walt, and he became Clyde. He would dress in these outlandish outfits, [and] teammates started to call him Clyde.

FRAZIER: I'm known for my sartorial splendor—that's how I became Clyde. When I go to a tailor or a fabric store, I tell them to show me something they think nobody will wear. That's what I'm looking for. I don't smoke, I don't drink, I don't gamble. My only vice has always been clothes. Whenever you see me, I'm dressed, because when I was growing up and I went downtown, I was not only representing my family, I was representing my race. That was drilled into me by my parents, my coaches, and everybody: "When you're out, you gotta show your best behaviors, you gotta look your best." That's something I'm still cognizant of. Whatever I do, I'm black, so I'm representing black people.

NELSON GEORGE: Frazier always says that basketball players look good in clothes because they're tall and lean and naturally models. The idea of the basketball player as a style icon, Clyde absolutely created that.

FRAZIER: I dreamed of being a star, but not in the world's greatest city, and when it happened, I just couldn't believe it. I could go East Side,

West Side, all over town. In the prime of my life—24, 25 years old, a champion, going out, dressing up, partying, going to Studio 54, a lot of attractive women around, driving a Rolls-Royce. I never dreamed that part. I never even liked the Rolls-Royce because they were black or gray, insipid colors. But then I met a guy at the shop, and he goes, "You can paint it any color you want." So my Rolls-Royce was antelope and burgundy. The hood, the top, and the trunk were antelope, and the sides were a bright burgundy. But something was still missing, so I put the gangster whitewalls on it. *Now, that's a Clydemobile!* I had the "WCF" plates—it was a fixture of the city. On weekends I used to get so many tickets 'cause I'd park on meters and just get out of the car. I was the first guy to have a sneaker named after him, the Puma Clyde.

MIKE VACCARO: I remember as a kid wanting to get Puma Clydes. In fact, I still have my Puma Clydes. In New York, that was a status thing.

MULLIN: I wore his sneakers, the low-top blue Pumas. He was the best player in New York at that time.

SILVER: We all loved Clyde, even in the suburbs. I wore Puma Clydes. It was a love of the Knicks. That was my team, no doubt about it.

After the 1970 championship, the Knicks remained in title contention, losing to the Baltimore Bullets in seven games in the 1971 Eastern Division Finals and the Lakers in the 1972 NBA Finals. Two trades reshaped the Knicks at the beginning of the 1971–72 season: they acquired Earl Monroe from their Eastern Division rivals, the Bullets, and center Jerry Lucas from the San Francisco Warriors. While many expected Monroe to clash with Frazier in the Knicks' "Rolls-Royce backcourt," the guards' games blended harmoniously, and together they led the team to a second NBA championship in 1973.

CALVIN MURPHY: I'll tell you about Earl "the Pearl" Monroe. We called him "Black Magic." He had all kinds of names. Playing against him the first time, I told him, "Earl, I don't care about you getting 50, but if you start dancing on me, I'm gonna bite you. I'm not playing. My momma's up in them stands." The spin was the beginning of showtime on the court.

FRAZIER: When you play with Earl, you don't want him to score on you, 'cause he does it with flair. Whereas Jerry West is just gonna hit the jumper, Earl is gonna put this little extra thing into it that pisses you off.

JULIUS ERVING: When you saw Earl play and the way things flowed from him, there was a Globetrotter aspect to it. But this wasn't a Globetrotter playing the Generals, this was the best players in the world and the best league in the world. Earl was a showman—efficient, effective, smart as can be.

BILL WALTON: When we were in college, we would be in our dorm room watching Earl Monroe do things that nobody had seen before. His sense of balance, his sense of flow, his sense of being the pinball wizard out there—coming up the court, seeing something, and being able to spin right through it.

ALBERT: Earl Monroe was magnificent as a Baltimore Bullet—really something the NBA had not seen, with spinning moves, wild dashes to the basket, and pizzazz.

BOB RYAN: Earl was about spins, change of direction, stop-and-starts, and *spins*. But coming out of it, shooting with perfect balance. That was amazing—the beautiful shot coming out of that spin.

FRAZIER: Earl perfected the spin—spinning and winning. He captivated everybody with that move. Only way you stop it is keep him in front, because he's like a top. You gotta stay right behind him so he can't spin. Nobody has ever really mastered the way Earl the Pearl did it, 'cause of his footwork. He was a maestro with that move. And he could be coming full speed down the court and still pull that move off. That's devastating.

MURPHY: When he made that spin, he carried the ball. He carried it past you, over you, around you. I'm saying it was illegal 'cause he went around me 100 times with that move.

MONROE: The spin was instinctive. I would juke you, then place my right foot between your feet, and then spin with that right hand like everyone else would, but then I would push the ball with my right hand. That way, I'm head and shoulders past you when I come out of the spin, so the only way you can stop me is if you put your arm out, and if you put your arm out, then that's a foul. I could juke you and go right, or I could come down and juke you and then spin. The main thing was leaving you in the middle as I'm going by.

PETER VECSEY: One of the most underrated [rivalries was] the Bullets and Knicks. The matchups were unbelievable.

FRAZIER: Earl the Pearl was my nemesis. This guy, he didn't know what he was going to do [with the ball], so how could I know when I'm trying to guard him?

MONROE: In Baltimore, we regarded the Knicks as an Antichrist.

ALBERT: What were the challenges of Earl Monroe coming from the Baltimore Bullets to New York? The Knicks players themselves were apprehensive. He was known as a shooter and a scorer, and here's Earl Monroe joining Walt Frazier in the backcourt.

FRAZIER: When Earl came, I was upset. We needed a center. Willis had been injured for a couple years. People were saying that we'd never work together, we'd need two basketballs, get rid of Frazier.

MONROE: I was apprehensive coming in, but when I had my meeting with [Holzman], his remark was, "I'm glad you're here, and I know we won't have any letdowns." That was refreshing.

ALBERT: The feeling on the Knicks was that Earl was a mystery man. They thought they were gonna get someone with entourages and all kinds of requests. They had no idea what to expect.

BRADLEY: The press talked about there won't be enough balls for Earl Monroe and Walt Frazier to play together. Never once was this an issue. Earl came to the Knicks, we played a certain way, and he played within the structure. And there were moments when he became magic. I remember a game against Milwaukee when Kareem [Abdul-Jabbar] and Oscar [Robertson] were with the team. We were 19 back with 6 minutes to go, and people started leaving the Garden. Then Earl took over, and we won.

PHIL JACKSON: He moved to the side, but there were times when he stood up and said, "OK, it's my turn." And Clyde was able to say, "You're right."

FRAZIER: I really didn't change—Earl did. To his credit, he became a team player. When he was with the Bullets, they wanted him to shoot 30 times a game. He didn't have to worry about defense. Coming to the Knicks, it was different. He had to move the ball more, play defense, and he did that.

ERVING: [Monroe] could score 40, 50, or 60, but he made that ultimate sacrifice when he goes to the Knicks. He's like, "Now I'm playing a team game, and we don't need a guy to score 30 points every night."

MONROE: As I come into New York after four years in Baltimore, it was easier to give that up than it would have been as a rookie. Coming into the league, it's all about proving yourself. Once you feel you've proven yourself, then you can give back.

BRADLEY: Earl demonstrated that he was a true team player. He and Clyde worked well in the backcourt. There was never any friction, never any looks, nothing. I don't even know which one of them averaged the most points. I don't think anybody looked at that. As a teammate, he was a wonderful human being, always upbeat and positive.

FRAZIER: Actually, when he came to the team, I had my best year. I averaged 25 points, and everybody said it was because Earl the Pearl came and psyched me up. But I watched him in practice—how he moved his feet, how he always seemed to have one more dribble, one more move. I copied that, and it worked for my game.

ALBERT: [Monroe] comes to New York and he [and] Clyde end up deferring to one another. The players really started to like him, because Earl was a good passer, and the Garden crowd was thrilled by his moves. On behalf of Walt Frazier, I must say how well he received it. They are good friends to this day, and a lot of people did not think that that would happen.

After their careers, the '70s Knicks went their separate ways. Bradley entered politics and represented New Jersey in the U.S. Senate for 18 years before running for president in 2000. Frazier became the beloved, loquacious color commentator for the Knicks, all the time preserving his flamboyant fashion sense. Jackson won 11 more NBA championships as coach of the Chicago Bulls and Los Angeles Lakers. Reed spent another two decades in the league as an executive with the New Jersey Nets and New Orleans Hornets. But no matter where life after basketball took the members of the 1970 and '73 champion New York Knicks, they carried the bonds they formed with them.

FRAZIER: I'm often asked the difference between the two teams, '70 and '73. In '70, we personified *team*. You can't mention Frazier without Bradley, without DeBusschere, without Reed, without Barnett. The '73 team was more talented. We had Earl the Pearl, Jerry Lucas, Dean "the Dream" [Meminger].

MONROE: To be a champion in New York makes you an icon. People saw you in the street and on the subway. We were a part of the fabric of New York, and that made us live on, generation to generation. Even the guys that weren't so-called stars are still remembered fondly. Dean Meminger, rest his soul, was a New Yorker, and people remember him for the role he [played] and the great Game [7] he had in Boston [in the 1973 Eastern Conference Finals] to take us to the championship. Henry Bibby, Harthorne Wingo—people remember those guys. Not to mention Dick Barnett, Jerry Lucas, Bill Bradley, Dave DeBusschere, Walt and Willis, and so forth.

ROSEN: Bill and Phil read books, Dave DeBusschere drank beer and hung out in the bar, and Clyde was Mr. Slick with his Rolls-Royce and the beautiful women. His women used to come in about midway through the game, and players on the opposing teams used to go, "Wow, look at Clyde's babes." He *was* New York, the height of wealth [and] sophistication. Red Holzman dressed schlumpy. He didn't have tailor-made suits, and he was kind of gruff. He was a New Yorker, no pretense about him, and Knicks fans were hungry. All these things just clicked, and the way they played was so irresistible.

ALBERT: On the court, it was chemistry. The perfect mix of players.

FRAZIER: Basketball 100 years from now will still be about passing, dribbling, shooting, teamwork, defense. Look at the [2014] Spurs—they played like the old Knicks. It never changes.

RYAN: Imagine the vintage Knicks with the three-point shot. Imagine DeBusschere and Bradley—and *Lucas*! Lucas would've been a devastating three-point shooter.

BRADLEY: To this day, we feel close as a family. Our lives have gone different ways, but those moments when we went to the top together bond us in a way that doesn't happen in a political campaign. A campaign is simply winning an election, but when you win a championship, it's unquestioned. Most of life is gray—this is black-and-white. You've won it, and the chills are going up and down your spine, your fists are flowing in the air. You have a smile that aches, and you realize you're the best in the world. It lasts about 48 hours, then you go and do it all again.

FRAZIER: My relationship with Phil [Jackson] is terrific, like my relationship with Bill Bradley. These guys never change, no matter what their status. If I was in Washington and I called Bill, he'd tell me to come on in. I get to his office, there are 20 people waiting to see him, and I walk right in. Then I was just sitting there, talking for hours, and the secretary is calling him every 10 minutes. Same thing with Phil when he was coaching. I could walk right in the locker room when he was with the Bulls or the Lakers. I call him "Action Jackson" 'cause on the court he was all elbows and making things happen. He's got 11 rings, and he's still the same guy.

BRADLEY: It wasn't until I was a Knick that I was aware of the complete joy of the game.

PAT VS. GENO: Icons Divided

When she wasn't tending to crops or milking cows on her family farm in Clarksville, Tennessee, Patricia Sue Head was honing her basketball skills by trading elbows with her three older brothers on the makeshift court her father constructed in a hayloft. When it came to basketball, she was primarily self-taught; there were no female coaching networks to connect her to notable peers such as Jody Conradt at the University of Texas or Billie Moore at UCLA (and earlier Cal State Fullerton).

Head (later Summitt, after her marriage in 1980) was just 22 years old when she accepted the head coaching job at the University of Tennessee in 1974. The job, which paid $250 a month, also entailed driving the team van and washing her players' uniforms. At Tennessee, she accomplished the unthinkable: transforming a male-dominated Southern football school into a women's basketball powerhouse. The success of the Lady Vols was unprecedented, with routine sellouts amid national fanfare. Summitt's iconic status prompted leaders from all walks of life to seek her counsel, from Air Force generals to championship football coaches. She won 1,098 games and 8 championships, but like her trusted friend John Wooden, Summitt waited an excruciating 12 seasons before she raised her first championship trophy. From there, she emerged as the face of women's basketball, the most endearing and admired figure in the game.

SALLY JENKINS (Coauthor, *Sum It Up*; Columnist, *Washington Post*): Normally, transformational figures in sports tend to be athletes—like Billie Jean King or Muhammad Ali. Oddly, the single most dynamic figure in women's basketball for 30 years was a coach.

NANCY LIEBERMAN: Pat Summitt was amazing not only for her courage but what she stood for. She was rooted in integrity. And she was gonna push you.

JENKINS: Off the court, Pat was a gracious, mild, nonconfrontational Southern lady with impeccable manners. On the court, she was a colossus, a complete monster whose personality seemed to be breaking every barrier.

TAMIKA CATCHINGS (Small Forward, University of Tennessee Lady Vols; 2011 WNBA MVP): Those two sides of Pat weren't an act. She was the most genuine and authentic person there was.

KARA LAWSON (Guard, University of Tennessee Lady Vols; 2007 WNBA All-Star): The SEC and Tennessee love women's basketball because of Pat Summitt. She changed an entire region of the country.

JENKINS: I remember asking Pat in 1996, "Are you a feminist?" She said, "No. I'm not a sign carrier. I'm not a yeller. That's not my style." This was sort of bugging me. So what is Pat? After several weeks of hanging around, I told her, "I know what you are. You're a subversive."

ANN MEYERS: The impact she made in young people's lives as a teacher and a mentor was remarkable—even for young *men* at Tennessee.

CATCHINGS: She's building this powerhouse out of nothing in the South . . . and that's where her grit and tenacity come into play. She decided, "If I'm gonna be here, I'm going to make this the best program ever."

JENKINS: People forget what she had to put up with. Guys screaming "Bitch!" from the stands. Guys who are supposed to be Tennessee fans yelling, "Go back to the kitchen!" I was walking with her on campus a couple of days after she won her fifth championship. This Southern administrator said with a smirk, "Did you win?" When he walked away, I said, "What was that about?" and Pat answered, "That's his way of telling me, 'I don't think what your team just accomplished is worth knowing.'"

LAWSON: When she walked into our living room for my home visit, it was different from all the other coaches.

JENKINS: There are a handful of people who can walk into a room and be the single most electric personality. And on top of it, Pat had real substance.

LAWSON: I was a freshman, and one of the early drills we did was one-on-one full court. Semeka Randall, who was a wonderful player, was guarding me. I come down and take a three because I'm a good three-point shooter, and I'm thinking I'm probably not gonna have a great shot at getting by Randall. I shoot an air ball. And you could hear a pin drop in the gym. There was awkward silence, and then Pat just went off on me. I remember thinking, "Welcome to Tennessee."

MICHELLE MARCINIAK (Point Guard, University of Tennessee Lady Vols; 1996 NCAA Champion): There was always this little part of you that thinks, "Maybe she won't yell at me. Maybe if I work really hard . . ." But then you mess up and you get The Stare.

LAWSON: I might have set the program record for getting The Stare. Her stare is so powerful you can feel it without even seeing it.

CATCHINGS: The Stare is so much worse than actually getting yelled at.

MARCINIAK: She only used it when she needed to make a strong point. She wasn't doing it to get attention. She did it because she genuinely felt, "You need to listen to me right now."

JENKINS: For many years, Pat was always the bridesmaid. It took her a long time to figure out what she was doing wrong. After she coached the U.S. team to gold in the Olympics in 1984, her own father told her to retire and have a baby. She had a lot of self-doubt whether she was good enough.

MEYERS: In the early days, that tenacity and aggressiveness she had as a player? She brought it as a coach. There were stories about them losing and flying home with players still in their uniforms at three in the morning. There were practices where kids were throwing up in trash cans. But as Pat grew, I think she had more patience. She never lost the intensity, but she became softer.

JENKINS: She knew she overworked some of those early teams because she wanted it so bad. She thought more was more. She realized later that less is more. And then she started to win championships.

Luigi "Geno" Auriemma immigrated to Norristown, Pennsylvania, from Montella, Italy, when he was 6 years old, perfecting his English by reading the back of cereal boxes. He was a backup point guard for his high school basketball team, in part because he wasn't diligent enough about working on his game, a shortcoming Auriemma later shared with his Connecticut players when they asked why he drove them so hard.

When he took the UConn job in 1985, the basketball court was located in the middle of a track in the field house frequented by students, faculty members, and hurdlers. When they weren't dodging track athletes, the players maneuvered around buckets carefully placed by assistant coach Chris Dailey to mark the puddles from a leaky roof.

Connecticut's record in the three seasons before Auriemma arrived was an aggregate 27-56, including a woeful 4-28 in the Big East. Within 6 seasons, Auriemma led the Huskies to the Final Four.

CATHY RUSH: I was running a girls' basketball camp in the Poconos. My camp director, Phil Martelli, had a friend named Geno Auriemma. We're in the office, and Virginia coach Debbie Ryan calls Phil and says, "I have this assistant's position. It's going to pay $10,000 to coach the women." Phil says, "I really want to coach men." In that instant, Geno walks in. He's in short shorts, an Italian T-shirt, high socks with three stripes. He had been teaching basketball outside all summer. He's got these beautiful blue eyes and this brown hair that's getting a little bit of blond streaks in it, and Phil, in typical Philadelphia fashion, goes, "Yo, Geno, you wanna coach at the University of Virginia?" And Geno says, "I don't know, let me call [my wife] Kathy." He ends up going to Virginia for $10,000. And, as they say, the rest is history.

GENO AURIEMMA (Head Coach, University of Connecticut Huskies): I remember playing Tennessee while I was an assistant at Virginia and getting a technical foul because I was ripping the officials at halftime. It was such a big thing to beat Tennessee, and—people probably say the same thing about us now—you know you're going to get screwed. The place is packed, and you're not getting any calls. Debbie Ryan goes down to the locker room, and I go at the refs. Pat had come out to do the exact same thing, only I got there first. I'm killing these guys, and she's just nodding her head. The guy hits me with a T, she just turns around, walks away. I'm like, "Damn, I'm in big trouble." We come out for the second half, and they're shooting free throws. Debbie looks at me, and I go, "I forgot to tell you I got a T." That was my first encounter with Tennessee, and I thought, "It's different playing these guys. You have to beat who they are on the floor, and you've got to beat what they stand for, and you've got to beat all that tradition."

LAWSON: Tennessee basketball was a circus. When Pat walked out to the bus, it was like being with the Beatles or Elvis. You never knew who would show up in the locker room. You'd come back from warming up, and Hillary Clinton might be in there.

JENKINS: Pat says she's coming to Washington for a speaking engagement, so we meet for dinner. I ask her, "Who did you speak to today?" She says, "The CIA."

AURIEMMA: When I applied for the job at Connecticut, there was nothing. But I didn't care. I never asked, "Where do you guys play your games?" And they never showed me, because they didn't want to have to show me. I didn't even say, "Do you guys have a locker room?" They were happy I didn't ask, because they didn't have one.

DIANA TAURASI: I hated practice at UConn. I'd be nervous the whole day. Especially when I was a freshman and I was still trying to prove myself. Svetlana [Abrosimova] and Shea Ralph were in front of me. If you follow basketball, you know they're two of the best ever to play. They would kick my ass left and right. I couldn't cross half-court dribbling the ball.

It was almost embarrassing how little confidence I had. But it's all a big plan. Coach breaks you down, breaks you down, and then when March comes, he brings out the sword and crowns you, and you're ready to go. And then March Madness is kind of easy.

REBECCA LOBO: It's very difficult to play for him early on, when you don't understand yet why he is constantly yelling at you. Nothing you can do is good enough. He doesn't let anything slip, especially if you're a player he thinks can be special.

TAURASI: We can go 22-0, and you don't feel good. We watch film, we've just beaten Virginia Tech by 40, and it's, "You missed that block-out." Or "Diana, you can't keep anyone in front of you." I'm like, "C'mon, it's just one play." But to Coach, one play is everything.

LOBO: Women's basketball wouldn't be where it is without the relationship between Coach Auriemma and Coach Summitt. It was fascinating. What he said, what she said, it was all great drama, and the games played after the drama were even better than the buildup.

LAWSON: There might not be two people on the planet who pushed each other's buttons better than Pat and Geno.

CHERYL MILLER: You got two great coaches who, depending on which way the wind was blowing, liked each other, didn't like each other.

AURIEMMA: It was a perfect storm, the way [the rivalry] evolved. ESPN was saying, "We would like you to play in a game on Martin Luther King Day." They call a couple of schools whose programs were really, really good, and they turned it down. Finally, they said, "What about Tennessee?" I said, "Pat Summitt has a reputation for playing anybody, anywhere. She'll do it."

MARCINIAK: People want me to comment on how impactful the UConn thing was, but at the time, it really wasn't. There was no history. Tennessee was good, and UConn was coming up the ranks. We had no idea what it would become.

LOBO: We came from out of nowhere. It's not Tennessee, who had been to a bunch of Final Fours. It wasn't Louisiana Tech, that had been to a bunch of Final Fours. It was UConn, been to one Final Four, with a charismatic coach and players that people could really relate to that ran the gamut in terms of their backgrounds.

AURIEMMA: Tennessee is No. 1 in the country, and we're No. 2 in the polls. We don't watch any film of Tennessee because I don't want my players to see them play and say, "Wow, those guys are really good."

LOBO: There was definitely an energy that was building: "This is Tennessee! How good are we going to be compared to them?"

AURIEMMA: We show up for the game, and Gampel [Pavilion] is jammed. People can't get in. I remember watching the game on TV afterwards, and you couldn't hear the announcers it was so loud.

LOBO: I remember feeling like once we got a few minutes in, "We can win this game. Yeah, they're wearing orange and this is Tennessee, but we're good enough to beat them."

AURIEMMA: We win the game, and the players are on the floor in a pile at midcourt as if we had just won a national championship.

LOBO: I went back to the locker room, and somebody came in and said, "All the fans are still here. Come back on the court." They're playing Aretha Franklin's "Respect" over the speakers. It was like a house party.

MARCINIAK: We didn't know about any of that. We went to the locker room, got our stuff, and left. Whenever we lost, it was so painful. Whether we lost to the best or the worst team in the country, Pat handled it the same. She made it hurt for about two or three days. She let it simmer. It was, "I'm going to make this hard on you emotionally. I'm going to come barreling down on you mentally. I'm going to make you watch film over and over and over, until you tell me for the 50th time, 'I got you, Coach.'"

AURIEMMA: We knew how good Tennessee was, we knew how good a coach Pat was, and that's why beating them felt so good, because you weren't just beating anybody. That's why losing to them hurt so badly, because you knew that was the one game you were gonna be measured by.

LOBO: We end up playing Tennessee for the national championship that year [1995], and I remember Jen Rizzotti getting ticked off before the game because Tennessee was stretching around the center circle on our half of the court, and she asked them to move and they wouldn't. This is probably one of the reasons they lost—you don't tick off Jen Rizzotti.

MARCINIAK: The thing I remember about that UConn team was how balanced they were. Rizzotti was an amazing point guard, Lobo was a monster at the four, and they got great contributions from players like Carla Berube.

LOBO: The day after the championship game we get on a charter plane, and as we're landing they said to us, "There's some people waiting to see you." There's about 6,000 people at Bradley Airport with signs. We're looking at one another like, "This. Is. Crazy." We get off the plane, meet all the people, get onto a bus, and as we're driving on Route 84 there are people stopped on the overpasses with giant signs spray-painted on sheets. We were joking, "This is like the O.J. chase."

AURIEMMA: Tennessee had been the standard-bearer all that time. They were like the gray gunslingers in the Old West. Lots of people came through town and took their shots, but when it was over, they were the ones still standing.

JENKINS: Pat really had no vanity. She had pride, but no vanity. If you beat her, she used it. She wasn't embarrassed to lose to UConn. She knew the quality of the team. And, like all the great ones, she used it as fuel.

LAWSON: The next year, the Final Four was in Charlotte, and Tennessee played Connecticut in the semis. It was one of the best games ever—back and forth, back and forth. Tennessee ended up winning in overtime, then beating Georgia for the championship. It was great redemption for Michelle Marciniak, who took that loss in '95 so hard.

JENKINS: I remember asking Pat in 1996, "Do you like the UConn coach?" She said, "I do. He's funny, he likes a cocktail, he's engaging. And he's a very good coach. But we are very different.'"

A trio of Tennessee talents called "The Meeks"—Semeka Randall, Chamique Holdsclaw, and Tamika Catchings—restored order to the Lady Vols' universe with dominant title runs in 1997 and 1998.

The Huskies countered with a championship in 2000, then again in 2002, with their own stable of stars posting a 39-0 mark: seniors Sue Bird, Swin Cash, Asjha Jones, and Tamika Williams, and a sophomore dynamo named Diana Taurasi.

Taurasi, who went on to be the most decorated women's player of her generation, finished her career winning two more championships, in 2003 and 2004, both at the expense of Tennessee in the title game. Asked to explain his team's dominance, Auriemma answered, "We have Diana, and you don't."

As the rivalry intensified between Tennessee and Connecticut, so did the friction between the two coaches. Auriemma coined Summitt and the Lady Vols "the Evil Empire," a moniker no one in Knoxville found amusing. When Summitt spent time with Villanova coach (and close Auriemma pal) Harry Perretta to learn his motion offense, Auriemma cracked, "Harry left me for an older woman," then joked about the two of them sharing a hot tub.

It was no longer just about basketball. It was personal.

JENKINS: Pat was famously generous with money, but it was more her emotional generosity that separated her. And that was the real stumbling block for her with Geno. She felt more generous towards Connecticut and couldn't understand his lack of generosity towards her program.

AURIEMMA: So you're Tennessee, and all of a sudden no one wants to talk about how good you are. They just want to talk about the fact that those Connecticut guys beat you, and it doesn't sit well. And if you're not careful, it becomes very emotional, and it becomes more than just a basketball game.

LAWSON: It got so the Connecticut fans knew the eighth or ninth player on our bench, and our fans knew all of their players. I couldn't wait to play in those games.

JENKINS: There were little things that started to happen. Tennessee got upset by Xavier in the round of 16 [in 2001]. It was a bad loss, and Pat was furious. The team hadn't worked hard and took Xavier lightly. After the game, Pat said, "I'm more disappointed *in* them than I am *for* them." During the off-season, someone from Tennessee said, "I want you to see this." The person faxed over this paper with Geno's hand-writing. He had written, "I knew Tennessee was going to get upset by Xavier, and I knew Pat was going to blame her players." Pat faxed it to Geno and asked, "What's this about?" He never got back to her.

AURIEMMA: I think a lot of it has to do with who I am and what I'm like, and who Pat was and what Pat was like. I would venture to say that if I was a woman and had a really good team, I don't think it would be as contentious as it became, but I rub people the wrong way.

JENKINS: When Geno started taking shots and being petty, it really bugged her. Pat was no saint. But she genuinely had regard and respect for his program. She didn't understand the combativeness.

AURIEMMA: I think Tennessee thought we were just like Louisiana Tech or Old Dominion or USC or Texas. "Have your fun, but 15 years from now you'll be back where you belong and we'll still be where we are." And it didn't happen that way.

MILLER: You would hear Geno say something, and Pat would say some-thing—a little jab here, another there. It was great for women's basket-ball. We want [to] be politically correct, but it's always good to have a little animosity.

CATCHINGS: Preparing for UConn was different. The focus, the approach, the whole vibe was more intense.

LAWSON: My first UConn-Tennessee game was my freshman year in Knoxville. It was sold out, 25,000 people. We scored a layup off the jump ball. It got tipped back to me, I threw a pass ahead to Tamika Catchings and she scored, and the crowd was so loud that I couldn't hear my own voice.

TAURASI: When I played my first game in Tennessee in 2000, it was hot. They just didn't like each other. And you could feel the tension in the locker room. The games were mean.

CATCHINGS: It's funny, while you are going through it, you hate UConn. "Hate" is such a strong word, but you don't like anything about them. It's not just the coach—even the players. That's what makes great rivalries.

JENKINS: The coaches are in Indianapolis for a big summer tournament. Pat is eating at St. Elmo Steak House. Geno is sitting a few tables away. Pat could hear him. He's railing on about "Pat Summitt this, Pat Summitt that." It got uncomfortable, so Pat got up and left. [DePaul coach] Doug Bruno, who had been sitting at Geno's table, came running after her. He said, "Pat, don't pay any attention to him. He doesn't mean anything by it."

AURIEMMA: At one point, it got very, very personal.

JENKINS: There was a famous exchange at one of their big games that was caught on television, where Geno pulls Pat over and says something in her ear. He told her, "Don't listen when people say I don't respect you. That's not true. I do respect you." But stuff kept happening. She told him, "If this bullshit continues, I'm not going to play you."

TAURASI: I hit a game winner [in 2003] in overtime against Tennessee. Then I walked to their bench and let them know we took the crown. I said, "This is my fucking house!" which I probably didn't have to say, 'cause they knew already.

AURIEMMA: There was a point in time where it didn't matter if we beat Tennessee every single game for the rest of eternity. It wouldn't have mattered. There was nobody in women's basketball that was ever going to think of Connecticut the way they thought of Tennessee, ever. And I think our players and our coaching staff were pissed about that.

JENKINS: That's absolutely true, and it's a good observation by Geno. Pat would ask me, "Why is he doing this?" And I would say, "Pat, no matter how much he wins, you're Billie Jean King. You are larger than life. No matter how much he wins, he can't attain that."

TAURASI: It probably got a little bit uglier than Pat wanted. She never was much of a confrontational person. Coach Auriemma was the new kid on the block. He wanted to carve out a piece of history for himself, and like a young player or a young coach, you have this inner anger and you wanna get things done, and sometimes you act in a way that you shouldn't.

MARCINIAK: Pat had built something really special. She was on top of the world for a really long time. So to have someone challenge her . . . Geno knew which buttons to push.

TAURASI: Whenever coaches got into it with him, I'd be thinking, "That's a bad idea." Because it doesn't sway Coach Auriemma at all. He will not lose sleep.

LOBO: Sometimes you're thinking, "Oh, Coach, really? You had to go there?" There were times when I wanted to say, "Pat, just give him heat. Come back at him. Don't be so nice."

MARCINIAK: Everybody would have loved to see Pat come back at him, but she just wasn't going to get caught up in that.

MILLER: People were texting and calling up each other: "Can you believe that?" It was wild. If you were a women's basketball fan, you were by the watercooler, deciding whose side you were on, pleading your case.

AURIEMMA: What the outside world wanted us to do was compete like that and then go to dinner and have a great time. I'm saying, "Where does that happen? What part of the world, in any sporting endeavor, when you've got two fierce rivals like this, do they really enjoy each other's company?"

MARCINIAK: Pat used the controversy to motivate herself. Geno didn't change her at all. She was still the same person.

AURIEMMA: When we were at coaches' clinics or at meetings, there was never any, "Yeah, there goes Pat Summitt. Screw that, I ain't talkin' to her." It was always, "Hey, how you guys doing? How's everything? Blah-blah-blah." It was never as bad as people thought it was. It was just never as good as they wanted it to be.

MARCINIAK: You have this humble, graceful, respectful coach that had done it her way. Now Geno comes in and he's always talking, knows how to get a reaction out of her, but Pat wasn't going to play that game.

AURIEMMA: When they said, "We're not playing anymore," that was a personal decision that Pat made for whatever reason, and it didn't go over well with anybody, obviously.

JENKINS: I'm sure there are two sides to every story, but Pat thought Geno cheated. Tennessee had been recruiting Maya Moore since middle school. She was an Atlanta kid. Pat had an issue with Maya and the ESPN tour she got during her visit with Connecticut, which was not the usual 10-dollar tour. Maya had a sit-down with producers, had interviews with executives, and Pat felt the implication was, "If you come to Connecticut, there's potential here for other things down the line." Then the mom moves there and winds up living in a nice town house. Whether the NCAA was going to bring a case or not, Pat felt what went on was outside the rules. Her way of dealing with it was to cancel the series.

AURIEMMA: The happiest people when that series ended were the other coaches around the country. I remember they asked [Texas A&M coach] Gary Blair, "Who do you think's going to win the national championship this year?" He said, "I don't care as long as it's not Tennessee [or] Connecticut."

For nine seasons, from 1998 to 2007, Tennessee was on the outside looking in, as Auriemma and UConn amassed trophies. Some speculated Summitt and the Lady Vols had won their last championship—until Candace Parker obliterated that narrative by leading them to back-to-back titles over Rutgers and Stanford in 2007 and 2008.

The 2008 championship would be Summitt's last. At first, she dismissed her memory lapses as a side effect of the powerful medication she was taking for crippling rheumatoid arthritis. But her friends and family sensed something was amiss, and in 2011 Summitt finally agreed to a battery of tests that revealed a diagnosis of early-onset Alzheimer's disease. Summitt stepped down from coaching in 2012 and established the Pat Summitt Foundation to raise awareness of the disease. She died in June 2016 at the age of 64.

That October, an emotional Parker won her first WNBA championship with the Los Angeles Sparks. As the cameras captured the celebration, a sobbing Parker declared, "This one's for Pat."

LAWSON: I noticed something was different with Pat well before her diagnosis. She would repeat things, or I would tell her something, and she would ask me the same question maybe an hour later.

MARCINIAK: I visited her at her house in Knoxville. It was before we knew anything about [her health]. I had a conversation with her late at night. It was one of [the] best conversations we had, the most real she had ever been with me. We talked about family, faith, who we were as people. It was the first conversation I had with her as a real friend. The next morning, I was having coffee in the kitchen with one of her friends. Pat walks in and says, "Hey, Michelle, you sleep OK?" I said, "Yes, I'm just telling [your friend] Florence about my family." Pat says, "Michelle, how is your family doing?" The hairs on my arm stood on end. She had no recollection of our conversation from seven hours earlier.

CATCHINGS: I got a call from Pat in 2011. It was late at night, and that caught me off guard. She normally goes to bed early. I'm thinking, "What's wrong?" I pick up the phone, and she says, "Hey, Catch, I gotta tell you something. I don't need you to be worried about me. I'm gonna fight this, and I'm gonna win." I don't know what she's talking about. I ask her what she means, and then she tells me the diagnosis. "But don't worry," she's telling me. "I'm gonna beat this." And I believed her. Because whenever she told me she was going to do something, she did it.

LAWSON: One of the first things Pat said when she was diagnosed was she was not throwing a pity party. She was going to attack it. Are there people who can't afford to pay for certain treatments? Are there areas of the country where diagnosis needs to happen earlier? Are there areas that need to be lobbied for more funding?

JENKINS: Geno was incredibly generous when Pat got sick. He wrote a note to her home. At the Denver Final Four [in 2012], she was still able to travel a little bit. UConn was practicing, and Pat walked into the arena to see a friend. Geno saw her and came over and gave her a big hug. He wrote a big check to her foundation.

MARCINIAK: Geno has grown tremendously. You have to scratch and claw to arrive, but once you do, you deal with things a little differently. He was probably too proud in the beginning to say he was jealous of Pat, but now he can appreciate her instead of competing with her.

LAWSON: When Pat stopped coaching, part of me was sad, because so many women in the next generation would not have the direct influence that Pat had on us.

JENKINS: I thought, "OK, she's going to lose her memory. She may look at a trophy or a ring and might not recall the details of it." But I never imagined Pat would stop having the ability to talk to me. That was the most excruciating part.

MARCINIAK: I still came around, but it just broke my heart. One of the most uncomfortable things is carrying on [a] conversation with someone you love so much, who you've known your whole life, and it's a one-way conversation.

JENKINS: We talk a lot about Pat's legacy. Pat essentially transformed the model for women in this country from ornamental to active. She taught every young woman who came within 10 feet of her that you don't let anyone define you. You become a strong, individual, independent young woman. She put a lug wrench in our hands and taught us how to change a tire. She gave women muscles.

From 2009 to 2017, UConn won it all six times, including back-to-back un-defeated championship seasons spearheaded by Maya Moore in 2009 and 2010. Breanna Stewart topped that by leading Connecticut to three straight championships from 2014 to 2016. Today, Tennessee is no longer the Hus-kies' only daunting opponent. Notre Dame and coach Muffet McGraw have proven to be worthy sparring partners both on and off the court, while South Carolina and coach Dawn Staley, champions in 2017, have built a program with staying power. Stanford has been a consistent threat for two decades, and Stewart was prevented from winning four championships in four years when Mississippi State pulled off a shocking upset over Connecticut in the 2017 NCAA semifinals.

Along the way, Auriemma surpassed both Summitt and Wooden by win-ning 11 championships. And he's not going anywhere.

AURIEMMA: Winning for Rebecca Lobo was especially gratifying. For Diana and Maya Moore and those guys, it's boring because when they came in freshman year, they told me, "Look, you don't worry about me.

I'm gonna win four national championships, and this is how I'm gonna do it," and then they walked around like that every minute of every day.

TAURASI: Coach was always so cocky, but it was also an act to take the pressure away from the team. "Put it all on me. I got it. All you worry about is winning."

AURIEMMA: The big story now is if we *don't* win. That's a lot of pressure for the players to deal with. They just signed up to play basketball and go to school and be like normal kids. Except they're not normal—they're really good basketball players. This idea that you have to win every game, that wears on you after a while.

CATCHINGS: When we played for Pat, we thought she was the best coach ever. And that's how the UConn women feel about [Geno]. I hope someday they play each other again, because it was great for women's basketball.

AURIEMMA: People say to me now, "What motivates you to keep doing this?" If we win again, I don't think it will change me, but in the last 10 minutes of the game, there's going to be some kid who is gonna sit there and say, "Man, this is what I've been dreaming about my whole life." You can't put a price on that.

MILLER: If you don't like Geno, if you think he's cocky, he's arrogant, he talks too much, he thinks too highly of his program and himself, then beat him. He has every right to be arrogant. He has every right to be cocky. He's great for the game. Why not celebrate him? Because he's a man? Sorry, people. You can't have it both ways. He's our Wooden.

THE AGITATOR

Cheryl Miller sharpened her basketball skills in her Southern California driveway as a means of survival. When older brothers Saul Jr. and Darrell were done knocking her around, she'd take out her frustration on her younger, skinnier brother, Reggie, whose only retort was to launch his signature jumper from behind their mother's rosebushes.

As Miller grew older, she couldn't understand why her moves, which she meticulously emulated from videos of Dr. J and Oscar Robertson, were whistled for traveling. "That's when I realized there were different rules for men and women," she said.

That notion was driven home when, as a senior at Riverside Polytechnic High School, she scored 105 points in a game. "It was, 'How dare you leave her in?'" Miller said. "I learned early on it was OK for me to score 20, but it wasn't a man's 20. My 20 wasn't good enough. OK, I'll score 50. That's not good enough? OK, I'll score 105. And then I get killed for that. I couldn't win."

Miller wasn't just a jump shooter. She was a ferocious offensive rebounder, as adept at diving into the seats after a loose ball as crossing over and leaving would-be defenders in her wake. She played hard all the time, and she played with flair. "She played like a guy," said Reggie.

Miller was recruited by more than 200 colleges, but back then, players had to pay their own way for official visits, and her family couldn't afford to fly her to prestigious programs across the country. She chose nearby USC after clicking with coach Linda Sharp and meeting with twins Paula and Pam McGee, who informed her, "You can play two years *with* us or two years against us."

In Miller's freshman season, USC played Louisiana Tech, the school she had dreamed about playing for, in the national championship. Tech, led by point guard Kim Mulkey and center Janice Lawrence, built an 11-point halftime lead. Sharp calmly announced to her team that they would press to scratch their way back into the game. "I'm thinking, 'Are you kidding me? Our press is horrible,'" Miller said.

Miller and Cynthia Cooper led the USC comeback, clinching the Trojans' first championship ever.

As Miller's notoriety increased, so did her struggles with handling fame. Female stars had no road map, and Miller's confidence was often branded as arrogance. "Being recognized was becoming a burden because I didn't know how to be me," Miller said. She huddled with her idol, Ann Meyers, who told her to separate the player on the court from the person off the court.

Miller embraced Meyers's wholesome approach with the same enthusiasm that she endorsed the swashbuckling style of Nancy Lieberman. "The cocky, arrogant, flashy, finger-pointing, beating-the-chest, raising-the-roof Cheryl? I blame that all on Nancy," Miller said. "I loved Nancy's game because Nancy knew she was good, she was gonna let you know she was good, and then she was gonna show you why she was so good. Her showmanship was impeccable. She reeled you in without saying a word, just by the way she walked.

"So Ann Meyers is my Mother Teresa and Nancy is my Satan. And the thing they both have in common is, they love and respect the game."

In Miller's sophomore season, she led USC to the championship again, this time against Tennessee and the legendary Pat Summitt. Miller declared that if the Trojans won, she'd do a cartwheel at center court. She kept her promise after USC's 72–61 victory (and her Most Valuable Player award), an antic that did not sit well with Summitt, who became her Olympic coach that summer.

During a Team USA scrimmage in Taiwan, Miller was low-bridged by an elbow and kicked the ball out of frustration. Summitt yanked her from the game. At halftime she reamed each player, one by one, but skipped Miller, who silently heaved a sigh of relief.

As the team ran out for the second half, Summitt said, "Oh, wait. I forgot one person. One special individual who thinks she's bigger, better than the whole team. Cheryl Miller, can you come here, please?

"Now, let me tell you something, missy. I will win or lose a gold medal without you, do you understand me?"

Miller nodded, then turned to go. Summitt grabbed her and asked, "Where are you going?"

"The second half is about to start," Miller answered.

"Yes," Summitt said. "Without you."

The two met the next morning, with Miller apologizing for her outburst and Summitt conceding she was an "old dog, still learning new tricks."

Miller promised to tone it down. As she walked out, Summitt asked, "Are we square?"

"Yes, Coach, we are," Miller answered. "Oh, by the way, you couldn't win a gold medal without me."

"Probably not," Summitt agreed.

They won gold together that summer in Los Angeles. Miller celebrated by jumping into the arms of teammate Anne Donovan, the quiet yet forceful center who exemplified poise under pressure and was a kinder, gentler leader. She knew that her teammate Cheryl Miller was the best player in the world.

Three years later, during a pickup game at USC, Miller injured her knee on a fluke collision. "The knee goes, the doctor comes in, 'Have a nice life,' and that's it," Miller said.

With her playing career cruelly cut short, Miller turned to broadcasting and coaching. Now, decades later, she is remembered as a meteor of the women's game—a brilliant, shining light that came and went too fast, too soon.

YOUR HEROES' HEROES

The greatest players to ever lace up a pair of sneakers started off like pretty much every other kid who picked up a basketball: they dreamed of playing like the legends of their time. The experience of working on your game, imagining playing alongside or against your favorite player, or even pretending that you are that player is universal.

LeBRON JAMES: I pretended to be the superhero that was in real-life form, Michael Jordan. Sticking my tongue out and flying across the street, wishing I could dunk. And at that time I wasn't coming close.

KEVIN DURANT: Shooting around by myself, I would pretend it was Game 7 of the Finals and I was on the same team as Michael Jordan. That's when I really fell in love with the game, when I would simulate different scenarios. I knew I was pretty crazy—definitely on a different level from my friends mind-set-wise, and that's what made me who I am.

STEVE NASH: Isiah Thomas was my favorite player growing up. Obviously, I idolized Michael Jordan, but Isiah, you don't see him dunking every night, outmuscling people. I gravitated toward him—the skill, the dexterity, the competitiveness, the son of a bitch, the grit and fight and clutch, and more than anything the imagination to make plays out of nothing.

STEPHEN CURRY: I loved watching Michael Jordan play. I loved watching my dad [Dell Curry]. Muggsy Bogues was also a favorite. But Reggie Miller, he just mesmerized me. He never stopped moving, always found a way to get open, and made big shots. When me and my brother would be in our backyard playing, I envisioned myself in a Pacers uniform, playing like Reggie.

CHRIS PAUL: When I was in fifth grade, my dad had a basketball court built for me and my brother in our backyard. We played every day, one-on-one [and] then two-on-nobody. We would lower the goals and it's me and him going on a fast break, and we're Jordan and Pippen throwing each other lobs. We used to play against two imaginary people. We never lost—that is unacceptable. And when we heard my dad pulling into the driveway, we hurry up and [raise the rims]. He'd get mad because we went through about three sets of goals, dunking all the time.

SHAQUILLE O'NEAL: When I started playing, I'm like 9, 10 years old, I'm not that tall, and I'm pretending I'm Dr. J. I got the Converse. I'm trying to finger-roll. Then a guy named Magic Johnson comes around. He's 6'9", and at this time I'm 6'9", so I wanna be Magic. Then as I got taller, there's a guy named David Robinson. He's running the floor, and he had this little spin that he did, so I called my friend [and] said, "Meet me at the park." We set up a garbage can, and the first 100 times I failed. I'd go back and watch Robinson. How's he getting [there]? OK, he's waiting for the contact. When the guy pushes, then he spins. Now I got that. Patrick Ewing, he's mean, making faces, intimidating people, I gotta add that to my game. [The] last piece of the "Shaq" character is Rony Seikaly. When he dunks, he gets his legs so high it's intimidating. So when I start dunking, I would lift my legs up. Michael Jordan had [the Jumpman] emblem, and I always said to myself, "If I make it big, my emblem is gonna be the Rony Seikaly aka Shaq dunk." And voilà!

KOBE BRYANT: One day I was Magic. Next day I was Bird. Then, when Michael came around, I was Michael. Then I was Hakeem [Olajuwon], Charles [Barkley], [John] Stockton. I moved from player to player, from Dennis Johnson to [John] Havlicek to Elgin Baylor, Oscar Robertson—I can go on and on.

STEVE KERR: I wanted to be like Magic, but that was kind of far-fetched. I was nothing like Magic. Totally different game. Growing up in L.A., every kid wanted to be Magic Johnson, so we all sort of pretended to be him. In the end, I turned out to be John Paxson, which worked out pretty well.

PAUL PIERCE (Small Forward, Boston Celtics; 10-Time NBA All-Star): I was born in Oakland. I moved to L.A. when I was like 8 years old, and I had a chance to watch Magic Johnson, the Showtime Lakers. That's when I really fell in love with basketball. In Inglewood, I lived about one and a half miles from the Forum. Sometimes we would just walk to the parking lot and see if we could catch a glimpse of the guys coming in. We would go to the Forum Club, and we noticed they weren't coming in there, so we moved to the tunnel, and we could see them driving down in the fancy cars. We'd be like, "There's Magic! There's Michael Cooper." The Forum had this side door that the custodians used to go in, [with] a stairwell that led all the way up to the top floor. Sometimes the door didn't close all the way, and we'd sneak in. We didn't have tickets, so we'd sit down until somebody came and took their seats, then get up, go find another seat. I probably sat in every seat in the Forum during that period.

MAGIC JOHNSON: Those were the days. I would be out there, playing by myself. I would come down: "Wilt Chamberlain fakes baseline, he comes through the middle and shoots the ugly finger roll. It is good!" And then I would be Dave Bing: "He comes off the pick-and-roll shooting that beautiful jump shot. And it's good!"

DAVE BING: Elgin Baylor grew up in the same neighborhood in Washington, D.C., that I grew up in, so I was a little Elgin Baylor. He wore number 22 in high school; I wore 22 in high school and college. Elgin could jump out the gym, do everything, and that's the guy I fell in love with and tried to pattern my game after.

JULIUS ERVING: I used to pretend I was Wilt Chamberlain, get around the hoop and do a finger roll backwards. Then when I saw Elgin Baylor play, that was an eye-opener. Even till this day, Elgin's game was probably the most influential—strong, rebounding the ball, handling in transition, making plays around the hoop, up and under, left hand, right hand, body control, hang time. Elgin, he was like a guy from another planet.

CHARLIE SCOTT: The first basketball player that really intrigued me was Elgin Baylor. I watched him on television, and it was like watching poetry.

RICK BARRY: My biggest idol was Elgin Baylor. When I was in college, there was a magazine, and there was a picture of me driving to the basket and then a picture of Elgin Baylor, and—it was unbelievable—we were in the exact same body position. I thought that was the coolest thing ever. Elgin was my hero, and to [eventually] play against my boyhood hero, it's amazing.

MARK JACKSON: Anybody that was raised during that era, you always went to the playground and dreamed of being somebody else. I was making spin moves, fading away like Earl the Pearl. Smiling and doing interviews on the sideline, just like him. I watched Magic Johnson turn his back, bringing the ball up the floor, making incredible passes, and I went to the park and tried to do those things. It gave birth to a dream, to a desire, to a hope.

BEN JOBE: I studied Bob Cousy, thought he could do no wrong. And Marques Haynes, the Globetrotter, I could imitate everything they did.

SONNY HILL: I used to take a coat hanger, put it on the closet door, take a sock, and I'd shoot the sock through. I remember listening to basketball games when the great Joe Fulks, the Babe Ruth of basketball, played for the Philadelphia Warriors. Then came Paul Arizin with the classic jump shot. I remember listening on the radio, and I would be shooting the basketball—or the sock—through the rim of the hanger.

DOUG COLLINS: When I went to the school yard, Jerry West and I were playing one-on-one. And the beauty of it is, Jerry West never beat me. It always came down to the last shot, and if I missed, he fouled me [and I] went to the line for two free throws. If I missed a free throw, somebody stepped in the lane too quickly and I got another one. Jerry West never beat me.

NOLAN RICHARDSON: Oscar Robertson, Wilt Chamberlain, Bill Russell—I would imagine they were trying to block my shots or I'm taking them to the hoop. That's one thing I enjoyed—I beat every one of those guys. I never took somebody else's name and said, "OK, I'm Oscar Robertson." I was Nolan Richardson. I felt like I could play 'em.

LARRY BIRD: I always pretended like I was playing against someone else, not being someone else. You always play until you make the last shot and win the game. That's just how it is.

MIKE KRZYZEWSKI: I pretended to be on a team. It was Krzyzewski going down the court, Krzyzewski hitting the shot in the last 5 seconds, Krzyzewski missing but getting fouled and going to the free throw line. I always won in my imagination, and at times I would cheer out loud. I'm sure people walking by the playground said, "That kid's nuts!" Yeah, I *was* nuts.

CALVIN MURPHY: When I was growing up, the older people that lived around the area used to think I was crazy. I would visualize I was Oscar Robertson, Hal Greer, all these great players. I'd be talking to myself: "He's coming down the floor. Oh, he's got him out of position! He goes between his legs. He falls back, it's 2!" They would hear me on the playground and say, "There's something wrong with him." But I had a dream.

CHARLEY ROSEN: No imaginary drama. When I was shooting by myself, I was just concentrating on making the ball go in the basket.

ISIAH THOMAS: I always emulated my older brothers. My brother Lord Henry Thomas was really good in high school, and a guy by the name of Sammy Puckitt, and they would light it up against each other. I remember standing up on the track—those old gyms where the track would go around—and I would be looking down, watching those two go at it. Then, on the pull-up bar we had—the bar was the basket—I would roll up a sock and imitate everything they did.

DANNY MANNING (Head Coach, Wake Forest University Demon Deacons; 2-Time NBA All-Star): My father [Ed Manning] played professional basketball in the NBA, ABA, and overseas. I remember [when] my father played for the Nets in the ABA, going to practice and sitting on the stanchion of the goal. Julius Erving would dunk and the goal would just shake.

RICK CARLISLE: I grew up in a small town on the border of Canada in New York State. We didn't have cable television, so the mystique of the NBA was larger than life. I followed it through magazines, and my early heroes were Chamberlain, Dr. J, Bobby Jones. The irony was, my favorite players were all guys that had the kind of game I could never have. And maybe the coolest thing that happened to me when I made the league was the first time Dr. J said hello to me. A couple of hours before the game, I was shooting around, [and] my ball bounced over to him. He grabbed it, pitched it back, and goes, "How you doing, Rick?" When you come face-to-face with your heroes and they acknowledge you, that's a larger-than-life moment.

THE GREATEST OF ALL TIME

CHARLES BARKLEY: Michael Jordan is the greatest basketball player ever. [He was] not unbeatable, but he was the best I ever played against. When I played for Philadelphia, we beat them like 12, 15 times in a row, but that was not in the playoffs. The difference is, if you got a guy who's got superior ability, can you beat him four times in a week? There's a reason Michael's Bulls won six, Bird's Celtics won three times, Magic's Lakers—you're talking about some of the greatest to ever play the game.

JIM BOEHEIM: Michael Jordan was going to beat you. He was so ferocious, and he defended and had a nasty streak. He had 47 against the last-place team in the league, and they asked him, "Michael, you're up 30, why?" And he said, "There's some guy out there watching me tonight for the first time. And I want him to go home and say, 'I saw Michael Jordan. I saw the greatest play.'"

DAVID THOMPSON: I knew that Michael admired me and talked about patterning some of his game after mine. When he was playing with the Bulls, I was working with the [Charlotte] Hornets. I'd do pregame clinics, and I'd have guys come in and talk to the kids. I'd get Michael, and it was amazing. When he'd tell them I was his idol, they'd look at me in a whole different light.

MEL DANIELS: I don't believe that Michael Jordan was born on earth. I think he's an alien, because some of the shit he did was unbelievable. I went to scout Michael against Atlanta. On a fast break, Michael came down the right side of the floor, they passed him the ball at the three-point line, he took two dribbles and went in the air. He brought the ball down, switched hands around Dominique [Wilkins], and dunked it with his left hand. I came back, Donnie [Walsh] said, "Get your scouting report?" I said, "The only way you're gonna beat these sons of bitches is to kill number 23."

BILL SIMMONS: It was different to see [Jordan] in person. To be in the building with him was like nothing else. There was something different about the way he carried himself. Jordan always knew everyone was staring at him, taking pictures, and that's how he lived his life. He was the biggest celebrity we had other than like Michael Jackson, and it never affected his basketball. Look at how Michael Jackson went crazy, Britney Spears went crazy, all these people went crazy from celebrity, and he somehow channeled it back into hoops and was better and better and better.

DON NELSON: There was a time when I had Sidney Moncrief, and I thought Sidney was as good as Michael. I was wrong. Michael was incredible. The things that he could do and the competitiveness he had on the floor—jeez, the guy never stopped.

JULIUS ERVING: My last three years overlapped with Michael. He's at the top of the list in terms of being an assassin. The look in his eye, the determination—Michael was phenomenal in that regard. He was that guy.

PETER VECSEY: [Jordan] was blossoming, but I didn't really pick up on that, and now I'm seeing him at the Garden against the Knicks, and he reminded me of Julius [Erving]. The first time I saw Julius dunk, it was like, "Oh God!" The first time I saw Michael playing pro ball, it was like, "Oh God!" So I wrote a column and really glorified him. I compared him to all the greats, and I said as long as he's healthy, he is going to be one of the top players of all time. I was proud of that one.

AHMAD RASHAD: The first time I ever heard of Michael Jordan, I was with [tennis great] John McEnroe. We're laughing and talking and he goes, "Hey, have you seen this guy from North Carolina?" Two or three days later, we watch him, and I'm thinking, "This guy is unbelievable."

BOB RYAN: Michael was ruthless. His desire to win was as strong as anyone's has ever been, certainly in the non–Bill Russell category. In the end, *nobody* would cut your heart out faster than Michael.

RASHAD: When you start talking about his career, how great it was—it never was not great. Michael Jordan was the most relentless basketball player I have ever seen. He'd give you 30 points, and he'd guard your best guy and shut him down the entire game. And he never took a night off! He plays 82 games eight times during his career, 80 games the other time—who does that?

HOWARD GARFINKEL: I get a call from Roy Williams: "We have a player, and we think he's very good, but we wanna see him play against the best players at your camp. Could you please get him in?" I said, "Coach, I'm sorry, camp is sold out. Tell you what: We have a program called Waiters. We want to get the best players, so we [have] 25 camp workers waiting on the tables, and I think I can get the kid as a waiter if he can come for two sessions. They pay half price, the waiters." He came, and you wanna know his name? It was Mike Jordan, not Michael. Mike Jordan came, and he was fantastic.

ROY WILLIAMS: The spring of his junior year in high school, I started calling coaches around the state, trying to get the best players to come to our camp that summer. It's hard, because they got to pay, but we were fortunate enough to get Michael's school. It's Sunday afternoon, I was in Carmichael Auditorium, and he was with me for a couple of hours. I came back and told [UNC assistant coach] Eddie Fogler I just saw the best 6-foot-4 high school player I've ever seen. There's no way I knew he was going to do what he did, but I thought he was an unbelievable prospect, and it ended up that he had a heart that matched his ability. He had a toughness, the will to win, the focus that made him the greatest to ever play the game, and it's a great, great part of my life, even though I was a small part of it.

DAVID FALK (NBA Player Agent): Michael's skill level was dramatically enhanced under Dean Smith. When Michael was a sophomore at [North]

Carolina, he was a tremendous offensive player. He told me he thought about leaving school early, and Dean brought him in and basically said, "You stink on defense. Come back for your junior year, and I'll teach you." And he became maybe the greatest defensive player at his size.

WILLIAMS: We were doing a conditioning program in the fall of his freshman year, and he said, "Coach, I want to be the best that ever played here." I said, "Well, you got to work harder than you did in high school." He says, "I worked as hard as everybody else." I said, "Excuse me, I thought you just told me you wanted to be the best. Those don't go together." Two days later, after the conditioning program—I tried to bury them—he said, "You wait. You'll never see anybody outwork me. And he lived up to that. Nobody *ever* outworked him."

BILLY PACKER: [North Carolina] was ranked No. 1 in the country to start the season—big deal, *Sports Illustrated* cover, Dean Smith and your starting five. No, it was the starting four. Michael Jordan, being a freshman, didn't get in the picture. That's just the way [they] do it: you're a freshman, you will carry bags, you will do what you're told. And if you talk to Michael about that, probably it annoyed him, but it did help him become the great player that he is.

PHIL FORD: You have to be born with a certain amount of ability, and if you're born with that ability, the harder you work, the better you are. Michael was born with a gift. I don't care—all of us could work 24 hours a day, 7 days a week, and 365 days a year, and not be able to do some of the things he can do and not be born with that competitive heart. And Michael worked as hard as anybody. Listening to Coach Smith tell stories about him, it didn't matter if it was a drill or five-on-five—he always wanted to be the best. And when you have Coach Smith teaching—how to be a good teammate; what's a good shot; Michael, get to the offensive glass; Michael, you've got to defend; Michael, see man and ball; Michael, turn it on . . . And Michael, with all that ability, accepted that. It was a two-way street between him and Coach Smith.

PACKER: The night before Michael's last game in college, when they lost to Indiana, Bobby Knight says [to me], "Can I beat this team?" And I say no. He said, "I don't think so, either, but I'll tell you one damn thing—I'm going to do two things to find out. First, they're not getting any of their backdoor cuts. Second, I don't think Michael Jordan can shoot the ball. I'm going to play him from 15 feet and in. If he can make a 16-foot shot, let him score 40." . . . So now it's time for the Olympic team in '84. Bobby says to me, "My biggest problem is going to be Jordan, 'cause he'll make the team. How can I have my second guard not be able to shoot the ball?" So they have eight exhibition games leading up to the '84 world championships, and I was lucky enough to broadcast five of them for a local station in Indiana. The first game's up in Providence, and now Bobby likes Michael because he is such a competitor. Then he comes down to Greensboro, and we have a conversation and Bobby says, "The guy still can't shoot, but man, I love him. He's a fox-hole guy." The next game is in Indianapolis, and at this point the NBA has lost all three games, and Larry Fleisher, president of the NBA players association, he's had it. He packs the lineup. He's got Larry Bird, Magic Johnson, Isiah Thomas—everybody. It was a knock-down, drag-out game, but [Knight's team ends] up beating them. Imagine, today, getting a college all-star team to beat All-NBA players. It's not like the [pros] practiced for the game, but just think about that. The next game is in Milwaukee. They're two weeks away from the Olympics, and Oscar [Robertson] is coaching the NBA guys. Oscar says to me: "We're going to beat them. Anytime they come to the basket, we're putting them on the floor. On offense, we're going to clear out, and whoever their weakest defensive matchup is, we're going to take it to the basket." I said, "The way Bob coaches, they're not going to let you just do that." Well, the game turns into a bloodbath. Guys are knocking guys down and Bobby is getting hot, and he and Oscar come real close to meeting at center court for a fight. I'm talking about a real fight, not an arguing match—this is how brutal it's getting. So Michael is driving to the basket, he gets fouled by [Mike] Dunleavy and cuts his face. No foul is called, the ball goes out-of-bounds, Bobby grabs it and refuses to give the ball to the referees. They throw Bobby out of the game.

Now, this is only being televised in Indianapolis. If this was a national game, Bobby might have had problems staying on as coach. So they come back out on the court after everything settled down. Michael's got the cut on his face, and he turns the NBA players upside down in the next few minutes. He does things I've never seen him do. It turns out he always could do them, he just played under the controlled environment of North Carolina. By the time we get to Phoenix—that was the last game, the kids ended up being 8-0 against the NBA—Bobby puts his arm around me and says, "I'll tell you one fuckin' thing—the guy is going to be the greatest player who ever lived."

RYAN: Michael's ultimate forte was putting the ball in the basket. Passing was secondary: he could do it, but it wasn't what he lived for. Other guys lived to see everybody else happy, and I believe the biggest difference between LeBron James and Michael is that Michael did not win a championship until he learned to share, and LeBron did not win a championship until he learned to accept the responsibility of being the best player on the floor.

FALK: When LeBron went to Miami to play with [Dwyane] Wade and [Chris] Bosh, he wanted to win a championship. I [asked Michael Jordan], "You ever consider teaming up with Larry Bird and Magic Johnson?" Michael looked at me like I was ready to go to the loony bin. He said, "Are you kidding me? I wanted to kick their heads in every day."

His Airness: Michael Jordan, Nike, and the Birth of the Modern NBA Superstar

RICK WELTS: When Michael came along, it changed the industry forever—probably the biggest fundamental change in how players were marketed in the history of sports.

ADAM SILVER: Nike, together with Michael, transformed the business. Recently, Mark Parker, the CEO of Nike, said to the NBA Board of Governors that running is the heart of Nike but basketball is the soul.

And, no coincidence, Mark Parker started as a shoe designer working on Air Jordans. And talk about Michael as a brand—Jordan brand is now a multibillion-dollar division of Nike.

RASHAD: When Nike decided to use Michael to endorse their product, the entire sports marketing world changed. Nobody had done that. It was a big risk to put all your marbles behind one guy, but for them to have done that with Michael, and for him to soar the way he soared, that may never happen again. [Nike cofounder] Phil Knight is quick to say, "Nike, in part, is here because we signed Michael Jordan."

FALK: I was working at [the sports management firm] ProServ from the early '70s. There was a senior partner named Frank Craighill, and he had developed a relationship with [Dean] Smith. Back then the coaches controlled the selection process of agents for their top players. The company had developed a track record of doing a good job for Carolina players, and Smith recommended us. That's why we got Michael.

DAVID STERN: David [Falk] deserves credit, because he was negotiating for his client in a way where he anticipated that his client's fame and celebrity would outlive his playing career, and he turned out to be very right.

FALK: With Michael, I had to do his shoe deal, and he wanted to go with Adidas. He wore Converse at Carolina, but he loved Adidas. I wanted Michael to sign with Nike because I had a strong relationship with [former Nike executive] Rob Strasser. The problem was, Michael had no interest. He didn't know Nike. I couldn't even get him on the plane to Oregon and make a presentation. So I appealed to his parents. I said, "Look, if we're gonna manage your son, he's gotta trust me. I wouldn't ask if this wasn't worthwhile." Finally, his mother made him get on the plane. We went to Nike, and they had made a VHS tape of Michael's highlights in college and the Olympics to the Pointer Sisters' song "Jump," and Michael is transfixed on the screen. We spent the day at Nike, and Michael didn't move a muscle. So we're about to fly home, and I turned to Michael and said, "So what'd you think?" He looked at me and said, "No more meetings. This is it."

WELTS: I think David Falk represented a different prototype of [an] agent, one that wasn't just focused on collecting a percentage of a player's salary, but one that could see where this was going. Michael Jordan had the personality and the talent to be a brand in and of himself.

FALK: I can remember sitting down with Michael and his parents at the outset of this Nike relationship. I like to get parents involved at the beginning, because the player doesn't know you from a hole in the wall. He knows you represent him, but he doesn't have a personal relationship with you. You haven't done anything to earn his trust. So we're sitting down, and I said, "There's two ways we can approach this shoe deal. We can sign with a shoe company, and we can sign clothing and split it all up—Tultex for socks, JanSport for bags, somebody for hats, somebody for sweatbands—and you'll probably make more money in guaranteed dollars. Or we can give everything to one company, and they can promote you as an entity. Long term, if it works, you'll make way more money having everything integrated.

MIKE VACCARO: Nike was [a] genius in being able to target a player who was so transformative—not only his ability but [also] his appeal.

FALK: When Nike signed the deal, they had no confidence whatsoever that this would work. They never had a player that had a line in basketball, and so they put a clause in the contract that at the end of the third year, if they didn't sell $3 million worth of products going into the fourth year, they could terminate the line. The first year, they sold $130 million.

WELTS: Converse had been the traditional shoe company. They ran the famous Larry Bird/Magic Johnson ad with the "off-the-ball, off-the-wall, into-this, into-that." That was pretty good, but this was a completely different approach. That was an approach to sell shoes. Nike had an approach that each player had unique characteristics that they could bring out through marketing. They created an aura around that player that extended way beyond athletic ability. It was not separable from his athletic ability—he had to be a great player—but it enhanced how people looked at those players and made them much more.

FALK: When Magic came in in '79, the overwhelming feeling on Madison Avenue was that there were rampant drug problems and that the [NBA] was too black. When we pitched Michael Jordan in 1984, it really hadn't changed. We went to some of the major companies, and they said, "What are we gonna do with an African American basketball player?" I would say, "Gosh, when I walk into a McDonald's or an establishment serving Coca-Cola, I see a lot of African American people buying your product. Why isn't [Jordan] a good ambassador?"

SIMMONS: I hate to say it, but I really think they didn't feel comfortable that you could market black athletes to white people. With basketball, there was this tipping point that needed to happen, where for years it was always, "The league's too black; they're drugged out; it's not gonna work on TV." It was like every awful stereotype.

STERN: There was always tension, because Nike, their opening view was, "This is about the athletes, and *attitude* is important." And attitude was everything I was trying to *not* emphasize. I'll never forget when Reebok had a deal with Kenyon Martin, and they put him on a post office "Wanted" poster. I said, "We're trying to show our guys in the best possible light, and you'll do anything to sell *sneakers*." That has [since] changed completely, and Nike participates in a most positive way.

FALK: So we had to sit down and make a deal. I told Strasser, "If you want to sign this young player at Nike, I want you to treat him like a tennis player." We had represented a lot of tennis players in the early '80s, and [they] all had their own line of rackets, shoes, clothes. Strasser said, "We're willing to give him this line of shoes and clothes, but what do you want to call it?" And I looked at him like, "Are you kidding? I want to call it Michael Jordan." What does any other athlete call their line? He said: "No, we can't do that. Michael's 21 years old, and he's a basketball player. No one's going to seriously think that he's [going to] become Christian Dior, Oscar de la Renta." Rob thought the credibility of just slapping a label on a line didn't work. So [Nike] will make the line, but you've got to come up with a name, and the name can't be Michael Jordan. I'm thinking to myself, "How do you identify the personality with the line without using the name?" So I'm sitting in my office on a hot summer day, and all of a sudden—don't ask what inspired me—I'm thinking air. Michael plays in the air. I got it! We're gonna call it Air Jordan.

VACCARO: The logo was him flying with a basketball in his hand, and who doesn't want to be able to do that? And they look different from any other shoe. When you wore them, people knew you were wearing Air Jordans.

RYAN: Nike and Phil Knight and Spike Lee's commercial—Mars Blackmon! I can still see him hanging on the rim! I grew up in the era of the Chuck Taylor Converse All Stars, and that was fine, but it pales in comparison to the sneaker world now. The basketball shoe is such an important cultural item, and Michael Jordan having that kind of personal influence on the business of basketball is astonishing.

SIMMONS: Jordan, when he shaved his head, he basically created the shaved-head industry. He really did. Who else? It wasn't Gene Hackman in *Superman*.

WELTS: The Nike moment of brilliance in those early years was when the NBA banned the shoe Nike made for Michael Jordan. The problem was the coloration of those shoes didn't conform with [league] rules, but Nike realized they had hit the jackpot. This shoe [supposedly] created such an unfair advantage for Michael Jordan that the NBA had to ban the shoe. And there never has been a better marketing campaign in my life than the shoe that gives Michael Jordan his superhero powers.

STERN: At some point, we said, "We need a rule on shoes. It has to be black or white and one of the team's principal colors." Or something like that. And Nike turned around and said, "This is the shoe that was banned by the NBA. It must be that it makes Michael too good."

ARN TELLEM: Nike was a significant partner to the NBA in basketball's huge growth and popularity, and a lot of it is those commercials that we all remember—"Be Like Mike." They not only elevated Michael but elevated basketball.

ALLEN IVERSON: When that commercial came out—"I Wanna Be Like Mike"—I literally did. He was everything to me.

VACCARO: When that became as popular of a brand as it did, he stopped being just a basketball player, and he became an icon. There's a difference. Iconic athletes tend to be forever. You can argue that there are a lot of quarterbacks better than Joe Namath, maybe a lot of boxers who could compete with Muhammad Ali, but those were iconic figures, not only in sports but in popular culture. And Michael Jordan certainly took his place there.

SILVER: I was in China with Michael in 2015, and it was the first time Michael had been to China in 11 years. When Michael walked onto the court in Shanghai, it was as if people were seeing a person they didn't believe could really exist. Yao Ming got a big applause, but it wasn't like Michael's. People were swooning when Michael came out.

STERN: Air Jordan is so fascinating to me, because not only was it taking the best-known athlete in the world and making it his brand, but it was a brand that was designed, promulgated, and massaged to exist well beyond his playing career. That tells you what impact NBA players can have on business and society.

NELSON GEORGE: I don't know that black players owe anybody anything, but when they do make a statement, it's important. In this respect, Michael Jordan has been disappointing as a role model. I will never forget—I think it's Harvey Gantt—there was a black politician [running for Senate] against Jesse Helms in North Carolina, and Jordan did not publicly endorse this guy. I'm saying to myself, "Here's a chance to get rid of one of the most un-reconstructive racists in the U.S. Senate"—and that's saying a lot, you know. Maybe [Helms] couldn't have been taken out, but to be on the side of right ... and [Jordan] didn't do it. That disappointed me. What? He's gonna make a couple million dollars less if rednecks in that state don't buy his sneakers? He's got his own life, and I respect him immensely, but his lack of advocacy, coming from a point of almost untouchability in terms of his public respect, is sad. He was basically Oprah before Oprah. He was that big and that ubiquitous, and he hasn't reached to leverage that in the way that I would have liked.

FALK: Today's players I'm not sure have an appreciation for the barriers that Michael had to break down on Madison Avenue. Basketball was not prime-time, and African American players didn't have their own shoes and didn't do Sara Lee and Coca-Cola and McDonald's. He broke down all those barriers.

SILVER: Michael gets knocked for being too much of a commercial entity, for not being multidimensional. But what Michael Jordan single-handedly created—the fact that he came from where he did in North Carolina, that he's now in a club of billionaires that own NBA teams—[that's] more than Babe Ruth ever did.

The Jordan Era

ROD THORN: I first realized we had something special in Jordan during the '84 Olympics. Jordan was electric. Everybody was talking about him. Then he comes to us in Chicago and we have the first practice, and I wasn't there for some reason. I get a call from one of the assistant coaches, and he said, "Congratulations, you didn't mess the draft up this year." And when we started exhibitions, everywhere we went, people were lining up to see Jordan. This is before he ever played an NBA game! We start the season, and I can't say that anybody was prescient enough to know he was gonna turn out to be what he turned out to be, but after one month, you knew you had an All-Star.

VACCARO: It wasn't just that he was extraordinarily gifted. It was that he had great coaching in college, and that when he exploded on the NBA after an unforgettable '84 Olympics, he seized the day immediately with his talent and his will.

THORN: Going into the draft where we ended up taking Jordan, we were floundering. There was a coin flip between Houston and Portland [for the top pick]. Whoever won was gonna take [Hakeem] Olajuwon. If Portland won, Houston would have taken Jordan, because they had Sampson. Portland, on the other hand, had Clyde Drexler and Jim Paxson. Drexler was a tremendous wing player, Paxson was good, too, and their feeling was if Sam Bowie passed a physical, they're gonna take him. So that left us with Jordan. We were unbelievably fortunate that the right team won the flip and that Portland felt they didn't need other wing players. . . . Dean Smith said to me at the time that Jordan would be a better pro than he was a college player.

FALK: I don't think Coach Smith had any idea how good he would be. I don't think the Bulls had any idea how good he would be.

THORN: I would not have drafted Bowie, because Bowie had some injuries and our medical people felt that [they] might show up again. Had we not gotten Jordan, I would've drafted Sam Perkins and passed up Charles Barkley, because my feeling was there's no way he could do in pro ball what he had done in college. He was too small. I got lucky on a couple of counts there. I get a lot of credit for picking Michael Jordan, but that's also the draft that I picked [Olympic track-and-field star] Carl Lewis. It was the last round, and [former Bulls owner] Jonathan Kovler said, "Do you have anybody you think can make the team here?" I said no, and he said, "Let's pick Carl Lewis. We'll get some publicity out of it." That's the reason we did it, but it goes on my record.

STEPHEN A. SMITH: The Jordan era began when he dropped 63 on Boston and Bird called him the closest thing to God.

RYAN: In the first game against the Celtics in the 1986 series, Michael Jordan had 49. It was a piggy 49, a ball-hoggy 49. In the second game of the series, he had 63 in a double-overtime loss, and it was a very team-oriented 63. It was his ultimate coming-out party, though the Celtics did win the game. The most telling statistic is that the Celtic who fouled him the most in that game was Bill Walton, which means [Jordan] had beaten the defense several times and Walton stepped in from there. He wore out Dennis Johnson, he wore out Danny Ainge, he just destroyed people. Larry Bird, after they had played in the very first game that regular season, declared that this was a whole different phenomenon, that this guy is the best player [he'd] ever seen. After one game! Great ones, they know each other.

SIMMONS: We've never had a better team than the '86 Celtics, and they couldn't stop Jordan. They had Dennis Johnson, one of the best defensive guards of that generation. They had all these big guys protecting the rim. And they didn't know what to do [with Jordan]. It really did feel like basketball was going somewhere else when you watched that series. Bird recognized it. After, he was like, "The guy is unbelievable—God disguised as Michael Jordan."

GEORGE GERVIN: I played with Michael Jordan his second year. If you saw his speech at the Hall of Fame, he mentioned me, 'cause he thought me, Isiah, and Magic had something against him [at] the '85 All-Star Game.

Heading into the 1985–86 season, the Bulls traded David Greenwood to the San Antonio Spurs for Gervin, then 33, and released Jordan's close friend, forward Rod Higgins. "I have no comment on the trade," Jordan told the press at the time. "Just say I am unhappy." The previous season, Gervin was rumored to have been part of a plot by NBA veterans to embarrass Jordan, then a rookie, at the 1985 NBA All-Star Game. While fellow Eastern Conference All-Stars allegedly froze Jordan out of the offense, they also supposedly planned to leave Jordan alone to guard Gervin, his matchup on the Western Conference All-Stars, without offering any help on defense.

GERVIN: Yeah, I got something against you, young fella—I'm playing against you! I want to hold you to no points.

ISIAH THOMAS: I defy anybody to look at that tape and say Dr. J, Moses Malone, Larry Bird, and I conspired to freeze Michael Jordan out. This is what I try to remind everybody: Michael Jordan wasn't the guy he was in the '90s. At that time, Dr. J, Larry Bird, George Gervin, Kareem [Abdul-Jabbar]—those were the guys who were winning championships.

GERVIN: I was on [Jordan]'s team. When [the] Spurs let me go, it was over for me. I'm living out my contract with Chicago. He got a 14-year vet coming in, and he was mad 'cause they traded [Rod] Higgins and Higgins was his boy. First day at the press conference, people ask me, "Ice, when you see Michael, what you gonna say?" "What you think I'm gon' say? I'm saying the same thing I say to you: 'What's up?' I'm confident in who I am and what I have accomplished in the league. He ain't done nothing." That's how I looked at it. I knew his potential was scary, 'cause I got a chance to see him. And then he broke his foot, so I went into the starting lineup, let him see the old man at work. I remember in Dallas, I got 35 at [the] half, and I saw him over there clapping. I end up with maybe 44, 45, and he came to me laughing and said, "You got tired, old man." I say, "Look here, young fella, I was just showing you how it used to be. You ain't done nothing." See, I'm talking about before he became that guy we all love. I have nothing but admiration and respect for him. I got his shoes on right now. I didn't at that time, though, 'cause he was a little punk.

SMITH: Magic and Bird, they come take the league by storm, and all of a sudden Michael Jordan and the Jordan era arrived. But before that, the Detroit Pistons were not only winning back-to-back NBA championships, they were selling out the Pontiac Silverdome. They were playing in front of 60, 70, 80,000. And people were glossing over that because they wanted to leapfrog from Magic and Bird to the Jordan era.

THOMAS: It bothers me when the writers of history change the narrative. In the '80s, Jordan wasn't the guy that he became in the '90s. It was still Kareem Abdul-Jabbar, Julius Erving, Larry Bird, Magic Johnson, and the Detroit Pistons. Those were the teams that won championships in the '80s. So when they stick Jordan and Chicago in there, that's when we say, "Wait a minute, that's not the truth." When you say the '80s and omit the Pistons, that's just wrong.

Before the three-peats, before the dynasty, Jordan and the Bulls had to dethrone the reigning back-to-back NBA champions, the Bad Boy Detroit Pistons, led by Isiah Thomas, Bill Laimbeer, and head coach Chuck Daly. Detroit eliminated Chicago from the playoffs in three consecutive seasons, from 1988 to 1990, and the Bad Boys reserved a special set of "Jordan rules" for the Bulls. The strategy referred to a mix of defensive schemes intended to prevent Jordan from finding a rhythm, along with fouling him hard whenever he beat his primary defender. The rivalry became even more acrimonious when the Bulls finally defeated the Pistons in the 1991 Eastern Conference Finals, and the Pistons players left the floor without shaking hands with Jordan and the Bulls.

DOUG COLLINS: [When] we played Detroit, it was always an amazing environment. Detroit had Isiah, the legend *from* Chicago. Michael [was] now the legend *of* Chicago. Isiah had the better team. The frustration Michael would feel at losing to them was a process that everybody had to go through. Michael, Scottie [Pippen], Phil [Jackson], Horace [Grant], Pax [John Paxson], they had to scale that mountain.

RYAN: The Pistons talked. They allowed themselves to be quoted about the Jordan rules, which I thought was playing with fire, but it worked for a while.

CHARLEY ROSEN: The Pistons really were the Bad Boys. You know the code: You foul a guy hard, but you don't do anything to threaten his career. You don't low-bridge him—when he's up off his feet, you don't take his feet out. But those Pistons did things like that. They would hit a guy after a whistle.

COLLINS: Just watching the pieces grow up—to watch Michael get in that weight room and lift and get strong, because the punishment he had to take when he played the Pistons and the Knicks and the Heat . . .

RASHAD: Michael didn't all of a sudden become the biggest winner. [There] was a road to that, and every time he got knocked down, he got up stronger. Remember when he developed that 15-foot fadeaway? He didn't have that before. When Detroit beat 'em, he started getting stronger and bigger.

SCOTTIE PIPPEN (Small Forward, Chicago Bulls; 7-Time NBA All-Star): It was different then. The league was more physical, and the Pistons were able to take advantage of it. I had to adjust. As a young player, you can't just throw your weight around. I had to wait for my body to mature, and that was true for Michael and Horace, too.

COLLINS: The disappointing thing through that whole situation was when Detroit left the floor early the year when the Bulls knocked them out—[after] all the years that we had to shake their hands.

THOMAS: Boston and Detroit—our players were very friendly. We learned a lot from Boston—how to win, how to persevere. So we're beating them in Detroit, we're getting ready to close the chapter on their run, and they start walking off through the middle of the court. McHale and I shake hands, and the Celtics walk off. We didn't think it was a big deal. They were the kings, and we were not about to feel insulted. I don't think you heard one player out of our locker room talk about the Celtics not shaking hands, because it was respect from us. So fast-forward, the whole Chicago thing—we felt that the way we treated the past champions, the way we treated the Lakers and Celtics when we dethroned them, we gave them their respect. We always said great things about them, even in the process of dethroning them. Chicago, in the process of dethroning us, they were trashing us in the newspapers, television, and we felt like, "This ain't cool." As champions, we thought we should have been treated better. Now, should we have taken the high road and shook hands? Yes, but we didn't.

The Bulls went through three head coaches—Kevin Loughery, Stan Albeck, and Doug Collins—in Jordan's first five NBA seasons. Although Collins coached the Bulls to the Eastern Conference Finals in 1989, he was replaced the following year by Phil Jackson, who would eventually lead the Bulls to their championship form.

COLLINS: I first started watching Michael the year he had that 63-point game. Stan Albeck was the coach. Chicago had talked to me about being an assistant to Stan, and I was doing broadcasting. I said I can't make that lateral move to come in as an assistant—I gotta make some money. But I started watching Michael that year. Stan got let go after that, and they hired me to be head coach.

ROSEN: I think the primary job of an NBA head coach is to get along with his superstar and to get the superstar to buy into his system. If a superstar puts the stamp of approval on the coach, everybody has to follow.

COLLINS: The first time I met Michael [was] that year he had broken his foot and missed all but 18 games. When he came back, he played in a minutes-restricted thing. I had just been named head coach, and I met Michael in the summertime at the doctor's office to re–X-ray his foot. I said maybe it'd be a good idea to rest this summer so it can heal completely. I had a stress fracture, it never healed right, and it ended up costing me my career. I'll never forget the look he gave me. He said: "Are you gonna be my coach? Well, let me say something to you, respectfully. First of all, that's my foot, not yours. And I'm gonna play, 'cause I love to play." He said something I always tell coaches: "If you got a thoroughbred, you better let him run. 'Cause if you hold him back, eventually he stops."

FALK: Doug is an incredibly bright, insightful guy, but he's so intense, and Michael's a very steady kind of person. Doug is very emotional. It was one of his strengths, but it was also one of his weaknesses.

COLLINS: I love Michael Jordan. I coached him for five years, [and] every single night that guy gave me everything he had. I looked at him and I said, "I gotta grow into a position where he'll trust me." I had to come every day with the idea that I know what I'm doing. Chuck Daly said, "There's three things you can't fool: kids, dogs, and NBA players. They know if you know what you're doing."

VECSEY: Michael had no problem with Doug. They lost in the finals of the East [Collins's last] year. They were on their way up. But Doug was exhausting everybody with his personality. He walks that line—you know, insanity and genius. Things would go bad, he'd change a million things, 20 new plays every day, and he was causing some grief. I'm not saying Jordan and he didn't get into it—they did—but Jordan was fine with him. [Collins's] mistake was, he got into it with [Bulls GM Jerry] Krause, and anybody who got into it with Krause was gone eventually.

COLLINS: When I was fired by the Bulls, it was the first time in my life someone told me I wasn't needed. It was devastating. And you know when I got over it? I got over it the next year in the playoffs when Detroit beat the Bulls. It was like, "Well, they didn't win a championship this year, either." I carried it with me every single day. My kids were here, the Bulls became a raging success, Phil won six championships. But it was a gift that I gave my children—I wanted them to see that I had nothing to hide from. I wanted them to understand the heartaches that go with it. I did a radio show four times a week, and the whole topic was the Bulls. Everybody was always looking for that touch of bitterness or sour grapes, and I think the thing people admired was they never felt that from me. [Bulls owner] Jerry Reinsdorf, to this day, is one of my dear friends. I have six championship watches in my trophy case that he gave me, with a note to every one, saying you're a part of all these championships. Did I lift the trophy? I did not. But I played a role in them getting to that point, and I'm proud of that.

SIMMONS: Let's be honest, [Jackson] probably shanked Doug Collins. He was the assistant on that team, and all of a sudden he has the job.

FALK: Phil came in with the low-key Zen approach, and I think it really appealed to Michael.

BILL BRADLEY: When we were playing together, I never thought Phil was going to be a coach. But looking back on his attitude and the way he played the game, all the attributes were there. He was highly analytical. When he had his spinal fusion, he sat next to [Red] Holzman for a year on the bench. He was totally unselfish. He found a unique way to relate to each of his teammates as human beings, and he was a fierce competitor. And if you look at his success, all of those can be traced back to when he was a player.

PHIL JACKSON: When I got to the Bulls in '87 [as an assistant under Collins], the two other assistants were Johnny Bach and Tex Winter. Both of them had been playing basketball in the '30s, went to college in the '40s, gone to World War II, and came out and became the youngest basketball coaches in America. They had a history of the game right up to the seams in the basketball. As a coach, I got a secondary education with these fellows who [had] almost 40 years in the business.

STEVE KERR: Everything [Phil] did was different, but it was genuine. Whether it was meditating or watching a film in a room full of Native American relics. When you first get there, you look around [and] go, "Is this guy for real?" And you quickly realize he is, and he's teaching us about bonding together, about mindfulness on the court, about being competitive as a group. Phil could pull that off because it really does come from his heart. Phil generated a sense of the team being bigger than the individual, which is a cliché, but it always felt like there was a bigger goal, something special that we were pursuing together.

RASHAD: Phil takes great pride in always moving forward, staying in the moment, and being able to talk his teams into his philosophy. When Michael and Phil were in Chicago, they had a relationship that was just beautiful. He knew that Michael had to have his freedom, and Michael knew that Phil had to have the triangle.

JACKSON: Having coached on my own for four or five years, running a variety of offenses—flex, the Hawk offense—I didn't enjoy the box that you got put into by running those. The triangle wasn't anything new. Pete Newell ran a triangle with California, Bill Sharman won championships [with the triangle]. Wilt Chamberlain set a record with assists as a center, leading the league out of a triangle offense. These were very basic parts of basketball: overload one side, have an opportunity on the weak side. It was something Tex had really thought out—how to create angles so players mentally saw the correct angle to set up a pass; what you have to put in players' minds so they understand the sequences all follow one another. And my college coach, Bill Fitch, instituted this offense my senior year of college. There was no name attached to it, and Bill didn't give us any idea where it came from, but I actually played it.

ROSEN: When Michael Jordan bought into the triangle, everybody had to. When Michael Jordan saw that Phil knows what he's doing, everybody had to shut up and listen to Phil.

RASHAD: Fourth quarter, you never saw the triangle. Up until that point, it would work. But the fourth quarter is Michael Jordan.

JEFF VAN GUNDY (Head Coach, New York Knicks/Houston Rockets; NBA Analyst, ESPN): I don't think Phil Jackson's gonna be sending me a Christmas card—and I'm not sending him one—but I have great respect for his abilities as a coach. In fact, I think his coaching gets narrowed down too much to the triangle and Zen versus he was a brilliant defensive coach. In Game 2 of [the Knicks'] '93 series against [the Bulls], we were pounding them with the Starks-Ewing pick-and-roll, and that's how [John] Starks's dunk came. Jordan jumped high side, they hadn't practiced it, so Starks got the running start and hammered it on Grant and Pippen. But it changed the series, because Games 3 through 7 [they adjusted], and we weren't nearly as good. So even with 11 championships, I don't think Phil has gotten his due.

VACCARO: When you look at Phil Jackson's body of work, I am not going to be one of those guys who gives an asterisk because he had the best players. You need great talent to win a championship. Look at how many championships Chicago and Los Angeles won [with those rosters] before he was coach. Zero.

SIMMONS: Here's the defense for Phil Jackson: he was able to manage Michael Jordan, who was a brutal teammate and supercompetitive and had a way of just ruining guys.

The tales of Jordan's insatiable will to win are endless. From opponents to teammates to unsuspecting fans, Jordan challenged them all. And when they tried to answer his challenges, Jordan used it to fuel his competitive fire.

JACKSON: Mike would go in the locker room and pinpoint the mood of the team: "You guys are playing tentative. Let's get with it!" There may have been a turned-over chair or a demonstrative act. Not breaking things, but I will come in the locker room after meeting with my coaches and go, "Hmm, the air is charged. Something happened in here." That didn't happen often, and he wasn't the kind of guy that would berate his guys. Sometimes he'd kid big guys about their hands, or he'd tell guys, "If I give you the ball, make the next shot."

PIPPEN: Michael never went after me. Now, when you talk about some of our teammates, he made people uncomfortable in the heat of the moment, but that's part of being on a team. One minute guys are in each other's faces, and the next minute the same players are hanging out.

VACCARO: The stories that emerged—it was almost an irrational competitive fire, to the point where he would get into it with teammates. And not just when he didn't think they were playing well, but in practices where he thought a guy had taken a cheap shot, or a guy had made a lucky shot and his team had won a scrimmage.

COLLINS: The guy won every drill. He won every scrimmage. He had a motor that ran like nothing I'd ever seen. As badly as I wanted to win, he wanted to win more. It was funny—sometimes he'd walk by the bench and go, "You wanna win? Get so-and-so out. He don't wanna play tonight."

One of Jordan's most publicized instances of challenging his teammates came during the 1995–96 preseason, when an argument between Jordan and Bulls guard Steve Kerr escalated into a fight.

KERR: Michael was not easy on his teammates. I think his theory was that if you couldn't handle the pressure he put on you in practice, there's no way you'd handle the stress of the Finals. He lifted the intensity at practice every day. That year, training camp was incredibly competitive, and that particular day got a little ugly. We were guarding each other, and I remember feeling disrespected, so I went back at him. It was a typical training camp scuffle, and the whole thing ended quickly, but because it's Michael Jordan, we're still talking about it 20 years later.

VACCARO: Kerr himself obviously burns as a competitor, so you can see how those two might've been a little combustible. But Jordan is the alpha dog—probably in every relationship Jordan ever had, he was the alpha dog—and whatever Kerr did that angered him, there was no restraint there. He punched Steve Kerr, and Kerr laughs about it now, but you gotta figure that in the moment, that's not something you take lightly, when Michael Jordan takes a swing at you.

JACKSON: Leadership [comes] in many different forms on different teams. Bill Cartwright could be that character that's supporting everybody. Scottie Pippen became a really good leader, because the team was like his family. He had 12 or 13 siblings: "Hey, this is [how] I grew up, part of this collective whole." Michael Jordan could drive a team.

RASHAD: There was never any excuse for losing. It was just in your brain: "We're not allowed to lose."

SIMMONS: There's 9 or 10 games a year where it's like a back-to-back or a four-in-five-nights, and you're just not gonna win. Jordan didn't have "schedule losses." He was homicidally competitive. They'd be down 10 and somebody would say something on the other team, or he didn't like the way somebody looked at him, or some fan made fun of him—he'd grab some fuel from somebody, and all of a sudden they're up 3 with a minute to go. There's some stat: from November 1990 all the way through when Jordan finished playing with the Bulls, he never lost three games in a row.

MARV ALBERT: Michael would get motivated by the slightest provocation. There might be a woman in the front row heckling him, just an innocent woman thinking, "This is the way it is at basketball games," and he would point at her and say, "This is what I'm gonna do now."

VACCARO: He hated losing so much, and he didn't hide it. You could tell when he was angry. You could tell when a competitor annoyed him. You could see, in the [1997] Finals, when Karl Malone won the [league] MVP, that he wanted to prove everyone who voted for Malone wrong.

RASHAD: When Michael played against Clyde Drexler [in the 1992 Finals], everybody tried to say these guys were the two best individual basketball players. [Michael] said [later], "The point I wanted to make is, I'm way better than him."

RYAN: Nothing stirred Michael's competitive juices more than someone being touted as an antidote to him. He won all the challenges. Against Portland in the Drexler comparison, [he had] the three-point barrage in the first half [of Game 1] with that famous look of his.

SIMMONS: Game 1, '92 Finals, I've never known how to interpret the shrug. Everyone interpreted it as, "I'm so hot, can you believe this magic?" I interpreted it as, "Clyde Drexler? Really? That's the best?"

RYAN: Let's not forget '93, the Phoenix series. This is Barkley's MVP year, and Michael rose to that challenge as he always did. Barkley, at his absolute peak, doing everything he possibly could to win, [and] he couldn't get it done.

ALBERT: At NBC, we'd always sit down with Michael before the game, and he would give sound bites. Once, he felt that I was too favorable to Gary Payton, that Payton had something to do with stopping Michael.

RYAN: Nobody's going to be able to look us in the eye and say, "I stopped Michael Jordan." That didn't happen. Nobody ever *stopped* Michael Jordan.

RASHAD: I'll never forget when they were playing against Seattle, [Jordan] came [out] after a game and said, "You know what? Gary Payton asked if he could have my shoes after the game. Right there, I knew I had him."

Although the Bulls are remembered for winning six NBA titles in the 1990s without an All-Star center, Chicago's championship teams surrounded Jordan with strong supporting casts that included fellow Hall of Famers Scottie Pippen and Dennis Rodman, as well as Horace Grant, John Paxson, Toni Kukoc, and Steve Kerr, among others.

BILLY CUNNINGHAM: Michael Jordan went six years without achieving anything, and all of a sudden there's a phenomenal draft for Chicago— Grant and Pippen—and they were the pieces that needed to be around Michael. They became a phenomenal defensive team without a dominant center.

KERR: They were incredible defensive players. They would switch and guard whoever they wanted. Johnny Bach called them "the Dobermans," along with Ron Harper and eventually Dennis Rodman. It was an amazing defensive unit, and Michael and Scottie were at the forefront of that.

SIMMONS: Jordan basically created a mini-me. By the mid-'90s, Pippen was like Jordan had given birth to this perfect wing person for himself. They even ran and moved the same way. Name another NBA player who literally gave birth to a sidekick. It's never happened.

RYAN: Michael's clearly the most important component, but he doesn't win without Pippen. Six-foot-seven, enormous wingspan, ballhandling skills, defensive aptitude—I'm not gonna downplay Scottie Pippen.

KERR: Michael and Scottie were perfect together. Michael was the killer; Scottie was the facilitator. Michael was the closer; Scottie set the table. Michael was hard on everybody; Scottie had a much softer touch. Everybody loved playing with Scottie. He'd get you the ball, he always had something nice to say, and it was a good contrast, because Michael might rip you, and Scottie might pat you on the back.

PIPPEN: Over time, it was like a marriage for us. We spent so much time together in the gym, in the weight room, off the court, our friendship naturally evolved. He started to realize, "Here's a guy who is willing to work as hard [as] I do."

SIMMONS: I think "Pippen" should be a noun—the perfect sidekick. He always understood Michael was the guy, and Pippen's job was to do everything he could to help Michael and the Bulls win.

In the summer of 1993, following the completion of the Bulls' first three-peat and the shocking murder of Michael's father, Jordan announced his retirement from the NBA, along with his intention to become a professional baseball player, starting with the AA Birmingham Barons. Jordan would return to the NBA midway through the 1994–95 season, but during his year-and-a-half absence, the Bulls became Pippen's team. Pippen exceeded expectations in the role, leading Chicago to 55 wins and placing third in the 1994 MVP voting. But the period without Jordan also led to the most infamous moment in Pippen's career—a 1994 Eastern Conference Semifinals game against the New York Knicks, where Pippen refused to enter the game for the last possession because Phil Jackson designed a game-winning play for Toni Kukoc.

KERR: My sense was that Scottie was comfortable in his role until Michael left to play baseball and it became Scottie's team. It was a different role for him, and he was ideally suited to play the role he did when

Michael was on the court. He could score, obviously, but that wasn't really his game. He wasn't looking to attack all the time, particularly in the half-court. So when Michael was gone, it was tough for Scottie, but he figured it out and had one of the best seasons I've ever seen.

ALBERT: This is 1994. Michael Jordan was in retirement, so Pippen and Kukoc are the key players for the Bulls. Game is tied, Knicks had come from 22 down, but it's Chicago ball. Pippen refuses to go into the game because Phil Jackson called the last-second play for Toni Kukoc, and Pippen took it personally. They run the play, Kukoc hits the game-winning shot, and the Bulls run off the floor.

RASHAD: Phil came up with a play for Kukoc, and then Scottie wouldn't play, which is almost unheard-of.

RYAN: It's a low point, and it's something that many have held against him. I don't think he's ever sufficiently apologized or admitted that he was out of line.

PIPPEN: The competitive fire in me took over. I wouldn't handle it the same way, but I would still make my point. I felt Phil overused his power against me, like he was trying to make a point that didn't need to be made.

SIMMONS: Pippen wants to be the hero, but they design the play for Kukoc. He gets mad, has a bad moment. I don't condone what he did, but I get it. He carried them that whole year. They won 55 games without Michael Jordan. He had earned the right to take that shot. But he took it personally, and he made a mistake. Afterwards, the players go in the locker room, and [if you're] Phil Jackson, how do you handle that? These guys feel like Pippen quit on them.

ROSEN: They came into the locker room, and Phil stayed out. He let Cartwright handle the situation, and Cartwright and everybody else was like, "What did you do?" to Pippen. They shamed him. That's the key to the way Phil coached—you create an environment where the players can monitor themselves, because a coach is wearing a tie and a jacket, sitting on the bench. It has to come from the players.

SIMMONS: He didn't go in. He let the players talk it out, and there's a famous story [of] Bill Cartwright just screaming at Pippen, tears coming down his face: "You let us down. This is my last chance and you quit on us."

ALBERT: There was such respect for Bill Cartwright—just the fact that he was upset about Pippen letting the club down really put the message forward.

RASHAD: It was one of these things that normally you don't get past—a scar that lasts the rest of your life. Which goes to show that Phil Jackson was a master psychologist. They squashed it and moved on. I always felt like Phil had such a wonderful atmosphere around that team, that they were a family and could get over arguments.

The Bulls welcomed an unlikely contributor for their second three-peat, from 1996 to 1998: the live-wire, Technicolor-haired, Bad as I Wanna Be Dennis Rodman. A former member of the Bad Boy Pistons coming off a disruptive two-year stint with the San Antonio Spurs, Rodman found a home with Jordan's Bulls.

RASHAD: You can have a person who may have questionable character off the court but tremendous character on the court. Dennis Rodman was a wild, crazy guy. But when he played? He was 100 percent there. No matter if he had been out two days and never slept, when that game started, that guy was rock solid. Rodman might have been the best defensive player I've ever seen.

KERR: We all loved Dennis. He didn't say much during practice, but during games he was a monster—his rebounding and defense, the way he'd get in his opponents' heads. The off-court persona was something he generated and promoted, and most of it was exaggerated.

SHAQUILLE O'NEAL: A weird legend. Can't say nothing about his tattoos, but earrings in the nose? Just weird. However, when it came time to do his job—and I've seen it personally with the Lakers—he's gonna get you 20 rebounds. He would come in late on game day, with like 10 minutes to play, eating chicken and rice. Everybody else is in uniform, [and] he'd come in [in] his loud clothes, loud hat. Walk out of the meeting while Coach was talking, go in the back and take a cold shower, and he'd just come out and get 25 rebounds. Then, after the game, put his clothes on, go to the club, and when you go in the club, the most beautiful people in the world are sitting around watching him.

ROSEN: Dennis Rodman is a being unto himself. All the crazy stuff—getting drunk and passing out, wearing a wedding gown, doing crazy stuff to his hair, and piercings all over his face—that's his business.

KERR: It got a little bothersome in the third year, where Dennis started to get restless. He ran off and did some World Wrestling Federation thing during the season, and then he got suspended for kicking a photographer. That would bother us, because we're trying to win games and he would create the sideshow, but it was the perfect team for him because there was already a circus going on.

COLLINS: A guy like Rodman has to be in the right environment; otherwise he can be a huge distraction. When he got to Chicago with Michael and Phil and Scottie, they said, "We don't mind what you do, but when you come here, you're on our time. We're playing for championships."

Jordan may be the greatest scorer in NBA history, but many of his most unforgettable and impactful plays came on passes to teammates for clutch shots, whether it be feeding Bill Wennington for a game winner against the Knicks in his first trip back to Madison Square Garden after returning from retirement in 1995, or finding Steve Kerr for the go-ahead basket in Game 6 of the 1997 Finals against the Utah Jazz to clinch the Bulls' fifth title.

ALBERT: Michael coming back to the Garden was thrilling. You had the feeling that the Garden was actually rooting for Michael Jordan. They were happy to see him back, and they always appreciated greatness in New York. Now, he was not always cheered, particularly during the era where the Knicks had a shot to win the championship. But when he came back from his baseball hiatus and played his first game at the Garden, that was a huge event, and he puts up 55 points. Then it comes down to the last shot, and he gives the ball to Bill Wennington.

COLLINS: Michael was between the foul line and the dotted area, and Patrick [Ewing] stepped up to block [him], and Michael dropped it right down to Wennington and he laid the ball in to win the game.

RASHAD: You would've thought that he would take the last shot. 'Cause he had taken all the shots before and 'cause he's a superstar. And to see him pass it to Wennington, you realize that's a team guy. After that pass, you got an inside look of what Michael's all about. He was about playing hard and winning. He would do whatever it took to win. If it meant shutting down your guy, he'd shut the guy down. If it meant he had to score 40 points, he'd score 40. And in all the games I saw him play, I never saw him play a *bad* game.

THORN: I was at the game when he made the pass to Wennington, and my feeling was, "Why is he passing the ball to him?" Game winner. Those guys see things others can't.

RASHAD: Of all the things Michael Jordan did during that time, he never separated himself from the team. If he had 60 points, it was still *us*. He was excited because they came through: "My man stepped up and knocked that thing down!" That solidifies your team.

O'NEAL: My favorite basketball clip in the world: Michael Jordan sitting on the bench, tired as hell, and he looks at Steve Kerr and says, "They're doubling me all the time. I'm going to kick it to you." And Steve looks back at him and says, "I'll be ready."

KERR: Michael was always thinking a step ahead. He knew that John Stockton, the guy who was guarding me, was the most likely guy to double-team him based on the play we designed and where I was gonna be located. Earlier in that series, Stockton had stolen the ball from him on a similar play, so he realized what was likely to happen.

O'NEAL: Mike pump-faked, Stockton jumped, he kicked it to Kerr: nailed it.

KERR: It was pretty simple: we were gonna go to Michael in any clutch situation, and the rest of us had to be ready for whatever was coming next. Usually, he'd get double-teamed. Sometimes he'd score anyway, but he really learned to trust his teammates. Players approach the last shot in different ways. Some guys—Kobe Bryant, Michael Jordan—embrace it and can't wait to take it over and over again. Most players, like myself, sometimes they feel comfortable taking it, sometimes they don't. Sometimes you're not feeling good about your game, you're struggling a little bit, and the ball's coming your way and you're thinking, "Oh man, I may not make this." You have to go into those shots without a care in the world, and that's hard because everybody's focused on you. The only way you can be successful with clutch shots is just saying, "Screw it, I'm gonna let it fly." That's not easy. For me, it wasn't easy. I could get in my own head, so I had to allow myself to just play and enjoy the moment.

THORN: The mental makeup of the assassin, or any player who goes above and beyond, I think it's inherent. Some people just have that gene.

COLLINS: Greatness wants people around them that they can trust. Michael had to see you do it in practice to trust you. I used to talk to guys who played with Michael, and they said, "[If] you come into the game, you run a pick-and-roll, they trap Michael and he throws you the ball, you better knock that shot down. You might not see it next time if you don't make that shot."

KERR: That moment against Utah was the moment I earned Michael's trust. I hadn't earned it before that night and had been playing with him for a couple of years. I had hit shots, but I never hit a big shot in a huge moment like that. The game was tied, maybe 30 seconds left. We called timeout, designed a play for Michael, and he turned to me and said, "I know I'm getting double-teamed, so be ready." I just remember walking out on the floor and saying, "Don't feint. If you catch it, just let it fly." I had made a couple of shots in the quarter, I was feeling good, I was just gonna be aggressive and take the shot. I still remember—after the game he was interviewed and I think he used the words, "Tonight, Steve earned his stripes." And I thought, "Man, I thought I already earned my stripes!" But with Michael, you had to do it in the big moments.

The defining moment of Jordan's career: Game 6 of the 1998 Finals, trailing the Utah Jazz by 1 point with only seconds remaining in the fourth quarter. Jordan steals the ball from Karl Malone, dribbles past half-court, makes a move to the top of the key, and rises for the last shot.

SIMMONS: The weirdest situation of a team that actually won the title was probably the Bulls in '98, when all those guys were on one-year contracts and Phil Jackson wasn't talking to Jerry Krause. But they had Jordan, and I think Game 6 of the '98 Finals is the greatest game anyone ever played. That guy beat the Jazz by himself and won the NBA title. He had Scottie Pippen, who could barely move with a bad back. Dennis Rodman was like a reality TV show at that point. And he's in Utah, which was the toughest place to play. He was 35, the [Bulls] had just played three straight seasons, gone through two championships already—he played 304 out of 304 games over those three years. They have to win Game 6, 'cause you're not winning Game 7 on the road in the Finals. He just controlled the game. At the end, they're down 3, [Jordan] comes out of a timeout, coast-to-coast layup. Utah comes down, they throw it to Malone. Jordan runs by him, turns around, swats it.

SMITH: You saw Jordan sneak behind and strip Karl Malone, and then you *knew* he was not giving up the ball. You saw them spread out, and Jordan drove to his right, crossed over—you got to remember, we all watch the footage now and you see the push-off, but live, you didn't see the push-off, all you saw was the crossover—and Bryon [Russell] goes sliding. And then Jordan shot it and it hit, and you're like, "Oooohh-hhh!"

SIMMONS: It all happened in the same 40 seconds—there was no time-out, nothing.

SMITH: The crossover, Bryon goes flying, and then he shot it and held the pose. Man, it was great to be there. I could always say I was there for Jordan's last title.

PIPPEN: The last one, we really celebrated it. By that point, when we went around the country, we weren't just basketball players anymore. We were like rock stars. It was something we hated to see go away, but in that final year, we tried to make the best of it. Now there's all the Bulls fans who come up, let you know how much you impacted their lives, and they always end with, "We really miss it." Well, I miss it, too.

Jordan, Genius, and Raising Basketball to the Level of Art

CUNNINGHAM: When you look at basketball, it's poetry, it's an art. When you watch Julius [Erving] or Jordan or LeBron James, some of the things they do, it's like a ballet. Their movements—there's only a couple people on the face of the earth that can do these things.

COLLINS: When you watch the genius and the artistry and the greatness of these players, I've always said they can be in the greatest ballet of all time. If you took LeBron James and put him to music and let him dribble the ball—he's an athlete like you can't believe. Larry Bird, you break down his jump shot—it's like silk. Magic Johnson making the pass. Michael Jordan with his tongue out, going to dunk it here, putting it here, and bringing it over here. These guys are different than anybody else. They play to their own music.

THOMAS: Basketball at its best is an art, but it can't really be described by language. It's a combination of mind, body, and what we call soul really coming together in this great physical display that you don't find in any other part of our society. The mind, the body, really come into play in a spontaneous, rhythmic, instantaneous combustion. When we say, "Man, Michael Jordan did a 360!"—to be able to come down [the court] and instantaneously spin in the air and dunk—it's sublime.

MICHAEL GOLDBERG: In basketball, you watch and emulate the things other players do. Once one player can do a "wow" move, then every kid in every school yard tries to do that themselves. Those that can refine it, take it to the next level, and so on down the line. I would say that Elgin Baylor begat Connie Hawkins, and Hawkins begat Earl Monroe, and Monroe begat Dr. J, and Dr. J begat David Thompson, and Thompson begat Michael Jordan, and Jordan begat Kobe Bryant, and there's more begats going on.

THORN: There's so many players who were not only great, but they were artistic. Being an assistant coach with the Nets when Erving was at his height—he would do things every night that I would say, "Can you believe he just did that?" You know when you drop a cat, it always lands on its feet? One night in San Antonio, he's driving to the basket and he got undercut, and he's about five feet off the floor. Any of us would've landed on our neck, seriously hurt ourselves. He landed on his feet. Connie Hawkins, all the things he could do with the ball—I mean, who else could do that? Earl Monroe with his spins—who could do that? And then David Thompson. Jordan, he's the next tick up the ladder.

SMITH: There's always successors. How would MJ have known how to be MJ if there was no Dr. J? Would Kobe have been Kobe if there were no MJ? Would LeBron have come along if Kobe wasn't doing what he was doing? That's why you never diminish the pioneers in this game, because they show you a path to greatness that you otherwise may not have known.

COLLINS: I don't think there's any question that there's a genius factor in the great players. They see the game in a different light, they feel the game differently, they understand the game on a different level.

VACCARO: I believe there really is a genius to playing at the highest level. To take it to the ultimate level, you have to be able to outthink your opponent, to see things two and three plays ahead. Michael Jordan was like that, of course. It's hard to describe to somebody that doesn't play basketball what that means.

COLLINS: I had the opportunity to coach Michael [at the end of his career]. When Michael got older, he and I would meet before games. He would say, "From my standpoint, this is the way I can hurt this particular team. So the stuff you run for me tonight, make sure I end up with it over here or over here." Just the way he thinks the game—I've seen [it] with Michael, with Magic, with LeBron, with Bird. You get this combination of skill, competitive will, energy, toughness. You watch them play and you're like, "Man, I wish I could just be Michael for one day. Let me be one of those geniuses."

MAGIC JOHNSON: It's tough to get somebody that's a genius of the game. I think Michael Jordan and Larry Bird are the closest that we've seen. A genius has no weakness, no flaws, and both of them didn't have one weakness. A genius could figure out what you're trying to do against him: "Oh, you're doubling from the top? I got something for that. You're coming baseline? OK, got it." That's genius.

KERR: The thing that connects guys like Tim Duncan, Michael Jordan, Larry Bird—all the great players had an incredible passion for the game. They can't wait to get to practice. That's why it's hard for those guys to retire. They spent 15, 20 years coming to work every day, loving the competitiveness, loving the process, and then all of a sudden it's over. Not every player in the NBA loves the work. The superstars love the work. Look at Kobe Bryant—I don't know if anybody's ever worked harder. Steve Nash—the attention to detail, the focus, and the joy in the process of working and competing is something that runs through all great players.

LEN ELMORE: The great ones are differentiated from the near greats because [of] a confidence that is born through hard work, past success, and it develops a mentality: "I'm the only one that can get this done."

DANIELS: To have the confidence to do the job at hand at that particular moment. Reggie Miller had that. Michael Jordan had that. Elgin Baylor, Jerry West—they had that confidence. They understand their limitations, and to them, they don't have any.

VAN GUNDY: I think that little extra confidence you see in the champion is not *before* they win it, but after—they know they can win it. In that climb of trying to win a championship, if you've never done it before, there's always doubt. Was Patrick Ewing a champion? Yes, because he invested everything he had, and he came *this* close. He just wasn't better than Michael Jordan, and Jordan, at the moment of truth, was always the difference. Sometimes you're born at the wrong time, and your team comes together at the wrong time. These guys who lose—you're never gonna convince me that Patrick Ewing, John Stockton, Karl Malone, are not champions. Likewise, you're never gonna convince me that because a guy plays his role—as insignificant as it might have been—on a Bulls team, he's more of a champion than those guys. The way it is today, Ewing would have gone to Chicago and become a champion and played a role. I hate how guys are viewed like he didn't have a ring and that means he wasn't as significant.

MASAI UJIRI (President of Basketball Operations, Toronto Raptors; 2013 NBA Executive of the Year): Leaders are born. I can't even think of any other way. They have the feel, they have the mental toughness, they have the selflessness, and they have the selfishness, too. A time to say, "Screw everybody, it's time for me to take over." The great ones—Bird, Magic, Jordan—have it. They understand the time, the place, the moment. They understand everything.

COLLINS: Do you think Michael Jordan ever thought in his lifetime what was gonna be written or said if he missed the game-winning shot? Never. Greatness fears no consequence.

KEVIN DURANT: What makes LeBron and Kobe and Jordan different is, those guys try to rip your neck off. They gonna show you they can back you down, throw an elbow at you, shoot the jumper over you, and if you show weakness, they gonna exploit it.

SIMMONS: I heard a great story: It was a big game and they were coming out of the timeout, and LeBron was coming towards the scorer's table. [The opposing team] had to foul—the team was down—and the coach told the player, "Foul LeBron if he gets it." He said it knowing LeBron would hear and that it would bother him. If you said that to Michael Jordan, he would have taken it so personally. He would have come over and pulled your jugular vein out, and he'd be like eating your jugular.

RASHAD: Michael Jordan and winning are synonymous, and it's not an accident. I've never seen anybody rise to the occasion as many times as he has. *All the time.* Always! We played doubles tennis together one time and got beat, and he will never play tennis with me again. That's how competitive he is.

SIMMONS: The one bummer about the Jordan era: this doesn't go on his legacy, but he taught an entire generation who weren't as good as him to play like him. That generation was like, "I got this. Get out of my way. I'm gonna be Michael Jordan." And it infected the NBA for 15 years.

COLLINS: These stars think they can always win, no matter the score, the time, the circumstance. We're playing [Indiana] when I was coaching Washington. We were down like 25 going into the third quarter, and Michael had 8 points. I went to him and said, "I'm gonna sit you here, and if we make a run, I'll put you back in." Well, I wish the PR director had told me that Michael had like 800-plus games in a row that he had scored double figures. So we get blown out, and it breaks his streak. I go to the media, and they're like, "How do you think Michael is gonna feel about this?" I said, "Six championships, gold medals—Michael doesn't care about 10 points." So they go to Michael, and he supports everything I say. Now I'm sitting on that loneliest seat in the world—a head coach after a loss by yourself in the front row of the bus. Everybody got on, and Michael sits next to me and he said, "I need to ask you a question. Do you think I can still play?" I said, "Michael, you know how much I believe in you. I'm here with you to build something, and I definitely think you can still play." He said, "You did the right thing tonight—there's no need for me to go back in to score 2 points."

Fast-forward [to] our next game, two nights later. Michael scored the first three times he touched the ball. Timeout. Michael looks at me and he said, "We don't have to run any plays. Just play through me and don't take me out until I tell you." With about 2 minutes to go, we're up 20, he looks at me like, "I've had enough." I take him out, and he said, "Told you I could still play." You know how many points he had? Fifty-one. Came back the next game, had 45. He had 96 points in the next two games after he got 8, at age 40. I'm sitting there, and I'm like, "Do people really know what greatness is?"

THE NBA'S RELUCTANT REVOLUTIONARY

On March 12, 1997, the Philadelphia 76ers crowd sprung to its feet, cheering wildly with anticipation.

Rookie Allen Iverson preened at the top of the key behind the three-point circle, sizing up his childhood idol, Michael Jordan. As Jordan crouched in his defensive stance, Iverson dribbled in place, then crossed him left—"a little cross, to see if he would bite," AI would explain later—then whipped the ball between his legs and crossed over again, hard, as MJ, the game's greatest player, lunged at him in vain. Iverson stepped around the off-balance Jordan, sank the jumper, and the jubilant 76ers fans celebrated as though they had just won the NBA championship.

In reality, Philadelphia eked out only 22 victories that season, but Iverson, at barely 6' and 165 pounds, captivated the city with his fearless drives to the basket, his theatrical clutch shooting, and that crossover, which reduced legends to mere basketball mortals.

"I would challenge any basketball historian to come up with five guys who were greater warriors in NBA history than Allen Iverson," said Stephen A. Smith, who covered Iverson for the *Philadelphia Inquirer*. "And it wasn't just because of his performance on the court. Allen Iverson had to fight every day, mentally or emotionally. One minute it was with society, another minute it was with coach Larry Brown, another minute it was with a teammate, another minute it was with friends and loved ones, another minute it was the media, and it circulated time and time and time again."

Iverson had led Bethel High School in Virginia to state championships in both football (as quarterback) and basketball (as point guard) and was one of the most hotly recruited athletes in the country until a racially charged melee at a bowling alley on Valentine's Day 1993 landed him in the Newport News City Farm correctional facility. Although he was pardoned by Governor Douglas Wilder and released after four months, all the scholarship offers except one had vanished.

"There was no choice but Georgetown," Iverson said. "I got in a situation, and my mom went up to coach [John Thompson] and asked him to save my life, and that's basically what he did."

Iverson joined the NBA as the No. 1 overall pick in 1996. He grew out his hair and had it braided into cornrows, added numerous tattoos over the course of his career, and became the face of the hip-hop generation—a look that some fans, and sponsors, struggled to embrace.

"I'm pretty sure I rubbed a lot of people the wrong way in the beginning," Iverson said. "I didn't do anything to try to hurt anybody or disrespect anybody. I was just being me. I got cornrows because I was sick of [barbers] messin' my hair up on the road. I figured, 'If I get cornrows, I don't have to worry about that.' But people thought that I was doing it to be some gangsta tough guy."

David Stern said Iverson mirrored society's disposition. "There's music, there's fashion, motion pictures, and sports," Stern said. "Those are the four things that reflect culture and change attitudes. So if Allen Iverson wears his pants down to his ankles, then kids are wearing their pants down to their ankles. If somebody appears in a hat after a championship game with a tag hanging down, then the kids are wearing their hats that way. If two guys hug after the game, it's, 'Oh my God, a white player and a black player hugged each other.' Of course they hugged each other—they're teammates. That has a huge impact on society."

And yet the NBA initially resisted AI's influence. Stern instituted a dress code that Iverson claimed specifically targeted him. When *Hoop* magazine (a league publication) put Iverson on the cover in 2000, they airbrushed his tattoos.

"The tats were something that people weren't used to, so it was odd to them," Iverson said. "Everybody in the world has tattoos now. It's all right because I did it, and people accept it now. They know that just because somebody got a tattoo don't mean that they're some bad guy."

In his only Finals appearance, Iverson shocked Kobe Bryant, Shaquille O'Neal, and the Los Angeles Lakers in Game 1 of the 2001 Finals by dropping 48 points and leading the Sixers to a 107–101 overtime victory. L.A. would go on to win in five games, but not before AI's signature crossover grew in stature, this time with Tyronn Lue as the victim. As Iverson unleashed his murderous move, Lue fell, the shot swished through, and AI pointedly stepped over Lue as he turned up court.

"When your imagination's running wild, you figure out different ways to take [the crossover] to a different level," Iverson said. "When I crossed up Jordan, people thought it was something that I planned. I didn't—it was just a reaction."

Iverson's nomadic final seasons included stops in Denver, Detroit, Memphis, back to Philly, and Turkey. Along the way, he was involved in a bar brawl and domestic disturbances, was banned from casinos in Atlantic City, and struggled with alcohol and financial woes.

Smith believes the bowling alley incident forever shaped Iverson. "The moment you imprisoned Allen Iverson, you forever imprisoned him. Every day he wakes up, he is incarcerated, because there's somebody in his face, in his heart, in his spirit, in his thoughts, that's telling him what he can do, when to do it, how to do it," Smith said. "So he walks around with these battles."

"I've been defending myself my whole life," Iverson said. "I've gotta have rhino skin and deal with it."

THE GREATEST TEAM EVER ASSEMBLED

Although FIBA had plans to open Olympic basketball to NBA players even before the Seoul Olympics took place in 1988, the effort gained public approval after the games, where a Soviet team led by Sarunas Marciulionis and Arvydas Sabonis defeated Team USA's group of college stars, which included Danny Manning and David Robinson. It was the United States' first noncontroversial loss in Olympic basketball, and it set the stage for a team of professionals to seek redemption in 1992.

BILL SIMMONS: 'Eighty-eight was the worst. I'm still mad about the '88 gold medal. We had David Robinson, we had Danny Manning, we had Hersey Hawkins. We should have killed everybody.

DONNIE WALSH: The European guys were playing pro players. Russia, Yugoslavia—those guys were as good as our pros, and we weren't playing pros. John Thompson was coaching that team, and I'm thinking, "He has no hope. They're playing an NBA game out there." We had good players, but they hadn't had the experience that these guys had, and as a result they weren't playing the same kind of game. I remember thinking, "There's no way we can beat these teams—they're too experienced."

DANNY MANNING: It was very disappointing, not winning the gold. Your whole mind-set is, you wanna put that gold medal around your neck. You wanna hear the national anthem of your country. And we fell short of that.

DAVID ROBINSON (Center, San Antonio Spurs; 1995 NBA MVP): It was devastating to be the first USA team to not win a gold medal outside of some controversy.

SIMMONS: The problem was Thompson. He didn't pick Tim Hardaway, didn't pick Steve Kerr, didn't pick Rod Strickland. The team we put together was like, "We're gonna press these guys." And the Russians were like, "Great, this is the best news we've ever had." Sabonis was magnificent, but that was such a poorly picked team that I still blame John Thompson.

SARUNAS MARCIULIONIS (Shooting Guard, Golden State Warriors; 1988 Olympic Gold Medalist): Sabonis would help to bring the ball [up]. Always you can pass [to] Sabonis that he can pass you back. You know, to get into position to play half-court game.

ROBINSON: I thought we had a pretty talented team and we were going to be successful, but we lost in the semifinals to the Russians. It was a game we could have won, but we did not.

MARCIULIONIS: When [we] came to play semifinal against U.S., I really didn't expect to keep up with them. David Robinson, J. R. Reid— they're blowing teams away. And [Soviet coach Alexander] Gomelsky came to me: "Why are they better? Why are they better?" Gomelsky said before the game, "Do not allow them to dunk, because you just going to provide the energy if you allow them."

MANNING: They were a better team than us on that night. When you look back on the team we played against, they had a future Hall of Famer in Sabonis, and they had some really talented guards. They were well coached, and they had a great deal of experience. I played terrible. I could have scored more, could have done a better job defensively. I could have rebounded better. I didn't do enough to help our team win, and that haunts me to this day. After we got beat, it was the last amateur team. I like to say we paved the way for the Dream Team, 'cause we didn't fare so well.

Team USA's bronze medal in 1988 may have "paved the way for the Dream Team" as far as the American public was concerned, but the NBA still needed to be convinced.

MARV ALBERT: What was the Dream Team? First of all, it was FIBA that wanted the United States' professional players. The U.S. did not want it.

RUSS GRANIK: One misperception is that the NBA was anxious to get involved with the Olympics. We had no particular designs on the Olympics.

DAVID STERN: The '88 Olympics came and went. [The NBA] was not part of it. I do remember the American team ran into the Soviet Union and a united Yugoslavia—two hellacious teams. . . . But it wasn't that we were somehow determined to avenge the 1988 Olympic loss.

GRANIK: Coming out of '88, David [Stern] and I were like most basketball fans in the U.S., saying this is lousy because we really lost, unlike in '72, where it was debatable. We got beat, and that didn't seem to make sense, since we knew the best players were in the United States. But prior to 1988, we had some contacts with FIBA in the form of Dr. [Boris] Stankovic, the secretary-general, to talk about creating some competition where the NBA would play against international teams.

STERN: Russ and I had begun discussions with FIBA in either '86 or '87. Boris Stankovic said, "Look, it's a bit of an anomaly: we're in charge of all the basketball players in the world except for the best 350. So, would you do us the honor, if we open the Olympics up, to allow your players to play . . ." Now, remember, the big secret was that pros were already playing in the Olympics. If you played in Italy and made a million dollars, you were an amateur, but if you played in the NBA you were a pro. We said, "All right, let's work together, see how it goes."

DAVID FALK: Most people in America felt that the idea of sending amateurs to the Olympics had become outmoded. Most of these countries were subsidizing the athletes—they were pros, and we're sending college kids.

ROD THORN: From FIBA's standpoint, it would give a tremendous impetus to the world to have professionals play and particularly to have NBA players play, helping basketball grow. I think Commissioner Stern felt that also.

GRANIK: In 1989, FIBA voted to eliminate distinctions between amateurs and professionals, which opened the door for NBA players to compete in the Olympics. Shortly before that, David and I got a call from Dave Gavitt, who was then the commissioner of the Big East Conference, but also the newly elected president of the Amateur Basketball Association of the [United States of America], which was in charge of selecting and fielding the Olympic team. Gavitt told us, "There's going to be this vote, and since I work for the college representatives at ABAUSA, I have to vote against having pros in the Olympics. But it's going to pass despite our vote, and we gotta start talking about what role the NBA should have." We said, "Let's wait and see, and if there's something to talk about, we'll give it some thought."

THORN: If you recall, two countries voted against having professionals play in the Olympics—the United States and [the Soviet Union].

GRANIK: I don't think you can praise Dave Gavitt enough. If Dave was not head of USA Basketball in 1989, I don't know if things could've gotten together. There was a fair amount of shock among the college ranks, because the Olympics had always been theirs to run. NCAA people had always controlled international basketball from the U.S. standpoint. And it took somebody like Dave, who could say to the college community, "Look, this is inevitable. The amateur/pro distinction doesn't work anymore, and if we're going to put the best team together, we've got to work with the NBA."

STERN: We had a great relationship with Dave Gavitt, and we said, "If it isn't for '92, it's fine. We don't *have* to do it, we're not pushing it." It was interesting that the U.S. was against it and Russia was against it, because they didn't want to lose control of what they had, and therefore those federations voted against it.

GRANIK: Sure enough, at the FIBA meeting, the resolution passed overwhelmingly, and all of a sudden there were no barriers to NBA players competing in international competitions.

STERN: The vote came and went, and they said, "We're gonna open it up for '92." We said, "OK, we want to be good neighbors, we'll do it."

GRANIK: The NBA was not certain that we wanted to participate at the level we ultimately did. David [Stern] and I had a lot of conversations about it, and we felt we were in a difficult spot. Again, we had not lobbied for this. On the one hand, we saw lots of obstacles to participating and several concerns, but on the other hand, we felt that if we're being invited to have NBA players in the Olympics, if we say no, we're gonna look bad. Clearly, under player contracts the owners and the league could've prohibited players from playing in the Olympics, but we concluded that we really had to participate. Once we were gonna do that, we were gonna help the United States put together the very best team that it could.

FALK: I think it was a brilliant move by the NBA, both to reassert American dominance in a sport that we invented as well as to market the league internationally.

GRANIK: The NBA owners had to be convinced that it made sense to have players in this competition during the off-season. This was an opportunity to promote the league, particularly internationally, in a way that had never been done before, and that's certainly what David and I were advising them. That was handled pretty quickly and unanimously by the NBA Board of Governors. The first issue we had was, there was an upcoming world championship, in 1990, and now NBA players were eligible for that, and we all agreed we didn't want to rush. We weren't prepared, so let's make our focus the '92 Olympics in Barcelona.

ALBERT: The [NBA] saw the possibilities of what would happen from a global point of view, because basketball was starting to become significant overseas.

SIMMONS: When the Dream Team started happening, it was such a good stretch of the NBA to have a Dream Team, 'cause the early '90s was about as talented as the league has ever been. And the cool part was, "Who they gonna pick?" It was the greatest high school varsity decision of all time.

GRANIK: There was the issue of whether players would be willing to give up a substantial chunk of their off-season, but getting the players was never a problem. All the star players came to it with the same response, which was, "If you can get A, B, and C to play, then I'm in." Nobody wanted to be the only superstar on this team, but every superstar saw this as an opportunity to play with other great players that he'd really never played with before. What we did was, Rod Thorn and I started making contact with the players, and right away Magic Johnson said, "I'm in if you want me, and you can tell anybody you want that I'm in." Even Michael Jordan said right at the start, "I don't want my name out there for a while, but if you can put together the kind of roster you're talking about, I'll do it."

MAGIC JOHNSON: When the call came, I jumped at it. To play against the world's best every day in practice was a thrill for me, and also therapy at the same time.

ROBINSON: I was mixed about the idea of the pros playing in the Olympics. I like the idea of college players representing the United States. I felt like we were still very competitive in '88. I was disappointed that we lost, but I liked the idea of competition. I like the idea of "Hey, everybody's getting better, we better get better." So I had mixed feelings about the pros playing, but when the opportunity came in '92, there was no way I was turning that down. The opportunity to get that gold medal was like a prayer answered.

GRANIK: In the past, whether you played in the Olympics always depended on when you happened to be graduating or finishing your junior year of college. Some of the players had already played in the Olympics—Michael Jordan, Patrick Ewing, David Robinson—but either way, I think there was some element of "This opportunity to play for my country on a stage like this is something I can't turn down." I do think competitiveness and being able to be part of perhaps the greatest team ever put together also meant a great deal.

CHRIS MULLIN: There were a lot of different reasons why people were into it. Magic left school, right? He and Larry didn't play in the Olympics. Clyde [Drexler] left [college] in '83, so he didn't play in '84. John [Stockton] and Karl [Malone] were cut from '84. Michael [Jordan], Patrick [Ewing], and I were fortunate enough to play in the 1984 Olympics, so at that point you feel it's the only chance you'll get to represent your country, because it's only open to amateurs. Then, lo and behold, we lose in '88, the rule changed, and all of a sudden it's open to professionals. There's an opportunity to do it again. You think about the legendary players on that team—to spend a summer with these incredible players, to learn from them, it's mind-boggling.

CHRISTIAN LAETTNER: I was 22, I had been watching Magic and Bird and Jordan and Ewing play my whole life, and I looked up to every one of 'em. I'm saying to myself, "This is gonna be a great experience because I get to practice with these guys and play one-on-one with these guys, and then know and accept my position on the team," which was the 12th man, the lowest man on the totem pole. And I was perfectly comfortable with that.

MULLIN: From what I'm told, they asked 12 people, and 12 people said yes.

LAETTNER: I didn't even know if I belonged. Shaq could've very easily been on that team. Alonzo [Mourning] could've been on that team. I just knew that I was lucky to be chosen, so I was gonna take advantage of it by listening, watching, learning, and playing as much as I could.

RICK WELTS: I was lucky enough to be in charge of the marketing side. At the All-Star Game before the Olympics, the NBA orchestrated a secret photo shoot for *Sports Illustrated* to shoot our amazing athletes in these USA uniforms. Patrick Ewing was there, Michael Jordan was there,

Larry Bird was there, Magic Johnson was there, and all of a sudden the cover comes out: a picture that said, "Look out, world, this could be the next dream team." And there was the name. Some copywriter coined the name "Dream Team," which instantly stuck forevermore.

GRANIK: The Dream Team is a great name. I think the team still would've had incredible notoriety, but the Dream Team title was the cherry on top.

MULLIN: That's a good name for it because that was my dream.

GRANIK: Once we agreed we're going forward, we had to pick a coaching staff. First, we selected a committee, the majority of which were general managers that the league office asked to participate—the very best of the best, at the time, across the NBA. And the first mission of this committee was to pick a head coach and start talking with him about what kind of team we needed. We decided it had to be an NBA coach the first time around, to make sure the owners were comfortable, make sure players were comfortable. And it certainly was not an accident that Chuck Daly was appointed coach of the Dream Team.

QUINN BUCKNER: The hiring of Chuck Daly was because he's clearly got enough skill, but the question is, who's best at managing personalities? Isiah Thomas was a strong-willed man. Dennis Rodman. If you go up and down that [Pistons] team, they had guys who were extremely strong-willed. Chuck was able to manage that and win championships with it, so they felt like he was the right guy to manage a team full of Hall of Famers.

GRANIK: [Chuck] was one of the most universally liked and respected people across the NBA. He had a reputation for getting along with players that had a certain ego level, and getting [them] to submerge their egos and play well together. And Chuck was just great with people, and we needed someone who was willing to do press conferences, go to cocktail parties, and do all the public things that were gonna be necessary if the NBA was going to achieve what it hoped out of this effort, and if USA Basketball was going to be happy with the image projected.

PETER VECSEY: Chuck Daly was the perfect guy to be around superstars. You know, make it fun, keep their egos in check, not too much practice, not too much talking. But the strangest thing is that Chuck did not include Isiah. I've talked to Isiah about that, and he won't go there. Chuck could have had him—they told him he could have four picks. Now, if you have four picks, you don't have to worry about saying, "Make sure you get Jordan and Magic." Isiah was the guy he should have said number one. Won him two championships. How can you not take him? What does it say that Chuck Daly didn't take him?

ISIAH THOMAS: I don't know, I really don't know. There've been a lot of people to take credit for keeping me off the team. All I know is this: I wanted to participate. I wanted to be on the team.

ALBERT: He should have made the team. There's no question. Nothing has been ever proven about that, but it appears that they didn't want him.

THOMAS: Well, at that time, if the criteria was supposed to be the players who had done the most for the game, players who won championships and elevated the NBA—the Pistons had won two championships, Jordan had just won his second, Magic had four or five, Bird had three—those were the champions at that time. I think people were outraged [that I wasn't chosen], but that's how it was. My life has been the salmon swimming upstream, and sometimes the bear gets a claw on you.

SIMMONS: Isiah's one of the best 25 players ever, and he didn't make it. Did he not make it 'cause Jordan said, "I'm not playing if he makes it"? Yeah, partly, but they also had John Stockton and Magic Johnson, so it's not like they weren't set at point guard.

AHMAD RASHAD: Was that after the [Pistons] walked off the court or before? After. OK, there's the fallout. When you're gonna walk off the court and not shake hands, there's gonna be fallout somewhere.

STEPHEN A. SMITH: I think it's unfair for Isiah Thomas to be blamed for everything, but some of it was him because of his stubbornness, because of his willingness to fight, because of him being loyal to a fault. Walking off the court against Chicago without shaking guys' hands, that wasn't Isiah Thomas's idea, but Isiah was willing to go with it and stand with his teammates, not realizing that the Jordan era had become so significant. Anybody who went against him was a pariah.

RASHAD: Chuck Daly didn't pick him, end of story. Now, there's other stuff that happened, but the bottom line is, it's Chuck's pick, [and] he didn't pick him. Maybe Michael wouldn't have played if Chuck picked [Thomas], but he could've picked him. Chuck made that decision because of chemistry. For Isiah, I would think that'd be one of the most disappointing things in his whole career, that he wasn't a part of that.

SMITH: I don't know of many things more egregious in NBA history than Isiah Thomas being left off of the Dream Team. If there were ever a situation where somebody should have been arrested for making such a decision, it was that, and I respect every damn body who was on that team. But don't tell me that John Stockton or anybody else outside of Magic and Jordan deserved to be on that Olympic team more than Isiah Thomas.

THOMAS: Actually, you know what? It *was* a dream team. When I wasn't selected, I rooted for the Dream Team. They were great players and they won the gold medal, and at the end of the day, that's what you're supposed to do.

STERN: What people forget is the criticism we got for this team. Everyone said, "Oh, the NBA is ridiculous. They're putting together this overkilling team to smash the rest of the world."

ADAM SILVER: As famous as that team is now, the fact was these were a group of professionals that were widely perceived as beating up on inferior players. And whether it was the *New York Times* or *USA Today* or mainstream sportswriters and editorial writers, they were largely condemned. And we were aware that outside the United States, the reception was completely different. People were falling in love with these players. It wasn't just the basketball. This was a piece of Americana. It was fashion, it was style, it was the music that came with them.

WELTS: The biggest challenge in trying to get the Dream Team to the Olympics in 1992 was the fact that the United States had not qualified. Because we had not done well in international competition, there was no automatic path. In fact, there was a [qualifying tournament] that involved teams from Central and South America to determine who was gonna represent our region at the Olympics. Russ Granik somehow made a deal with the bandits that owned the rights to that tournament to move it to Portland, Oregon. We knew we had something special by the time we got to that tournament because the first team that came out of the locker room to play the U.S. came out with their cameras to take pictures of Michael Jordan or Larry Bird or Magic Johnson, whoever it was.

ALBERT: When the Dream Team played in the Tournament of the Americas in Portland, the first time they walked onto the court I got chills. It was the greatest team in the history of sports. Then, that first game they beat Cuba by 50 or something like that, and you knew they were going to knock everybody off, because the other countries were not ready for that. I remember going to Monaco after Portland, because [the Americans] were playing a series of exhibition games, and they played against France. There was a little French guard who [was] defending Michael, and they ended up pushing and shoving, screaming at each other, taunting. It was getting ugly. The game ends, the U.S. wins by 30 points, and the little French guy comes over to Michael and says, "Can I take a photo with you?" Of course, Michael has his arm around him, and they took a photo. You just knew something different was happening 'cause the photos started.

WELTS: To be the one who had the opportunity to head the marketing side of it was a dream come true. We could go to companies and say, "This is who's gonna represent the United States in basketball. Wouldn't you want to run a national super-promotion around that?" And the answers were "Yes, yes, yes! Sign us up."

STERN: People forget—it was not an easy Olympics, despite what it appeared. One day, Charles [Barkley] gives the Angolan an elbow and says, "I just wanna show the brother what it's like in the hood," or something. And then Michael puts the American flag over his Reebok Olympic uniform because he's a Nike guy? Or the players were gonna refuse to step to the podium if they were forced to wear the Reebok uniform. But Charles is Charles, and it was fun.

MULLIN: The thing that was amazing was how quickly it became a team. We had a few practices in San Diego that were kind of choppy. Everyone was getting out of each other's way, and then all of the sudden, everyone got into their roles and Chuck Daly was the perfect orchestrator, and it became a team.

P. J. CARLESIMO (Assistant Coach, 1992 U.S. Men's National Team): Everything was aligned. You had some guys at the peak of their career, some guys nearing the end, some of the young guys. . . . I've been lucky. I've had some of the greatest experiences you can imagine. But those couple months, beginning in San Diego and then Portland and the week in Monte Carlo before we went to Barcelona, you can't get close to that.

ROBINSON: Playing basketball with that team was a dream. Smart players at every corner. The game was easy, it was competitive, it was intense. It was really basketball in its purest form.

CARLESIMO: It was incredible from day one how focused those guys were and how seriously they took it. They took no prisoners from the first practice to the end.

MULLIN: Larry and Magic were pretty much our leaders, vocally. Physically, probably Michael and Charles—the way they dominated on the court. But each and every game, in the locker room we'd say, "Let's try to play a perfect game. Let's set the bar so high for the people behind us

Moses Malone jumped straight from high school to the ABA in 1974, when he inked a $1 million contract with the Utah Stars.
Associated Press Photo/Robert Houston

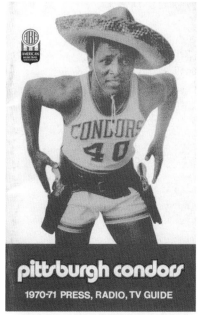

Forward John Brisker was one of the ABA's most dangerous scoring threats—and an even greater threat to punch out his opponents.

Lynette Woodard's decorated résumé includes 3,649 points at Kansas, a stint with the Globetrotters, and a gold medal with team USA in the 1984 Olympic Games.
Tony Duffy/Getty Images Sport/Getty Images

From the streets of New York City to the subway, Walt "Clyde" Frazier exuded style. *Associated Press Photo/Richard Drew*

Even as a reserve forward for the New York Knicks, Phil Jackson exhibited a free spirit that would earn him the moniker Zen Master as a Hall of Fame coach. *George Kalinsky*

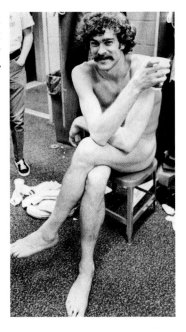

Isiah Thomas listening to coach Bob Knight during the 1979 Pan American Games. Thomas would help lead Knight's Indiana Hoosiers to an NCAA title in 1981. *Associated Press Photo*

John Thompson coached the Georgetown University Hoyas from 1972–99 and led the school to its only national championship in 1984.
Associated Press Photo

Cheryl Miller won back-to-back national championships with USC in 1983 and '84.
Associated Press Photo/Alvin Chung

Pat Summitt coached Team USA to a gold medal in 1984, but it would be three more seasons before her Tennessee players hoisted her to celebrate her first national championship with the Vols.
Peter Read Miller/Sports Illustrated/Getty Images

Connecticut coach Geno Auriemma describes his complex relationship with longtime rival Pat Summitt as "never as bad as people thought it was, but never as good as they wanted it to be."
Hartford Courant/*Tribune News Service/Getty Images*

Larry Bird, pictured here on October 24, 1988, accepting the MVP trophy after the Boston Celtics defeated Real Madrid in the 1988 McDonald's Championship, became known throughout the world for his gritty physical play and signature clutch shooting.
Andrew D. Bernstein/ National Basketball Association/Getty Images

The Los Angeles Lakers, led by coach Pat Riley and all-time greats Magic Johnson and Kareem Abdul-Jabbar, won five NBA championships in the 1980s and introduced the world (and number-one fan Jack Nicholson) to Showtime.
Associated Press Photo

The impeccably coiffed Pat Riley epitomized the style and glamour of his '80s Showtime Lakers.
USA TODAY Sports Images

Lithuanian Šarūnas Marčiulionis, one of the first European players to leave the former Soviet Union to join the NBA in 1989.
Mitchell Layton/Getty Images Sport/Getty Images

Michael Jordan celebrates knocking down The Shot over the outstretched arms of Cleveland guard Craig Ehlo in the Game 5 clincher of the 1989 playoffs, one of many clutch baskets His Airness delivered in his iconic career.
Ed Wagner/Chicago Tribune/Tribune News Service/Getty Images

The Dream Team won gold for the United States in the 1992 Barcelona Olympics and inspired a generation of basketball players around the globe.
Andrew D. Bernstein/National Basketball Association/Getty Images

David Stern (pictured with LA Sparks star Lisa Leslie and commissioner Val Ackerman), vowed that "failure was not an option" for the fledgling WNBA.
Jennifer Pottheiser/National Basketball Association/Getty Images

Hakeem Olajuwon came from Nigeria to play college basketball at the University of Houston before becoming the Number 1 overall pick in the 1984 NBA draft, selected by the Houston Rockets.
Manny Millan/Sports Illustrated Classic/Getty Images

Coach Gregg Popovich assembled a group of unselfish stars from all corners of the world who fostered a culture that came to represent an NBA model of success and consistency.
USA TODAY Sports Images

Kobe Bryant and Shaquille O'Neal, two of the game's most dominant supernovas, left us all wondering what could have been had they stayed together.
Lori Shepler/2002 Los Angeles Times. *Used with Permission.*

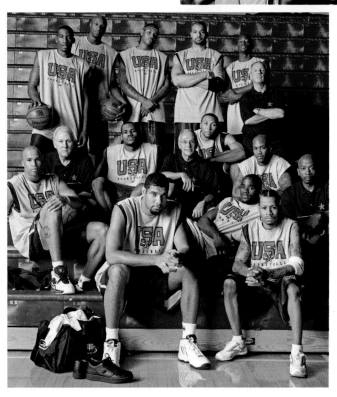

The 2004 men's national team, led by head coach Larry Brown, won bronze in Athens and became the first NBA-backed Olympic team to fall short of a gold medal.
Michael O'Neill/Contour RA/Getty Images

Splash Brothers Steph Curry (left) and Klay Thompson revolutionized "small ball" by dialing up a barrage of long-range three-point bombs with spellbinding accuracy.
Elsa/Getty Images Sport/ Getty Images

While NBA commissioner Adam Silver (right) admired the work of his predecessor and mentor, David Stern, he proved to be fearless in imprinting his own stamp on the league.
Scott Halleran/Getty Images Sport Classic/Getty Images

Even as a young high school player at St. Vincent-St. Mary High School in Akron, OH, LeBron James (far left) had already been branded The Chosen One.
Phil Masturzo/Akron Beacon Journal/Tribune News Service/Getty Images

that we play this special brand of basketball." We kind of knew we were going to win, but [we said], "Let's not settle for that. Let's play unselfish, let's move the ball, include everybody, and set this high standard."

JOHNSON: We were practicing hard, and then we got out there, and I was able to do my thing, to be Magic. I wanted the world to see me as the same guy as when I left [the NBA]. I was gonna be *that guy* on the Dream Team—and I was able to do that. I didn't know I would help people [with HIV] around the world by playing for the Dream Team.

LAETTNER: I loved the role I had on the Dream Team because I didn't have to play good for us to win. There's no pressure. I carried the bags when they told me to, I got them doughnuts and cigars. Half of them were really good to me before the first practice, and half didn't warm up to me until after the first practice, once they realized I wasn't too soft or I wasn't a prima donna, and that I was willing to pick up their dirty towels. Then they were all great to me. Even Jordan, you know, 'cause of the Carolina and Duke thing. But it was fun being the rookie. There were times where I was the practice dummy for Chris Mullin or Larry Bird. Bird was a little injured, and he and I would play one-on-one to get the rust off him. Then there were times when Mullin didn't practice, so the coaches would say, "Go down there with Laettner and get the rust off." I was like a puppy dog, waiting for them to come down and play one-on-one with me.

ROBINSON: I bonded with all of them, even Karl Malone. Karl was Utah Jazz, our [the Spurs'] hated rival. They were, execution-wise, the team we wanted to be. And certainly our biggest headache in our division. So that was a surprise to me, that I ended up liking him so much. We were in the gym, lifting weights together, and I'm watching Karl and thinking, "There's a reason why that guy looks [like] an animal. He works like an animal." And Charles Barkley was in the gym with us, and we were in there hanging out, got to be great friends.

SIMMONS: Barkley was the breakout star of the Dream Team. I love All-Star Games and the Olympic stuff, because you see guys that you might have pigeonholed a certain way and then you watch them with good players and it's different. Barkley had been carrying a lousy supporting cast, and that was one of the only times he had a team.

LAETTNER: Barkley was skinny on the Dream Team. But the power the guy had in his legs was just unbelievable. I've never seen anyone 6'4" defend the rim like he can. He would let people get all the way to the hoop and then at the last second block their shot.

PEJA STOJAKOVIC (Shooting Guard, Sacramento Kings; 3-Time NBA All-Star): I watched every single game. They were so dominant athletically, so dominant fundamentally. Everything they did, it felt [like it] was out of this world. That it can't be copied. The way they move the ball, the way they play defense, the way they ran the floor, and then they also were individually very strong, so it was really hard for any team to not only play against them but just to compete against them.

MARCIULIONIS: You know, we [Lithuania] wanted to—how do you say—not be beaten badly, but it didn't happen. Health-wise, we didn't get hurt, we saved our energy, but we lost embarrassing. What can you do?

FALK: You had these guys over there, the best America could offer, winning by an average of 50 points a game. And you watch these teams asking for autographs after the Dream Team beat them. It was almost like men against boys, but it made the point that reasserted American dominance in worldwide basketball.

SIMMONS: When they picked the team and you saw who was on it, it was just unparalleled. We didn't realize until the actual Olympics started that it sucked to watch, 'cause they were so much better. It was like watching a high school team play a fourth-grade team.

ALBERT: Croatia gave 'em a game for a little while, and then it was over. Toni Kukoc was playing for the opposition, and at the time there were rumors that the Bulls were going to sign Kukoc, who was then considered the best player overseas. Pippen was very upset because there were numbers being thrown around, and Pippen was in the process of getting a new contract, and the numbers did not measure up to what Kukoc was supposedly going to get. So Pippen and Jordan decided they were going to double-team Kukoc throughout the game. Kukoc never could get the ball. They blanketed him, and he was so frustrated, and of course the United States won easily.

RASHAD: Michael and Scottie shut down Toni Kukoc, just because the owner had said that he was better than them. They wouldn't even let him dribble.

VLADE DIVAC (Center, Los Angeles Lakers/Sacramento Kings; 2001 NBA All-Star): I was watching the finals when Croatia play Dream Team, and definitely it was a statement: "You gonna be our teammate, but you have to earn your respect." Toni took it the right way, and when he joined the Chicago [Bulls], he was a big part of their success.

ALBERT: Red Holzman used to say, "You think it's easy to win a championship, but how many things can go wrong?" Chuck Daly was well aware of that, and he did a phenomenal job. They won by these astronomical scores. He *never* called a timeout.

STERN: The success of '92 surprised me because it was such a big deal. Being in Barcelona as Charles walked down the Ramblas and was followed by hordes of kids, and every place they went . . . They put together a great team, which was legendary as some combination of the Kirov ballet, the New York Philharmonic, and the Beatles.

ALBERT: Anytime they'd come out of the hotel, there were throngs, thousands of people, waiting just to get a gaze at them as they walked onto the bus.

ROBINSON: We were definitely rock stars. Staying in the best hotels, security everywhere, going to the game with police security down the wrong side of the road. We had incredible attention everywhere we went. We had Olympic athletes waiting outside their rooms and outside the bus to meet us, and it was really an amazing experience.

BOB RYAN: When I started covering this league in 1969, I never would've believed there would be players representing over 40 countries in the NBA. That's a wonderful development. It's broadened the talent pool, it's revitalized interest in basketball and the Olympics. Clearly, there were other antecedents and pioneers, but people must understand: the Dream Team was the turning point in all this.

BUCKNER: It's really what fostered global basketball. David Stern saw it and the late Dave Gavitt—they understood, "Let's grow the market. Let everybody play." And the reason there's so many good international players in the game is, they watched Larry, Magic, Michael, Charles, and that 1992 Olympics.

CHARLES BARKLEY: I get all these young guys coming to me from overseas saying they started playing basketball because of the Dream Team. Whether it's Steve Nash, Dirk Nowitzki, Tony Parker, Nene [Hilario], all those guys. That's probably one of my proudest accomplishments, not that I'm taking credit for it. I think it's really cool they're here, 'cause you want the game to be worldwide. Now Europeans play the game like we do. Back in my day, they didn't know how to play street ball. They played a very fundamentally sound game. But now there's no intimidation factor. They play with us all the time.

DIVAC: The Dream Team set the bar. They show the talent, and they show what basketball player can do on the floor. When I grew up, I had the chance to see maybe one or two [televised] games—delayed, not live. But after the Dream Team, [basketball] became very popular.

STOJAKOVIC: I think every kid at that time, they were watching the Dream Team. They wanted to imitate their moves in the playgrounds. Personally, it gave me motivation to work harder on my game and one day hopefully playing at that level, in the NBA, and it happened.

MASAI UJIRI: To non-Americans, the Dream Team was the moment that changed everything. Nobody had seen anything like that. The NBA was known to the world on VHS tapes; it was known on TV. The NBA was something unreachable, untouchable. And here you are, bringing it to play against the world: Michael Jordan, Karl Malone, Magic Johnson, all these guys on one team, here for the world to see.

MARK CUBAN: We all point to 1992 as being this great linchpin, but it wasn't the fact that we were in the Olympics, it was what happened with technology, what happened with media. It was when cable really started to explode, and when we started to get all these sports channels. People like to point to all these athletes that, because of the '92 Olympics, they got into basketball. What's a 7-footer in Germany going to do? Become a racecar driver? What's a 6'6" guy or 6'7" guy out of Argentina going to do?

YAO MING (Center, Houston Rockets; 8-Time NBA All-Star): I'm sorry, I have to tell the truth: in '92 it didn't mean a lot for us. Because TV broadcast is not very popular in China yet. The basketball games, especially in '92, the Dream Team didn't play against Team China, so they didn't get broadcast in China.

SILVER: The reaction abroad was what made them the true Dream Team. Part of what I did in my early days at the NBA was sell NBA rights outside of the United States. After the Dream Team, all of a sudden, these were some of the biggest stars on the planet. And there was a very different sense of who the NBA was and what these players stood for and the recognition that this was something much bigger than sports.

FALK: Basketball is played, I think, in over 200 countries now. You have more people today that play basketball every day in China than there are people who live in the United States. So exporting basketball on a global televised stage was a genius move by David Stern, and to do it the first time, you're not going to experiment, you're going to send the A team, you're going to send a team that absolutely can't lose.

GRANIK: The Dream Team had a huge impact on the NBA's brand and the growth of that brand internationally. Up until that point, people that might be interested in basketball had some awareness of the NBA. But [they] did not have a real hook to follow it the way they did after 1992.

MULLIN: Looking back over my career, it's the one thing that, above everything else, sticks out. It's the association with those great players, the great coaching staff, and the tremendous impact it had. David Stern told us that at the time. It's funny, too, when someone says, "Twenty years from now, this is going to mean so much," and you're like, "Maybe . . . I guess." But then, sure enough, you hear Pau Gasol say the first time he really watched basketball was the Dream Team. It's almost like this fantasy that happened, and you got all these great memories.

PIPPEN: The whole experience was incredible. It was so special to be around Larry and Magic—guys I had idolized. Just to have the chance to hang with them, to play alongside them, that's something I will never forget. One of my favorite moments was when Barkley would come to shoot at our end, and Michael and Larry and Magic would tell him, "Shoot somewhere else. This basket is only for people who have rings!"

LAETTNER: To be standing on the pedestal and getting a gold medal, representing your country, was the greatest feeling. But I have to admit, even more than that was to be on the podium with those guys—not the 11 greatest players ever, but the greatest basketball team ever assembled.

WE GOT NEXT

The quandary of advancing a women's professional league from a fanciful notion into a viable enterprise left some of the game's greatest stars sidelined in the prime of their careers.

The Women's Professional Basketball League (WBL) lasted just three years, from 1978 to 1981, despite showcasing the star power of pioneers Carol Blazejowski, Ann Meyers, and Nancy Lieberman. When the WBL ceased operations, founder Bill Byrne lamented the lack of revenue, fans, and corporate backing. Fifteen years later, the American Basketball League (ABL), hoping to capitalize on the popularity of the 1996 gold medal U.S. women's Olympic team, kicked off to great fanfare.

The ABL had no chance. Within months, NBA commissioner David Stern, who had been mulling over the idea of a women's pro league for years, decided to throw his considerable weight behind the WNBA. The ABL offered higher salaries, but the WNBA, which opted to play in the summer months, utilized the NBA's vast resources to steamroll its fledgling competitor, which folded after two seasons.

Over the next decade, Stern became the WNBA's fiercest—and most stubborn—advocate. Failure, he informed his staff, was not an option.

VAL ACKERMAN: I really believe the plan for the WNBA was in David Stern's brain from the time he became NBA commissioner. It wasn't a question of if. It was only a question of when.

DAVID STERN: Years before, I had actually authorized somebody to spend a little money to analyze whether basketball was doable for women. An old friend, Jimmy Drucker, who was the commissioner of the [minor league] CBA [Continental Basketball Association], had put on a couple of games with a lower backboard and the women in spandex. The

Australian women's Olympic team wore spandex in 1996 in [the] Atlanta [Olympics], so you could imagine the conversations that went on.

RICK WELTS: David Stern, Russ Granik, and myself debated for a long time whether the next big thing to do would be to start what's evolved into the NBA Development League or to start a women's sports league.

STERN: It's hard to start any league, but it's particularly hard to start a women's league.

WELTS: What put us over the top was the idea that American women were the best athletes in the world, but they failed in major competitions because of the lack of preparation they had prior to those big international events. . . . The NBA agreed to fund putting those players together for almost a year leading up to Atlanta, and they were amazing. They never lost a game all over the world.

CAROL BLAZEJOWSKI: During that time, Val Ackerman was busy writing the business plan for the WNBA. David [Stern] was out talking to the owners of the eight charter teams and saying, "Here's why you should have a team in your market."

ACKERMAN: David Stern is the best salesman in the world.

BLAZEJOWSKI: David Stern told ownership, "You have dark arenas. You can now use these dates and put programming in there and build a new audience. You know your current programming appeals to men and to boys and to the male demo, right? You can now appeal to a broader target audience—women, children."

WELTS: I think we got a little bit lucky. The American women in Atlanta were incredible. Every corporation in America was looking for a way to get on that women's sports bandwagon, and the WNBA became the most visible way for a company to express their interest in women's sports.

ACKERMAN: The time was right, and more importantly, women's college basketball was reaching a zenith, with the Tennessee-Connecticut rivalry taking off in the early '90s and ESPN taking an interest in the women's game. The data showed rising participation rates for women in the youth, high school, and collegiate levels.

LYNETTE WOODARD: I had retired. I was working on Wall Street, but then I hear about this league. The rumor was getting bigger and bigger.

ACKERMAN: There had been women's pro leagues that started and stopped in the years after Title IX; none of them made it. But none of them were supported by the NBA.

REBECCA LOBO: The ABL was starting in the fall of 1996 after the Olympics. Then we hear about the WNBA. It's a summer league? There are only eight teams? What is this all about?

LISA LESLIE: I thought it would be a reversible-jersey kind of league where we would play at Long Beach State. I had no idea it was gonna be such a first-class league, where we would play at the Forum, where the Lakers played.

WELTS: I think the best promotion campaign ever done was "We Got Next," which was taking the NBA playoffs and creating a promotional campaign featuring the launch of the WNBA.

LOBO: Sheryl Swoopes and I signed our contract in the NBA offices, then we went and had our picture taken in front of the Twin Towers holding our WNBA jerseys. It was a really exciting time for women's basketball.

WOODARD: All the fanfare and all the support, it was amazing—better than the dream.

STERN: Some of the more skeptical media said, "Well, this thing is gonna last for a year." And then they said it's gonna last for two. I didn't become a champion of the WNBA fully until I realized that there was sort of this "gentlemen's agreement" amongst the gentlemen that this sport couldn't make it.

ACKERMAN: We had a great, diverse mix of fans. We had young girls, lesbian fans, we had dads and daughters, we had basketball fans that were in withdrawal because whomever they were rooting for on the men's side was dark. We had young boys coming to games, which was great because they were now looking up to these women.

ANN MEYERS: I'll never forget. When I was living in Huntington Beach, I saw a young boy, about 11 years old, wearing a New York Liberty number 11 Teresa Weatherspoon jersey.

DIANA TAURASI: I used to go to the Great Western Forum with my dad to watch the Lakers. Then one night, he took me to watch Lisa Leslie play with the Sparks. When I got to see actual women play, it was like, "Wow, this is interesting. Maybe I wanna do this."

BLAZEJOWSKI: It was a turning point in the way society viewed women athletes.

STERN: The idea that it's OK for women to sweat and indeed throw elbows at each other was a liberating experience.

BLAZEJOWSKI: I was an exception versus the rule as a young girl, and often ridiculed for who I was. But now it was safe, cool to be an athlete, accepted to be an athlete, and the W was the platform for that growth.

CHERYL MILLER: It was justification of many, many years of excellence, decades of excellence for women. Finally, we had a league of our own.

BLAZEJOWSKI: I was named GM of the New York Liberty. On Opening Day, when we played Phoenix, you worried about everything *but* the game. I worried, "Are people gonna come see us play? Are sponsors gonna get the value they think they're signing up for? Are the television partners gonna get the viewership and be happy with what they see? Is the media gonna come out, and are they gonna trash us?"

ACKERMAN: As the fans were coming into Madison Square Garden, you could feel the electricity in the building. I just remember looking over at David [Stern], who is very rarely speechless. He was looking around, taking it all in, and not saying a word.

LOBO: It's our home opener at Madison Square Garden, and the lights go down for the introductions. They play this really cool video as they are announcing us. It was so loud in that arena, we couldn't hear our names over the PA. For it to be that loud at a women's game at Madison Square Garden, of all places, will always remain one of my absolute favorite memories of my WNBA career.

MILLER: The DNA of women's basketball was right in front of you. You had Nancy Lieberman playing, Lynette Woodard was playing, I was coaching, Ann Meyers commentating on the game. That's the backbone of women's basketball right there.

ADAM SILVER: Our first decade, we fought with "Joe," on talk radio, saying, "Me and my buddies could kill these women in a weekend game." They did not understand the level of talent.

STERN: I used to have meetings with the Associated Press sports editors every year. [I'd] get into fights about the W, almost preordained. "So how do you decide," I said, "how much you cover the W?" They'd say, "Well, it's a little bit of art, a little bit of science." I said, "You know, that's what people said with respect to keeping blacks or Jews out of particular places."

SILVER: I think [one mistake we made] was that we tried to conform the image of this league to what we thought fans wanted.

LOBO: People were wondering why the WNBA was putting commercials together with women leaning against racecars in leather pants. It didn't really make sense, but I think it reflected the fears in society in general at the time. The WNBA didn't want to be seen as a gay league because they didn't know if [a] women's professional basketball league could survive that.

TAURASI: The first video shoot I did in the WNBA, they had me put my hair down, lipstick, I had a fucking halter top on. I never felt so bad in my life. And I was like, "I'm not doing that."

SILVER: What we realized is, there's a certain wholesome quality to these players, and that's how it should be enjoyed. I think we initially shied away from the authenticity of who these women really are. These powerful, multidimensional, fascinating women, who struggle in their own lives, do great things, do bad things, but at the same time play this incredible game.

LOBO: If somebody knew I was a basketball player, one of their first questions used to be, "How many of your teammates are gay?" Now the first question is never, "Is she gay or straight?" It's, "Can she play?"

SILVER: I'm both exhilarated by what we've done and disappointed there's not more mainstream acceptance of the league.

TAURASI: In 2009, we played the Indiana Fever in the Finals. They had Tamika Catchings, who was incredible. We walked into Game 1 in Phoenix, and there were 20,000 people in there. It was awesome.

TAMIKA CATCHINGS: I remember thinking, "Wow, we've finally made it."

TAURASI: At the time, it was the highest-rated Finals. It went the full five games, so there was that suspense, that drama. But then the [last] game ended, and it was never talked about again.

LESLIE: We're always saying, "Hey, we're over here, playing this game that we love." We never make the kind of money that the last guy on the bench in street clothes would make. I had the same work ethic as Kobe Bryant, and I was probably a much better teammate.

STERN: Take a look at the NBA in 1966, 20 years in. Our arenas were empty—a gross revenue of nothing. Struggling as a league. Right now, the WNBA is a baby league. It's only 20 years old.

TAURASI: Twenty years is a long time. I think it's time to ramp it up. It's too good of a game, there are too many great players, and there are too many great stories that aren't being told.

MEYERS: When I go to camps to speak to young girls and say, "Who's your favorite [basketball] player?" they still tell me, "LeBron James and Kobe Bryant." I tell them, "No, you have to tell me Diana Taurasi or Maya Moore or Brittney Griner. These are the women you want to be."

TAURASI: There's a gender bias. Our USA Basketball team has won five Olympic gold medals in a row. No one cares. We'd probably be better off losing, which is sad, you know?

ACKERMAN: The good news is, the WNBA has now established this great pipeline—women's college basketball—so whether it's Brittney Griner or Elena Delle Donne or Skylar Diggins[-Smith] or Breanna Stewart, I think the world will take interest.

BECKY HAMMON: In 2016, women were still making more money by far overseas than playing in the WNBA. At some point, those salaries have to get up to par.

MEYERS: As a young kid, we didn't have professional women's basketball, so I followed John Havlicek and Bill Russell, but these young girls have role models, and they need to support them.

CATHY RUSH: You have to send people to high school games and college games so you're building the WNBA from the bottom up.

CATCHINGS: You just gotta market it better. You gotta be creative in putting together a better plan. For six to seven months, when they do cross promotion with the NBA, you hear a lot about the WNBA. Then, for the next five months, you don't hear anything. Nothing. It's like starting over again.

TAURASI: You get mad. You work so hard, you play the sport that you love for so long, it's frustrating the support isn't there.

LESLIE: It's not our fault we were born girls. We just want to play, too.

HAVE GAME, WILL TRAVEL

Basketball can transport you places you never imagined. For American women who finish their college careers and yearn to continue playing professionally, that often means grabbing a passport and hitting the road.

Minnesota Lynx star and 2017 WNBA MVP Sylvia Fowles's nomadic basketball journey has taken her to Russia, Turkey, and China. Because the WNBA season lasts only a little over four months and the league pays its best players a maximum salary of just $110,000, most of the women play overseas during the off-season, with foreign teams offering in excess of $1 million per year for elite players.

It makes for convoluted alliances. Consider the Lynx, a linchpin of the WNBA, who won three championships from 2013 to 2017. While Fowles linked arms with Minnesota teammate Maya Moore to win the WNBA title in 2017, just months earlier they were squaring off in the Women's Chinese Basketball Association playoffs, with Fowles starring for the Beijing Great Wall and Moore for the Shanxi Xing Rui Flame.

Adjusting to a foreign language, culture, and customs can lead to isolation and loneliness, but female professional ballers must also contend with prejudicial attitudes in countries where women might widely be considered inferior, or even subservient.

"If you told me 12 years ago that I would have spent [a decade] in Russia, I would have said, 'No chance,'" said Phoenix Mercury guard Diana Taurasi.

Taurasi spent her first pro season in 2005 with Dynamo Moscow, and while her roster included former UConn teammate Sue Bird and Indiana Fever center Tammy Sutton-Brown, Taurasi counted the days to go home and vowed never to return. But after her final game, Spartak Moscow owner Shabtai von Kalmanovic approached her and promised, "If you come back next year, I'll show you a different side of Russia."

"Shabs," as his players affectionately dubbed him, was a business-man, concert promoter, and former KGB spy who spent 10 years in a Russian prison for selling secrets. He shared his past openly with his players and strived to make their time in Russia as elegant as possible. He set them up in a palatial villa with an indoor pool and a personal chef, arranged for them to have cocktails with Giorgio Armani, and took them on spending sprees in Paris. He lured a who's who of great talent to play for him, including Bird, Fowles, Tamika Catchings, Tina Thompson, four-time WNBA MVP Lauren Jackson, and, yes, Taurasi.

"Shabs was the Don King of women's basketball in Europe," Taurasi said. "He wanted basketball to be a show. He wanted people to go to a basketball game and at halftime see the best singer in Russia, the national anthem sung by the Madonna of Estonia."

One cool evening in November 2009, Taurasi and her teammates went to Shabs's office to pick up tickets to a Beyoncé concert. When he wasn't there to greet them, they knew something was wrong. They later learned that Kalmanovic, while stopped at a traffic light just outside the Kremlin, had been shot 18 times, a murder that police designated "a professional hit."

Taurasi left the team at the end of the year and played in Turkey the next two seasons. She returned to Russia in 2012, signing with UMMC Ekaterinburg.

Shortly after leading the Phoenix Mercury to a 2014 title, Taurasi, one of the most successful and recognizable faces in the game, announced that Ekaterinburg, which gave her an annual salary of $1.5 million, would pay her to sit out the WNBA season. "It was a really hard decision," said Taurasi, "but it was [at] a point of my career [where] I couldn't say no."

WNBA players union president Nneka Ogwumike, the former Stanford star and 2016 league MVP with the Los Angeles Sparks, has acknowledged it's a pressing issue for the league. Players remain loyal to the WNBA because it remains the best competition in the world, but the toll of playing in the WNBA after playing a full season overseas is physically and mentally taxing.

Dallas Wings guard Skylar Diggins-Smith decided to pursue off-season modeling and television deals in lieu of playing overseas. Diggins-

Smith, the former Notre Dame supernova, is hardly just a pretty face. She was a 2017 first-team All-WNBA selection and is one of the premier young point guards in the game.

Yet most WNBA players aren't afforded such opportunities, and so they learn to cope with subzero windchills in Russia, as Mercury center Brittney Griner has, or to appreciate the rich history of Krakow, Poland, as New York Liberty star Tina Charles did from 2012 to 2014. And then there's Fowles, who during her stints with the Beijing Great Wall has learned to navigate Chinese culinary delicacies such as snake soup, tuna eyeball, and chicken testicles.

When you love the game, it's worth it.

THE BASKETBALL WORLD BECOMES FLAT

One hundred and eight international players started the 2017–18 season on NBA rosters. That means more than a quarter of the league's players are foreign. The globalization of basketball and the NBA has been one of the most dramatic developments in the sport over the past three decades, with MVP- and All-Star-caliber players like Steve Nash, Dirk Nowitzki, and Yao Ming following in the footsteps of pioneering European stars Sarunas Marciulionis, Vlade Divac, and Drazen Petrovic. Despite being raised in countries as far apart as Canada, Soviet Lithuania, Turkey, and Nigeria, many of these players had similar experiences growing up outside the United States: they often came to basketball after playing other sports, particularly soccer, in their youth; they played in cold gyms, built their own courts, and shot soccer balls when basketballs weren't available; and they looked at the NBA as a distant, almost unreachable dream.

PEJA STOJAKOVIC: Nineteen nineties. I was 13 years old [when] the documentary of Michael Jordan came out. *Come Fly with Me.* I think all the kids playing basketball at that time were in love with that tape—just watching Jordan and trying to imitate.

VLADE DIVAC: I was a very skinny, dark kid from small town in Serbia back in '78 when I started playing basketball. Everybody called me "Wilt," and I didn't know who the guy was, but obviously later on I was very proud of that nickname.

TONY PARKER (Point Guard, San Antonio Spurs): My idol was Michael Jordan, and I wanted to play in the NBA. Coming from France, I was a long shot, 'cause back in the day there was not a lot of Europeans in the league and no European point guard.

SARUNAS MARCIULIONIS: In Lithuania, basketball is number one sport forever. Kaunas was basketball capital of Lithuania. And that's where I got first introduction with basketball when I was kid. Kaunas pride is Zalgiris team, with Modestas Paulauskas as a superhuman, superplayer. It was a family tradition to sit by the TV set, watching basketball game. I was 5, 6 years old. I couldn't understand. I know there's running, shooting, and I remember names. Sometimes my dad would [yell], "Aargh, why they miss!"

HAKEEM OLAJUWON (Center, Houston Rockets; 1994 NBA MVP): In Nigeria, basketball was like a clique, a closed circle that I didn't know until I started playing. Then you find out there are local legends that are not known by the masses. Soccer was a passion and hobby. Playing competitively, to be a professional, was a long shot. Team handball was really my sport, [but] handball was very small. So many schools never play. So handball was dropped [at my school]. They canceled the sport. Then the coach invited me to the basketball team at my high school, even though I didn't know the rules. When he saw me, he immediately gave me the job description: "Stay right here in the middle, block everything that comes in, don't listen to the rules."

DIRK NOWITZKI (Power Forward, Dallas Mavericks): My sister and mom both played hoops, and my dad played handball. To us boys in Germany, hoops was more for women, and the real men played handball. I didn't change my mind until I was 12 or 13. I joined a club team, and I loved it. Something about the game just grabbed me, even though I had no skills in the beginning. I also played tennis, and I was bored by myself all the time. I liked going on the bus to the road games, being with teammates, and going through ups and downs. And my first dunk. That really sealed the deal.

OLAJUWON: I was selected to the state team from my school, and the coach was trying to get me to dunk. I thought he was kidding—jump and dunk? I'd never seen anybody dunk. I was looking at the goal, and it seemed so high. I didn't believe it could be done. The team was standing under the basket and they encouraged me to try, and I was not comfortable, so he let it go. Then, the second day, we were standing in the same position, and I kept looking at the goal. I started to believe this could be done. I just took the ball, went straight up, dunked, and everybody was shocked. Once I did it, all I wanted to do is dunk.

YAO MING: Thirteen years old—sometime around there is when I start enjoying sports academy in Shanghai. I not really *left* home, but I go back home once a week. You can describe that [as] lucky compared to other kids. They probably can go home only once a year. So I stay in the academy with a bunch of kids, play basketball every day, and go to school in the morning. We basically are training all day and play for either province or city or maybe national team. Starting [from] 14 years old, we train all day—conditioning, strength, and basic skill. Game experience a little bit. Of course, we also go to school to study grammar, language, mathematics, all kind of stuff. Money is very little, but we're all looking for a chance to serve for country.

DIVAC: In Europe, you start playing soccer. That really helped me on the basketball court. Soccer helps your footwork. Being a tall guy, feet are sometimes slow, and soccer develops that part of your game.

STOJAKOVIC: We all did play soccer; it was just something that we had to do. It was part of our society. I did play soccer all the way till I couldn't find any soccer shoes, and it did help me with footwork and agility.

ENES KANTER (Center, New York Knicks): I wanted to become a soccer player because every player in Turkey wanna become a soccer player. But then they're putting me in at goalkeeper 'cause I was too big, so I was tired of soccer and wanted to do another sport. Then I start basketball, and when I was a little boy, we didn't even have a basketball. I was playing basketball with a soccer ball.

STEVE NASH: Being a soccer player as a kid, you *have* to connect [with your teammates], 'cause there's more players on the field and you play with your feet. I think international players have more of that mentality:

"We *have* to do this together. We have to share." Whereas if you didn't grow up playing [soccer] and you grew up playing basketball in the playground, you're playing a lot of one-on-one, two-on-two, and there's tons of space to jack my guy up and win this game.

MASAI UJIRI: In Africa, we grow up playing soccer. At 13, I started playing basketball. A lot of the kids I see now, they start to play at 14, 15, and then it's not something that has been engraved in them since the age of 8. The game hasn't grown [as much as it could in Africa] because there's a lack of facilities, there's a lack of infrastructure, there's a lack of teaching. I don't think we have the coaching at a high level, and so they drill and drill, whether or not they are drilling the right things. We are probably the tallest, most athletic. Everywhere you go there's 7-footers. The continent is too big, the continent is too great, the continent is too athletic. There's someone walking around. There is a Hakeem Olajuwon somewhere.

OLAJUWON: The Dream Shake was a soccer move. Soccer requires body movement where you're facing your goal and chasing the ball, and your opponent is chasing from behind, and you wanna turn around and go the other direction. He's chasing you from behind, so you have to misdirect your opponent, and after he turns, you make a U-turn. That is the foundation of the Dream Shake.

DIVAC: In Yugoslavia back then, every city has a club for different sports. Obviously, [for] basketball I was a member of the local club. I was there for three years and I developed some game, and then—I was 14 years old—I end up moving and leaving my parents to play for another team which is three hours drive from my hometown. I spend four years there, finish my high school, and became national team member.

STOJAKOVIC: Basketball was always one of the popular sports in our country, and we had good coaches. I think that was important in Yugoslavia—teaching fundamentals in youth basketball. Also, the national team of Yugoslavia had some pretty good players, and we looked up to them. Guys like Vlade Divac, Toni Kukoc, Dino Radja, Drazen

Petrovic—they were in their early 20s, and they were really good. Everybody growing up in Yugoslavia who was playing basketball looked up to them.

MARCIULIONIS: First time I came to play, I was 10. My parents decided that tennis and music school is not enough. I'm too much energy, so they take me to basketball. We used to have a public basketball school, [where] I started to get some fundamentals. Some gyms [were] pretty chilly in wintertime. Most gyms you could smoke inside, so even in Kaunas, at the end of second half the air [would be] like blue fog, hard to breathe.

OLAJUWON: I went to basketball practice, and I saw the guards handling the ball between their legs without looking at the ball. The movement was so magical. [I thought], "Wow, that is a cool sport."

MARCIULIONIS: We built our own court. Put the tiles and dragged the frame of [the] basket in place. Then—I had the measurement and it's easy—we made this backboard. To buy a hoop is no problem. And, I have to apologize—people who were sleeping on Sunday mornings, when you like, *bum, bum, bum* [dribbling noise]. People, they say, "Aargh! What is this kid doing? It's too early to shoot hoops!" And [near] a five-story building, this sound spreads out. But I hope they understand now.

NOWITZKI: How do you describe [my lifelong coach] Holger Geschwindner? I met him when I was like 15. He is a strange character. He's got different views on life and sports. But I think that's where I was successful with him, 'cause he doesn't do everything by the book. He taught me basically everything there is to know about basketball, and we've been working ever since. At 15, 16 I was really tall. I could move pretty decent, but I didn't have any shooting ability. And people said I was too weak, I should start weight lifting. He was saying that if you start too early lifting heavy weights, you hurt your knees, your joints, and your career will be short. We would do handstands—walk through the gym in handstands. And we'd do push-ups and frog jumps and all sorts of stuff. We did a rowing camp every year. He says it's good for the power and the arms. We fenced once. We tried all sorts of different stuff on the basketball court. One of his philosophies was basketball as a jazz band. You have five guys on the court, and the guy who has the ball is playing a solo. So everybody within the band or the team got their own skill level and has to do their own thing, but it has to be in sync. Five guys have to play together, read each other, and do their own things at times. He also thinks that basketball has a nice correlation with music: You're supposed to love the game. You're supposed to dance the game. You're supposed to dribble with the beat in your head. So he had us doing stuff where I'd have the ball, and his boy was under the basket playing the saxophone. I had to dribble and move with the rhythm and shoot the ball to it. It was strange, to say the least.

MARCIULIONIS: You want to leave your own country, Lithuania. You want to prove, "I can play against those guys. I can play in different level." I don't think money was biggest issue. Maximum stipend from my club was 300 rubles, which was equal to around 100 bucks a month. But for us, we were not poor. We're happy with our status; we were celebrities. . . . You know, [life in the Soviet Union] was so tight: you travel with the team, you have no passport, you can't change your money. All these years piles up, like, "I'm married, I have a kid, I'm 25 years old, I'm looking for another life."

For players coming to the NBA or U.S. college basketball from overseas, just getting to the United States is often a journey riddled with obstacles, whether it's the political pressure players faced in the USSR, the thorny process of obtaining a U.S. visa, or the decision all international players eventually make—to leave behind family, friends, and their homelands. During the twilight years of the USSR, Sarunas Marciulionis learned that "another life" might finally be available to him and his teammates on the Soviet national team. The Soviet government was considering a plan to allow its players to pursue professional careers outside the Soviet Union, but only if the team could defeat the United States and win gold at the 1988 Seoul Olympics.

MARCIULIONIS: We beat the United States, and that was our ticket to another life. [Soviet Lithuanian guard Valdemaras] Chomicius asked [Soviet coach Alexander] Gomelsky, "Are you going to help if we win?" And [Gomelsky] said, "You can't win only one game; you have to win gold medal," and then he is going to help us leave Soviet Union. So we had that internal motivation, very big and powerful, to have a different life. Final game in '88 against Yugoslavia, they had so much talent— Toni [Kukoc], [Dino] Radja, [Drazen] Petrovic, Vlade Divac. And we were down by 10 or 12 points after first half. They were about four years younger, so maybe that played a major role for comeback. That was biggest achievement for us—four years, eight years of hard work finally paid back.... So I was free agent. In '88, '89, because Soviet government want to have good relationship with Ted Turner, they supposed to send us—[Alexander] Volkov and me—over [to the NBA]. And Donnie Nelson convinced me that San Francisco was a nice place, that [the Warriors] are a restructuring team with playing time. That was my decision—I go with him. And all these lawyers, Gomelsky, other lawyers—each of them had a piece of my first contract. I don't know how much they cut, but that doesn't matter. For me it was most important to get a ticket, go on the plane, and start new life. I'll survive either way.

DON NELSON: There was a lot of work to be done to get [Marciulionis]. [My son] Donnie went over to Lithuania and actually moved into his house and stayed with him for months to make sure we didn't lose him. I wanted to know everything he did and what kind of guy he was, and Donnie had all the information. Then we went through the long struggle with the governments to have him join the NBA.

YAO: Well, I didn't go to Madison Square [Garden for the 2002 NBA Draft]. I stayed in Beijing for national team training camp, but I went to watch it live in the morning. We have some information, we know it's pretty high possibility that Rockets would draft me. But still there's a question mark before it becomes reality. So a little bit of confused, a little bit of a hesitation, but when my name's being announced, it's exciting mixed with relief. Also pressure, because the challenge is right around the corner.

NOWITZKI: Everything happened so quick after that [1998 Nike] Hoop Summit, where I happened to have a great game. The hype was crazy, people saying I'm a lottery pick all of a sudden. My head was spinning. I didn't know what to expect, and then Dallas selected me at [No. 9], and they put a little pressure on me. I told them, "I'm not sure I want to come yet. I'm barely 20. I'm really skinny. I'm just not sure I'm ready." They were worried that they gonna waste their pick on somebody who doesn't even come, and they said, "Before you make a decision, we'll fly you to Dallas. You look at everything, meet some of your teammates." So I met Mike Finley, Steve Nash, and Nellie [Don Nelson] threw a big party at his house. It was phenomenal, and I remember they wanted to know in the morning—yes or no. So Holger and I were sitting at Nellie's pool most of the night, discussing. We went through the pros and cons, and at the end, we came out saying, "You can try, and if it doesn't work out, you can always come back to Europe and play at a high level."

KANTER: It was tough, especially the first two months. I was 17 when I came to America. My brother was 15. You're living with your parents your whole life, and then you come from a different country, and the food is different, people are different, language different, and culture different. I couldn't understand people. But I was like, "This is my job now."

OLAJUWON: Angola, this is where I was discovered. I was Most Valuable Player in a juniors tournament, and there was a coach for Central [African Republic], his name is Christopher Pond. He asked me, "If I arrange for you to go to the States, can your parents buy tickets?" I said, "Well, the most difficult thing is to get a visa. If my parents see the visa, they'll buy me a ticket." The next day, Christopher Pond took me to the consulate, [and] the consul general said he cannot give a visa unless [I] have some university saying they'd give a scholarship. So [Pond] called [University of Houston] coach [Guy] Lewis from the consulate: "Coach

Lewis, I have a player for you. You're going to love him." He was so confident. Coach Lewis was telling him, "If he's as good as you say, we'll give him a scholarship." Which is what the consul general wanted to hear. So he gives me his card, and he sent me back to Nigeria to get my visa in the embassy, to come to the United States. [Before I left], Christopher Pond gave me two more schools: "If you don't like Houston, look at St. John's and North Carolina State." . . . Going through the airport, my brothers, my family, realized that now I'm leaving to America for college. You're going to America, you don't know anybody—it was scary. I went to New York [first], and when I came to the airport, I was just wearing a shirt and pants. The breeze, the cold breeze that comes when that door opens—I ran back inside because I'd never experienced that kind of cold before. When I saw the weather, I knew I can't live here. So I changed my tickets for Houston. Coach Lewis thought I was supposed to spend two days in St. John's, [but] I came early to Houston. I go to the airport, made a phone call: "Coach Lewis, this is Akeem [later Hakeem]." And he remembers: "Akeem, where are you?" "I'm in Houston." "Where?" "At the airport." "Well, take a taxi to the basketball office." When I came to Houston at that time, the weather was beautiful. I said, "Wow, this is perfect."

Sarunas Marciulionis and Drazen Petrovic were seasoned professionals by the time they started their NBA careers, while Dirk Nowitzki, Hakeem Olajuwon, and Enes Kanter began their American basketball careers while they were still teenagers. No matter when they arrived, however, international players in the NBA have all had to adjust to the speed, strength, and skill of the American game.

OLAJUWON: When I came to the U.S., I've never seen American basketball, and my impression is, "They can shoot from anywhere—they won't miss. They can close their eyes and just throw it in." I was not sure [if] I can play at that level. Are they that good?

STOJAKOVIC: We looked up to United States in basketball. There was always a gap between Europe and U.S. Everything looked one or two seconds faster than we played. I don't know if it's because of the athleticism, but definitely you could sense that basketball had started in U.S., and you could sense they had advantage over some countries.

DIVAC: In late '80s, when I moved from Europe to United States, I call it two different sports. They have the same name, but they are totally different. American basketball is more physical, more speed. It's dunks, crossovers, and fundamental things are secondary. And international is more finesse and fundamentals. When you have those two styles, I think the physicality and speed is going to always be on top, but when you merge those two, you'll have a good product.

KANTER: When I think about American game, I always think about dunking—"show" basketball. People overseas said, "In the NBA there is no defense; it's all about show." But after I came here, I realized that not all of it is true. There is crazy defense! There is a lot of dunking, but at the same time there's players who are really skilled, who can shoot the ball, put the ball on the floor.

MARCIULIONIS: We didn't pay much attention to slam dunk, because we didn't have those breakaway rims. If you try to dunk, you in trouble if you break glass. Oh, you in big trouble! So expensive.

OLAJUWON: It was a relief for me when I saw the level of the pros. I went to a Rockets game, and I came home so excited because the pros missed some shots. I see people, they drive to the basket, I say, "I must be missing something. How come that shot isn't blocked?" I see opportunities that should be rejected, but it scores. The next day, the reporters ask me, "You were at the Rockets game, what do you think?" I told them, "I think I could block four shots I saw."

MARCIULIONIS: I came into Warriors organization, [and] so many people really care about me. They didn't spoil me, but I felt comfortable, and I didn't expect that. I thought [it was] going to be like on the street— you have to fight every step. The Soviet national team was much worse than Golden State. [Chris] Mullin, Mitch [Richmond], and Timmy [Hardaway]—all these guys really patient.

DIVAC: [My first NBA game], I played against Sacramento Kings. It was an exhibition in Hawaii when we had training camp. I was happy. It's hard to describe my feelings back then. A kid that was born in small city, 30,000 people, and I end up in NBA. It was a great feeling. I had a lot of pressure because I was the first European to be drafted and join in same year. I had to prove that we can play, and I'm glad I did a good job.

STOJAKOVIC: I remember scoring 2 points and not playing very well in my first NBA game, but it was great experience.

KRISTAPS PORZINGIS (Power Forward, New York Knicks): Going up against Kobe, LeBron, Steph Curry—at first you're like, "Wow, I'm here." But always in my head I'm like, "I'm part of this. I can't be starstruck." We're all the same, we compete on the basketball court. But those are the guys that I looked up to and learned the game from, and that's why it was special moment to be on the same floor with them for the first time.

NASH: Danny Ainge was my first coach [with the Phoenix Suns]. He'd see me in practice every day and we'd play one-on-one a lot, and I dribbled by the bench and he'd say, "Take him, take him!" That's a big vote of confidence for a guy [backing up] Jason Kidd and Kevin Johnson, to have a coach be like, "Don't run an offense. Just go at him." There was a time where [Dallas Mavericks head coach] Don Nelson got tired of me downplaying my abilities, and he'd come in after a game and say, "If you're a dominant motherfuckin' player, dominate." To have a Hall of Fame coach not bat an eye calling you dominant, that was huge for a short guy from Canada.

MARCIULIONIS: You have to earn playing time, right? And during the time you're on the floor, you have to be maximum productive. So if I would start taking long shots, it's a lottery. It means you will go back on the bench. My performance had to be most productive. That means you have to penetrate, you have to get fouled, go to basket, finish or shoot free throws. That's how I can earn minutes.

PARKER: Coach Pop, the first four or five years, I felt like he was a European coach. Because he screamed so much and cursed at you. When me and Manu [Ginobili] came, it was normal for us, because in Europe they scream all the time. [Most] NBA coaches, they don't scream that much because there's a lot of egos. I felt like [Popovich] was a Serbian coach, cursing the way he does. I think it worked, because I came from Europe, so for me it's the same. And Timmy [Duncan] was unbelievable because all he cares is winning, and he just went with all that screaming. I was like, "If he's gonna scream like that at Timmy, then if he screams at me, I can't do anything."

NOWITZKI: The first year was a lockout year. So after I got drafted, I didn't sign a contract. I went home to Germany and played for a few months, then in January we got a call from [GM] Donnie [Nelson]: "You gotta come the next day." I didn't know all the plays or the defensive systems, and I was basically thrown into cold water: compete against the best of the best with a 10-day training camp, no summer league. I had a couple good games early, but once the routine set in, I was struggling. They used to call me "Irk" because there was not a lot of defense going on. I would be guarding somebody in the post, right in front of the opposing bench, and I just hear everybody saying, "Take him. He can't guard you!" I had to work hard on getting stronger and keeping people in front of me.

YAO: [My rookie year], people would not miss any opportunity to try a dunk on me. Or crossover—just pass by me, maybe make a shot right in front of me.

NOWITZKI: Doubt creeps in. I think that's normal when you struggle. But it never really got that far that I would say, "I'm out of here. I want to go home." I was lucky. I had great teammates. Steve [Nash] and Mike Finley—I think they saw sometimes I was struggling, and they supported me.

DIVAC: Being with the Lakers and having Magic [Johnson], James Worthy, Byron Scott, A. C. Green—those guys helped me feel better about those differences: culture, language, style of play.

STOJAKOVIC: There were moments my first year where I wanted to go back [home]. When I wasn't sleeping and I doubted myself and I thought that I made a bad decision coming over. But I always thought that tomorrow is a new day, there will be more opportunities. I was lucky I had Vlade, who went through similar things, and he was making me understand the pace of the game, the schedule, competing against the best, just being ready and focused every night.

DIVAC: Peja [Stojakovic] is so talented, especially with shooting. I think he was lucky to end up in Sacramento with me and my experience. I had to protect him. Usually, you give hard time on rookies, but Peja was coming from different country, and I try to help him.

NOWITZKI: My rookie year, we had 50 games in like two and a half months. Something crazy. By the last 10 games, we were basically eliminated from the playoffs, and Nellie came to me and said, "Hey, this is your time. There's no pressure, go have fun, try to get better." That was huge for me. I remember I had a 29-point game in Phoenix that gave me a lot of confidence. So I played summer league, played international basketball, and then in year two I was more comfortable. I found a spot to live, my English got better, everything came together, and I found it easier to perform on the court.

DIVAC: My English? I could say maybe a couple words, but most important thing was I spoke basketball language. That helps me develop my English off the court, and after the [first] year I was comfortable making conversation.

STOJAKOVIC: That's the hardest thing when you don't speak well. Even though the coaches and players wanted to give words of support, they couldn't because of language barrier. Basketball is always basketball, but not every day is a good day on a basketball court. Sometimes you need support from your teammates, from your coaches.

JEFF VAN GUNDY: I came [to the Rockets in] Yao Ming's second year, and he had a full-time interpreter, but he spoke—[coach] Rudy Tomjanovich coined this—"Yao speaks fluent basketball." In year one, he had his interpreter sitting next to him [during meetings], whispering exactly what Rudy was saying. I moved him out to another room so it wouldn't be distracting for the other players, and Yao wore an earpiece like [at] the United Nations. The [interpreter] heard what I said, and he would relay it back to Yao through his earpiece. By year three, there was no problem.

DIVAC: [Lakers announcer] Chick Hearn would ask me questions which I wouldn't understand, and I would just talk something different. One time he asked me about my life in L.A., and I thought he was asking about my wife. Even today my kids make fun of me when we take tapes from early '90s.

MARCIULIONIS: I had dog syndrome first two years. You know, dog understands, but he can't speak.

No international player looms as large among his contemporaries as Arvydas Sabonis, the Lithuanian center who anchored the powerful late-'80s Soviet national teams and who was widely considered one of the five best players in the world during an era when Michael Jordan, Magic Johnson, Patrick Ewing, and Hakeem Olajuwon were dominating the NBA. By the time Sabonis joined the Portland Trail Blazers in 1995, a ruptured Achilles tendon and chronic knee and groin problems had robbed him of much of his speed and explosiveness. He still managed to be a crucial starter for a Portland team that made several deep playoff runs and took the 2000 NBA champion Los Angeles Lakers to seven games in the Western Conference Finals, but most American fans never got to witness Sabonis's brilliance in the big man's prime. Perhaps that air of mystery has added to his legend—along with the fact that during his heyday, the large, one-liter bottle of vodka sold in Soviet Union liquor stores was commonly known as a "Sabonis."

MARCIULIONIS: I met Arvydas when we were 10 years old and he was asking me to show [him] the doors to the gym. We came to practice—that was my second day and his first day. That was 1974. He didn't know where the gym is, and he meets me at the corridor and asks where.

BILL WALTON: I saw Sabonis for the first time when he was 20 years old. I was in Europe conducting basketball clinics, and I saw this guy play in the [1985] European championships in Stuttgart, Germany. In the first half, he had a quadruple-double. He was the living combination of Kareem [Abdul-Jabbar], Pete Maravich, and Larry Bird. He was 7-3, lithe, and he could run and shoot threes and pass. He had uncanny vision and court sense, could rebound and block shots. He did everything. Arvydas Sabonis was the second-greatest young player I ever saw—Kareem being the best.

DIVAC: Somebody would say I'm crazy or stupid, but I would say [Sabonis] would be on same level like Michael Jordan.

KENNY SMITH: Arvydas Sabonis was healthy when we played against him in the [1986] World Championship. He was arguably—no, not arguably—he *was* the best center that I had seen at that stage. David Robinson couldn't do anything with him.

DANNY MANNING: When we played against Sabonis [in the 1988 Olympics], I remember him getting a rebound, coming down, and throwing the outlet behind his back. It was almost to half-court. Maybe it was Marciulionis that he hit in stride, moving down the court. It was a thing of beauty. He was the best passing big man I ever played against.

MARCIULIONIS: On [the Soviet team] he had to play as a center—only on the low post and only hook. They never developed his game. So he had to develop on his own. He loved to shoot threes with us guards, to play horse, and not too many 7'4" guys love to shoot. He also wanted to play one-on-one, so he picked up pieces from guards, [like] shooting or to see the floor—his passing game. He learned his finesse skills by playing with the small guys.

P. J. CARLESIMO: Most fans think of Arvydas when he played with Portland. If you go back and look at Arvydas in his early 20s, he was one of the most athletic bigs ever. He was so skilled. He had quickness, leaping, the whole thing. By the time we got him, he must have been

50 or 60 pounds more than when he played [in the USSR]. He just had so many surgeries, and his body changed. He couldn't move anymore, couldn't get off the ground. *Maybe* he could dunk. But I tell you what: he was so far beyond his prime, but he was still an excellent player. He'd throw behind-the-back passes. He could shoot threes. Not that anybody could dominate Shaq, but he could lean on Shaq. His feel for the game was unbelievable. Once a month, he'd get a rebound and see somebody streaking, and he would throw a behind-the-back like 60, 70 feet on a dime and lead the guy.

SMITH: He would have gone down like Shaq, like Kareem, like Wilt, in that vein.

BOB RYAN: The American public never got to see the Sabonis of legend. Yeah, he played here, but that was a couple of injuries and many vats of vodka ago.

ARVYDAS SABONIS (Center, Portland Trail Blazers; 1988 Olympic Gold Medalist): World is more free now. In that time, it was impossible for me to come to NBA. When political situation change, it [can] happen. I'm happy for [today's] young players who have chance to come try NBA. It's the top of basketball.

MARCIULIONIS: He injured his Achilles before '88 Olympics. He played in Spain for five or six years, became more accurate with the passes. So he became much more solid when he got to the NBA [in 1995]. You don't see Sabonis squishing ball at the backboard, throwing first pass and finishing on the fast break, slamming the ball. But you also don't see dumb turnovers. When he begins his NBA [career], he can play man-to-man game, he can face the basket, he can shoot, he can see the floor. So you can't say that [America] missed out—Sabonis had everything when he was 18. No! He developed everything, so when he came to NBA he had maximum of what he achieved, except his ability to run and jump. If he would go in '89, when I went to U.S., I don't know how he would play.

STOJAKOVIC: Even when he came into the NBA in his 30s, suffering from injuries, [Sabonis] was so skilled that he could dominate with his passing, with his presence.

MARCIULIONIS: I like to emphasize one thing: besides skills, he has this very sensitive passion to win. Until tears—he was shaking if he lose a three-on-three game. He take each game very seriously, wherever he plays. Horse or three-on-three or five-on-five—I don't remember player who would take so seriously each game.

CARLESIMO: For about six years, he was one of the best three or five players in the world.

It's been less than 30 years since pioneering international players like Marciulionis and Petrovic first broke into the NBA, but in that relatively short span, the foreign influx has changed the game. Players from Europe, Asia, South America, Africa, and Australia have battled negative stereotypes about their style of play to gain a foothold at the highest level of basketball, and in all likelihood, the legacies of foreign greats such as Yao, Nowitzki, Ginobili, and many others will inspire younger generations of players around the world to take up the sport and push basketball to new heights.

DIVAC: When I joined NBA, it was definitely a perception that European or international guys are soft. If you're athlete, it doesn't matter. You're going to have some label, and you have to prove them wrong. That was inspiration to get tougher, be faster.

KANTER: I definitely wanna prove more as a non-American player. People call Europeans soft, like, "They don't like contact," or, "The only thing they wanna do is shoot." I don't think it's true. European players work on their game and get tougher and tougher. Last night I played against Marc Gasol [from Spain], and he's one of the best big men in the NBA.

STOJAKOVIC: There is a stereotype of players from Europe being labeled right away as soft. But I think most of us never took that personally. I think we understood the criticism, and it actually motivated us to prove ourselves. First, to our teammates, our coaches—to earn their respect and playing time. And then to earn respect around the league. Now, seeing the success of so many international players in NBA, I think the "soft" label is not mentioned as much.

DONNIE WALSH: I don't think they're soft at all. A lot of these guys have been in wars, so they're tougher than anybody we got. Sometimes I see European guys come over here, and the athleticism and strength of the bodies in the NBA overwhelm them at first. What I hear from my European friends every now and then is they don't believe in weights. Well, weight training is a big part of the NBA, and I think they've got it down to a point where it's not harmful to the players.

SMITH: European players aren't soft. American players aren't. You're soft because you're soft, not because of where you were born.

UJIRI: Africa is different and Europe is different and Asia is different. When you go to Serbia, to that part of the world, basketball is taught in academies, in cold gyms, in places where you know it's tough. There is a mental toughness to it. . . . I drafted a kid from Brazil, and when we got to talk to him, I said, "Every American player thinks they are good enough to kick your ass." That's mental toughness for the American kids. They are edgy, and they play like they know the game, like they want the game. I love that. We can say all what we want about spoiled AAU basketball, but there's a tough edge about going to play pickup basketball with American kids: "I'm gonna dunk on you. I'm gonna take it to you." The mental toughness in Europe is different. They're taught in a gym: dribble this ball from here to there 800 times, every day, in the cold.

CHRIS MULLIN: To me, the trailblazer was Sarunas Marciulionis. He was the first international player that had a big-time role on a winning team. There were some guys that came in for a year or two and then went back because they didn't fit, but Sarunas, he was relentless, and guys didn't want to guard him. One year he played with us, he came off the bench and averaged 18 a game. I remember when Sarunas came, I figured: "International player, he'll be a jump shooter, kind of soft." Well, he was a driver and tough as nails.

AHMAD RASHAD: Marciulionis, "Rooney," was the first European to come to the NBA and not be intimidated. Guys told me he's one of the strongest they ever played against, and he never backed down from anybody. I think it really changed the way NBA fans started to look at European players. Him and [Drazen] Petrovic.

MARCIULIONIS: You don't fear what you don't understand, and I didn't have a clue [what NBA basketball would be like]. I just know that they have the same heads, same hands, same feet, you know?

PETER VECSEY: I heard about Petrovic before he came over [here]. Guys would play over there and talk about Petrovic—how good he was but also how nasty. I remember Jan van Breda Kolff telling me he spit at him during a game, he talked trash all the time.

STOJAKOVIC: Drazen was at that time the best player in Europe. His nickname was "Mozart."

DIVAC: He was, with Arvydas, probably the best player that ever came from international basketball to NBA. Drazen was scoring machine. He could score 40, 50, 60—you just couldn't stop him.

WALSH: I remember when Petrovic came over, you'd see him playing point guard and he wasn't having success. Then the Nets got him, and they decided they were gonna play him at two-guard. So he goes back to Europe and lifts weights, he comes back and he's got a body now, and he just started destroying the whole league. Of course, he got in a car accident and passed away [at age 28, in 1993], but he had been one of the great players.

SHAQUILLE O'NEAL: It's a funny thing about the NBA: any person that has a "vich" in the end of their name can shoot. Petrovic, Stojakovic, [Sasha] Danilovic—they all can shoot.

BILL SIMMONS: I'm always a fan of stereotyping countries by their basketball players. Like the Italians are a little feisty. Even [Andrea] Bargnani was feisty. He was a little trash-talker. He was very Italian. . . . I had a soft spot for Dino Radja because he was on the Celtics. He was pretty good—he had to be double-teamed one year. *And* he was a cigarette smoker, which I always respected.

MULLIN: The European players, their influence was passing. They played a beautiful team game, and teams they played on got better at ball movement, at being unselfish, looking for the open man, passing up a good shot and getting a great shot. Maybe, in some instances, they were not as physically gifted, so they had to rely on each other—how to use a screen, work together.

UJIRI: Some people say European teaching is more precise and touches the fundamentals, and you have less talented players having more success because they've learned the basics of shooting, passing, playing. Over here, there's that aspect, but there's incredibly more athletic ability.

STOJAKOVIC: I think it's a difference in philosophies, a difference in coaching. Basketball in Europe is more controlled by coaches. Here, it's more free, and it allows players to be more creative. But I have to mention that coaches here have one advantage of coaching better players. They can give them freedom. Coaches in Europe are working with less talent and trying to control the game more.

NASH: We're seeing the planet shrink. Information is ever present and available, so I think we're seeing the foreign game and the American game meet in the middle. You're seeing American coaches realize the way [international players] move the ball and play together is incredibly valuable. In the United States, the cultural influence highlights one-on-one. The bravado, the ego, the alpha dog—it's on *SportsCenter* and then it's on YouTube. There's the school of the game and the culture of the game in the school yard, and in the modern era I think we're seeing people value both.

ROD THORN: So many bigs now grow up shooting threes. The European influence—they've played an outside-in game for quite a while because they didn't have a lot of post-up players. But they taught their bigs skill. When you were growing up overseas, you worked on ballhandling, shooting, passing. You didn't just go down low and stay there.

SMITH: Well, the European game, it's face-up basketball. The influence is big, and it takes some of the size away from the game. You don't have to be 6-10 to be a power forward. It allows you to be more versatile in your positioning and more out-of-the-box in how you build your team.

JACK RAMSAY: The big man in Europe has typically been a player who can shoot from the perimeter, rather than have a strong post-up game. I think that showed the NBA there was a place for big men who could step outside and shoot the three-pointer.

NASH: Dirk [Nowitzki] is one of the most unique players ever. He was never explosive, but he had great feet. He was agile for his size. With his skill level and his ability to shoot, he got guys too close to him, so he could get around them. He was able to use his height and mobility and skill to create space, and to realize that, "If I just step back and lean on one leg, I'm too big for anyone to recover."

NOWITZKI: That one-footer fadeaway I developed later in my career. At the beginning, we always worked on two feet. It's all about balance in the air—you wanna get off two feet as much as you can. Then, as I got older, driving got harder—you get pounded. So I tried to create a shot that I could always get off without a lot of pounding. It helps that I'm 7 feet. All I need is a little step-back, then I could see the basket over the defender and usually get the shot off. What I try to do with my feet—the right leg that's going in the air has to point toward the basket. Then my eyes always focus on the rim. I never follow the ball with my eyes—try to really burn a hole into the front of the rim. I put the ball at the top of my head and release it from there, and when I do this quick step-back, I have to get the ball up as soon as I can to get a decent release. The rest is about touch, and if you shot a million jump shots in your career, I guess that comes natural.

PORZINGIS: That's why [Dirk's] so special. He made a move his own, and it's unguardable. What can you do against a 7-footer that's leaning back off one foot and hitting those shots? To be compared to Dirk Nowitzki, that's an unbelievable honor. He's a legend. He's done so many things for us Europeans in this league that made it much easier for me to come here and for people to believe in me.

TOM THIBODEAU: Yao Ming was pretty amazing. He played nine years, and each year he made significant jumps, to the point where there was a stretch where he was playing at an MVP level. He had that type of talent. Unfortunately [his] career [was] cut short [by injuries]. But for a guy that size to have the combination of touch, footwork, post moves, rebounding, intelligence, drive? He had it all.

RASHAD: If Yao Ming could've stayed healthy, he would've went down as one of the greatest centers of all time. He was 7'6", he could shoot left-handed, right-handed, great footwork, had a mean streak. He was a very nice, softy kind of guy, but not when he played. I remember Shaq telling me that he had a hard time against him because he had never played against anybody bigger than him.

VAN GUNDY: I don't think anybody's made to run up and down a basketball court that's 7'6". And the lower-extremity injuries often reoccur. It's unfortunate because Walton, Yao—it robbed them of some of their prime years.

DIVAC: It is unusual when you play against guys like Yao because he's much taller than you, but you just go back to your childhood when you were not that tall.

VAN GUNDY: [Yao] was the most diligent worker I ever coached. And Yao was one of the most beloved teammates of all time. His sense of humor was great, but to me the thing that set him apart was he was truly as happy for other people's success as he was for his own. After a game, a lot of players will feign like they're happy if another guy had a big game, but in reality they wished they hadn't had to sacrifice for that other guy to prosper. Yao was so happy when other guys had big games, and it's a very rare thing.

THIBODEAU: [Yao] did the right things each and every day. To me, that's the best type of leadership—just doing the right thing, saying the right thing, being a great teammate, and doing his absolute best. That's why I think he was able to walk away from the game with his head held high.

VAN GUNDY: To think what he did—coming from China to the United States to play in the NBA, not speaking the language, from a country that had never had a star like this. And remember, his first game in the NBA, he did not score. The perseverance this guy had, as a lot of people wanted to see him fail.

NASH: Yao's a beauty, a gentle giant. He changed the planet. [China's] the biggest country in the world, he's the biggest face in that country, and he made basketball their most popular sport. He introduced the NBA to the biggest market in the world, and that all being said, he was a pretty damn good basketball player, too.

PAT RILEY: There's a lot of world. There's only 350 million people in America. There's 7 billion people around the world. That's a lot of basketball players somewhere. They just need to be found.

THE LAKERS' ALPHA MALES

Shaquille O'Neal was driving too far—and too fast. That's how he cleared his head, to make sense of yet another sweep in the postseason for the Orlando Magic. In the 1995 Finals, it was Hakeem Olajuwon and the Houston Rockets that dismantled his young Magic team, which celebrated too long and too hard after eliminating Chicago in the Eastern Conference Finals.

One year later, the Bulls exacted revenge, with Michael Jordan, Scottie Pippen, Dennis Rodman, and Toni Kukoc humiliating Shaq and his team in four straight games.

Now it was the summer of 1996, and O'Neal was about to become a free agent. The Magic lowballed him on its initial offer, and the local paper was displaying a poll on billboards along the highway suggesting fans didn't think he was worth the money he was asking.

Los Angeles Lakers general manager Jerry West sensed an opportunity, and he went about convincing Shaq that he could revive the storied Lakers franchise. O'Neal was already making movies, recording music, and cranking out commercials in Hollywood. His agent, Leonard Armato, was based in L.A. and had been urging him to make the jump.

When he did, he had no idea he would be teaming up with a teenager who was raised in Italy, spoke multiple languages, and bypassed college to make himself eligible for the NBA draft. Lots of people told Kobe Bryant he was making a huge mistake, that only big men could make the jump from high school to the pros, but Bryant did what he'd always done: he bet on himself.

The most devastating—and volatile—duo in the game was coming to rescue the Lakers.

JERRY WEST: Shaquille spent a lot of time in Los Angeles in the summer. I got an opportunity to talk to him, and I said, "Look, we have better players than you do in Orlando. We'll win more here." I told him he'd be treated better here in Los Angeles than any place, because [Lakers owner] Jerry Buss let me really care for the players.

HAKEEM OLAJUWON: There are big men who are big but they play small, and there are small men who play big. Shaq is big and plays big.

VLADE DIVAC: The feeling playing against Shaq is you have to sacrifice for your team. You don't feel you can stop him, so you just have to do different things, even if you have to foul out. You have to do it because Shaq wasn't a good free throw shooter.

SHAQUILLE O'NEAL: When my father was teaching me the game, he always hollered three names. He would give me these little layups and he'd say, "You gotta block it like Bill Russell!" I smack it out, and he'd grab my shirt. "No! Bill Russell never did that! He blocked it to his guard, started the break!" I'm like, "Who the hell is Bill Russell?" Then he says, "You gotta learn the sky hook like Kareem!" I knew who Kareem Abdul-Jabbar was. "You need an unstoppable move like Kareem!" I would play in a game against some smaller kids, and I'd have 10 to 15 points. "You gotta dominate like Wilt!" I'm like, "Who the hell is Wilt?" "Wilt averaged 50 points!" So those were the three names that I would always have.

OLAJUWON: Shaq is very skilled, very agile, so your best chance was to run him and pick-and-roll, find ways to make him play the style of game that he doesn't like. For me, Shaq was the most difficult guy to play against.

DON NELSON: Nobody was more dominant than Shaq. He played for me in the [FIBA] World Games in 1994. He was the first center I had that said, "Coach, I don't want to start. Start the other guys. I'll come in whenever you need me." I said, "Boy, did you solve a lot of problems for me."

DIVAC: The flop came from [guarding] Shaq. When he caught the ball in low post and went over you, you just didn't have a chance. I tried to protect my ground and make sure that he didn't go through me. A lot of times the referee doesn't call that, so [by flopping] I would put pressure on them to make a call. I didn't have any other choice against Shaq.

WEST: After we signed Shaquille, I had to go in the hospital for two days. I was completely exhausted. I felt like I'd been in a boxing match for three weeks, there was so much pressure and stress.

O'NEAL: The whole Lakers thing kicked in when I walked into the Great Western Forum. Jerry West, who was all smiles when he signed me, had a frown on his face like he was upset. It was dark in the Forum, and as soon as we get to the middle of the floor, the lights on the jerseys come on, and Jerry West looks at me and says, "I know you got a lot going on, I know you like rapping and hip-hop and movies and all that, but I brought you here so your jersey will be up here at the end of all this. We can either look like geniuses or we can look like idiots. You decide."

WEST: When Shaq finally says, "I'm coming," I traded our starting center, Vlade Divac, for Kobe Bryant.

KOBE BRYANT: I had what in my family we used to call basketball fever. You just feel like you have to play all the time. It's almost like a sickness where you can't get enough of it, and it started for me at a really early age.

WEST: We worked out Kobe Bryant twice [before the draft]. After watching him once I said, "My God." You don't see a skill level from a young kid like this very often. Michael Cooper, who was an all-league defensive player, had been out of the game a year and a half, was guarding Kobe, and he scored on Michael like there was no one there.

O'NEAL: My first impression of Kobe was a kid with the "AND1" street mentality. He had a lot of tricks, between the legs, behind the back—it was all about him. Had no concept of pecking order. He was just a kid that's gonna get his. In high school, he was the man, so good he didn't need to go to college. Went straight to the pros: "Now that I'm a pro, it's mine." Age 18 and it's mine. So I was like, "No, no, no, no! It's not gonna work like that."

BRYANT: I was 18, 19 years old, and I understand it's pretty rare to take on a veteran, especially a person of that size. But this is the way I'm built, this is who I am. I'm not gonna sugarcoat anything. Our goal is to win a championship, and my job is to help us get there.

JULIUS ERVING: You tell Kobe he is not passing enough, next thing you know he's gonna have 15 assists the next game, just to show that he could pass.

O'NEAL: One time, Kobe did something crazy in the game, and [Lakers coach] Del Harris sat him down. One of Jerry Buss's guys came around the bench and said, "Jerry said to put him in the game." Because the fans were going crazy—"Ko-be! Ko-be! Ko-be!" So he does, and Kobe makes a crazy shot and the place goes crazy. They love this guy. He's an 18-year-old kid, he's flashy, they're seeing a little bit of Mike [Jordan]. His greatness came very quickly, and he wanted to assume a leadership position, but I wasn't having that.

PHIL JACKSON: One of the issues I had with Kobe was the fact that he wanted to be a leader, but he was very young when he came to the Lakers. He didn't have the capability of leading anybody. He didn't want to be with those guys, and therefore why would they follow him? So I said, "You want to be a leader, but you haven't found common ground." And he said, "They just talk about cars and girls and rap." I said, "Well, find a common ground, and the leadership will follow."

O'NEAL: Getting Phil Jackson to come to L.A.? I did that. I went upstairs and said, "Hey, this guy's won six [titles], he's a free agent, go get him." They said, "We've got Kurt Rambis. Let's keep it in the family." I said, "Forget that. I don't like the triangle, either, but the shit must work because he's got six rings running it."

DONNIE WALSH: After the 2000 Finals, I thought Kobe and Shaq were going to be together forever. It looked like the perfect match.

CHARLEY ROSEN: Phil's first championship in 2000, when they had Kobe and Shaq and A. C. Green and I don't remember who else, people on Phil's staff said that was one of the worst teams ever to win an NBA championship, and it was one of Phil's best coaching jobs.

JACKSON: At times, I was a better coach than I was a parent because I was more present sometimes with my teams [than with my kids]. My role as a coach was to say, "You're never stopping your education. If you're gonna be on this team, you're gonna get books, you're gonna get material, you're gonna have conversations. We're gonna talk about subjects that may be difficult, that may be current. It may cause you to be uncomfortable, but this is what we have to do." I gave the Hermann Hesse book *Siddhartha* to Shaq, and he said, "Well, this guy is just like me: he's beautiful, he's a prince, and he had many women in his life." I would kid the guys, "I want a book report," but Shaq was the only one that truly gave me one.

ROSEN: Young players, they have attention deficit disorder; they can't concentrate. Phil always kept them guessing; they never knew what he was gonna do. He's gonna come dressed in a tie-dyed shirt; he's gonna have a little plant that you water and it grows a Jerry Garcia head. He inserts crazy stuff into his training films like [Utah Jazz GM] Frank Layden, 350 pounds, running on the beach in a bikini, so they have to pay attention. One of the problems in the NBA is players tune out coaches. They say, "I don't want to hear this guy anymore." But they never knew what was coming next with Phil, so he held their attention.

O'NEAL: I used to come to practice some days, and Phil being a big man, he could tell by my walk if I was beat up. He sees me get beat up in the games, and he'd be like, "Give me 30 minutes on the treadmill, big man." But then he would always say, "But I need 30 tomorrow—if you don't get 30 tomorrow, you got to get back to practice." So I gave him 40.

BRYANT: Phil's influence was a very tactical one from the onset, which is understanding the triangle offense and the fundamentals of it. It wasn't coming in and saying, "OK, guys, we got to win a championship." It wasn't this rah-rah motivation thing. It wasn't a "Let's all get along" sort of thing. It was basic stuff: footwork, spacing, timing, be able to pass with your left, be able to make a correct bounce pass. He was absolutely obsessive about those details.

JACKSON: We had a knockout group of guys, really talented, but they just didn't quite have the wherewithal to win in the beginning. But they learned. By 2001–02, we just ran through the league, tore it up, we probably shouldn't have lost a game the final 30 games of the season.

ROSEN: They were good because Shaq was such a powerhouse. Tex Winter always said that Shaq had better footwork than Wilt.

WEST: Phil and I did not have much of a relationship. And I was the one who insisted that we hire him. He sort of was an isolationist, but obviously he didn't want to communicate with me. Which was fine, but I thought it was strange, because I thought one of the strengths of our group was that we really had good communication. For some reason, it just wasn't there, and I made a decision that I shouldn't be there anymore [in 2002] because he was more important to this team than I was.

From 2000 to 2002, Shaq and Kobe cut a swath through a series of Eastern Conference challengers: Reggie Miller and the Pacers (2000), Philadelphia 76ers supernova Allen Iverson (2001), and a New Jersey Nets team led by Jason Kidd (2002).

The Lakers were a dynasty in the making, except Shaq and Kobe, two self-described alpha males, clashed as they tried to share the ball, the points, and the limelight. Shaq was a dominant, fun-loving, free-spirited big man who freely admitted basketball was not his sole focus. Kobe was a singular talent who idolized Michael Jordan and thought of nothing but the game that had come to define him. When Bryant was younger, it was clear the Lakers were Shaq's team. But as he grew into his own, their conflicts threatened to derail their championship chemistry.

BILL WALTON: I never understood the dynamic between Shaq and Kobe, and it's the saddest part of my life as a fan and as a broadcaster and as an alum of this great game, because these two remarkable players couldn't figure out how to make this work.

ROSEN: Kobe and Shaq were always rubbing up against each other because Shaq bought into the triangle immediately and Kobe never did.

KENNY SMITH: These guys are like Felix Unger and Oscar Madison, but they live in the same house, so they just gotta learn to get along. They don't have to agree, but they have to learn to get along. They could have done a better job at it, honestly.

ROSEN: There was a Kobe faction and a Shaq faction, but there were more guys with Shaq. Guys would stand up and say, "We're not going to win with Kobe playing out on his own," and Kobe finally got up and said, "Well, I love you guys, blah-blah-blah." But Kobe always resisted Phil. He never really bought into the triangle. You can see that in a lot of ways. When he insisted on bringing the ball across the timeline and looked to create something before anything else—that is not the way the triangle is supposed to operate.

PAUL PIERCE: I don't think you could really tell there was an issue between the two. A lot of teams have players who don't get along, but when you get on the court, those things go away. They were able to put those things aside, so when they were on the court, they could accomplish what they needed to, which is what made them such a great tandem.

STEPHEN A. SMITH: Even though we all know and appreciate the greatness of Shaquille O'Neal, one of the most dominant forces in NBA history, we were not Kobe. We weren't waking up at 5:30 in the morning, we weren't working on our game religiously, we weren't fixated with the game of basketball the way Kobe was, and so he earned the right. He earned the right to have issues with Shaq.

PETER VECSEY: I think the Kobe-Shaq friction can be reduced to Kobe being possessed as a competitor and Shaq deciding when to play and when to show up. Seasons would start, and he'd decide to have surgery. Wait a minute—why didn't you do this in the summer? He wasn't in shape like Kobe. We've seen the same stuff with Kobe and Dwight Howard. If you're not serious, Kobe doesn't want any part of you.

GEORGE KARL: I thought Kobe was jealous of Shaq's dominance. Kobe wanted to be the guy and probably was the guy for 90 percent of the world, but it wasn't enough for Kobe. He wanted Shaq out of the way. There are certain players, and Kobe's one of 'em—and don't get me wrong, the list is long—that I call "spotlight-dominant." [Carmelo Anthony] was spotlight-dominant. James Harden, to me, is spotlight-dominant.

O'NEAL: There was one time Kobe and I almost came to blows [in 2004]. Because Phil had finally had enough. Phil never, never butted in. Phil knew that [the tension] made both of us play at a high level. But it just got to be enough for Phil to say, "Both of you be quiet. Shake on it right now." So we shake, then Kobe gets with his little broadcaster friend Jim Gray. I wake up the next morning, there's this article dogging me. So I call him and let him know: "Come to practice, I'm going to kill you." And he says, "All right, I'll be there." We get there, we get ready to square up, and Karl Malone and Gary Payton are already there and they say, "We've got to stop this." So they step in. As I've always said, if there were 10 instances where we were going at it, only 4 of them would be serious.

BRYANT: As players, we always differed, because I would try to bring the best out of him every single day and push his buttons. If we had a back-to-back, played Monday, Tuesday, practice Wednesday, I need him on that practice floor, and so I'm gonna do and say some things to make sure that your ass is out there. Some things may get underneath your skin, some things you might not like. We had a lot of friction from that, and that's really the core of our differences. It was work ethic—we didn't see eye to eye on that process.

O'NEAL: A lot of people think we had [a] beef, but if you look at the word "beef" and look at the word "turmoil" and look at two guys that are supposedly not gonna play together, you have to ask yourself, "Would they win three out of four [championships]?" And you also have to ask, "If they hate each other so much, then why, when Shaq wins his first championship, you see a guy full speed ahead run across the court and jump in his arms?" It's Kobe. If they hate each other so much, when Kobe twists his ankle and couldn't walk, who's the guy who said, "Jump on my back. I'll carry you to the bus." If they hate each other so much, why, at the [2009] All-Star Game, when Shaq's on another team and they get co-MVP and Shaq's with his son and the guy wants to give Kobe the trophy, Kobe looks at my little son Shareef and says, "Here you go, little man." So if there's [a] beef, it was an office beef. Office beef and real beef are two different things. If you come to your office and a guy's slacking around but he's putting up numbers, you agitate him: "Yo, if you dressed better, you'd get better results." The guy still wears the same suit and his tie is undone, but he's so pissed off that he's working even harder, he's getting purchase orders and his numbers are up. That's the kind of beef we had.

BILL SIMMONS: Those guys keep changing their stories. They hated each other, and for a few years they were like, "No, we didn't hate each other." You guys *did* hate each other; everybody knew you hated each other.

BRYANT: A lot of people would view [being ruthless] as a negative trait. For me, it was always pretty simple: our job was to win the game, and my job is to get the best from my teammates. If that means pushing certain buttons that others might not be willing to push, so be it.

CHRIS PAUL: People see Kobe and how he'll take the shot over three people. If he makes it, everybody loves him to death. If he misses, everybody's going to say he didn't trust his teammates.

SIMMONS: I think Kobe knows he's not a great leader, but he's really interested in the concept of leadership. He knew what his flaws were. He laid out, "Here's why we lost in 2008: we weren't tough enough; I was too easy on those guys; I wish I had been harder because we got bullied by the Celtics and I was too hands-off. So the next year, I came in and I was a bully to these guys."

In 2004, after the Lakers lost 4–1 in the Finals to a surprising Detroit Pistons team led by Chauncey Billups and Rasheed Wallace, Shaq was back in his Bentley, burning up the road. He could see the end coming. His relationship with Bryant had soured, and the Lakers had to make a choice—Shaq or Kobe. With Bryant enjoying the peak of his career, O'Neal knew which way it was going.

That summer, Shaq was traded to the Miami Heat. At his introductory press conference, he guaranteed a championship, and within two seasons, with Dwyane Wade in a leading role, he delivered.

Phil Jackson also parted ways with the Lakers over a contract dispute, leaving Kobe to go it alone. A rocky season ensued, and a frustrated Bryant asked to be traded. Instead, L.A. lured Jackson back into the fold, and together he and Kobe won two more rings, in 2009 and 2010. As Bryant savored his fifth championship, having dispatched a familiar foe in the Boston Celtics, he was asked what was most gratifying about it. Kobe replied, "I got one more than Shaq."

O'NEAL: I asked for three extensions while I was with the Lakers. I got them. Jerry Buss said, "No problem." Last extension I asked for, it was, "Ahhhh, you're getting older. We want you to go down." I just went to the Finals three out of four years, I'm not taking less money. That's not a conversation. So we lose to Detroit in the Finals, I'm figuring, "We'll come back; we'll get them next year." I'm eating cereal, Fruity Pebbles, having a good time. I turn on ESPN, and it's breaking news: [Lakers general manager] Mitch Kupchak says, "We will entertain calls for Shaq." Nobody called me, nobody called my agent. I thought that was super-disrespectful.

SIMMONS: The Lakers knew they were selling high when they got rid of Shaq. He had a shelf life at that point. You could see it in the '04 Finals—he couldn't bring it every night. He had one unbelievable game in that Finals, and I remember Phil Jackson said, "We just wasted a vintage effort from Shaq." He didn't mean it in a disparaging way, but it's the kind of thing he would never have said in 2000, because Shaq would have had that same game over and over again.

O'NEAL: I call them, and I said, "Look, it's over." I would have respected them more if they had called me into the office and said, "We want to go in a different direction."

STEPHEN A. SMITH: Kobe was perfectly content without Shaq, didn't even want to reflect on it, and wouldn't hesitate to call him a fat bastard. Because Shaq did have a vice, and that vice was Big Macs. Shaq likes Big Macs, and Kobe would be training and exercising and working on his game, and he'd come into the trainer's room and Shaq literally would be receiving treatment but he would also be eating a Big Mac, and it would drive Kobe absolutely nuts. He wasn't thinking about the fact that Shaq was the most dominant force of the modern era, that Shaq was a multiple champion, that Shaq helped him capture championships. Kobe wasn't thinking about that. Kobe was like, "This fat bastard."

SIMMONS: They trade Shaq, and Phil writes his book and he crushes Kobe in it. He really goes after him. There was one part where he talked about [Kobe's] sexual assault accusation and said, "When I heard about the charges, I can't say I was surprised." Phil clearly had a very low opinion of Kobe as a person, and if you read that book, your takeaway was [Phil] couldn't wait to just annihilate Kobe, and he'll never coach him again. And then he started coaching him again. And then they end up winning two more titles.

JACKSON: When I came back [in 2005–06], Kobe had to basically throw a fit, saying, "If you're not gonna start building a championship team, I want to be traded." Management got wind of it and we made a trade for Pau Gasol, and he was the right fit, the perfect addition for Kobe.

PIERCE: Guarding Kobe Bryant is like stepping in fire. You know he's gonna shoot, shoot, and keep shooting. He's gonna put pressure on you constantly. You gotta understand, he's gonna make shots. You just gotta stay on him, keep your body on him, get a hand up on his shot. You have to be where he is at all times, because he might take the next 15 shots. The key is you can't get down on yourself. He can wear you down to where he makes shots and you don't have any confidence in your defense. I kept saying to myself, "He'll miss this one. He'll miss the next one."

JACKSON: We played the Celtics in the 2008 Finals, and we lost one of the games on our home court. We had a 27-point lead, and we lost that game. The lead was in the first half and we couldn't hold it, and when we went in the locker room, Tex Winter said, "You just lost the series." I went, "Hold on, Tex, we have a lot of games left to play." He said, "No, the energy behind that game was enough devastation. They have a feeling now that they can beat you."

PIERCE: When we got home for Game 6, we were up 3–2 in the series, but we had to win one game. We knew it would be tough to beat us on our floor. We didn't want to leave anything up for grabs in Game 7 when you've got a guy like Kobe Bryant in the gym.

BRYANT: It's so complicated to win championships. Simple minds tend to look at very simple solutions and say, "They had Michael [Jordan], so they won," [or] "They had Kobe and they won." It is more complicated than that. It's all those pieces of the puzzle, how they fit emotionally, aside from even just an execution standpoint.

PIERCE: It's hard to see defeat in Kobe. He's a guy that's never gonna give up. But we saw it in the rest of the guys in Game 6. I remember one play right before the half, when Kevin Garnett and I got in a pick-and-roll. I threw it to KG, he caught it with one hand, went up, hung in the air for like four or five seconds, got fouled, and he knocked it off the glass with one hand, and-1. We went up 20 points right before the half. You could just see it on their faces. It was such a difficult shot that [KG] made, he fell to the ground, started pounding his chest. It was like, "I think we got this, fellas. They got the look of defeat."

JACKSON: In Game 6, Boston came out and hit all kinds of three-pointers in the second quarter. The [lead] got bigger and bigger, and I just let them go. I wanted our guys to remember it. That's what Willis Reed said to me that summer. We ran into each other, and he said, "You really let 'em burn in that playoff game. That was a lesson." I said, "Yeah, they were not ready. They didn't have the physical capabilities of standing up to that team at the time. But we're gonna see them again."

BRYANT: That Celtics loss was brutal—in the most beautiful way. We learned so much through that, and how to handle ourselves through the course of the season. I learned how to really push my teammates and prepare them to meet such a physical team in the Finals.

JACKSON: We weren't hardened, and we needed to be hardened. By 2010, we knew what it took for a championship run.

PIERCE: That was *definitely* a different Lakers team that we played in the 2010 Finals. They got a lot tougher. When you pushed them, they pushed back. You saw there was more fire in Pau Gasol, there was more fire in Kobe's eyes, there was more fire in all of them.

JACKSON: Kobe's maturation came later. He became a very good leader and could drive a team like Michael [Jordan].

O'NEAL: People ask me all the time, "If you could do it over, what would you do differently?" My answer is, "Nothing." We won three out of four. Me and Kobe. Best one-two punch in basketball.

KENNY SMITH: I don't think Shaq and Kobe ever valued each other as much as they should have. They were the two most lethal players ever put together in the history of the game, and they didn't even know it.

THE SPURS WAY

The San Antonio Spurs were on the cusp of cementing their case as the most enduring NBA franchise of the 21st century. After winning in 1999 with Twin Towers David Robinson and Tim Duncan, the Spurs, led by the innovative Gregg Popovich, evolved into a European-style team that won titles in 2003, 2005, and 2007. The franchise repeatedly drafted foreign-born gems who went on to long, productive NBA careers, flinging open the international doors to subsequent NBA franchises.

And now the Spurs' Big Three of Duncan, French point guard Tony Parker, and Argentinian whirling dervish Manu Ginobili were on the verge of eliminating the heavily favored Miami Heat in the 2013 Finals. The Spurs were up 5 with 27 seconds to play, prompting personnel at the Heat's home arena to begin placing protective ropes around the court for the inevitable celebration. "I was standing up with my arms folded, and I said, 'This is over,'" recalled Heat president Pat Riley.

Instead, a series of unfathomable events led to one of the most dramatic finishes in NBA history.

Missed free throws by Ginobili and the redoubtable young star Kawhi Leonard were the first cracks in the Spurs' seemingly impervious armor.

With San Antonio up 95–92 in the final seconds, Popovich removed Duncan for defensive purposes, a move that backfired when LeBron's three-pointer rattled off the rim and 7-foot Chris Bosh reached over the head of Spurs guard Danny Green to rebound it. He fired it to Ray Allen in the corner, who instinctively jumped behind the three-point line and buried the clutch shot.

"It couldn't have been in nobody better's hands," James said. "Thank you, Jesus Shuttlesworth [Allen's character in the movie *He Got Game*]."

"When Ray left the Celtics for Miami, we weren't really on speaking terms," said Paul Pierce, "but when he made that shot, I texted him and told him it was one of the greatest shots I've ever seen. People don't understand the difficulty of that shot. You have to have the instinct to know where the three-point line is, get behind it, and shoot it within milliseconds."

According to Riley, there was no luck or chance involved in the play, rather years and years of repetition. "Ray had practiced it so many times, he knew exactly where he was on the court," Riley said. "When the ball came to him in flight, he jumped behind the line, landed on his toes, and never took his heels to the floor."

Miami won in overtime, then won again in Game 7, leaving a devastated Popovich to explain why he pulled his Hall of Fame forward when it mattered most.

"Pop outsmarted himself by not having Duncan on the floor at the end," said Bob Ryan. "It was a mistake."

"Oh, he gagged," said Bill Simmons.

Riley understood the basketball logic—concern over Duncan being able to get to the corner to contest a three. "But he took his best player off the court, his best rebounder off the court, and his greatest winner off the court," Riley said. "And we ended up getting the rebound that we needed with him sitting on the bench. Now, how does Gregg reconcile that? I know what I would do. I would beat myself to death."

What the Spurs did was regroup over the summer and vow to commit to a new level of unselfishness. Ginobili, a free agent who had turned the ball over 8 times in that Game 6, took a 50 percent pay cut to return.

Before the 2014 playoffs, Duncan walked up to the whiteboard in the Spurs' locker room and wrote "16"—the number of wins needed to win it all.

The Spurs met the Heat again in the Finals, and the series was tied 1–1. "We were playing in our home building, we're defending champions, and there's no reason for us not to think we are in great shape," Riley said. "But then a freight train hit us."

With the Spurs whipping the ball around the perimeter, Miami's aggressive style of jumping the passing lanes on defense faltered. Chasing San Antonio's near-perfect ball movement left the Heat players exhausted.

Over the final three games—all San Antonio wins—the Spurs averaged 120.8 points per 100 possessions, an NBA record. "Their level of play went to another stratosphere," Riley said. "I said to myself, 'This is the greatest basketball that I've ever seen.'"

"Pop had them playing at a tempo that no one could keep up with," said James.

Popovich declared the 2014 championship the most satisfying of his career. The Spurs Way became the new blueprint for NBA team culture, with the next great franchise, the Golden State Warriors, taking copious notes. Once again, San Antonio was setting the tone for a new approach to the NBA game.

"It was the best basketball I've ever seen," former NBA coach Doug Moe said. "The first quarter [in Game 5] wasn't even over, and Miami quit. They knew they were done. To this day, I believe James left Miami because he didn't believe he could beat the Spurs."

"Guarding the Spurs' offense is equivalent to playing against five John Stocktons, because you can never turn your head," said Pierce. "Their offense is constant motion, and you cannot rest one second. If you're caught putting your hands on your knees, you're dead."

With Duncan retiring in 2016, San Antonio is undergoing yet another transition, but some things remain constant. "They are professional *Hoosiers*," said Shaquille O'Neal, "and they will fundamentally spank your behind to death."

THE NEW NBA: LeBron and Small Ball

When LeBron Raymone James was a high school junior, Sports Illustrated plunked him on the cover and declared him "The Chosen One." The teenager's response was to emblazon a "Chosen 1" tattoo across his back.

That fearlessness, fused with a breathtaking combination of size, speed, finesse, and basketball intelligence, earned LeBron the reputation as the most exorbitantly hyped NBA prospect in history.

James was chosen as the No. 1 overall pick in the 2003 draft by the Cleveland Cavaliers, the team in his home state of Ohio. Then he accomplished the unthinkable: he lived up to the extraordinary expectations heaped upon him, despite the jealousy of his own teammates and a steady stream of challenges from NBA veterans testing his mettle.

It took James four seasons to advance to his first Finals, where the Cavs faced long odds against a deeper, more talented San Antonio Spurs team. Tim Duncan, Manu Ginobili, and Tony Parker dissected Cleveland in a four-game sweep in the 2007 Finals, and James, who shot 35 percent from the field and 20 percent from three-point range, spent the long off-season honing his outside touch.

In 2007–08, another trio of stars aligned to thwart LeBron's path to a title. The Celtics lured Kevin Garnett to join resident All-Star Paul Pierce and recently acquired Ray Allen in Boston, and together they triggered the biggest single-season turnaround in NBA history.

Cleveland and Boston met in the Eastern Conference Finals that May, and in an epic Game 7 shoot-out, James's brilliance was surpassed only by Pierce's clutch shooting. "The Truth" led the Celtics to the 2008 championship, while "The King" went home empty-handed—again.

The two franchises met again in the 2010 playoffs, this time in the conference semifinals. During a Game 5 thumping, James appeared passive on defense and oddly disconnected from his teammates. It was a shocking lack of focus, and the image of LeBron chewing his nails on the bench as time *ticked off on the Cavaliers' season raised the question, What's wrong with "The Chosen One"?*

PAUL PIERCE: I heard about LeBron since he was in high school. A lot of NBA players went to go see him play. I remember thinking, "This kid is so good he could be in the All-Star Game." Then I'm like, "Whoa, nobody's that good, are they?"

PAUL SILAS (Power Forward, Boston Celtics/Seattle Supersonics; Head Coach, Cleveland Cavaliers, 2003–05): I was coaching Cleveland, and I didn't have a point guard. I watched this rookie dribble and pass the ball, and I said, "This kid is incredible." I made him the point forward, and he just took it, didn't question me at all, didn't say, "Coach, I don't know if I want to do this."

STEVE KERR: My guess is LeBron is [the] greatest athlete in the history of our sport, in terms of speed and size. As great as Michael Jordan was, LeBron's got 30 pounds on him.

PIERCE: When I matched up with LeBron, I wanted to go right at him. I remember thinking, "I'm gonna give this young kid a couple of 40-point games and let him know he ain't stepping over me. You're doing a lot of damage in the league, but you're gonna feel my presence each and every time we face each other." But he felt the same way, and that's maturity you didn't see from a young kid coming out of high school.

SILAS: All the people in Cleveland thought LeBron was going to be the best player, and the players that I had didn't want to hear that. They said, "He's never played before, so why does everybody think he's going to be the one to lead this club?" I saw the way LeBron played and the talent he had, and I knew. I would grab certain players and say, "Look, we have to win ball games, and if this man has it in his head you guys don't like him, it's not going to work." They wouldn't listen.

BOB RYAN: I go back to the documentary they did on LeBron at St. Vincent–St. Mary High School. You learned that it was important to him to be a part of the group, this same core group of buddies he'd known since grade school. He knew he was the best player and was not allowed to forget it, but he didn't use that as a weapon or as leverage against teammates. He still always wanted to be one of the guys. That's his instinct. I don't think that was true with Michael Jordan. Jordan was a virtuoso who had to accommodate himself. It was OK to be a part of this quintet, but Jordan's attitude was, "Get this straight: I'm getting the solos on this team." I don't think LeBron had that kind of attitude ever.

LeBRON JAMES: My childhood friends were the ones who were there for me when basketball was just pure and innocent. They saw me grow from the 9-year-old child to this 30-something-year-old veteran. They saw me before social media, way before coverage of high school kids or grade school kids being put on platforms or pedestals that they shouldn't be put on. They were along for the ride when things outside the sports world weren't all that fancy. So we all took hits, we all experienced adversity, and it made it a lot easier when I got to a point where I was covered by real bright lights that I knew who I wanted to be around.

SILAS: LeBron was just a kid. He wanted the respect of the other players. He wanted to learn the game, and he wanted to understand what the game was all about. I told him that takes time. I also told him, "The players that talk about you, you can't listen to them."

PETER VECSEY: LeBron's been able to get to the Finals how many times with whoever he's playing with. Playing with that first Cavaliers team, he had no talent, or very little talent, [around him]. The Cavs were slaughtered by the Spurs [in 2007] because LeBron didn't have enough help.

CHARLES BARKLEY: I've always said LeBron is more like Magic Johnson. Michael wants to kill you. Kobe wants to kill you. LeBron wants a triple-double. Now, they all work, and I think LeBron's a more rounded *person* than Kobe and Michael. His whole being is not about how many championships he wins. There's nothing wrong with Michael and Kobe's thinking, let me get that straight. People say, "Charles Barkley is trying to protect Michael Jordan's legacy," which needs no protecting. Only in America can you compare LeBron to Magic Johnson and his supporters are like, "These guys, they're just trying to hate on LeBron."

KEVIN DURANT: LeBron's mentality is different from Jordan['s] and Kobe['s]. I put it like this: LeBron James thinks, "How can I help my teammates, and how can they help me?" He gets everybody involved. He thinks about scoring 50 percent of the time. When he comes down the court, it's not score, it's assist, and then the next possession might be score, not assist. We talk about the "killer mentality" a lot. Kobe [and] Jordan will try to rip your neck off—they're gonna be physical with you, throw an elbow, shoot the jumper over the top of you, and if you show a sign of weakness, they gonna exploit it. LeBron is more like, "I'm gonna grind you out, I'm gonna make this pass, and then at the end of the game, it's gonna open up for me and then you gonna see who I am."

VECSEY: LeBron had his down points where we didn't think he had the guts to rise to the occasion. In those games in Boston where he lost, he seemed to come apart. The biting of the nails—you thought something was a little lacking. If I ever saw Jordan or Kobe bite their nails, I would be like, "Whoa!"

On July 8, 2010, LeBron James hijacked NBA free agency.
   Against the backdrop of the Greenwich, Connecticut, Boys & Girls Club, Cleveland's supernova announced in a live television broadcast on ESPN dubbed The Decision *that he would "be taking [his] talents to South Beach."*
   More than 13 million viewers tuned in, including Cleveland owner Dan Gilbert, who learned of James's decision to sign with the Miami Heat at practically the same time the rest of the country did. Even though James donated the $2.5 million proceeds from The Decision *to the Greenwich Boys & Girls Club, the backlash was vicious. In an instant, LeBron went from beloved superstar to vilified egomaniac for pulling a power play that smacked of insensitivity and self-importance. Gilbert blasted* The Decision

as a "cowardly betrayal," and local television outlets ran live footage of angry fans lighting James's jersey on fire.

Gilbert also released a scathing letter declaring, "This shocking act of disloyalty from our home grown 'chosen one' sends the exact opposite lesson of what we want our children to learn. And 'who' we want them to grow up to become."

In choosing the Heat, James had orchestrated the creation of his own Big Three by coaxing Toronto forward Chris Bosh to join him and guard Dwyane Wade to re-sign with Miami. The manufacture of this superteam rankled Magic Johnson and Charles Barkley, among others. "He'll never be Jordan," Barkley declared. "This clearly takes him out of the conversation."

The Decision may have torpedoed LeBron's favorability ratings, yet by flexing his free-agency muscles, the best player of his generation managed to ignite a new and unprecedented era of player empowerment.

BILL SIMMONS: *The Decision* drove more interest to the NBA than any other thing in the last 20 years. The lead-up to it—LeBron's bizarre performance in the playoffs [in 2010] that we'll never figure out, all the attention of "Where's he gonna go? Is he gonna backstab Cleveland?"— then he does this ridiculous show on ESPN.

DAVID STERN: We knew *The Decision* was happening. I got a phone call a day earlier, and we actually went up the chain at ESPN and said, "Please don't do this. Don't make it into a television show." So much for our clout with our broadcast partner. We knew it couldn't end well. I said three things: "*The Decision* was poorly conceived, badly executed, and poorly produced."

PIERCE: *The Decision* was something like I've never seen before. We were all holding our breath wondering where he was gonna play. You had never seen anybody announce a free-agent decision on national TV, so I think it kinda rubbed a lot of players the wrong way. Guys felt like, "He's taking this decision kinda Hollywood."

SIMMONS: The best player always determines some sort of outcome that has nothing to do with him as a player. With Jordan it was, "Oh, I can be more than a basketball player, I can be marketable" and "I can be 'the guy.'" That led to the whole one-on-one basketball that followed. So what's LeBron? He is "I'm empowered. I'm bigger than a team. I'm my own person. I'm gonna be a billionaire. I can pick what team I wanna go to, and I'm just gonna go there. I'm not gonna sign a long-term contract. I'm gonna take this year by year, and if I don't like what my owner does, I'm gonna go somewhere else."

STERN: I thought it ultimately portrayed LeBron in a light that he didn't deserve to be portrayed in. I always found him to be a very nice young man. I remember telling him when he left [Cleveland] that I'm proud of him, and when I gave him his ring I said, "I'm still proud of you." But I thought he was trashed in a way that was not his fault and could've been avoided.

JAMES: I realized that I shouldn't have done it that way when the season started. We saw so much negativity towards myself and to the group of guys.

STERN: My parents used to say, "It's not what you say, it's how you say it." They chose the wrong vehicle. They said it in the wrong way. All he had to say was, "I'm announcing . . . that I decided, all things considered, that I'm going to sign with Miami because I think I have a better chance to win a championship there." Period.

ADAM SILVER: *The Decision* was a bad idea, but I don't think LeBron was duped. LeBron is a very bright guy, and whether or not LeBron acknowledges he made a mistake, I think he owns it.

SIMMONS: He handled *The Decision* terribly, not understanding what that would do to the city of Cleveland, which hadn't won a title since 1964. It's the worst thing anyone has done to a fan base.

STERN: The worst thing was, I'm at a conference when it happened, and Dan Gilbert was at the conference, and I had to fine him $100,000 for that letter he wrote to LeBron, issuing the curse of Cleveland or something, which they didn't take down on their website until LeBron announced he was coming back—but they meant to.

SIMMONS: What's interesting is, two years later everyone forgot. LeBron won the title, great! How about when he backstabbed everybody?

JAMES: What hurt me more than anything is the backlash that my family was getting, and also my teammates. I put them in a tough situation because of something that I decided to do.

STERN: He made a mistake. "I'm taking my talents to South Beach." Come on.

SIMMONS: Miami became wrestling villains. The [team] became like the Bad Boy Pistons. Everyone was rooting against them, and you look at the ratings from that moment on, [they] went up, up, up. I guarantee if you ask Adam Silver, he would say it's the best thing that happened to the NBA.

SILVER: I defend LeBron forever in terms of his decision as a free agent to play wherever he wants, but I don't think LeBron James from Akron, Ohio, understood the significance of [doing the announcement in] Greenwich, Connecticut. I think they didn't want to mess with Knicks fans by doing it in New York. Connecticut was a neutral site in their minds. From ESPN's standpoint, handing over editorial control made no sense to me at all.

SIMMONS: After that, all of a sudden, players were all about keeping their choices open. "Oh, I'm Kevin Durant. I'm gonna be a free agent coming up. I have all these choices." They all have their company. They do their infomercial documentary that's terrible. They all do the same blueprint, and it's because of LeBron.

SILVER: The fact that LeBron James single-handedly can have double-digit millions of social media followers—whether he's tweeting or posting what his favorite shoe is, or his fashion interests, or his music interests, or posting a play that he thought was particularly interesting—I mean, my God, it's incredible. At the same time, these guys are being scrutinized every second of every day. Michael Jordan didn't live under that kind of spotlight, as famous and as prominent as he was. It's a different world for today's players.

SIMMONS: The thing that bothered me as a basketball fan and as somebody who's overcompetitive in general is that he's supposed to be trying to beat Dwyane Wade. Bird wanted to beat Magic. Russell didn't want to be on Wilt's team. [Dave] Cowens didn't want to play with Kareem—he wanted to beat him. Wade was one of the four best players in the league, and LeBron was like, "What if we join forces?" But it worked.

"Not 2, not 3, not 4, not 5, not 6, not 7 . . ."

LeBron James gleefully forecast the number of championships he expected to win in Miami as a capacity crowd at American Airlines Arena enthusiastically egged him on. Amid the smoke and pyrotechnics and dancers, Heat president Pat Riley winced.

A year later, the bravado felt hollow. While Miami advanced to the first of four straight Finals in 2011, the heavily favored Heat were upended by the Dallas Mavericks and superstar power forward Dirk Nowitzki, who, in almost the opposite manner as LeBron, had quietly re-signed in Dallas the past summer, without fanfare or television ratings.

While Nowitzki garnered Finals MVP honors, James averaged just 3 fourth-quarter points per game in the series, prompting Dallas coach Rick Carlisle to ask in the winning locker room, "How often do we have to hear about the LeBron James reality show? When are people going to talk about the purity of the game and what these [Mavericks] accomplished?"

That summer, LeBron enlisted the help of Hall of Fame center Hakeem Olajuwon to upgrade his post-up skills. The 2011–12 version of the Miami Heat returned stronger and more cohesive. Their trapping defense was a devastating weapon that forced turnovers and transformed them into demoralizing fast-break highlight shows, with James and Wade connecting for some of the most amazing alley-oop dunks ever seen in the NBA.

LeBron earned regular season MVP honors, then completely dominated Oklahoma City in the 2012 Finals, capping off his first championship with a triple-double of 26 points, 11 rebounds, and 13 assists in the clinching game.

Miami returned to the Finals in 2013 for a series against San Antonio that was steeped in drama. The Spurs blew a 5-point lead in the final 27 seconds of what would have been a championship-clinching Game 6, and James made them pay dearly for not closing it out. He was transcendent in Game 7, dropping 37 points on one of the best defenses in the game, adding a Finals MVP trophy and second straight ring to his arsenal.

"The King" had ascended his throne as the best player in the world.

RYAN: I was one of those who originally resisted the criticism [of LeBron] after they lost to Dallas. I did not want to accept that LeBron had shrunk in that moment of truth, even though I had seen him basically quit on his team against the Celtics the previous year. I still liked him enough that I was willing to overlook that. I now accept the idea that that's exactly what happened. He did, in fact, shy away from the ball against Dallas. But all I know is, he did not do that when he won the two championships in Miami.

SIMMONS: LeBron no-showed in all the games in Dallas. He was terrible. In Game 3, Wade was in full alpha-dog mode. At one point, he really got in LeBron's face and yelled at him and was like, "Hey! It's the Finals! Let's go, where are you?" And LeBron was just so far in his own head at that point. It wasn't until the next year, when Wade hurt his knee and couldn't do all the stuff that he could normally do, that LeBron went after it and Wade kind of begrudgingly settled into his role.

PAT RILEY: There are certain guys you want to have the ball in their hands because you believe they will make the right decision, they won't panic. LeBron and Kobe and Magic and Bird and Jordan, some of them have no shame. The consequences of making or missing will not affect them. They will move on to the next shot. I think sometimes with LeBron, he feels naked. And that's because he hasn't really been able to deal with—or he didn't early in his career deal with—the consequences of making, of missing, or maybe losing a game. And that's an inner thing more than anything else. I think a player eventually grows out of that, and I don't think LeBron has that feeling anymore at all. He might have had it earlier in his career, he may have had it with us the first year in Dallas, but now LeBron's fully clothed, he's fully armored up, and whatever he does at the end of the game is a game-winning, game-deciding play.

JAMES: It took sacrifice from D-Wade and I to make it work. For seven years, we had been the cornerstones of our own franchises, and now, how do we figure out how to share this but at the same time still play at an elite level and still feed our egos that got us to this point?

SIMMONS: LeBron and Wade were dueling banjos the first year. You could see it. "You shoot that time, I'll shoot this time." I've always been a believer in the alpha-dog theory in basketball. I didn't think it would work unless somebody became "the Pippen"—the perfect sidekick.

JAMES: I think maturity plays a huge part when you're trying to factor in two stars at the peak of their careers to join forces. D-Wade and I had a way of doing things without saying it. The chemistry and the energy that we had with one another didn't need to be talked about. We could just glance at each other, and we knew exactly what needed to be done—and that's both on the floor and off.

SHAQUILLE O'NEAL: LeBron is a born leader. Whenever you hear a player say, "My favorite part of the game is getting everybody involved," you know he has something special. I am so impressed with LeBron's ability to hold everyone's attention. That's what greatness is. That's why he won championships.

By 2014, the power had shifted again in the NBA, and predictably, it was directly tied to James's movement. Sensing his championship window was closing in Miami, James returned to Cleveland to team up with dynamic point guard Kyrie Irving and stretch big man Kevin Love.

Simultaneously, a new style of basketball was percolating on the West

Coast. Golden State Warriors coach Steve Kerr melded the philosophies of Phil Jackson's triangle, Mike D'Antoni's "7 seconds or less" offense, and Gregg Popovich's ball movement and defensive principles to create an electric "small ball" style that was as exciting as it was prolific. The catalyst was Steph Curry, a slight, baby-faced sniper who teamed up with marksman Klay Thompson to form "the Splash Brothers," the best-shooting backcourt in NBA history. With Draymond Green's fiery leadership and versatile skill set as the X factor, the Warriors emerged as the new darlings of the NBA.

Golden State met Cleveland in the 2015 Finals, and when both Love and Irving were lost to injuries, LeBron became the first player in NBA history to lead both teams in points, assists, and rebounds. Yet the Warriors won the series in six games, and Andre Iguodala, in a testament to Golden State's depth and versatility, was named Finals MVP.

In the 2016 Finals, the Warriors built a 3–1 lead against those same Cavs when their fortunes turned. In Game 4, defensive stalwart Andrew Bogut injured his knee and was ruled out for the remainder of the series, and the combustible Green was suspended for Game 5 after hitting James in the groin. James and Irving were spectacular in the final two games, bringing the championship-starved city of Cleveland its first NBA title.

Cavs-Warriors emerged as the new must-see NBA rivalry.

SIMMONS: Usually, the most popular player is the best player. This was one of the rare times [when that was not true], where Steph Curry was clearly the most popular player coming out of those 2015 Finals. Probably the most popular since young Michael Jordan. He's got his dad in the stands with the mom, he's got his pregnant wife, he says all the right things, he's a great interview, he's really fun to watch. . . . He's right out of central casting.

AHMAD RASHAD: Steph Curry puts the fear of God in everybody because nobody can guard him. He's gonna be so far out that you say, "He's too far out." Then he shoots a three-pointer. You come up, try to check that three-pointer, and now he makes you look silly. He's so much fun. He's so small—he's a little, teeny, frail guy—you can't believe what you are watching.

STEPHEN CURRY: I tell kids, "If you look on TV and see some of the great shooters in history, none of them are identical. As long as you can repeat whatever your specific form is every time, that's how you become more consistent." If Ray Allen shoots like himself five times and the sixth he shoots like Reggie Miller, I don't think Ray is gonna be very comfortable in that shot. Balance is the key to every shot, and there's not much that can be different in that respect. But when you look above the waist and see what a player's form is like, everybody has their own way to get into their shot.

KERR: There's a fluidity with Steph, and it makes no difference whether he has [the] ball or not. There's still an energy and a pace to how he plays. A huge part of what makes us tick is how Steph is so good without the ball.

VECSEY: Curry can go into the middle, penetrate, fool around with it, distort the defense, find the guy that's open that doesn't even know he's open yet. Then, when you need offense, he provides that, too. His range is unlimited. His ballhandling is everything [Pete] Maravich could do. He's a team player, and he's figured out the geometry of the game like a pool player.

CURRY: As a point guard, I like to be that maestro of the rhythm. When it's clicking and things are working—you work so hard to make that happen, you gotta enjoy it for a second before that moment passes.

JERRY WEST: Golden State can be down 7, and three trips down the court and they are 2 ahead. [The three-pointer] changed the game. But you need people that can shoot that three, and you also need coaches that understand that there's a time to shoot it and a time not to shoot it. When the court is really spread and somebody takes an ill-advised three-point shot, the [opponent] zips the other way for a layup.

KERR: Tex Winter was the first guy to verbalize to me that the way he evaluated players was to see if they would make a decision to dribble, pass, or shoot within two seconds. If you think about the triangle, the same thing applies. It's very patterned, but there are a lot of reads out of that pattern, and when it's clicking, everything's in rhythm. That's what we're after.

PIERCE: I've never seen a backcourt shoot this well. Both Steph and Klay are capable of making 10 threes a game. And if they get hot, you are done.

RASHAD: LeBron James is the most tremendous athlete I've ever seen in any sport. He's 6-foot-9, can run like the wind, can do everything. But on this side, you've got this kid Steph Curry. He's unstoppable. I guess you'd have to say on the defensive end, it might be a little bit different, but you know what? I don't even care who Steph's guarding, because he's gonna score more points than that guy. His defense is his offense.

KERR: We win in 2015, caught a break because of [Cleveland's] injuries. The next year, they catch a break when we lose Draymond and Bogut. I'm thinking, "Well, we're gonna have to go small for long stretches, and we don't like to go small for long stretches." Losing both Bogut and Green was a lot, but very quickly you realize it doesn't matter. You got to play whoever you got.

JAMES: The difference between a winning team and a championship team is detail. Paying attention to every single detail. Not during the playoffs but at the beginning of the season, in preseason, in training camp, and not letting something that's this big slip by, because if you allow it to slip by, then by the time you get to the playoffs, it'll be an avalanche.

KERR: I felt that year [2016], LeBron was dramatically better than the year before. I think it was a combination of years and years of experience and working on skills and covering his weaknesses. He was making threes and shooting a high percentage. The year before, I felt we had answers for him. We could go under screens. I'm pretty sure he shot in the 30s [on threes] in 2015, and he was over 50 percent the next year. We had no answer for him.

JAMES: Once I work up a head of steam, there's nobody who can stop me.

Kevin Durant's free agency in the summer of 2016 was not televised, but the agony over his decision was palpable. After entertaining suitors in the Hamptons, he chose to leave Oklahoma City for the Warriors and braced himself for the vitriol that followed.

He was branded a front-runner, a cop-out, a traitor, a liar. But after his first season in Golden State, he was crowned a champion.

Durant's length, versatility, and scoring ability elevated Golden State to new heights. The Warriors rolled over the Cavs in the 2017 NBA Finals, and Durant was named series MVP.

The ensuing off-season featured significant movement among elite players. Paul George and Carmelo Anthony joined Russell Westbrook on the Oklahoma City Thunder, Gordon Hayward and Kyrie Irving teamed up with Al Horford on the Boston Celtics, and Wade was reunited with LeBron in Cleveland, although by February he was shipped to Miami. All these moves seemed to be motivated by the same goal: finding a way to close the gap on the Golden State Warriors, who, with the addition of Durant, had seemingly lapped the field.

RASHAD: They kept asking Michael Jordan, "Who's the best between LeBron James or Kobe Bryant?" Michael said, "Kevin Durant," and people thought he was kidding. He wasn't. He told me, "This kid is unbelievable. Durant has a chance to be one of the great players of all time."

KERR: When you look at KD's ability to play without the ball, combined with Steph and Klay Thompson's ability to do so, that makes us hard to guard. What I love most about our star players is they really love to share the ball.

STEPHEN A. SMITH: When Kevin Durant, at 6-foot-11, is drilling shots from three-point range, it almost looks like a layup, he's so daggone long.

KERR: Working Kevin into our team was almost seamless. It took him two to three months to fully get comfortable, but all along I felt like he was a natural fit for us because of his ability to play without the ball and his desire to be über-efficient. I think Kevin takes more pride in being efficient that anything. He'd much rather score 20 points on 8 of 9 shooting than 30 points on 13 of 30 shooting.

DURANT: When you trust your teammates and you expect them to be there for you, that's a sign of strength. I think you're weak when you think you can do it all on your own.

PIERCE: Golden State not only shoots the three, they *make* the three. There's so much pressure when you have to guard teams all the way out past the three-point line because they're a threat to drive, and when you make them drive they're good finishers, and sometimes you just get caught. It becomes, "I challenged the three—what more can I do?" And then next time you get up on the three-point shot, they're driving to the hole.

STEVE NASH: The environment that Steve Kerr has created there is really, really special. The way guys interact with each other, the way they communicate, the way you know they show up and play for each other, and the way they work together is fantastic, and that is an invaluable commodity.

CURRY: The best is in the big playoff games, when you're out on the floor with the crowd going crazy, and you go on a 10–0 run or something like that. There's just no better feeling as an athlete or a competitor, to see that chemistry among a lot of different players on the floor.

BARKLEY: I look at the "new NBA" and it's "Who can beat Golden State?" We said Anthony Davis was the next great big man. Then it was Karl-Anthony Towns, then Kristaps Porzingis, and then Joel Embiid. We're always trying to find the "next guy." How about we just enjoy the guys we have?

BALL IS LIFE

There's a spiritual side to basketball. The court is a safe haven, a place where players can seek solitude or find community and lifelong friendships. The game can transport you: when you're in it, nothing else matters. It can help you survive the pain of losing a parent or develop the confidence to overcome a speech impediment. And whatever role the sport has played in an individual's personal journey, it becomes universal. Basketball becomes part of us, and it never leaves.

BERNARD KING: You can't play football alone, can't play baseball alone, but you could take a basketball and find a hoop anywhere in the country and play as long as you want. When you talk about the American game, basketball is the true American game.

CALVIN MURPHY: I played football, Little League baseball. I fought Golden Gloves. I was a national baton-twirling champion. I did everything. But as I was doing those things, my mind was visualizing basketball. Basketball is a drug. It's addictive. When you talk about the phrase "basketball junkie," that is true, and as the years go on, it gets worse and worse. You feel it in your DNA. A basketball junkie—it's not just someone that goes to the gym and watches. It's someone that wants to be a part of the game, someone that wants to develop his game and won't leave until he gets better. You go into the gym and say, "I'm gonna shoot 500 foul shots." And you didn't leave at 499; you left at 500.

ADAM SILVER: There is something special about this game, and I even think it's evolutionary. It's not an accident that the top two global sports both involve round balls, roughly the same size. One of them you kick, and one of them you use your hands. And I defy someone who's ever touched a basketball to walk into a room where they have a basket and a ball and not to shoot it. With a lot of interactive events we have around [the] All-Star [Game], we've learned [that] we can have the fanciest gadgets—push these buttons, bells go off, everything else—and then you have a basket and balls, and where do people go? They pick up the ball and shoot.

MARK CUBAN: I had my hip replaced. It doesn't matter—I'll still go out and shoot. I'll even limp over to pick up my misses. Some people play basketball because they want to. Some people play because they have to. I have to.

CHERYL MILLER: My two older brothers and their friends would come over and play in our front yard, against the garage. When the ball went into the bushes, [my younger brother] Reggie and I would fight—we would almost tackle each other trying to get the ball—just to dribble back and then inbound it for my brothers. They would let me dribble around, through my legs, and then pass it. They were like, "She's a baller."

RICK PITINO: You start out playing stickball or stoopball, and then all of a sudden in the second or third grade, you try out for a basketball team. You fall in love with that first layup and that first free throw, and it leads to the city game. You're always in the parks, playing basketball, and it catches you. It goes into your blood, and you play it for the rest of your life.

YAO MING: Around 17 or 18 years old, I felt those sounds: the shoes on the ground; the ball went in and scratch on the net; the ball pounding on the floor; the bodies physically hitting each other. That kind of sound really attract me, and that's how I started loving basketball.

PHIL FORD: I've always contended that to be good at it, you have to really love it. Don't get me wrong: to reach the pro level, you have to be born with a certain gift. But most of us that played professional basketball, we just loved it.

MEL DANIELS: I fell in love with it. I still have that desire to be around it. The passion doesn't leave, you know? It doesn't leave you.

BILLY DONOVAN: When you're a kid, you end up gravitating toward things that you feel you're good at, and I think the game built up my self-esteem. It taught me a lot of different things: how to work, how to be part of a team, how to be unselfish. At times, the only area in my life where I really felt a sense of peace, of accomplishment, of purpose, of being part of something, is when I played basketball.

CHARLIE SCOTT: Basketball meant family because basketball meant friendships. It was everything to me. It was the way I saw other people wanted to be with me. I spent my life as a loner, [and] basketball brought me a group of guys that I could be with at all times. Basketball was my survival.

JIM CALHOUN: When I was in ninth grade, we won the junior high school championship in Boston Garden. [It] was special for us because my dad watched the game. Well, a relatively short time thereafter, my dad died. I lost the most important person of my life. With the devastation of losing my dad, I became much more of a loner, trying to find meaning in my life. And the game became one of the few places that you could just go shovel the snow off and relive your dreams. The serenity, the isolation—I don't know if that makes sense, but it did for me. That's the love of the game.

MAGIC JOHNSON: When you're on the court, you get away from everything, everybody, the world. It's your safe haven, just you and your teammates. If there was anything else going on in my life, when I hit that court, I got two and half hours of joy.

KING: When you play, you forget everything else. You don't think about any issues, you don't think about any problems, you don't think about any friends, you don't think about family, you don't think about anyone. All you think about is the game.

JERRY WEST: I grew up in a house that was less than desirable to grow up in. A lot of tough punishment. And that was my escape—I had a basketball. That was my sanctuary, a place where I could feel special about myself.

BILL WALTON: Basketball has always been a sanctuary for me, a safe place to be on the stage. Being the quiet, shy, reserved stutterer that I am, once I got on the court, it was fine.

CHARLEY ROSEN: I was always the tallest kid in school, and if you're the tallest kid, you can't get away with anything. The little kids sneak around and do all kinds of stuff, but whatever you do, you're in trouble. People expect you to be more emotionally mature than you really are, more physically coordinated than you really are. I was uncomfortable and out of sorts and a little bit afraid to do anything, but on the basketball court, everything fit.

JOHN THOMPSON: I had a lot of voids in my life, and basketball gave me a sense of satisfaction, a sense of identity. You become different from just being who you are—you get identified with the game itself.

KARA LAWSON: Every significant milestone in my life comes back to basketball. I met my husband in Sacramento, California, where [he was] born and raised, because I was playing in Sacramento. When I look at the friendships I have through the game—if we went through my phone, everyone besides my family is some connection through basketball. Everybody I know is basketball. Everybody I enjoy talking to, somehow the conversation comes to basketball. I love the game. I will sacrifice things that I hold very dear to me—sleep and food—for basketball.

ISIAH THOMAS: I remember playing Biddy Basketball, and John McLendon came to talk to us, and my coach saying you're getting ready to meet one of the pioneers of the game. So John McLendon came in and I'll never forget, he held up the ball and said, "This ball can take you all around the world. You will meet kings and queens, and you will even have the opportunity to dine with presidents. But this is not just a ball; this is a game of values. If you learn the values of this game and play as you live, then you can be successful off the court."

GEORGE KARL: First time I remember [that feeling], it was in a high school game. You come together, you're ready for a big game, and the coach gives the pep talk. You get in the huddle, hands down together, and you could feel energy in that moment. I've felt that force in many different ways. I've felt that force crying after a loss. I've felt that force coming back from an injury and realizing [my] career might be over. The connection of being on a special team that contends for a championship. Those friendships and stories—even though we probably embellish them a little more every year—they're sincere. The reunions that you have are deeper and more soulful than normal friendships, because of the craziness of the competition we put ourselves through.

JOHNSON: When you come down and create a shot for your teammate and they score off that creation, that's a beautiful feeling. To me, that's basketball.

ACKNOWLEDGMENTS

FROM DAN: This book would not have been possible without the help of some exceptional young men who on an alternating basis traveled around the country with me while I interviewed about 110 players, coaches, executives, analysts, and thinkers who lived and loved the game: Lloyd Lochridge, Noah Malale, and Judson Wells. They were assisted by Eric Krugley and my longtime right arm, Joan Baird, in transcribing all these interviews, some as long as 150 pages.

Charlie Rosenzweig, "Mr. NBA," was my Magic Johnson in selflessly working overtime to open so many of these doors. Donnie Walsh, my go-to guy for anything and everyone that had to do with Indiana or UNC. Adam Silver, Russ Granik, Rod Thorn, and Michael Goldberg, who went too young and too fast, never hesitated if I requested a good word. David Stern's wisdom was steadfast, Paul Hirschheimer's energy unlimited. Carol Stiff—who to this day I've never met, but who loves and reveres the women's game—got her on speed dial.

My pals Wes, Bill Simmons, Rick Welts, Earl Monroe, Barry Watkins, Ernie Brown, Ira Berkow, Ken Sunshine, Liz Robbins, Frank Isola, Howard Beck, Garry Howard, C. J. Paul, Sal Petruzzi, Mike Bass, and my longtime friend and producer, Charlie Stuart never once blinked and always went the extra mile, no questions asked. No surprise that Bob Ryan handled most of the Celtics, Doris Burke zeroed in on UConn, the extraordinarily gifted Jackie MacMullan turned on her rolodex, and Danny Schayes and Chris Ramsay called their dads. Dr. Jack was my first interview at his home in Naples, Florida, his body riddled with the cancer he fought so zealously to defeat, and sat there for four hours teaching me about his 2/2/1 zone press, his offensive systems, and showing me the first criteria of being a great teacher of the game is clarity. Six weeks later, he left us. John Walsh, his neighbor and the editor of our time was helpful, and John Skipper, my friend and supporter at ESPN, who I miss greatly, were nothing but encouraging, 100 percent of the way. Connor Schell has been there.

Rob Pelinka, Molly Carter, David Falk, Rich Kleinman, Leon Rose, Andy Miller, Connie Unseld, Maverick Carter, Dan Schoenberg, Lindsay Kagawa Colas, Michael O'Brien, Jill Leone, Gary Moore, Andy Borman, Bill Sanders, all pros to me. Never asking for one thing and only there to assist.

Many of these interviews were made possible due to the generosity and flexibility of public relations professionals such as Ray Ridder, Matt Tumbleson, Jon Steinberg, Kenneth Klein, John Hayden, Sarah Melton, Arsalan Jamil, Mex Carey, Jon Jackson, Tom James, Matt Ryan, Steve Kirschner, Sarah Darras, Chris Clark, Tim Donovan, and Steve Kirkland.

Some of the number of interviews were conducted by a stellar group of dedicated and skilled journalists: Aaron Cohen, Brian Windhorst, J. A. Adande, Henry Abbott, Howard Beck, Jackie MacMullan, Frank Isola, Doris Burke, Garry Howard, Liz Robbins, Kirk Goldsberry, Ira Berkow, Bob Ryan, Pablo Torre, Sally Jenkins, and Leslie Visser.

Jay Mandel, my agent at WME, Nathan Roberson at Crown, and Rafe, whom along with Jackie MacMullan, spent God knows how many hundreds of hours pouring over my transcripts to make these voices coherent and heard for now and forever.

Everyone who did take the time, some such as Bill Russell and Oscar Robertson, each who educated and shared with me for more than five hours showed the spirit of champions. Everyone was gracious. Many, many home doors were opened. And all know their stuff. They didn't get to this level without having the brainpower and understanding of the intricacies of their love. Dolph Schayes, who was caring for his wife who wasn't doing well, passed. Moses Malone, a young and gifted man; Mel Daniels, a laugh, a storyteller, a handshake to remember; Howard Garfinkel, whose life was the game; Connie Hawkins, sweet and gentle; his savior, Roz Litman, with the heart and spirit of the Boxer; I am grateful to all of you, and wish you were here.

My friend, mentor, teacher, and father figure, the great Ben Jobe, who sat in at the lunch counters of Nashville, graduated from his beloved Fisk, coached at Tuskegee and seven other universities, winning more than 530 games, deserved of the Hall of Fame, for he helped to mold the lives and minds of countless boys and men—I miss you terribly: this project, this book and film is in your memory Ben, for honor and decency is who you are.

FROM JACKIE AND RAFE: This book is the result of the brilliance, innovation, and passion of Dan Klores. Thanks so much, Dan, for allowing us to become part of this truly inspiring project.

To Michael, Alyson, and Douglas Boyle, because as John Wooden once said, the most important thing is family and love; to Todd Balf, a superb writer, trusted confidant, and valued sounding board; to Ian Thomsen, who exemplifies everything that is right about the business of journalism and friendship; to Henry Abbott, who happily deals in relationships, not transactions.

To Mollie Glick, who was one of the only literary agents on the planet willing to take a chance on a 24-year-old who'd barely been published and was still living in Manila back in 2006; to coach Tim Cone, who gave that kid something close to a real basketball education; and to Caroline De Vera, whose companionship means more to that kid than anything in the world.

Thanks to Nate Roberson, our editor at Crown; to Jay Mandel of William Morris, who expertly brought this deal to fruition; and to Crown's team of Molly Stern, Tricia Boczkowski, Annsley Rosner, Tammy Blake, Julie Cepler, Melissa Esner, and Terry Deal.

Thank you, also, to the men and women who shared their stories, their insights, and their devotion to the game. Basketball is our love story, too.

INDEX